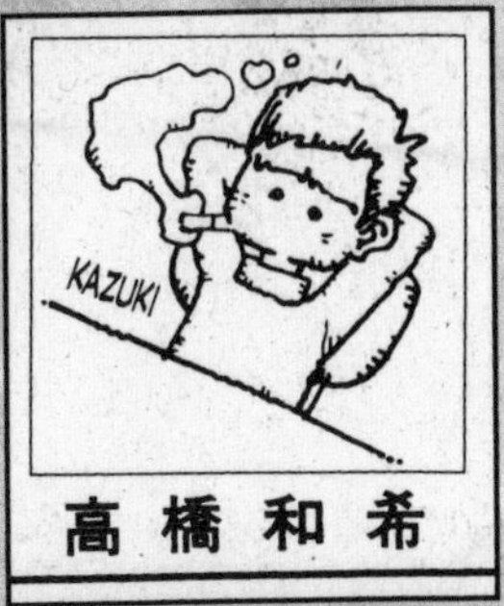
KAZUKI
高橋和希

KAZUKI TAKAHASHI

MR. KAGEYAMA'S JUST MOVED INTO A NEW WORKPLACE, AND BOTH HIS MANGA AND HIS PRIVATE LIFE ARE GOING INCREDIBLY WELL. PLEASE SEND HIM LETTERS AND CHEER HIM ON.

KAZUKI TAKAHASHI

Artist/author Kazuki Takahashi first tried to break into the manga business in 1982, but success eluded him until *Yu-Gi-Oh!* debuted in the Japanese *Weekly Shonen Jump* magazine in 1996. *Yu-Gi-Oh!*'s themes of friendship and fighting, together with Takahashi's weird and imaginative monsters, soon became enormously successful, spawning a real-world card game, video games, four anime series (two Japanese *Yu-Gi-Oh!* series, *Yu-Gi-Oh! GX* and *Yu-Gi-Oh! 5D's*). A lifelong gamer, Takahashi enjoys Shogi (Japanese chess), Mahjong, card games, and tabletop RPGs, among other games.

NAOYUKI KAGEYAMA

Naoyuki Kageyama was born April 12, 1969, which makes him an Aries, and is originally from Tokyo, Japan. He is the recipient of an honorable mention for the 1990 *Weekly Shonen Jump* Hop Step Award for his work *Mahou No Trump* (Magic Trump) and started drawing *Yu-Gi-Oh! GX* for *Monthly V Jump* in February 2006. Kageyama is a baseball fan and his favorite team is the Seibu Lions.

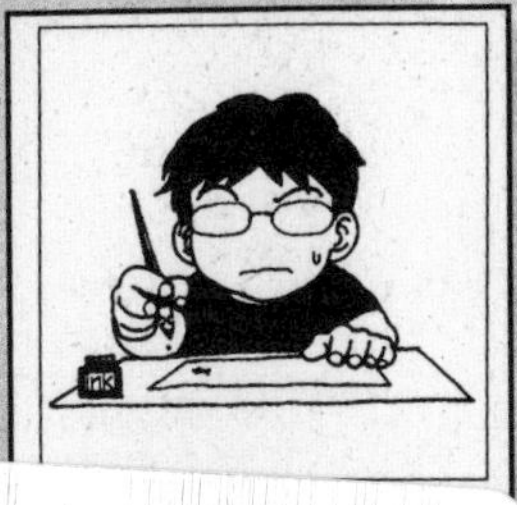
ink

NAOYUKI KAGEYAMA

MY DECKS: JADEN'S, MISAWA'S, MAC'S, CHAZZ'S (OJAMA DECK), AND THE D-HEROES! (WHY?!) THAT'S FIVE DECKS TOTAL. I'VE GOT TO MAKE DECKS FOR SYRUS AND ALEXIS, TOO!

YU-GI-OH! GX Volume 5
SHONEN JUMP Manga Edition

This manga contains material that was originally published in English in
SHONEN JUMP #81–84.

ORIGINAL CONCEPT/SUPERVISED BY
KAZUKI TAKAHASHI

STORY AND ART BY
NAOYUKI KAGEYAMA

Translation & English Adaptation/Kinami Watabe & Ian Reid,
HC Language Solutions
Touch-up Art & Lettering/John Hunt
Designer/Ronnie Casson
Editor/Jason Thompson

YU-GI-OH! GX © 2005 by Kazuki Takahashi, Naoyuki Kageyama
All rights reserved.
First published in Japan in 2005 by SHUEISHA Inc., Tokyo.
English translation rights arranged by SHUEISHA Inc.

Based on Animation TV series YU-GI-OH! GX
© 1996 Kazuki Takahashi
© 2004 NAS • TV TOKYO

Printed in the U.S.A.

Published by VIZ Media, LLC
P.O. Box 77010
San Francisco, CA 94107

10 9 8 7 6 5 4 3 2 1
First printing, October 2010

PARENTAL ADVISORY
YU-GI-OH! GX is rated A and is
suitable for readers of all ages.
ratings.viz.com

THE WORLD'S
MOST POPULAR MANGA

www.viz.com

www.shonenjump.com

Yu-Gi-Oh! GX

VOLUME
5
Ultimate Hero!!

Story & Art by
**NAOYUKI
KAGEYAMA**

Original Concept/
Supervised by
**KAZUKI
TAKAHASHI**

THE STORY SO FAR

WINGED KURIBOH

JADEN YUKI

CHAZZ PRINCETON

SYRUS TRUESDALE

BASTION MISAWA

ALEXIS RHODES

ZANE TRUESDALE
(KAISER)

DAVID RABB

REGGIE MACKENZIE (MAC)

ON AN ISLAND IN THE SOUTHERN SEA THERE IS AN ACADEMY THAT TRAINS THE
NEXT GENERATION OF DUELISTS—THE DUEL ACADEMY!

JADEN YUKI LEARNED ABOUT DUELING THROUGH A FATEFUL ENCOUNTER WITH THE
WORLD CHAMPION DUELIST, KOYO HIBIKI. ENTRUSTED WITH HIBIKI'S DECK, JADEN
TAKES ON ALL CHALLENGERS AT THE ACADEMY IN ORDER TO BECOME A TRUE
DUELIST! AT DUELIST ACADEMY, HE MAKES MANY FRIENDS, INCLUDING ALEXIS
RHODES, SYRUS TRUESDALE AND BASTION MISAWA. BUT HE ALSO MEETS FIERCE
RIVALS, SUCH AS CHAZZ PRINCETON.

WHEN SYRUS'S OLDER BROTHER ZANE "KAISER" TRUESDALE, THE CURRENT WORLD
CHAMPION DUELIST, RETURNS FROM AMERICA, THE ACADEMY HOLDS A TOURNAMENT
FOR THE RIGHT TO CHALLENGE HIM. SOON, THE TOURNAMENT COMES DOWN TO A
BATTLE BETWEEN CHAZZ AND JADEN. BUT AMERICAN EXCHANGE STUDENT REGGIE
MACKENZIE HAS COME TO THE ACADEMY FOR A MUCH MORE SINISTER REASON THAN
JUST WINNING...SHE IS SEARCHING FOR THE MYSTERIOUS "SPIRIT CARDS," SUCH AS
JADEN'S WINGED KURIBOH. AND REGGIE HERSELF IS JUST THE SERVANT OF AN
EVEN DARKER FORCE LURKING WITHIN THE HEART OF THE CARDS...!

Volume 5: Ultimate Hero!!

CONTENTS

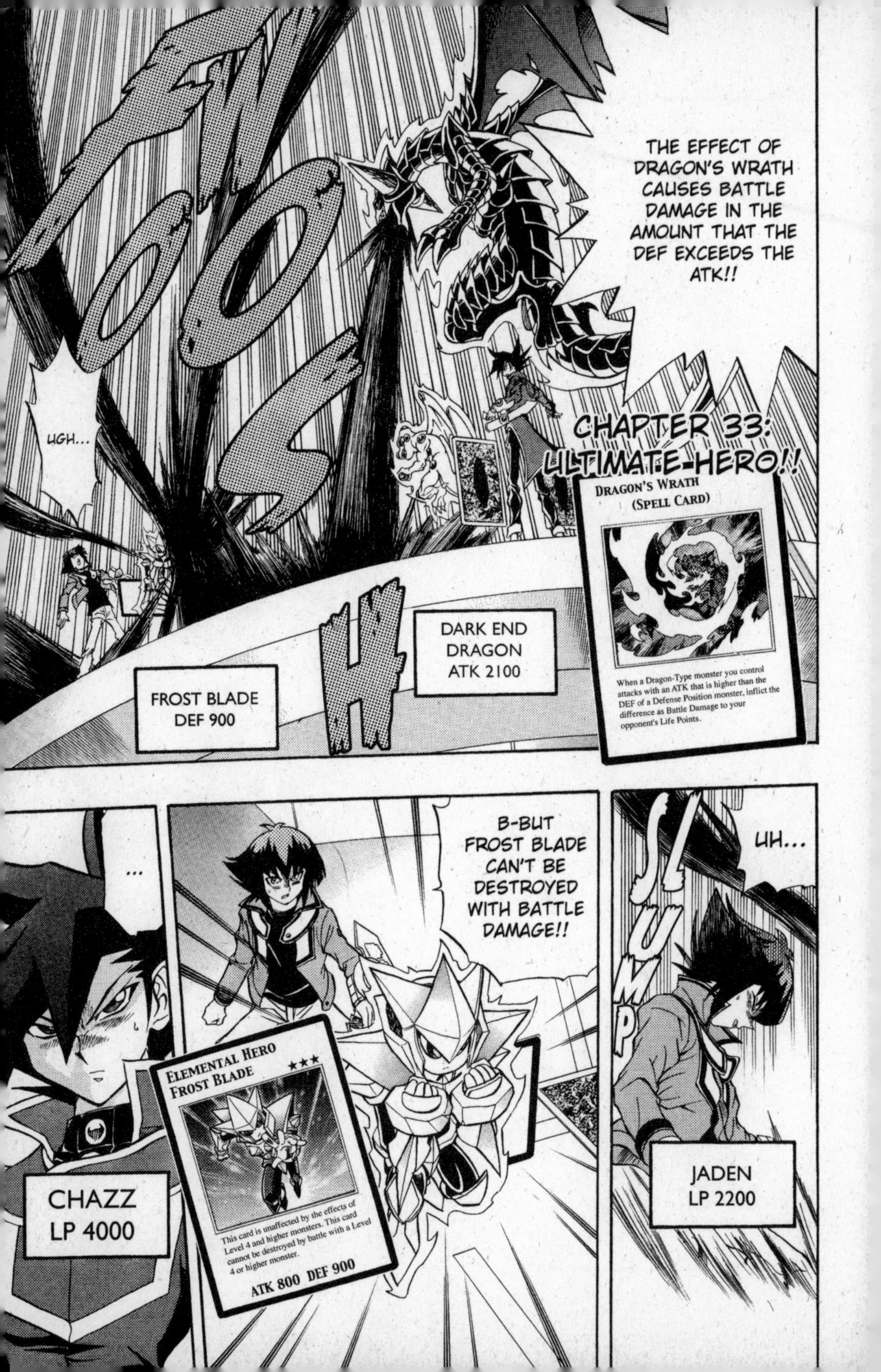
THE EFFECT OF DRAGON'S WRATH CAUSES BATTLE DAMAGE IN THE AMOUNT THAT THE DEF EXCEEDS THE ATK!!
CHAPTER 33: ULTIMATE-HERO!!
DRAGON'S WRATH
(SPELL CARD)
When a Dragon-Type monster you control attacks with an ATK that is higher than the DEF of a Defense Position monster, inflict the difference as Battle Damage to your opponent's Life Points.
DARK END DRAGON ATK 2100
FROST BLADE DEF 900
FWOOSH
UGH...
UH...
SLUMP
JADEN LP 2200
B-BUT FROST BLADE CAN'T BE DESTROYED WITH BATTLE DAMAGE!!
ELEMENTAL HERO FROST BLADE
This card is unaffected by the effects of Level 4 and higher monsters. This card cannot be destroyed by battle with a Level 4 or higher monster.
ATK 800 DEF 900
...
CHAZZ LP 4000

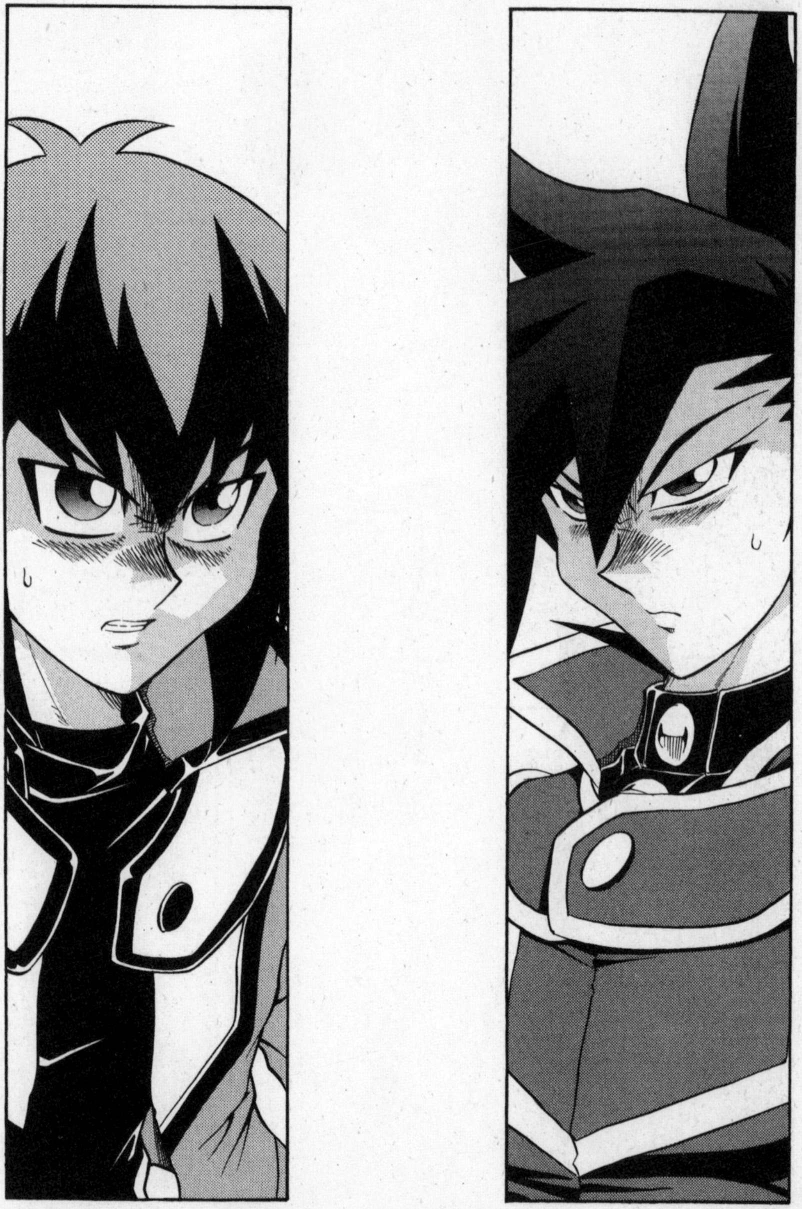

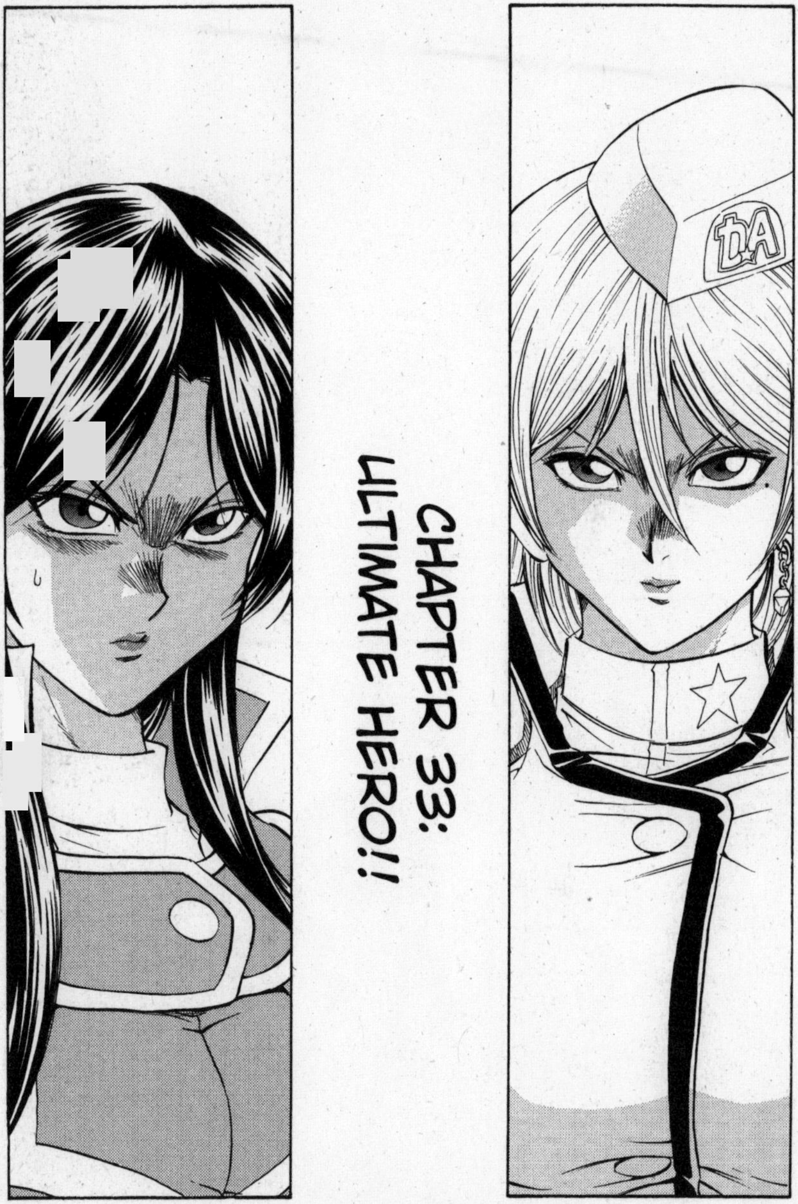
CHAPTER 33:
ULTIMATE HERO!!

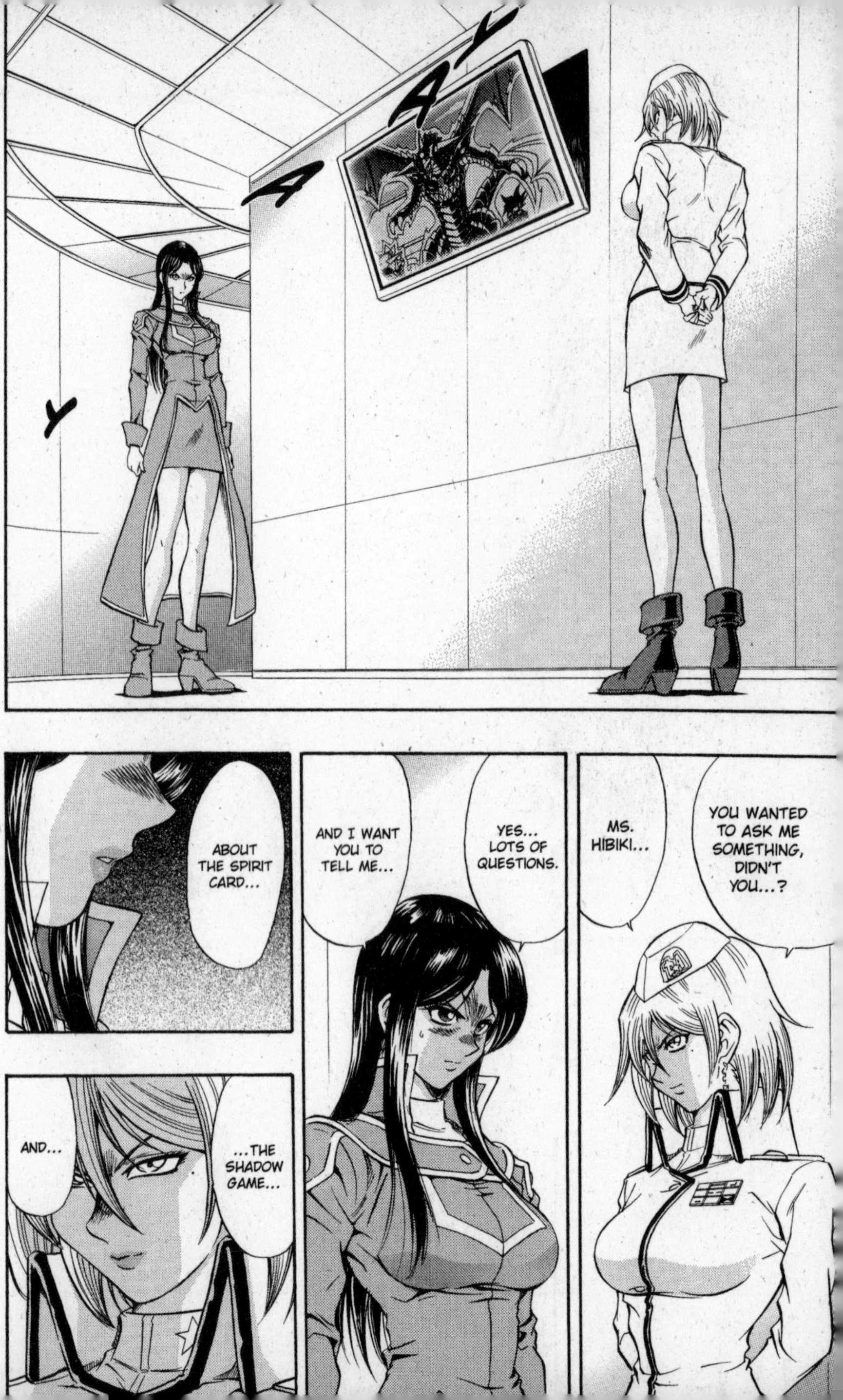
AAY
Y
YOU WANTED TO ASK ME SOMETHING, DIDN'T YOU...?
MS. HIBIKI...
YES... LOTS OF QUESTIONS.
AND I WANT YOU TO TELL ME...
ABOUT THE SPIRIT CARD...
...THE SHADOW GAME...
AND...

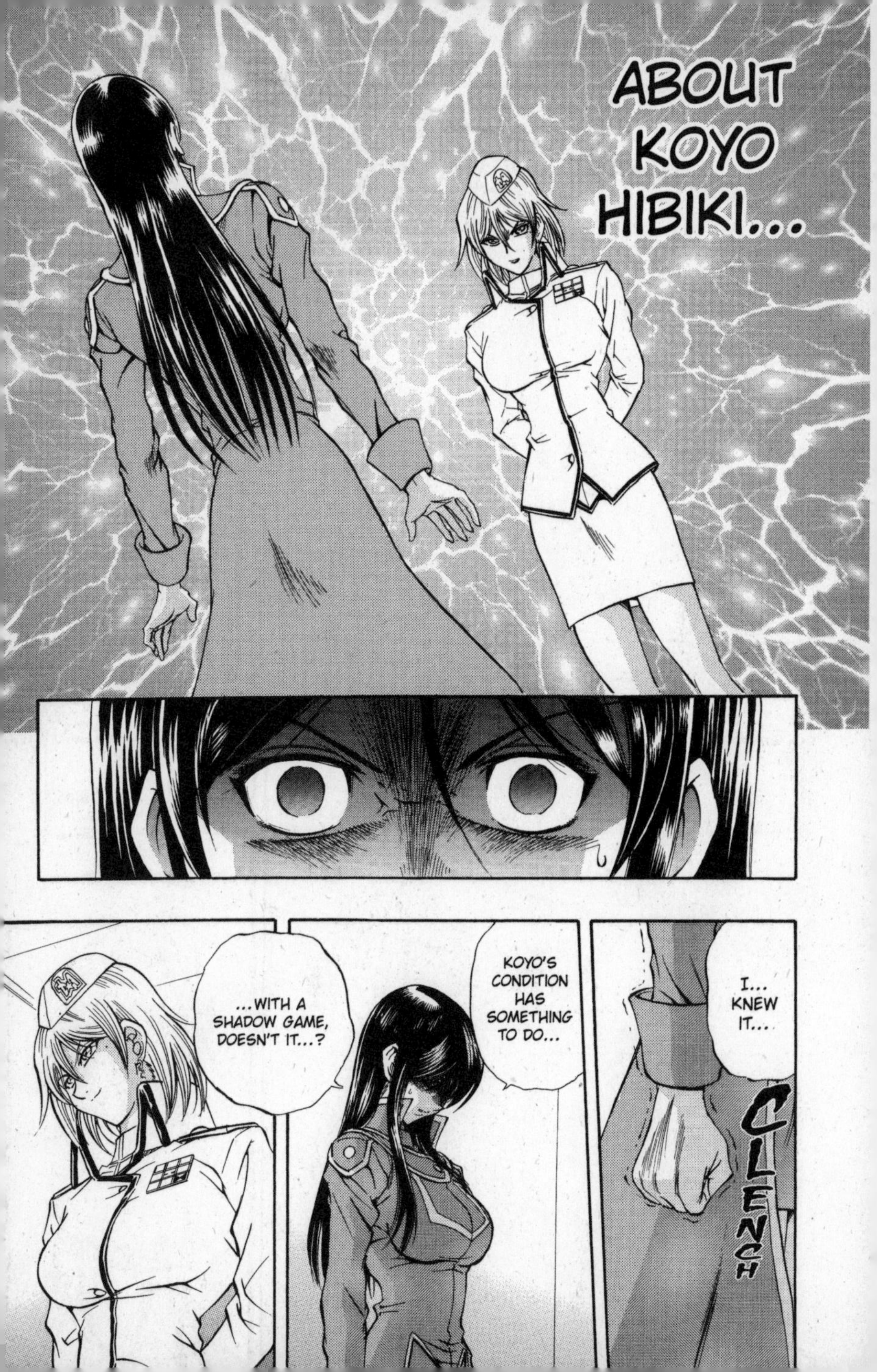
ABOUT KOYO HIBIKI...
I... KNEW IT...
CLENCH
KOYO'S CONDITION HAS SOMETHING TO DO...
...WITH A SHADOW GAME, DOESN'T IT...?

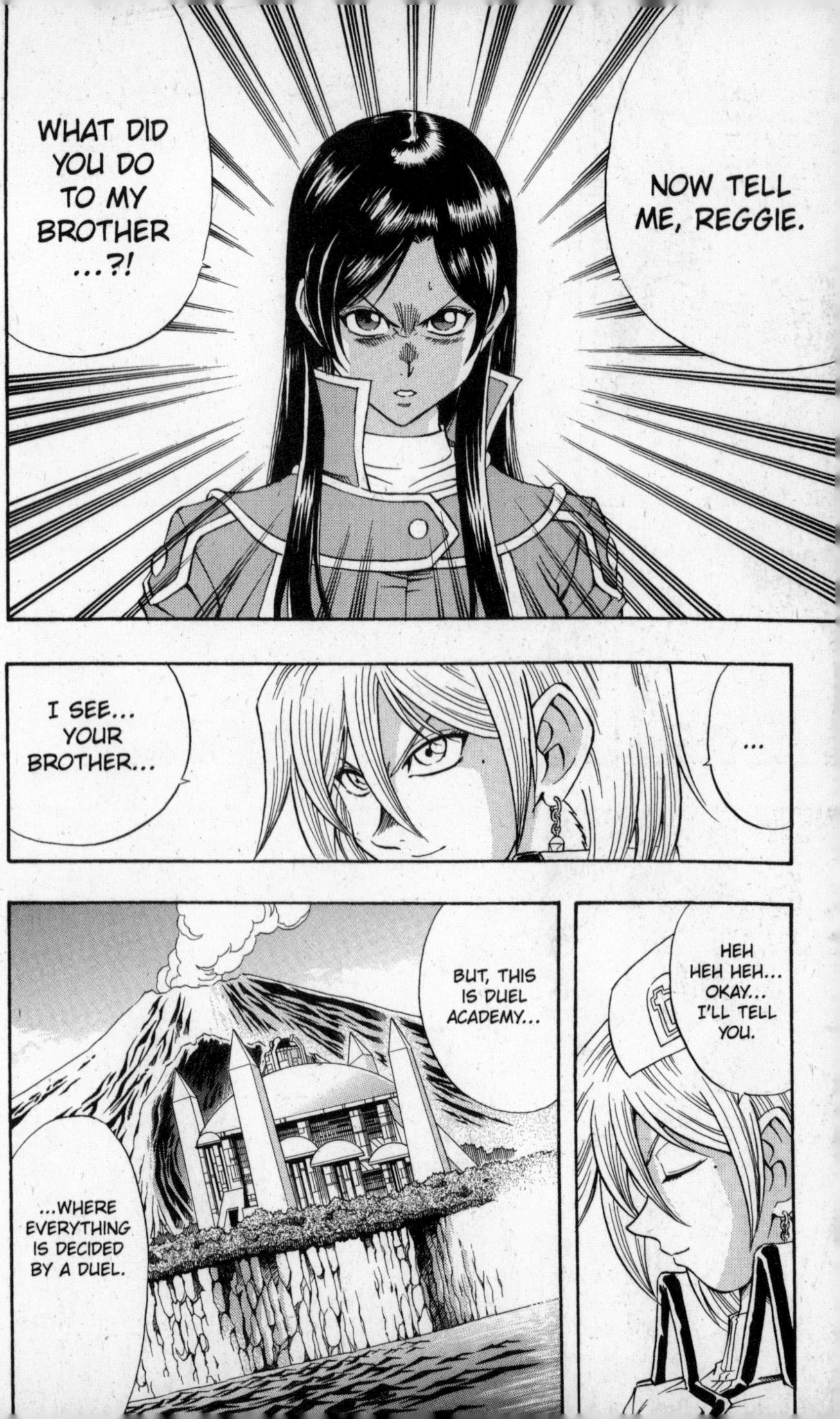
NOW TELL ME, REGGIE.
WHAT DID YOU DO TO MY BROTHER ...?!
...
I SEE... YOUR BROTHER...
HEH HEH HEH... OKAY... I'LL TELL YOU.
BUT, THIS IS DUEL ACADEMY...
...WHERE EVERYTHING IS DECIDED BY A DUEL.

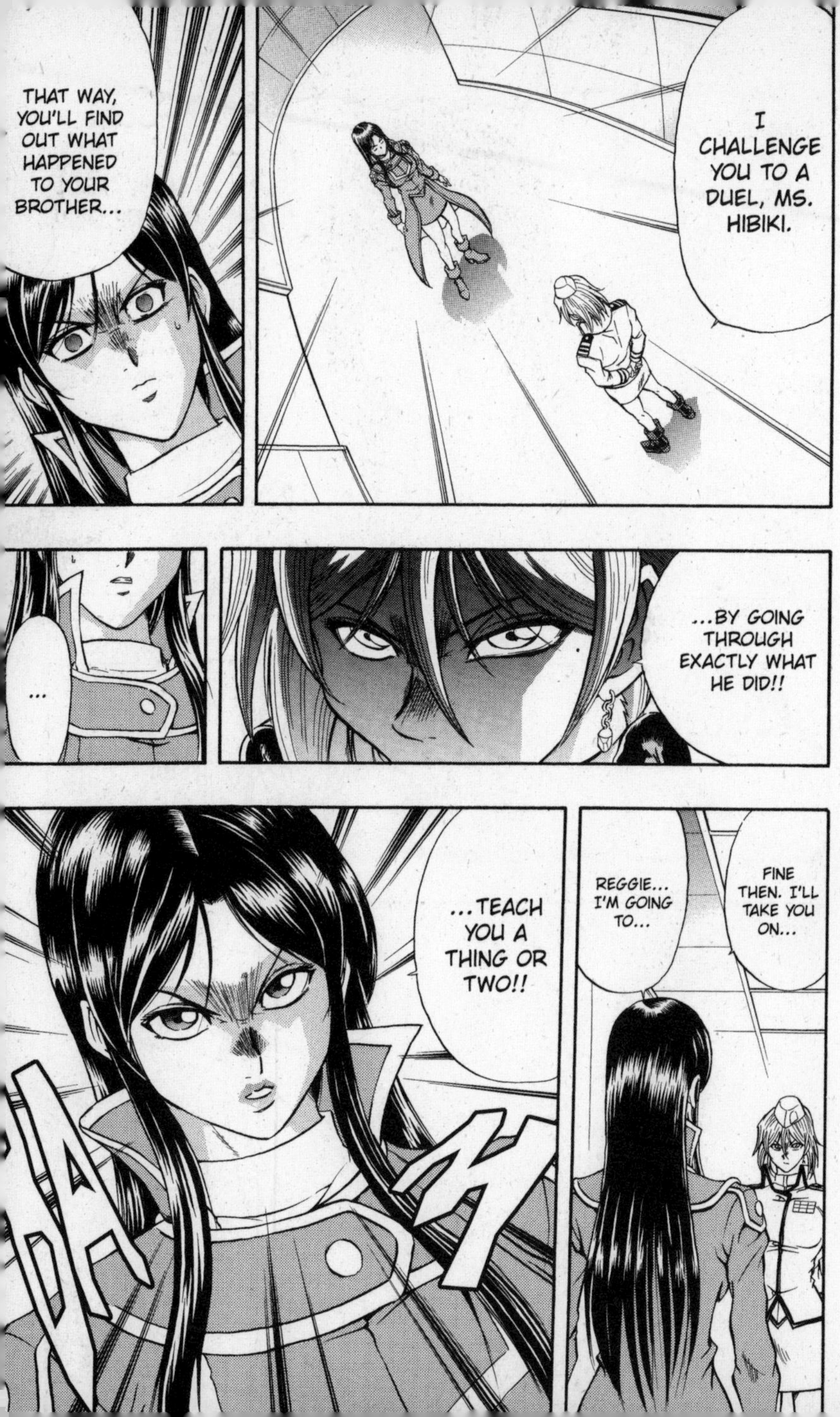
I CHALLENGE YOU TO A DUEL, MS. HIBIKI.
THAT WAY, YOU'LL FIND OUT WHAT HAPPENED TO YOUR BROTHER...
...BY GOING THROUGH EXACTLY WHAT HE DID!!
...
FINE THEN. I'LL TAKE YOU ON...
REGGIE... I'M GOING TO...
...TEACH YOU A THING OR TWO!!

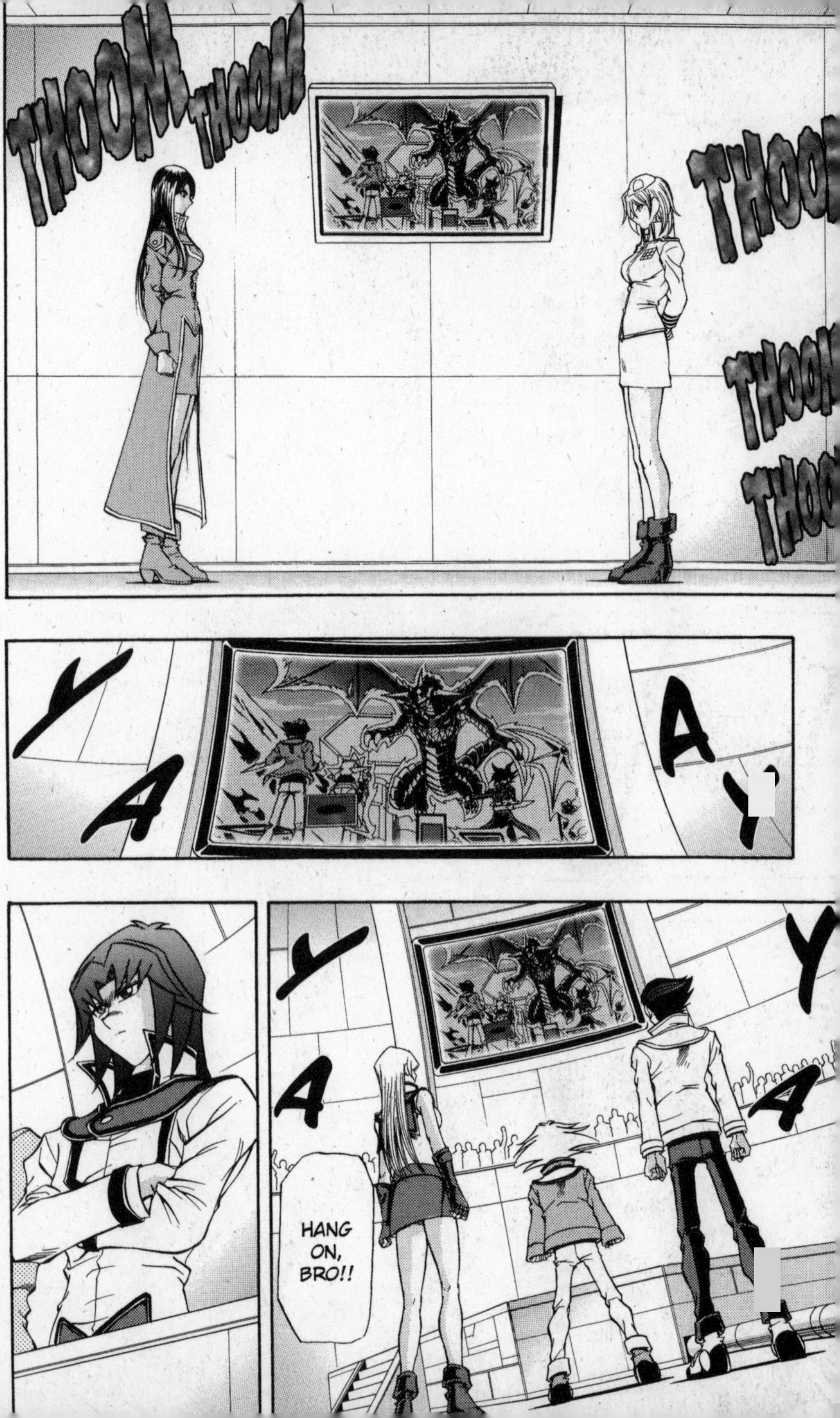
THOOM THOOM
AY
YA
YA
YA
HANG ON, BRO!!

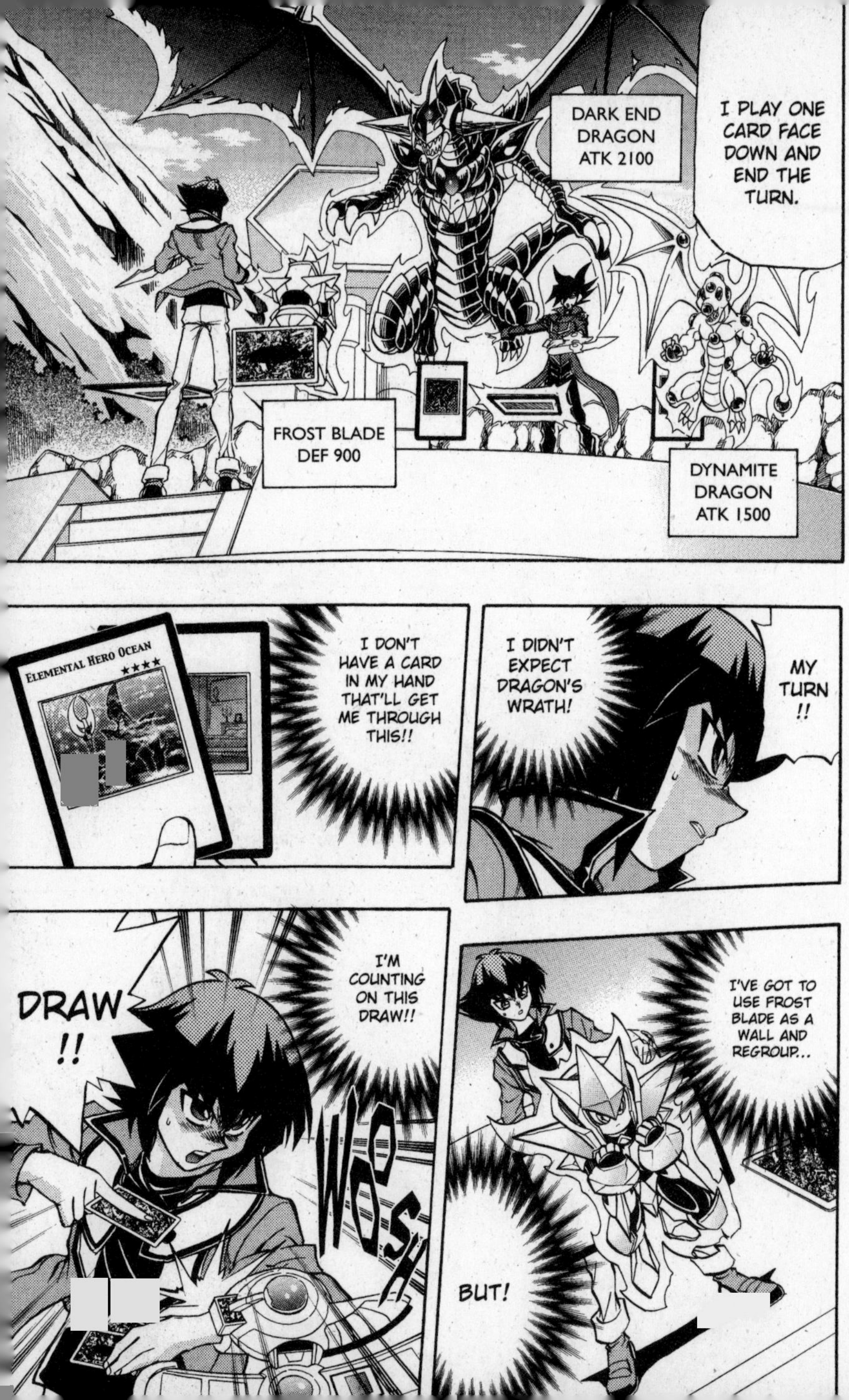
I PLAY ONE CARD FACE DOWN AND END THE TURN.
DARK END DRAGON ATK 2100
DYNAMITE DRAGON ATK 1500
FROST BLADE DEF 900
MY TURN!!
I DIDN'T EXPECT DRAGON'S WRATH!
ELEMENTAL HERO OCEAN
I DON'T HAVE A CARD IN MY HAND THAT'LL GET ME THROUGH THIS!!
I'VE GOT TO USE FROST BLADE AS A WALL AND REGROUP...
BUT!
I'M COUNTING ON THIS DRAW!!
DRAW!!
WOOSH

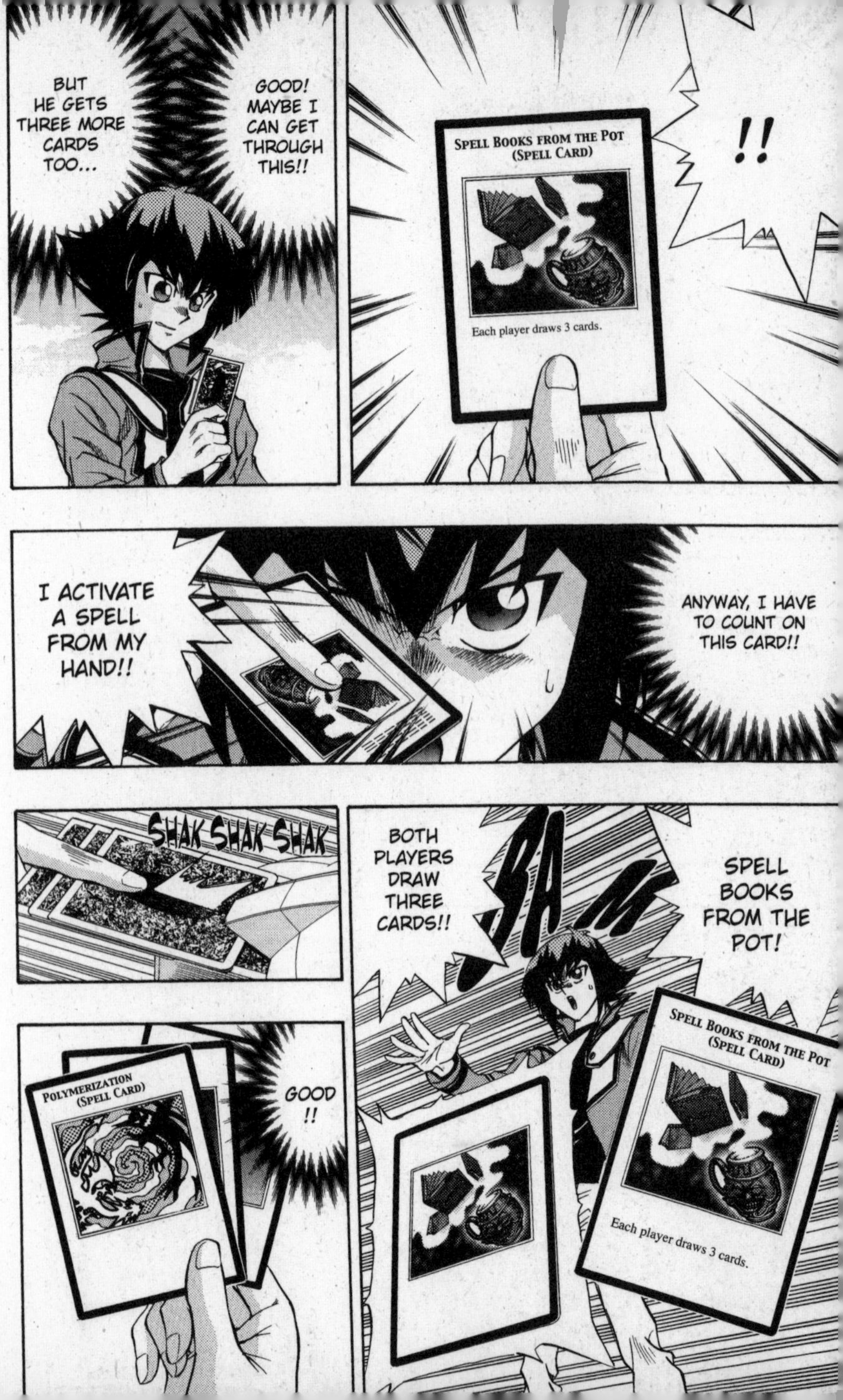
!!
SPELL BOOKS FROM THE POT
(SPELL CARD)
Each player draws 3 cards.
GOOD! MAYBE I CAN GET THROUGH THIS!!
BUT HE GETS THREE MORE CARDS TOO...
ANYWAY, I HAVE TO COUNT ON THIS CARD!!
I ACTIVATE A SPELL FROM MY HAND!!
SPELL BOOKS FROM THE POT!
BAM
BOTH PLAYERS DRAW THREE CARDS!!
SPELL BOOKS FROM THE POT
(SPELL CARD)
Each player draws 3 cards.
SHAK SHAK SHAK
GOOD!!
POLYMERIZATION
(SPELL CARD)

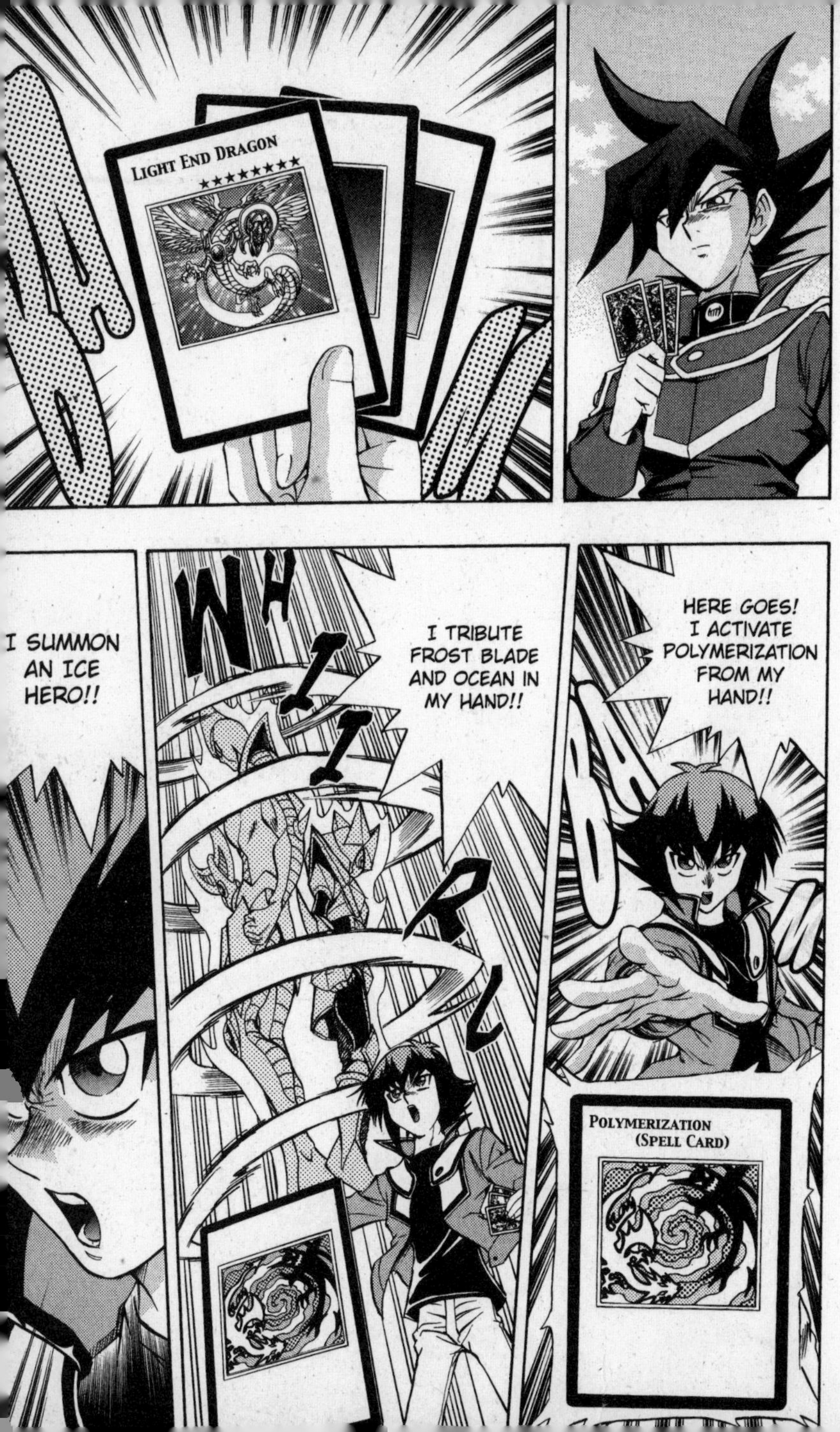
LIGHT END DRAGON
HERE GOES! I ACTIVATE POLYMERIZATION FROM MY HAND!!
POLYMERIZATION (SPELL CARD)
I TRIBUTE FROST BLADE AND OCEAN IN MY HAND!!
WHIIRL
I SUMMON AN ICE HERO!!

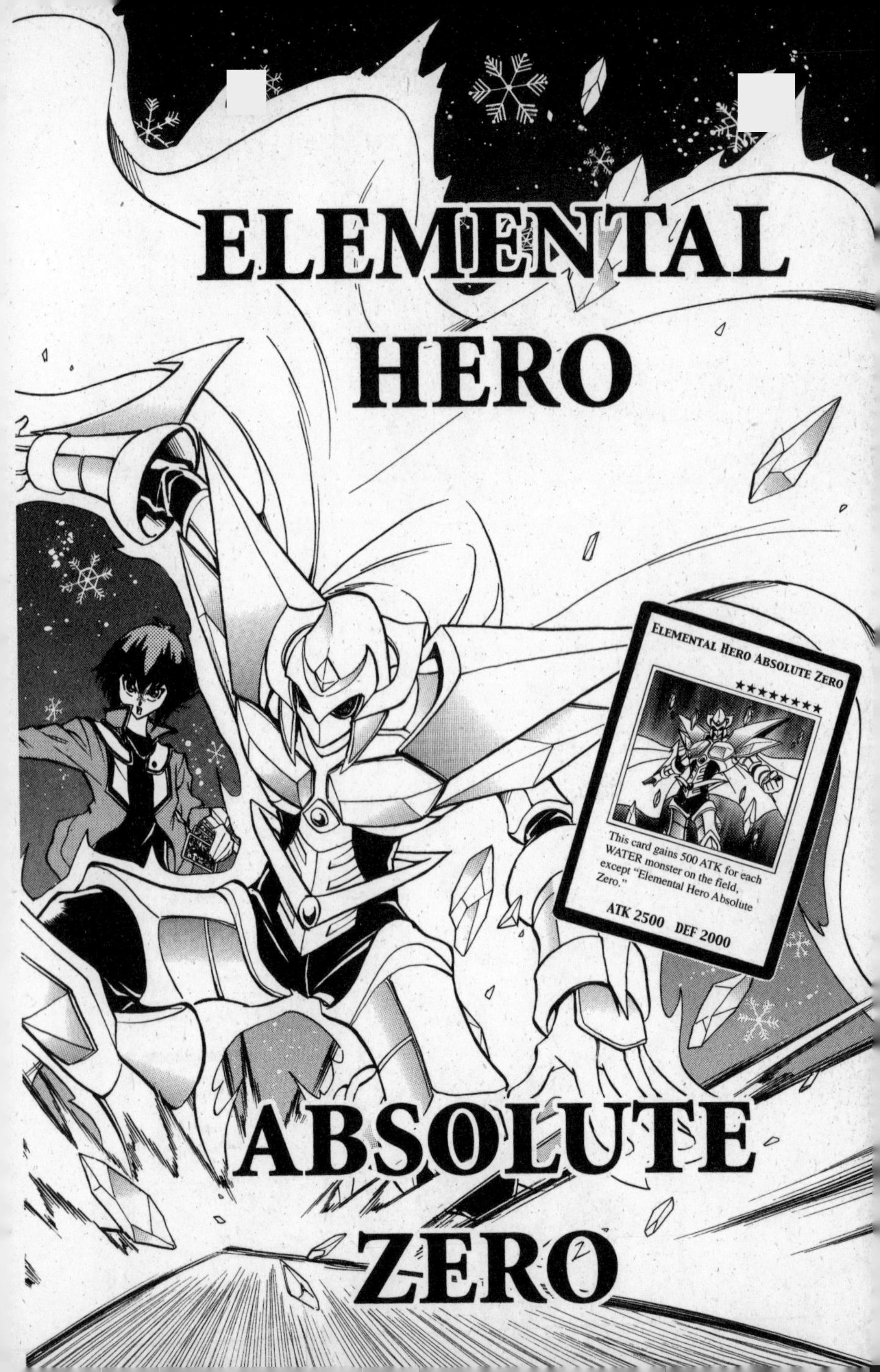
ELEMENTAL HERO
ELEMENTAL HERO ABSOLUTE ZERO
This card gains 500 ATK for each WATER monster on the field, except "Elemental Hero Absolute Zero."
ATK 2500 DEF 2000
ABSOLUTE ZERO

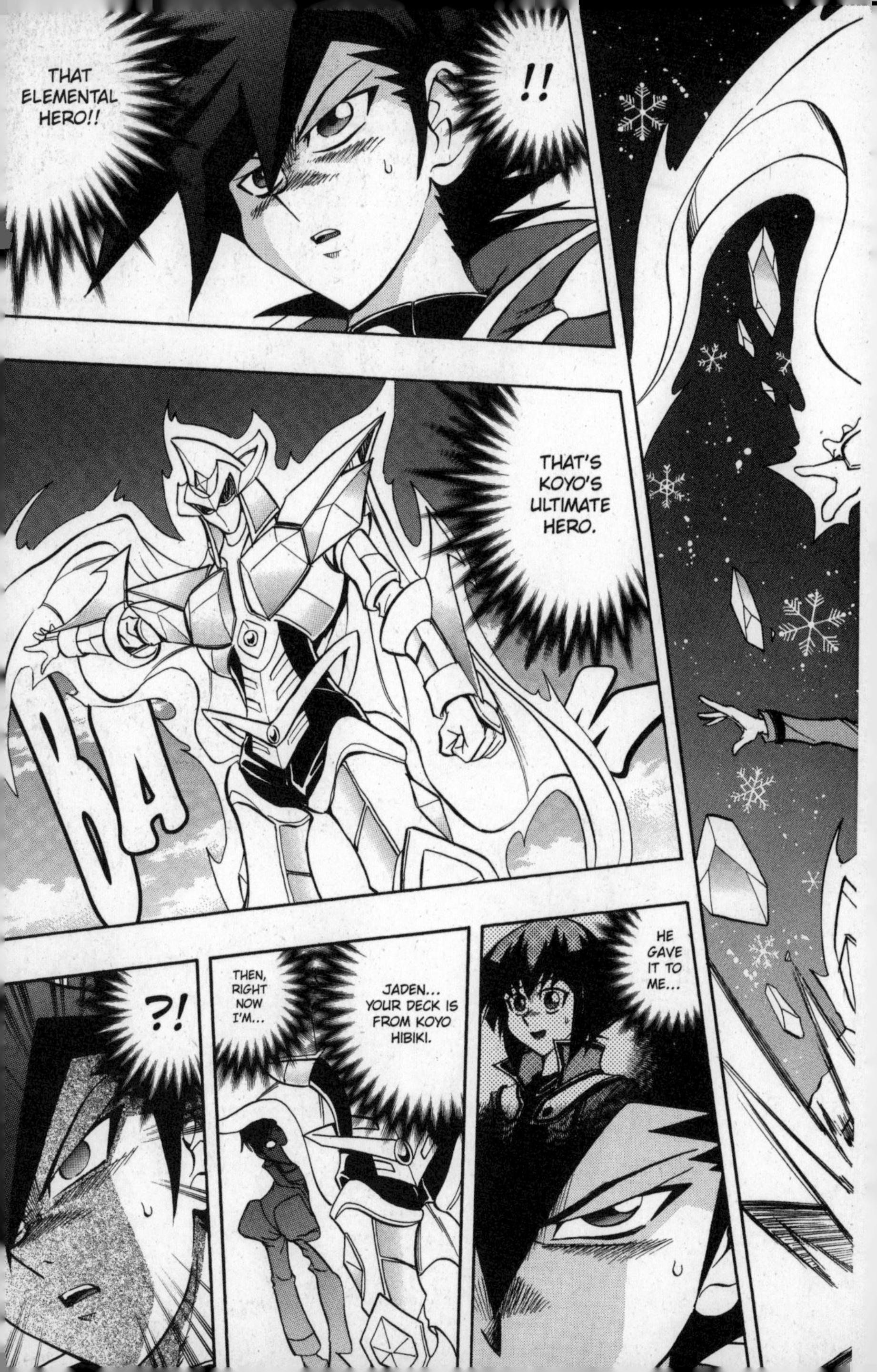
!!
THAT ELEMENTAL HERO!!
THAT'S KOYO'S ULTIMATE HERO.
BA
HE GAVE IT TO ME...
JADEN... YOUR DECK IS FROM KOYO HIBIKI.
THEN, RIGHT NOW I'M...
?!

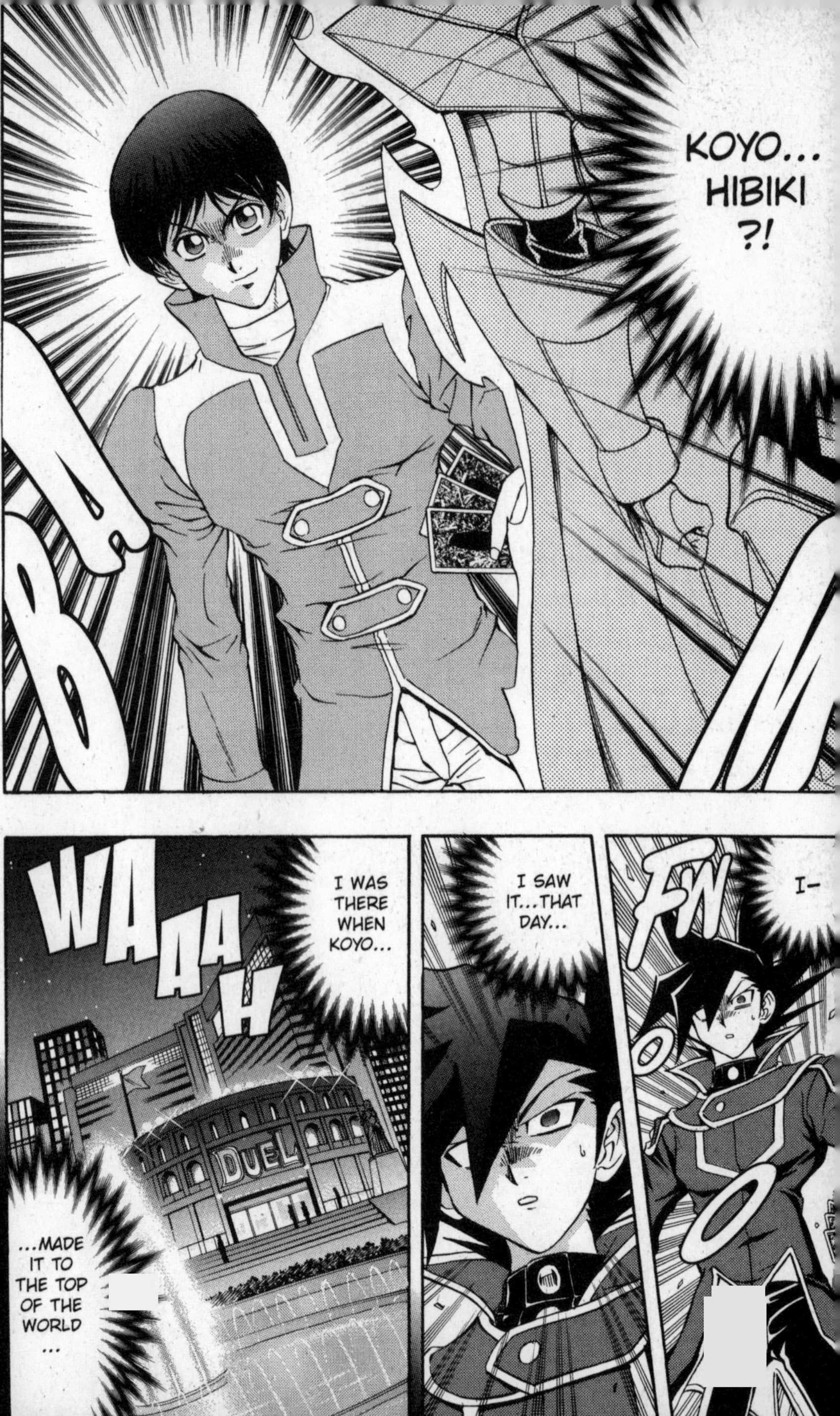
KOYO... HIBIKI ?!
FW
I–
I SAW IT...THAT DAY...
I WAS THERE WHEN KOYO...
WAAAH
DUEL
...MADE IT TO THE TOP OF THE WORLD ...

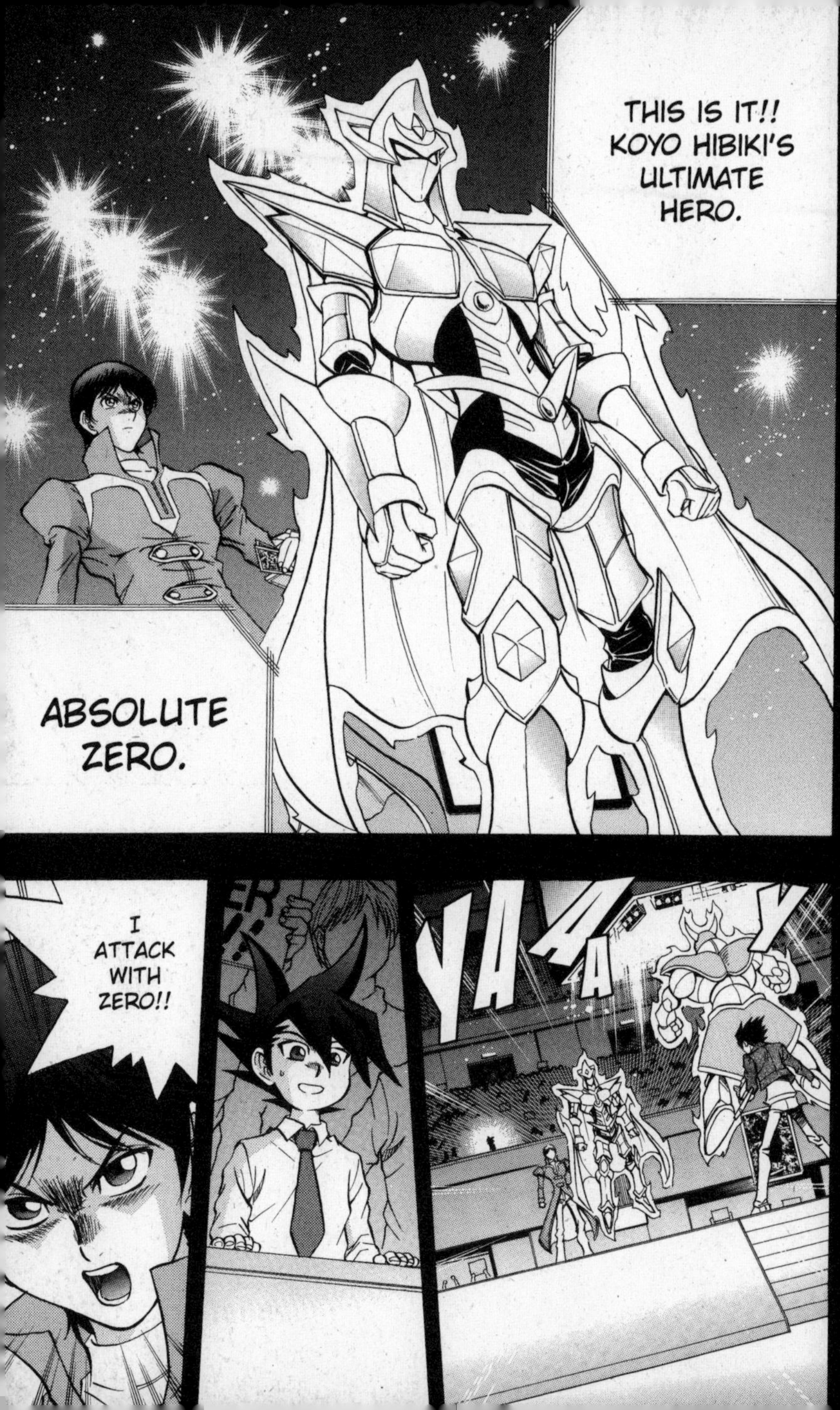
THIS IS IT!! KOYO HIBIKI'S ULTIMATE HERO.
ABSOLUTE ZERO.
YAAAY
I ATTACK WITH ZERO!!

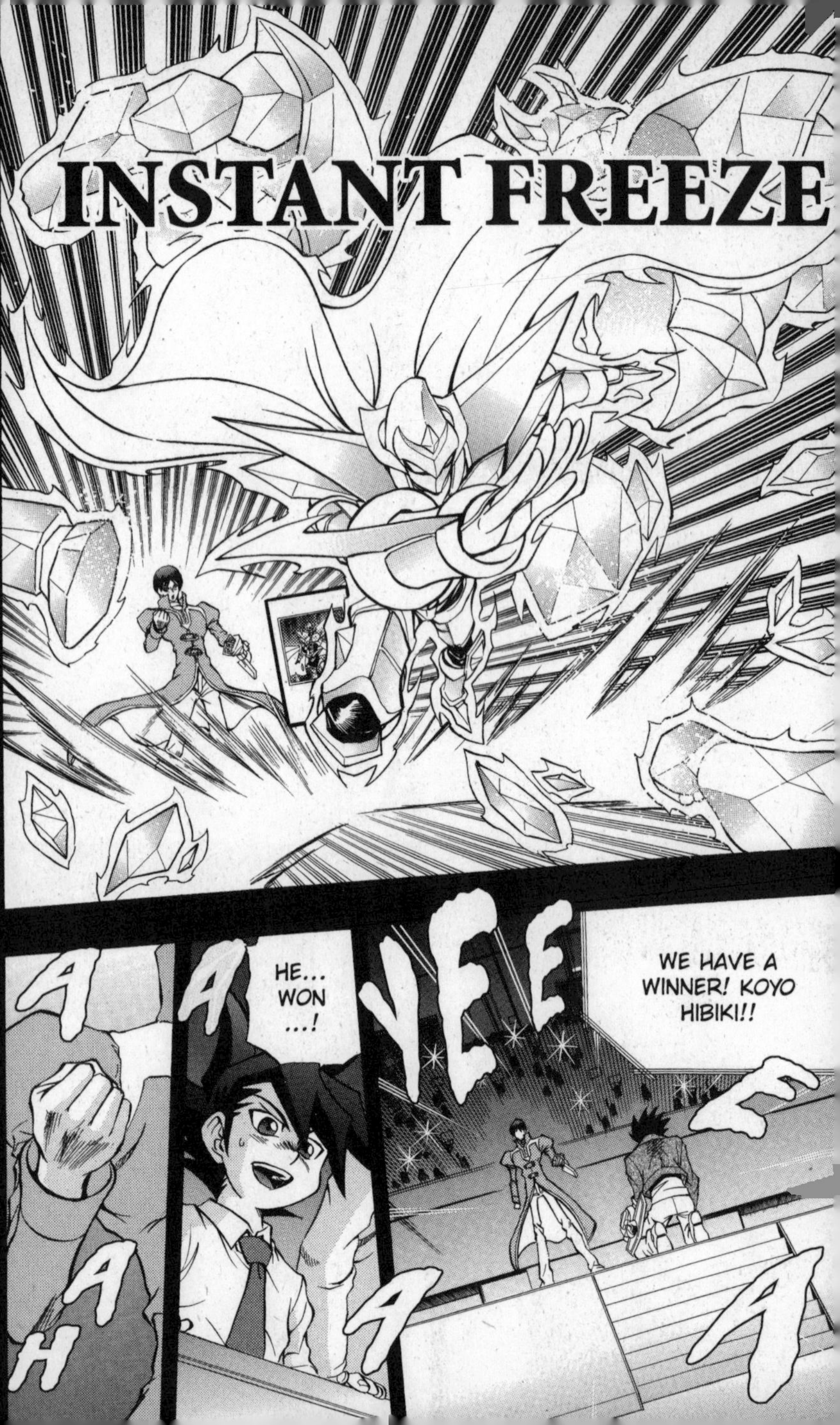
INSTANT FREEZE
WE HAVE A WINNER! KOYO HIBIKI!!
HE... WON ...!

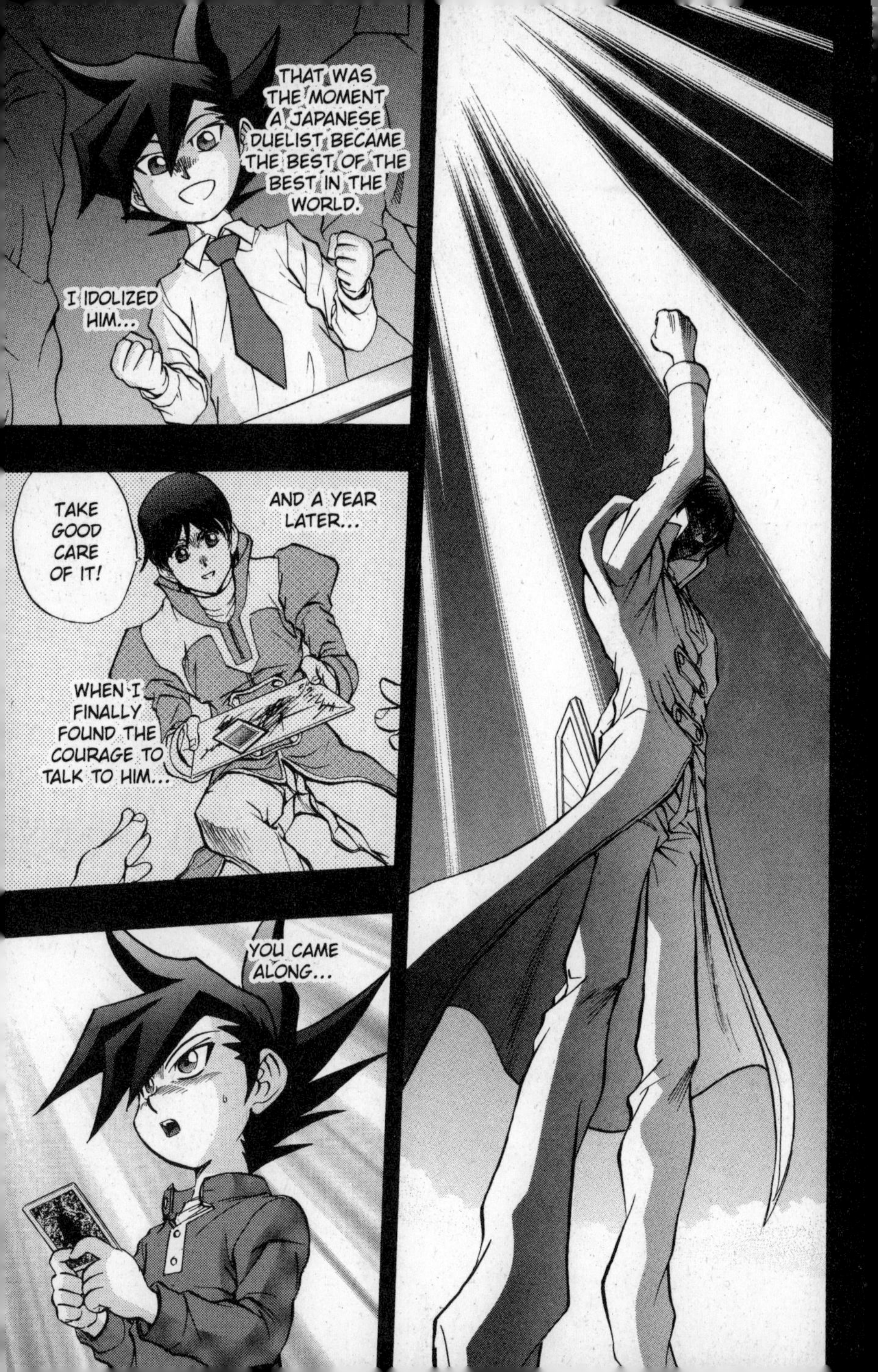
THAT WAS THE MOMENT A JAPANESE DUELIST BECAME THE BEST OF THE BEST IN THE WORLD.
I IDOLIZED HIM...
AND A YEAR LATER...
TAKE GOOD CARE OF IT!
WHEN I FINALLY FOUND THE COURAGE TO TALK TO HIM...
YOU CAME ALONG...

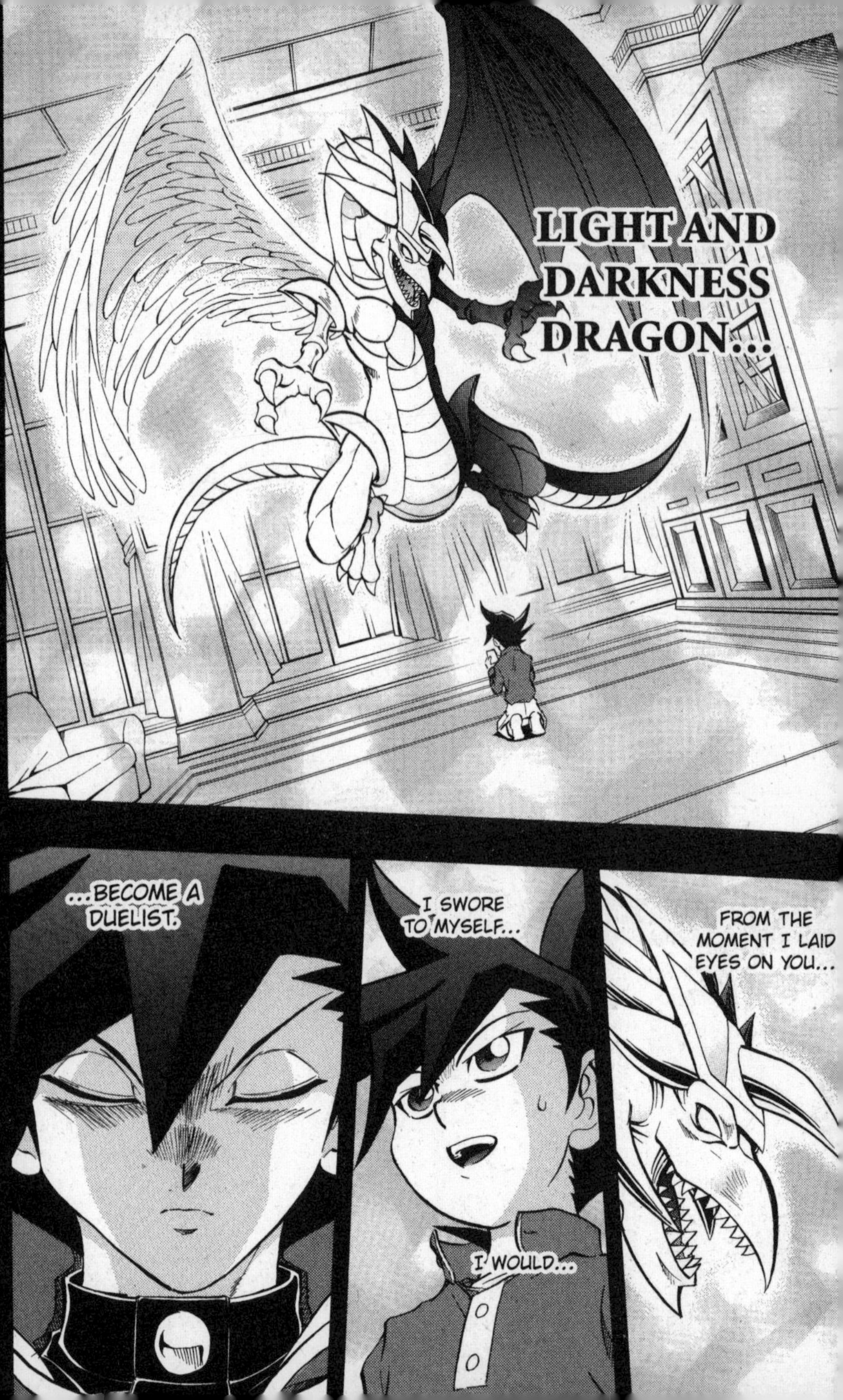
LIGHT AND DARKNESS DRAGON...
FROM THE MOMENT I LAID EYES ON YOU...
I SWORE TO MYSELF...
I WOULD...
...BECOME A DUELIST.

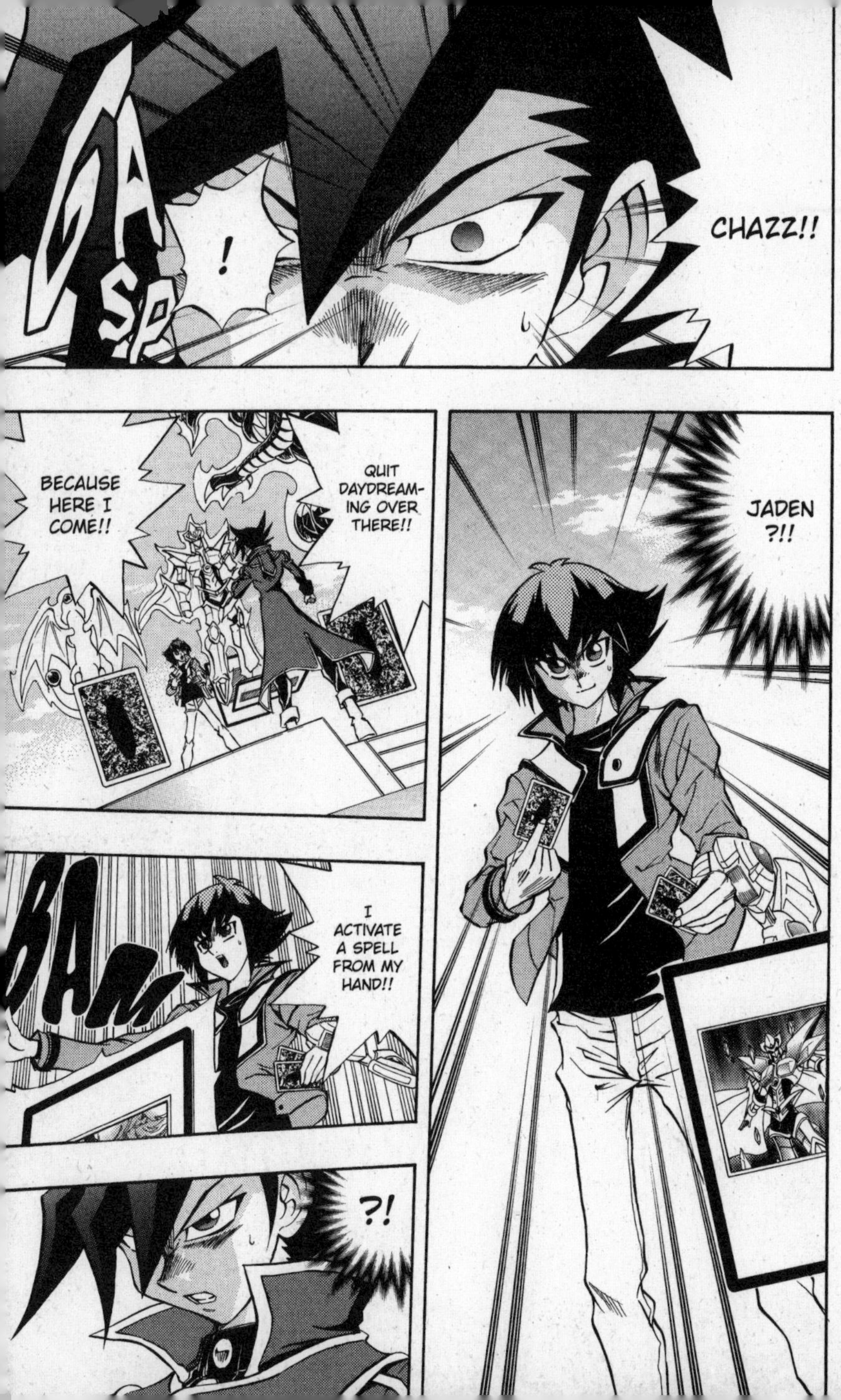
CHAZZ!!
!
GASP
JADEN ?!!
QUIT DAYDREAMING OVER THERE!!
BECAUSE HERE I COME!!
I ACTIVATE A SPELL FROM MY HAND!!
BAM
?!

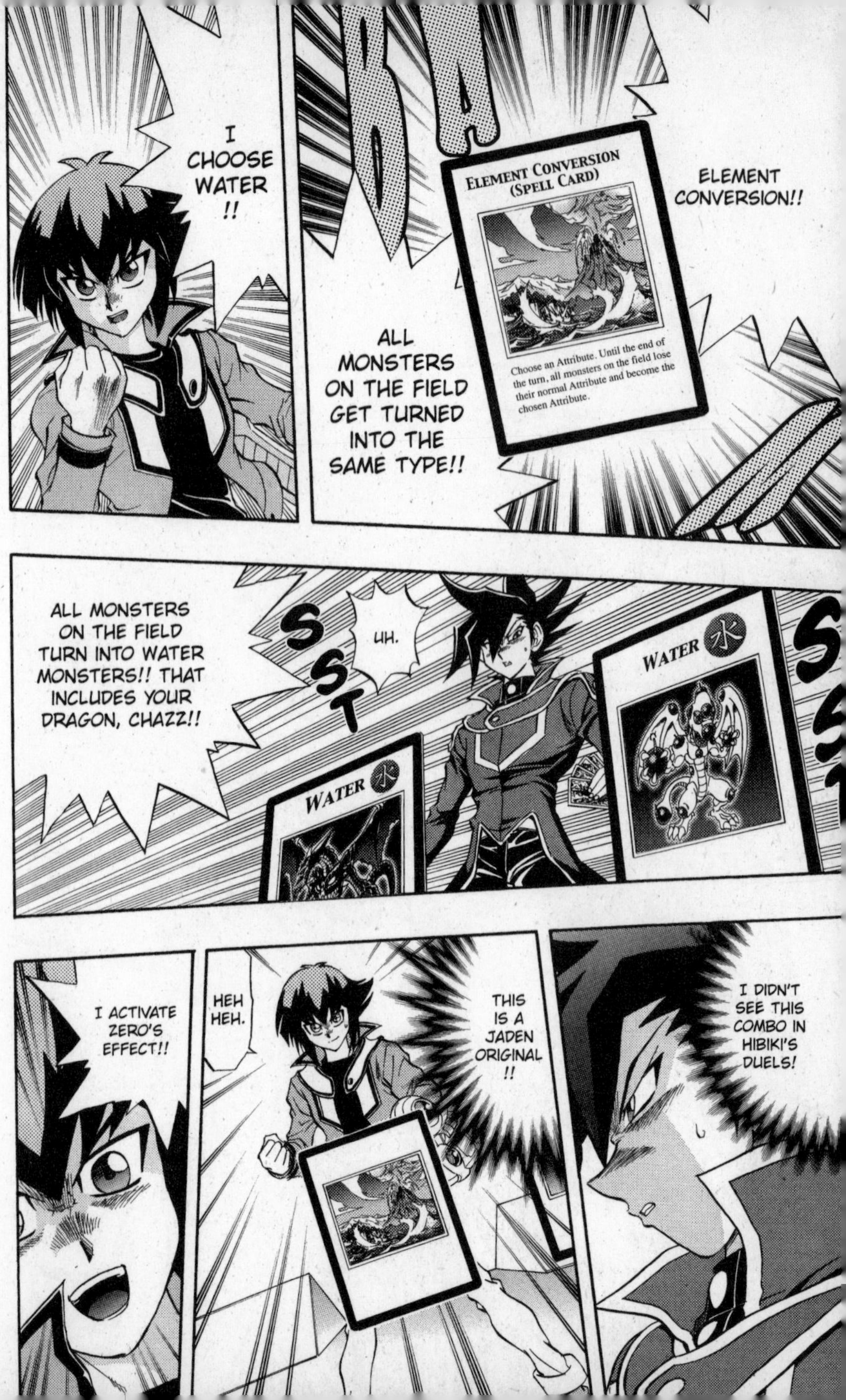
ELEMENT CONVERSION!!
BA
ELEMENT CONVERSION (SPELL CARD)
Choose an Attribute. Until the end of the turn, all monsters on the field lose their normal Attribute and become the chosen Attribute.
ALL MONSTERS ON THE FIELD GET TURNED INTO THE SAME TYPE!!
I CHOOSE WATER !!
SSST
WATER
UH.
WATER
ALL MONSTERS ON THE FIELD TURN INTO WATER MONSTERS!! THAT INCLUDES YOUR DRAGON, CHAZZ!!
I DIDN'T SEE THIS COMBO IN HIBIKI'S DUELS!
THIS IS A JADEN ORIGINAL !!
HEH HEH.
I ACTIVATE ZERO'S EFFECT!!

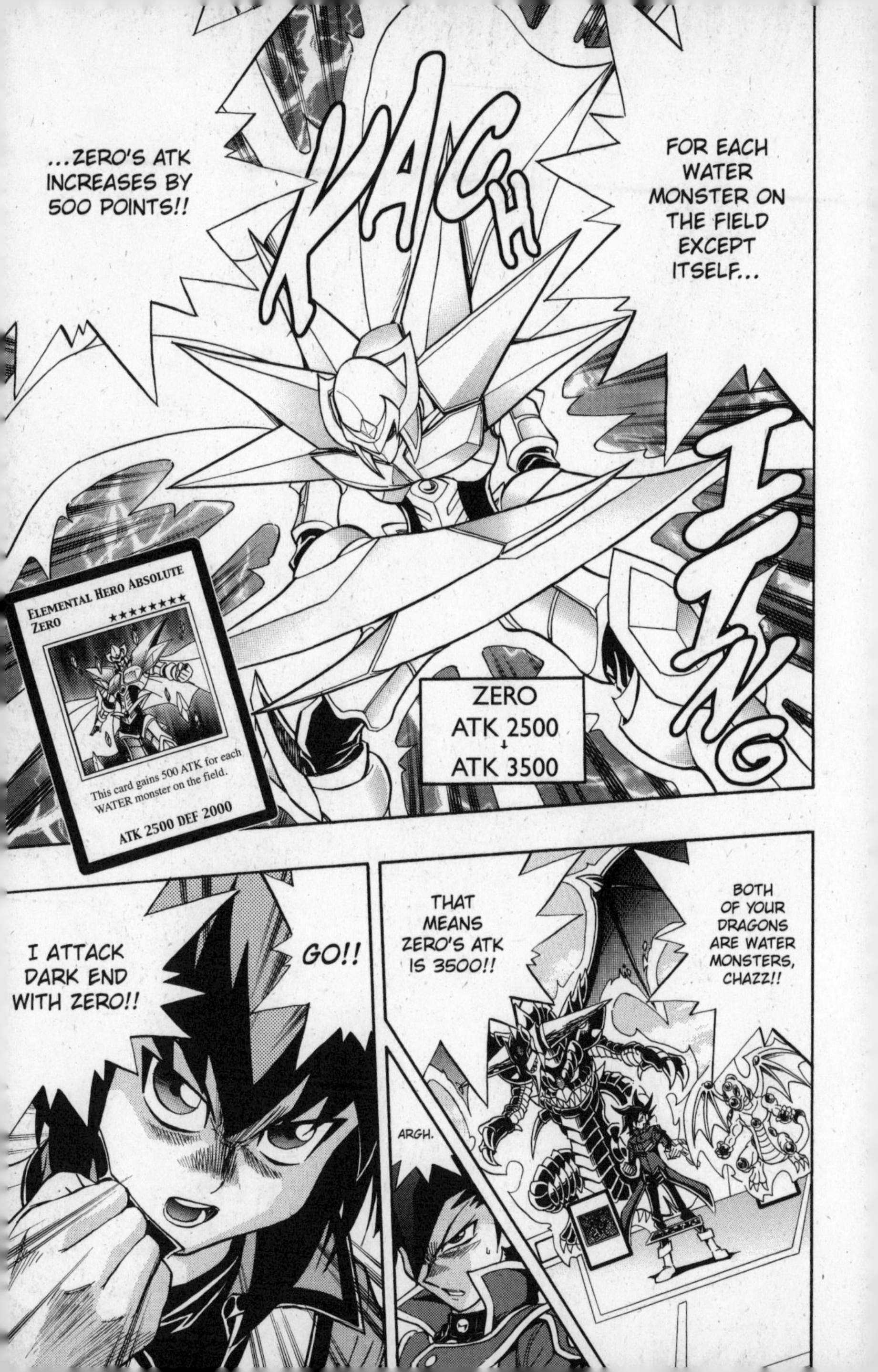
FOR EACH WATER MONSTER ON THE FIELD EXCEPT ITSELF...
...ZERO'S ATK INCREASES BY 500 POINTS!!
KACH
ZING
ZERO
ATK 2500
ATK 3500
ELEMENTAL HERO ABSOLUTE ZERO ★★★★★★★★
This card gains 500 ATK for each WATER monster on the field.
ATK 2500 DEF 2000
BOTH OF YOUR DRAGONS ARE WATER MONSTERS, CHAZZ!!
THAT MEANS ZERO'S ATK IS 3500!!
ARGH.
GO!!
I ATTACK DARK END WITH ZERO!!

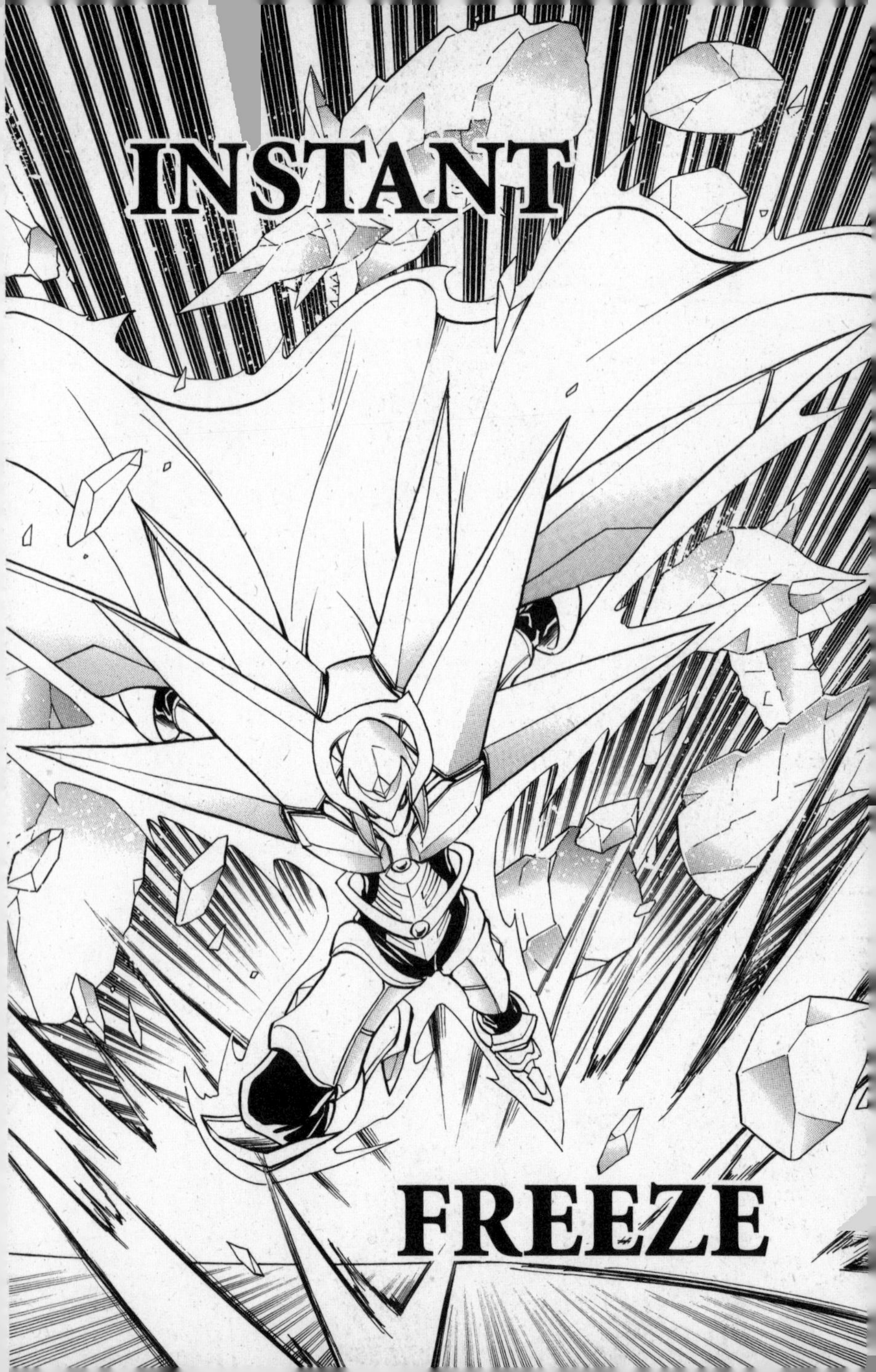
INSTANT
FREEZE

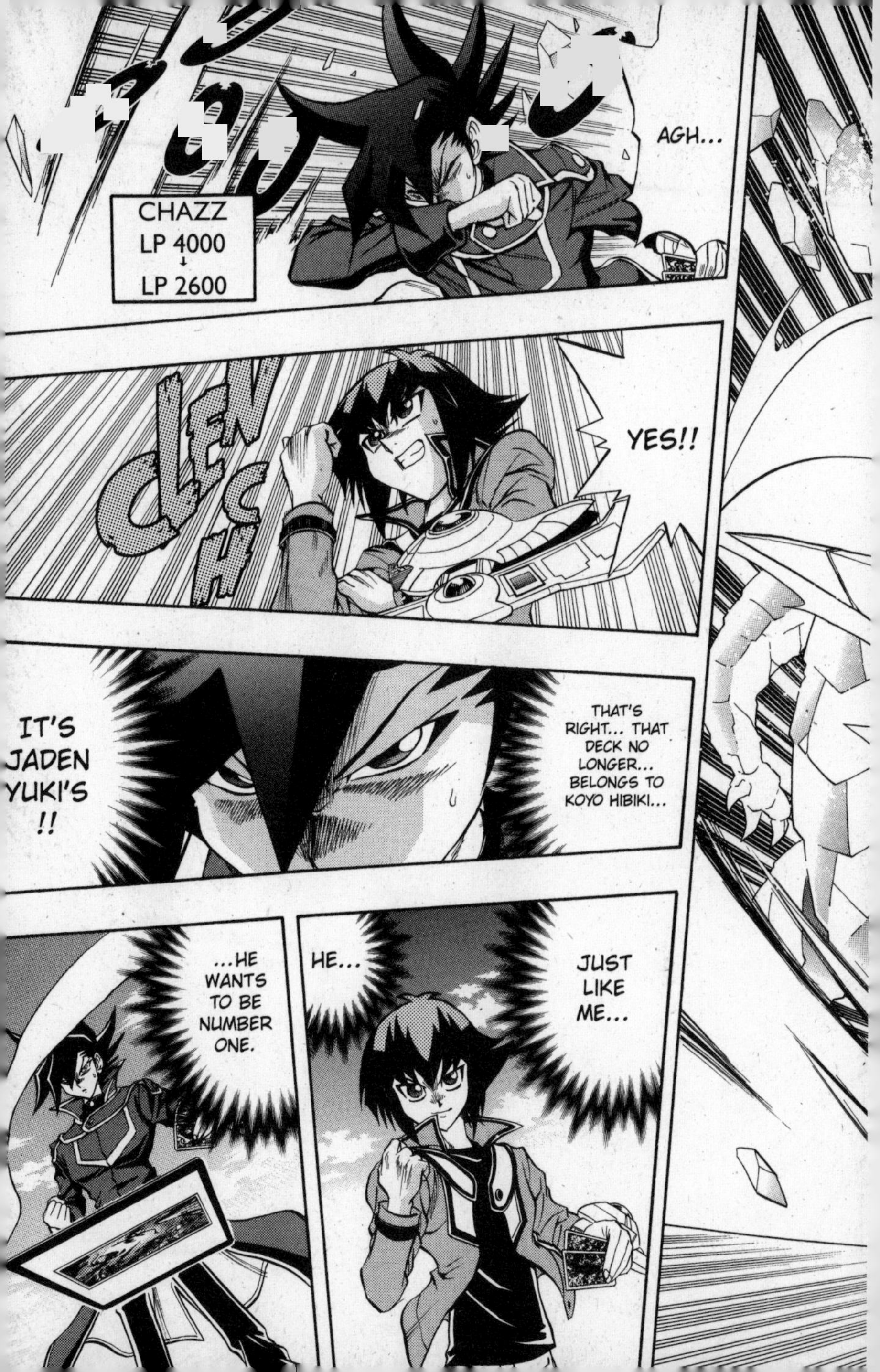
AGH...
CHAZZ
LP 4000
↓
LP 2600
YES!!
CLENCH
THAT'S RIGHT... THAT DECK NO LONGER... BELONGS TO KOYO HIBIKI...
IT'S JADEN YUKI'S!!
JUST LIKE ME...
HE...
...HE WANTS TO BE NUMBER ONE.

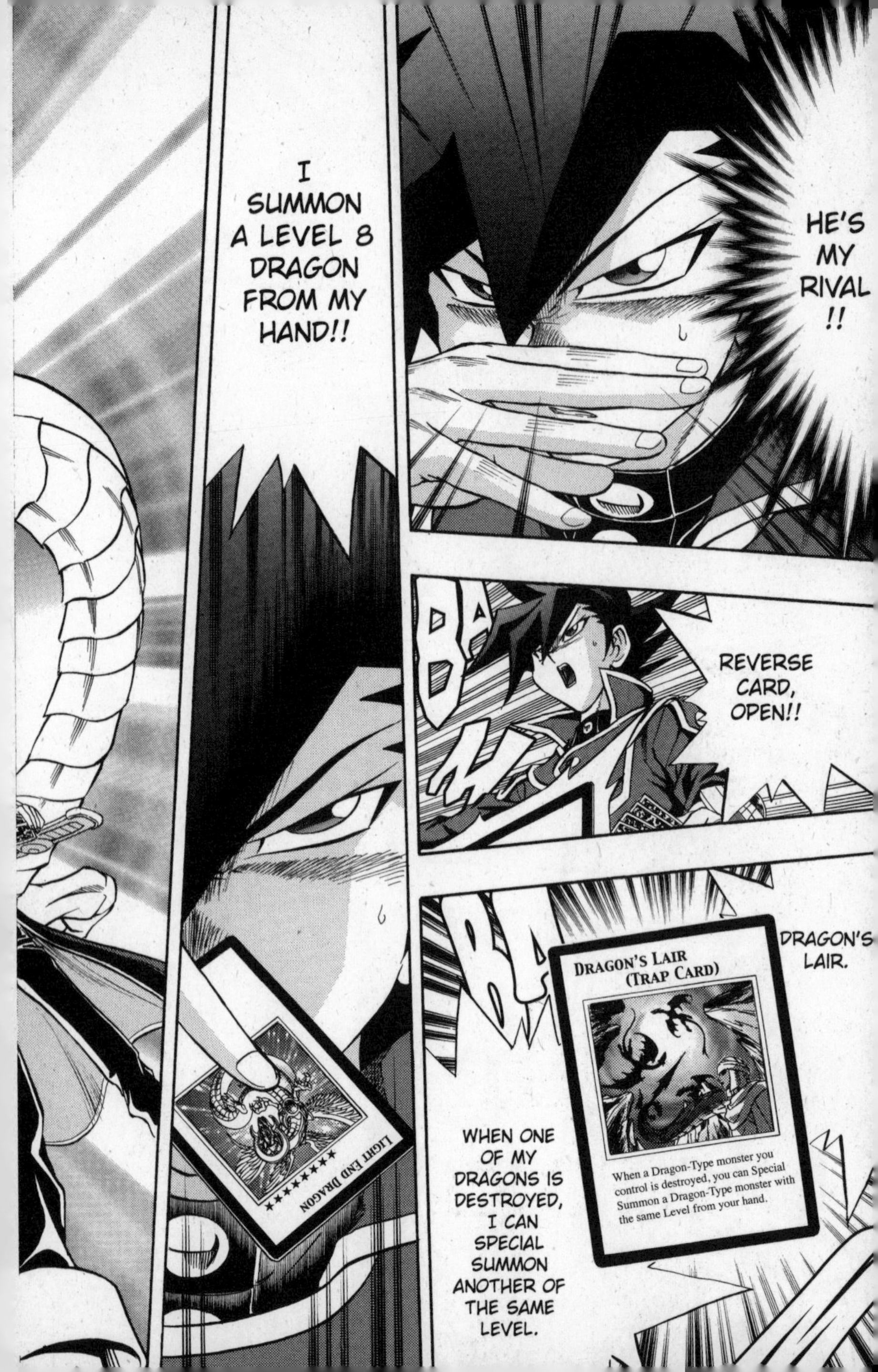
HE'S MY RIVAL!!
REVERSE CARD, OPEN!!
DRAGON'S LAIR.
DRAGON'S LAIR (TRAP CARD)
When a Dragon-Type monster you control is destroyed, you can Special Summon a Dragon-Type monster with the same Level from your hand.
WHEN ONE OF MY DRAGONS IS DESTROYED, I CAN SPECIAL SUMMON ANOTHER OF THE SAME LEVEL.
I SUMMON A LEVEL 8 DRAGON FROM MY HAND!!
LIGHT END DRAGON

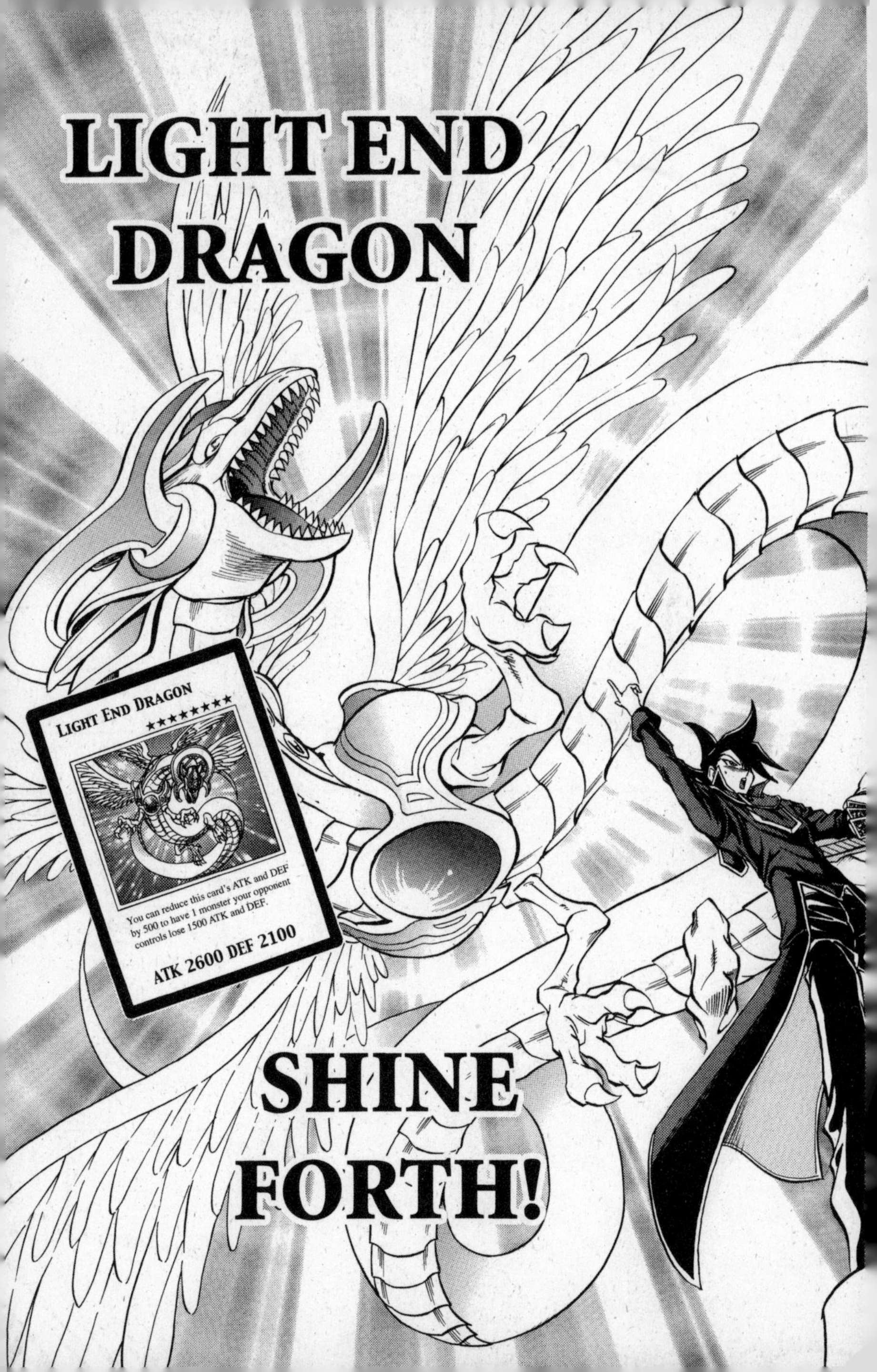
LIGHT END DRAGON
LIGHT END DRAGON
★★★★★★★★
You can reduce this card's ATK and DEF by 500 to have 1 monster your opponent controls lose 1500 ATK and DEF.
ATK 2600 DEF 2100
SHINE FORTH!

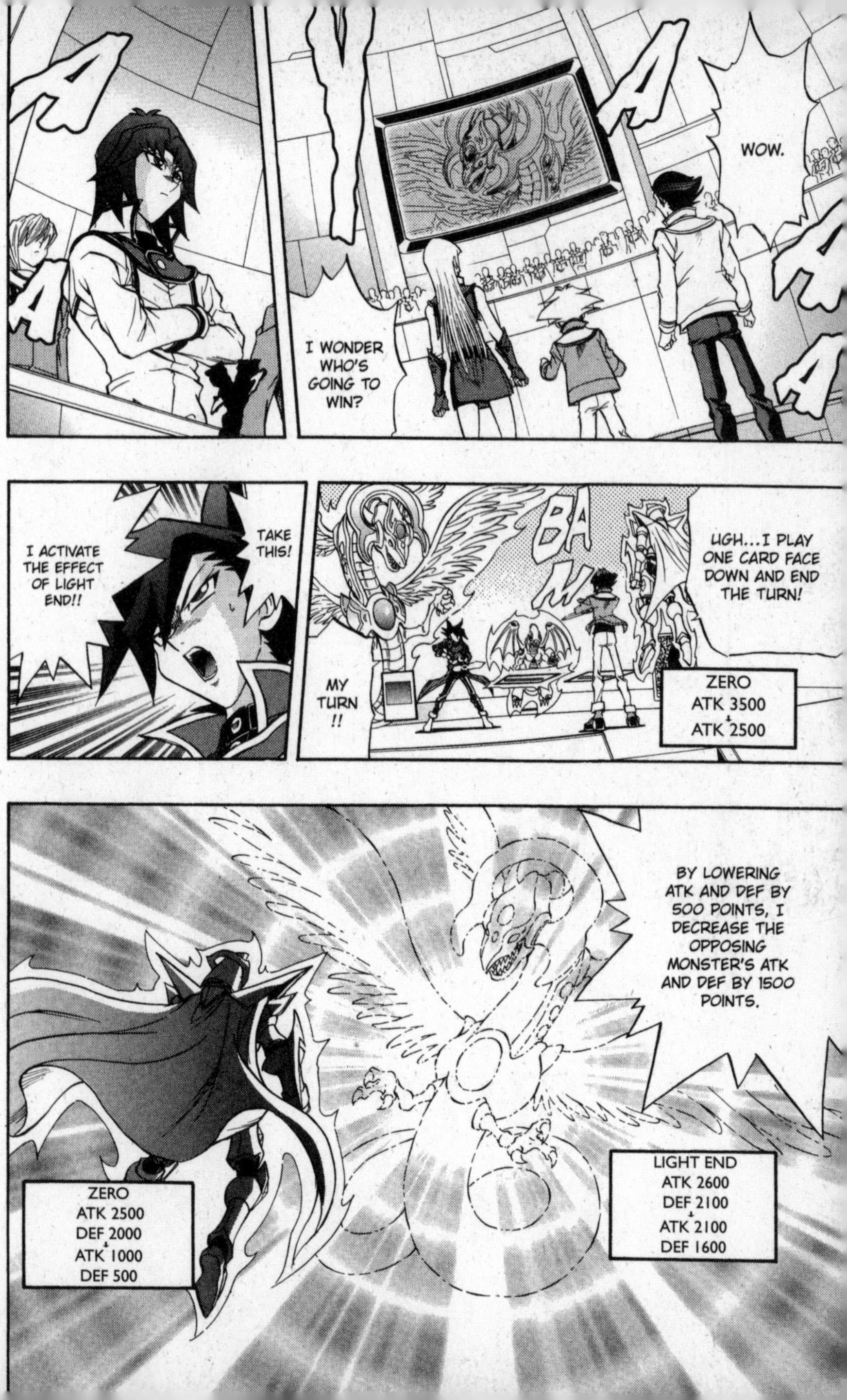
WOW.
I WONDER WHO'S GOING TO WIN?
UGH...I PLAY ONE CARD FACE DOWN AND END THE TURN!
BAM
ZERO ATK 3500 ATK 2500
MY TURN!!
TAKE THIS!
I ACTIVATE THE EFFECT OF LIGHT END!!
BY LOWERING ATK AND DEF BY 500 POINTS, I DECREASE THE OPPOSING MONSTER'S ATK AND DEF BY 1500 POINTS.
LIGHT END ATK 2600 DEF 2100 ATK 2100 DEF 1600
ZERO ATK 2500 DEF 2000 ATK 1000 DEF 500

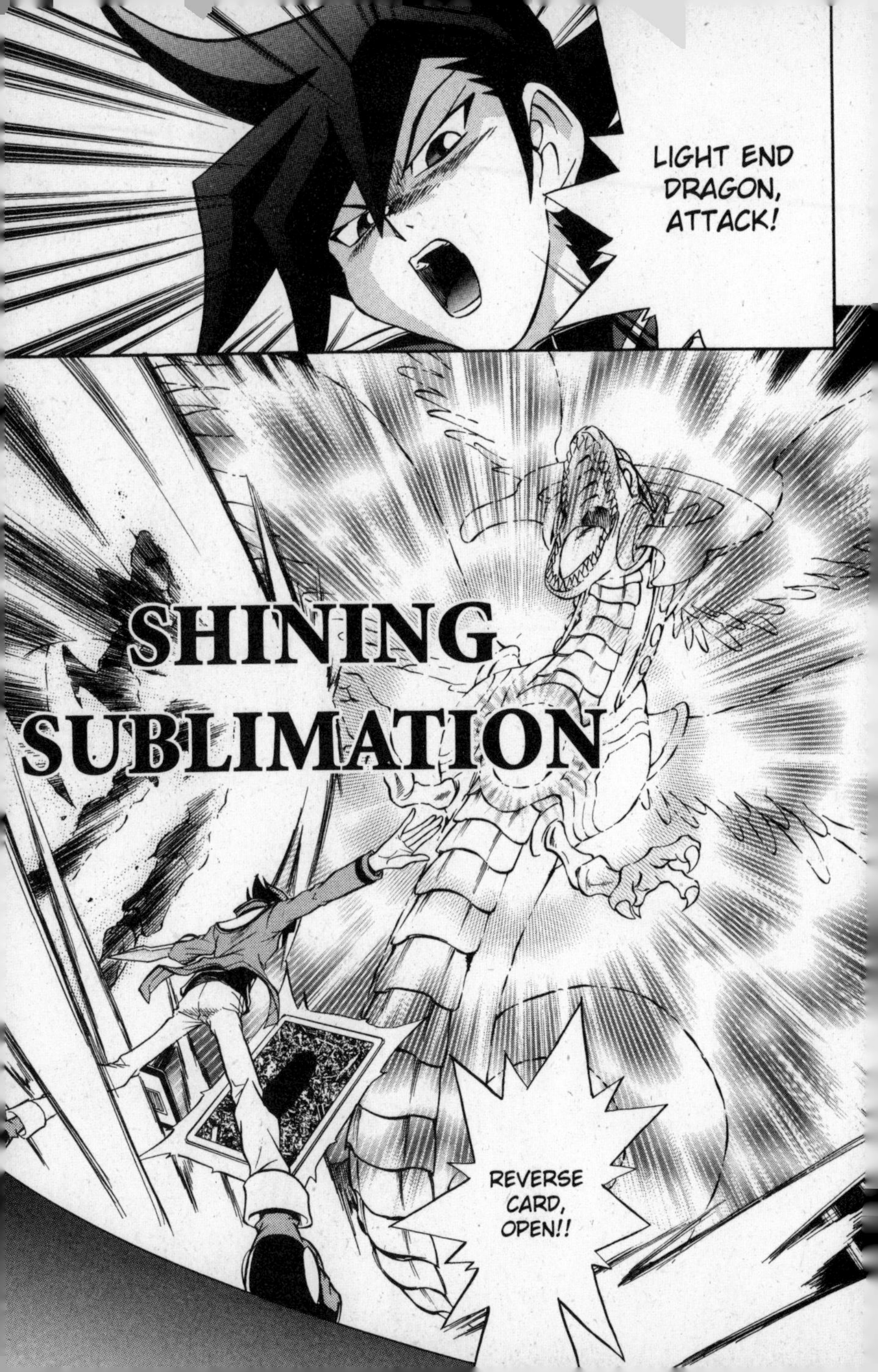
LIGHT END DRAGON, ATTACK!
SHINING SUBLIMATION
REVERSE CARD, OPEN!!

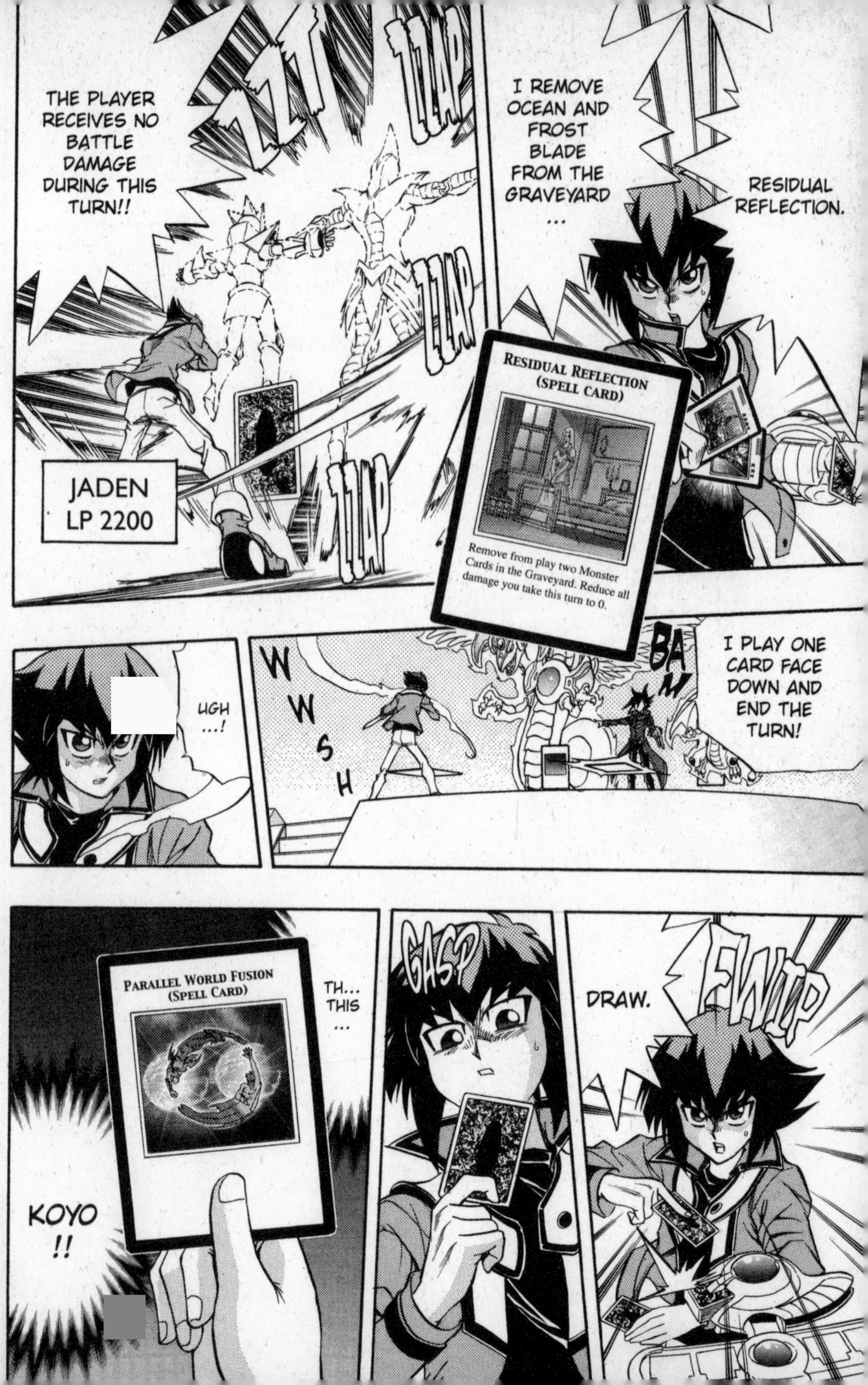

I REMOVE OCEAN AND FROST BLADE FROM THE GRAVEYARD ...
RESIDUAL REFLECTION.
RESIDUAL REFLECTION
(SPELL CARD)
Remove from play two Monster Cards in the Graveyard. Reduce all damage you take this turn to 0.
ZZAP
THE PLAYER RECEIVES NO BATTLE DAMAGE DURING THIS TURN!!
ZZAP
ZZAP
JADEN
LP 2200
I PLAY ONE CARD FACE DOWN AND END THE TURN!
BAM
WWSH
UGH ...!
FWIP
DRAW.
GASP
TH... THIS ...
PARALLEL WORLD FUSION
(SPELL CARD)
KOYO !!

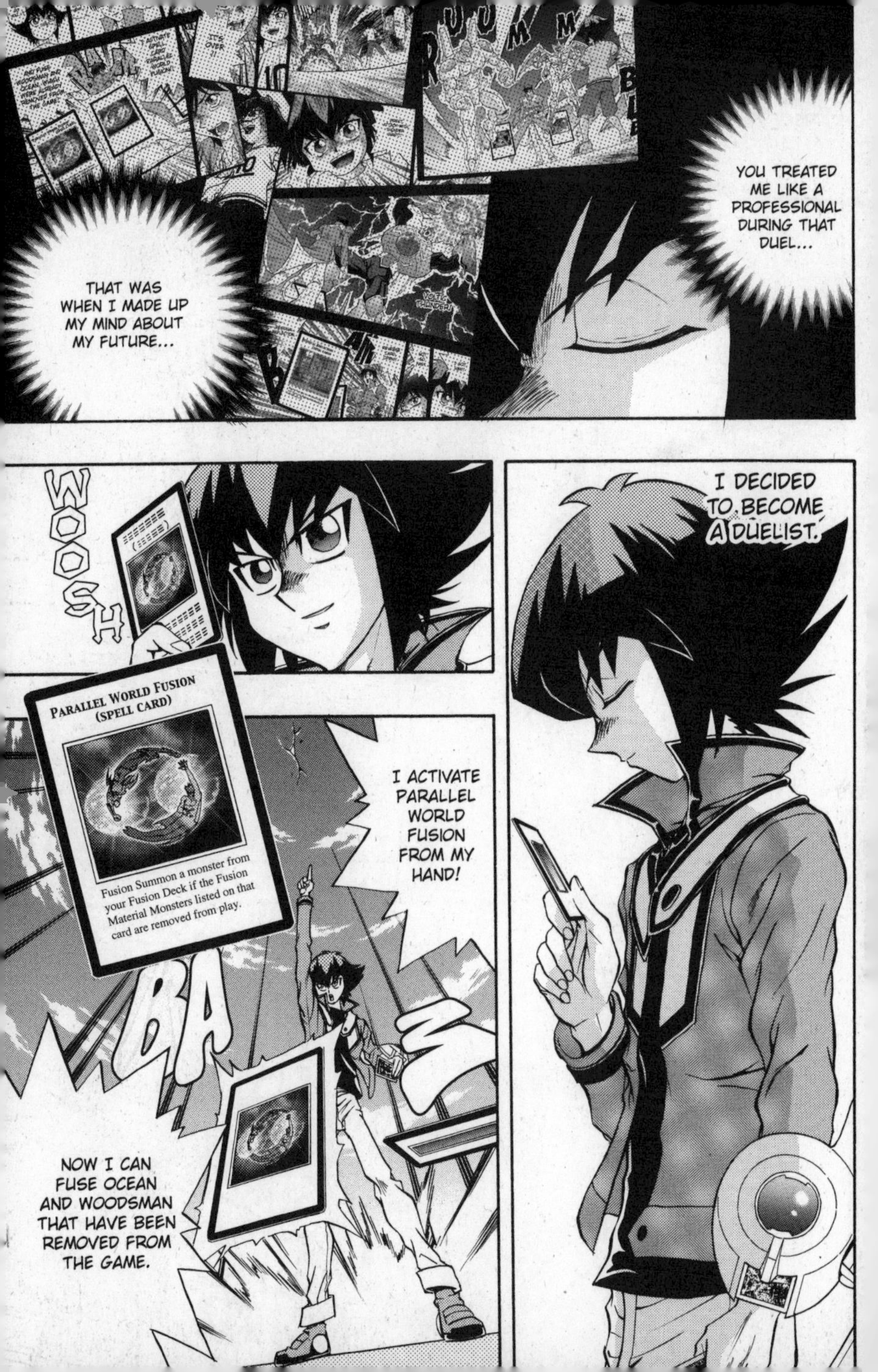

YOU TREATED ME LIKE A PROFESSIONAL DURING THAT DUEL...
THAT WAS WHEN I MADE UP MY MIND ABOUT MY FUTURE...
I DECIDED TO BECOME A DUELIST.
WOOSH
PARALLEL WORLD FUSION (SPELL CARD)
Fusion Summon a monster from your Fusion Deck if the Fusion Material Monsters listed on that card are removed from play.
I ACTIVATE PARALLEL WORLD FUSION FROM MY HAND!
BA
NOW I CAN FUSE OCEAN AND WOODSMAN THAT HAVE BEEN REMOVED FROM THE GAME.

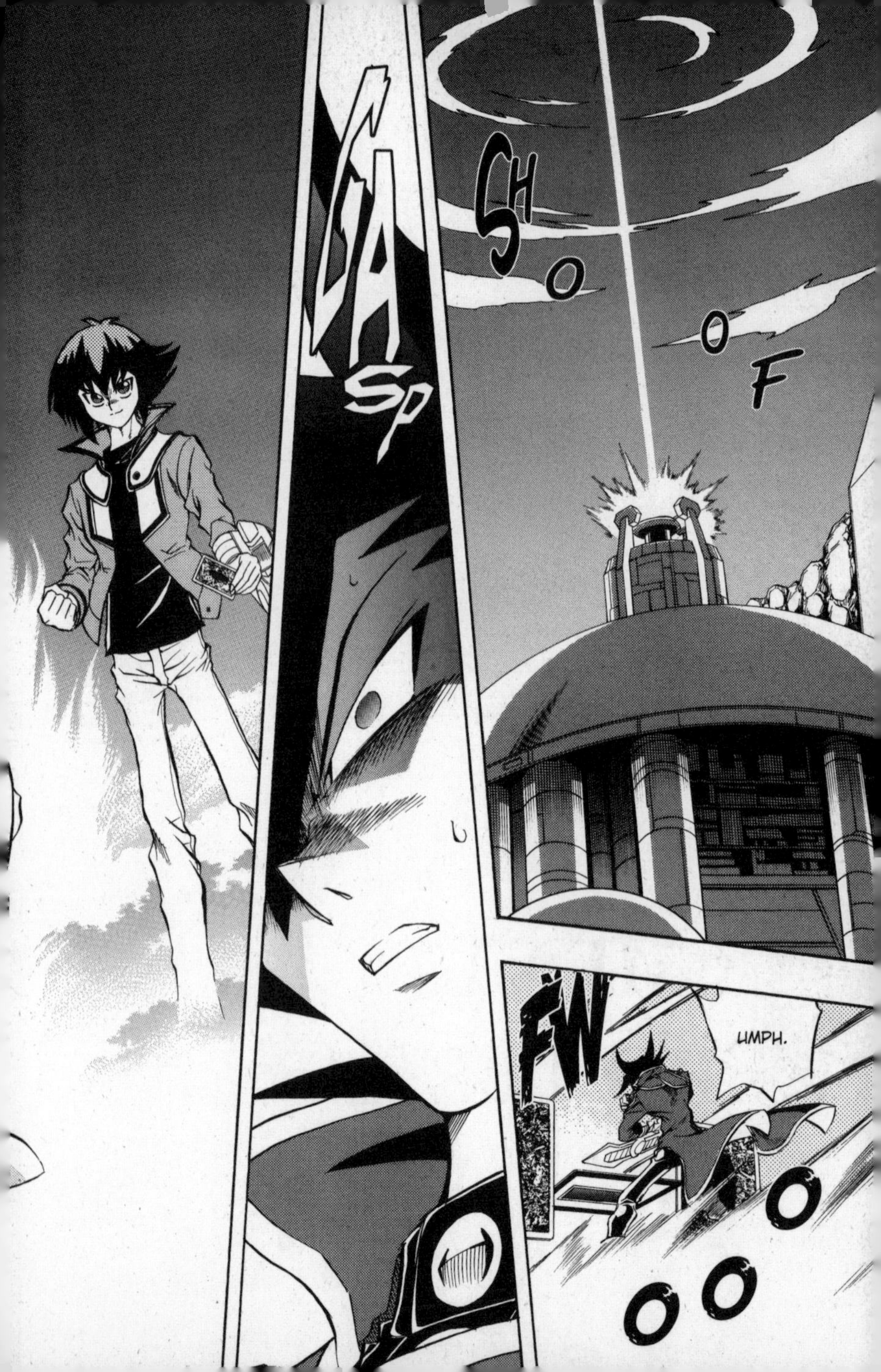
SHOOF
GASP
FW
UMPH.
OOOO

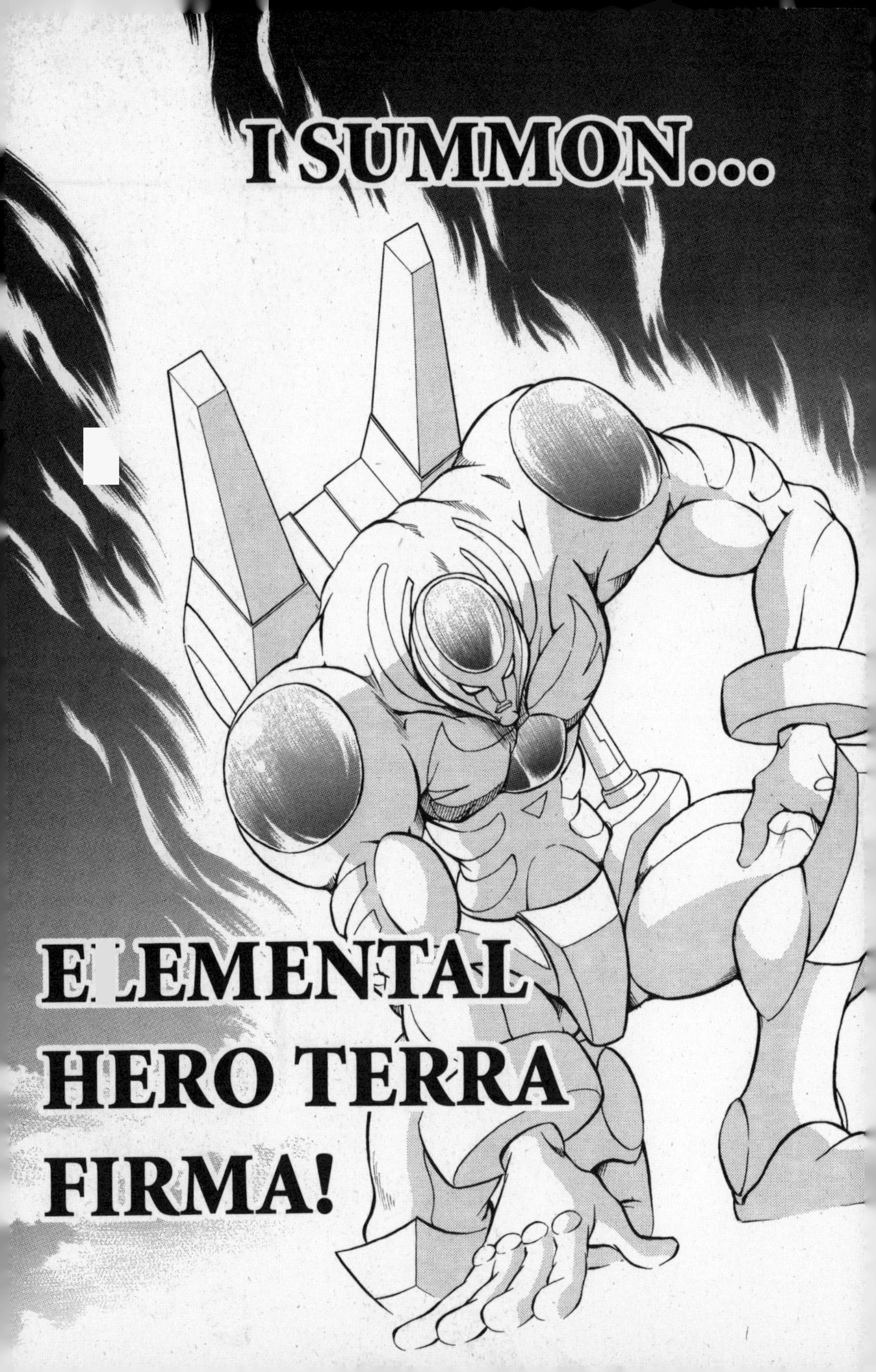
I SUMMON...
ELEMENTAL HERO TERRA FIRMA!

SYNCHRO SUMMONING

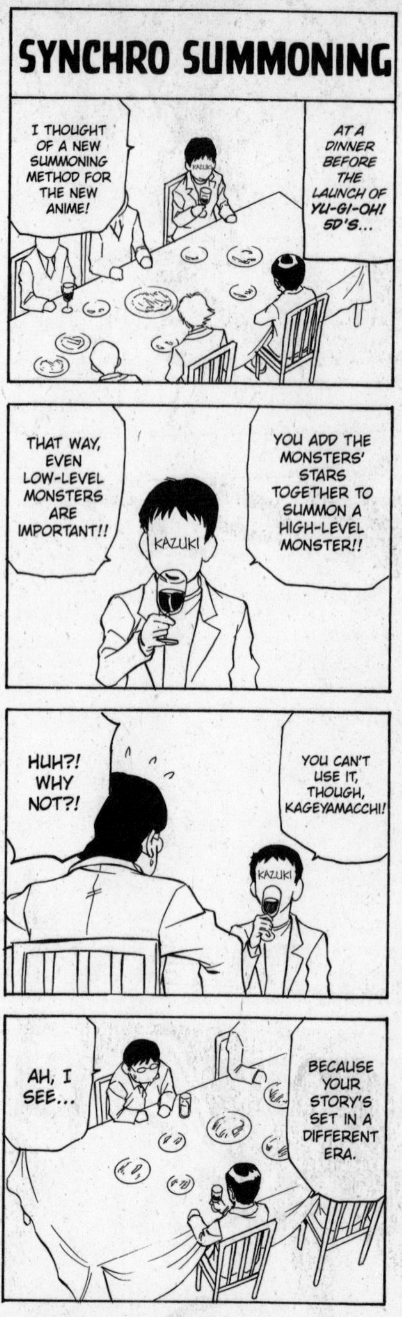
AT A DINNER BEFORE THE LAUNCH OF YU-GI-OH! 5D'S...
KAZUKI
I THOUGHT OF A NEW SUMMONING METHOD FOR THE NEW ANIME!
YOU ADD THE MONSTERS' STARS TOGETHER TO SUMMON A HIGH-LEVEL MONSTER!!
KAZUKI
THAT WAY, EVEN LOW-LEVEL MONSTERS ARE IMPORTANT!!
YOU CAN'T USE IT, THOUGH, KAGEYAMACCHI!
KAZUKI
HUH?! WHY NOT?!
BECAUSE YOUR STORY'S SET IN A DIFFERENT ERA.
AH, I SEE...

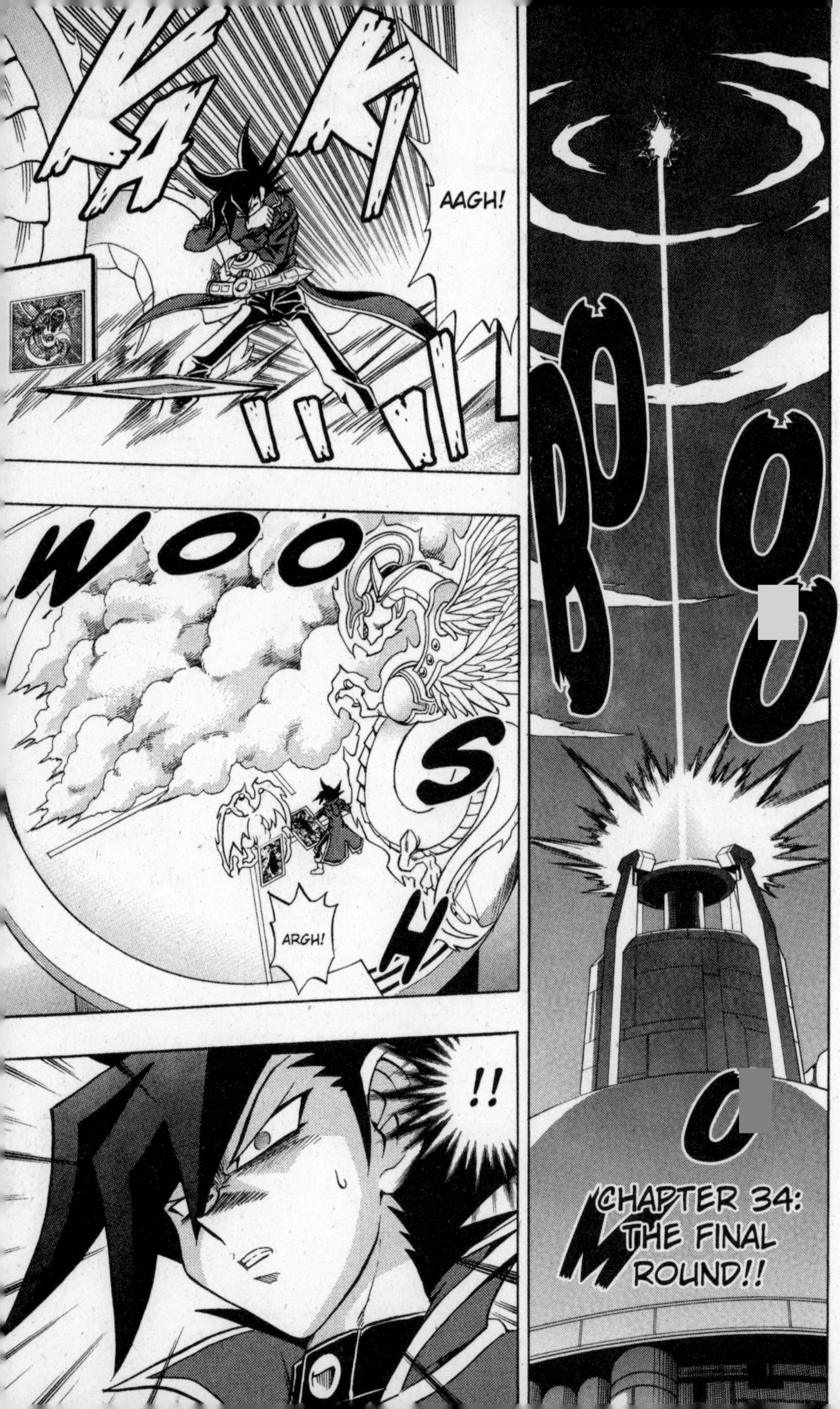
BOOOOOM
CHAPTER 34: THE FINAL ROUND!!
AAGH!
WOOSH
ARGH!
!!

ELEMENTAL HERO
TERRA FIRMA
ELEMENTAL HERO TERRA FIRMA
You can Tribute 1 face-up "Elemental Hero" monster to have this card gain ATK equal to the Tributed monster's ATK until the End Phase.
ATK 2500 DEF 2000
I SUMMONED ELEMENTAL HERO TERRA FIRMA

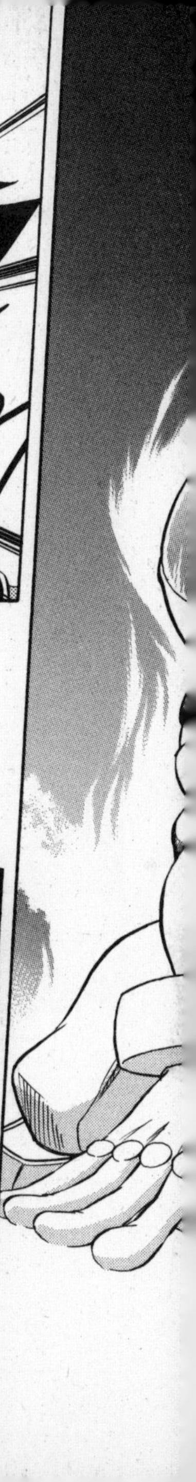

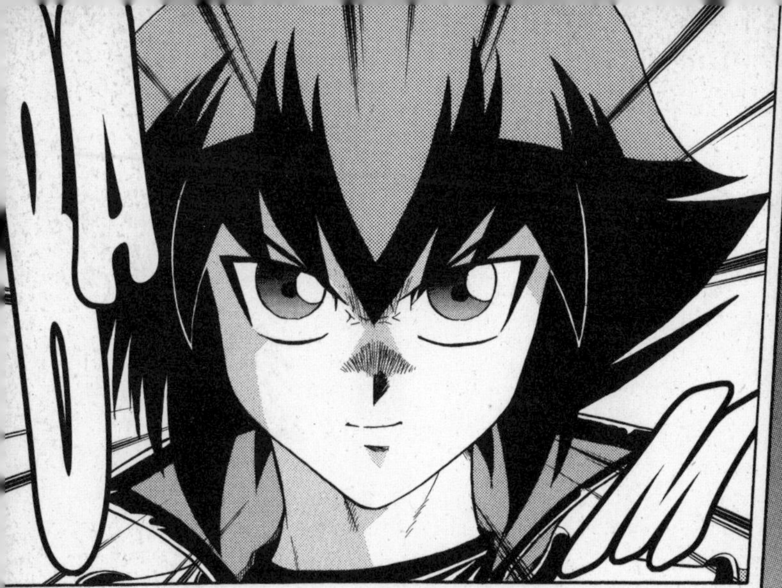

CHAPTER 34: THE FINAL ROUND!!

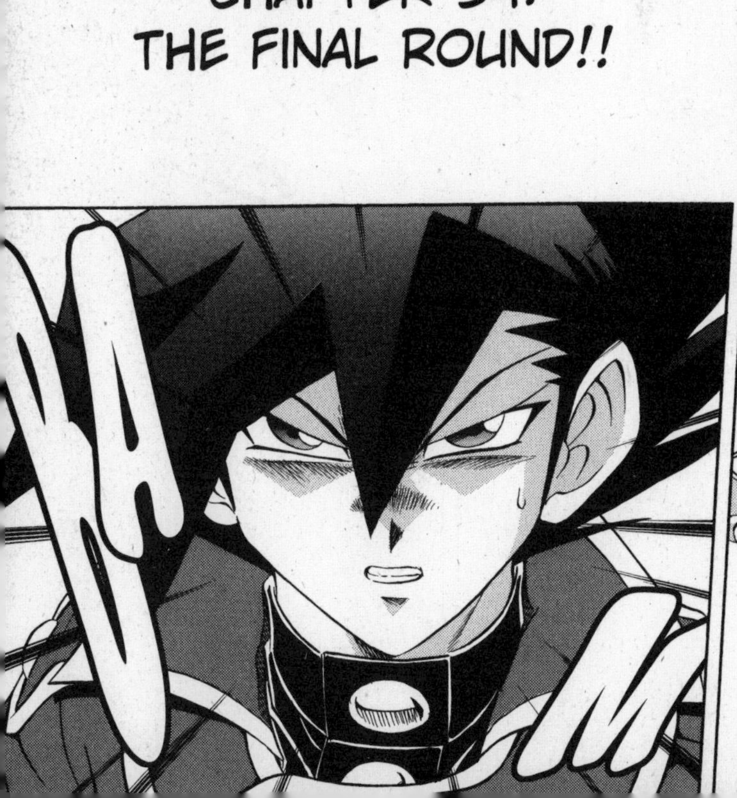

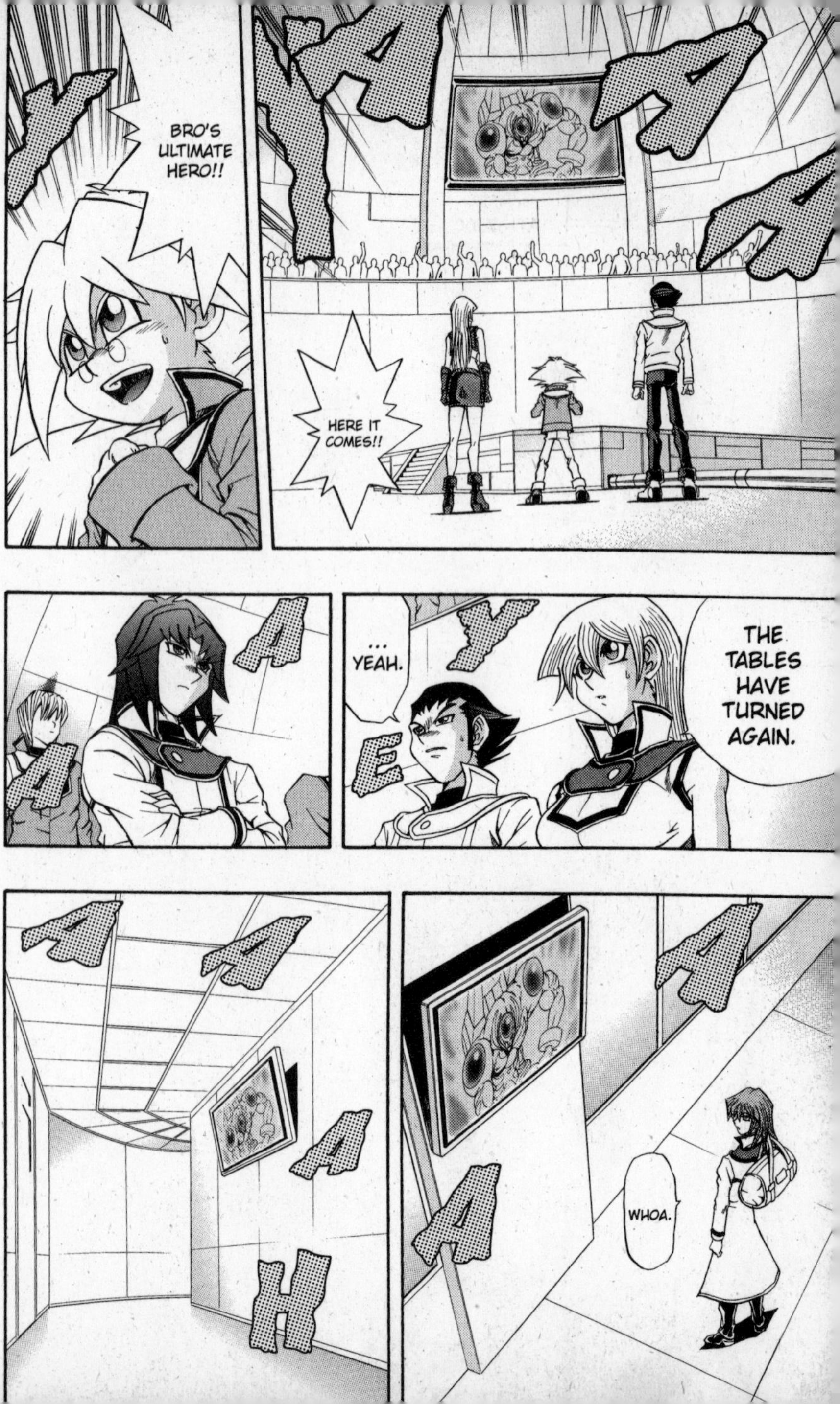
HERE IT COMES!!
BRO'S ULTIMATE HERO!!
THE TABLES HAVE TURNED AGAIN.
... YEAH.
WHOA.

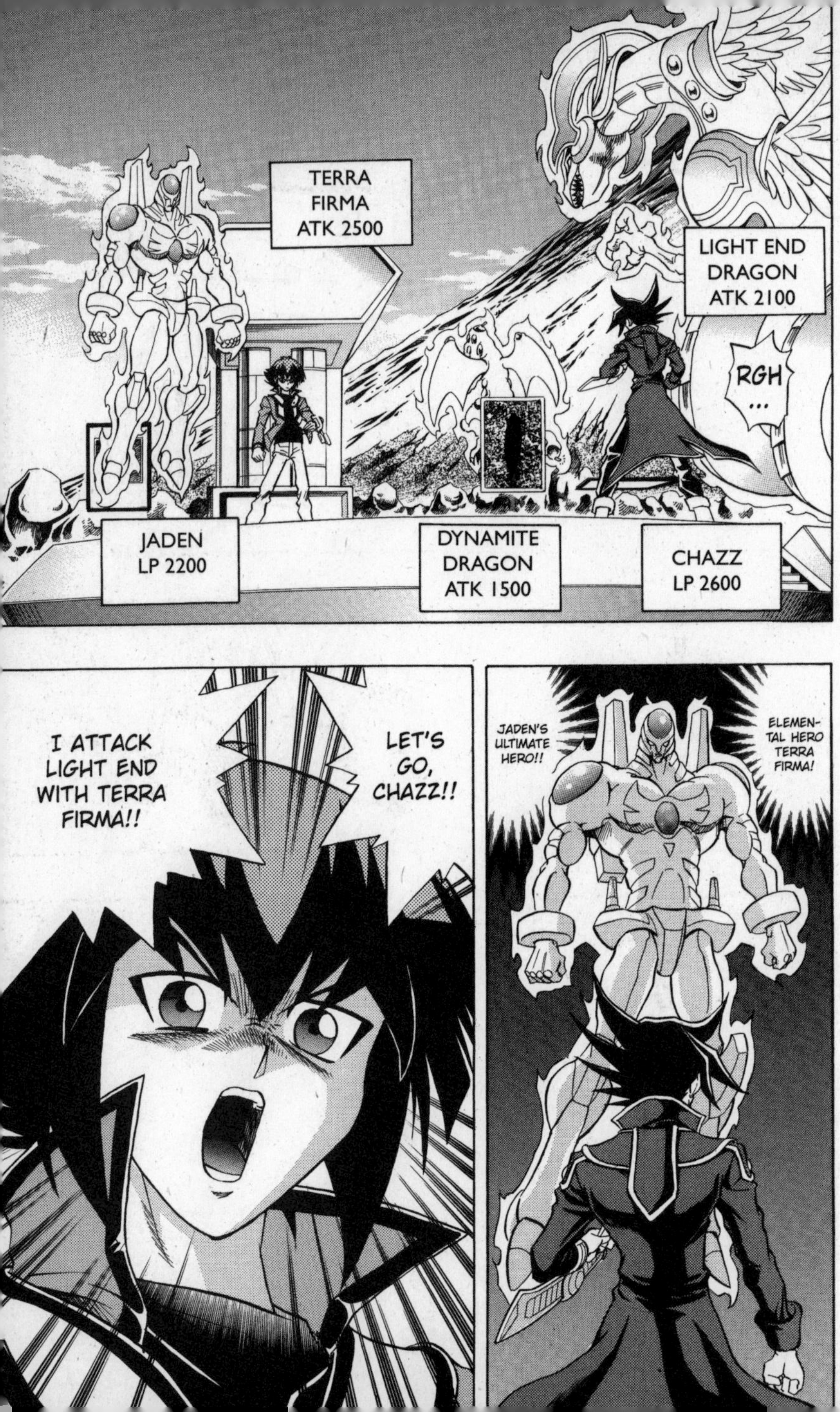
LIGHT END DRAGON ATK 2100
RGH...
TERRA FIRMA ATK 2500
CHAZZ LP 2600
DYNAMITE DRAGON ATK 1500
JADEN LP 2200
ELEMENTAL HERO TERRA FIRMA!
JADEN'S ULTIMATE HERO!!
LET'S GO, CHAZZ!!
I ATTACK LIGHT END WITH TERRA FIRMA!!

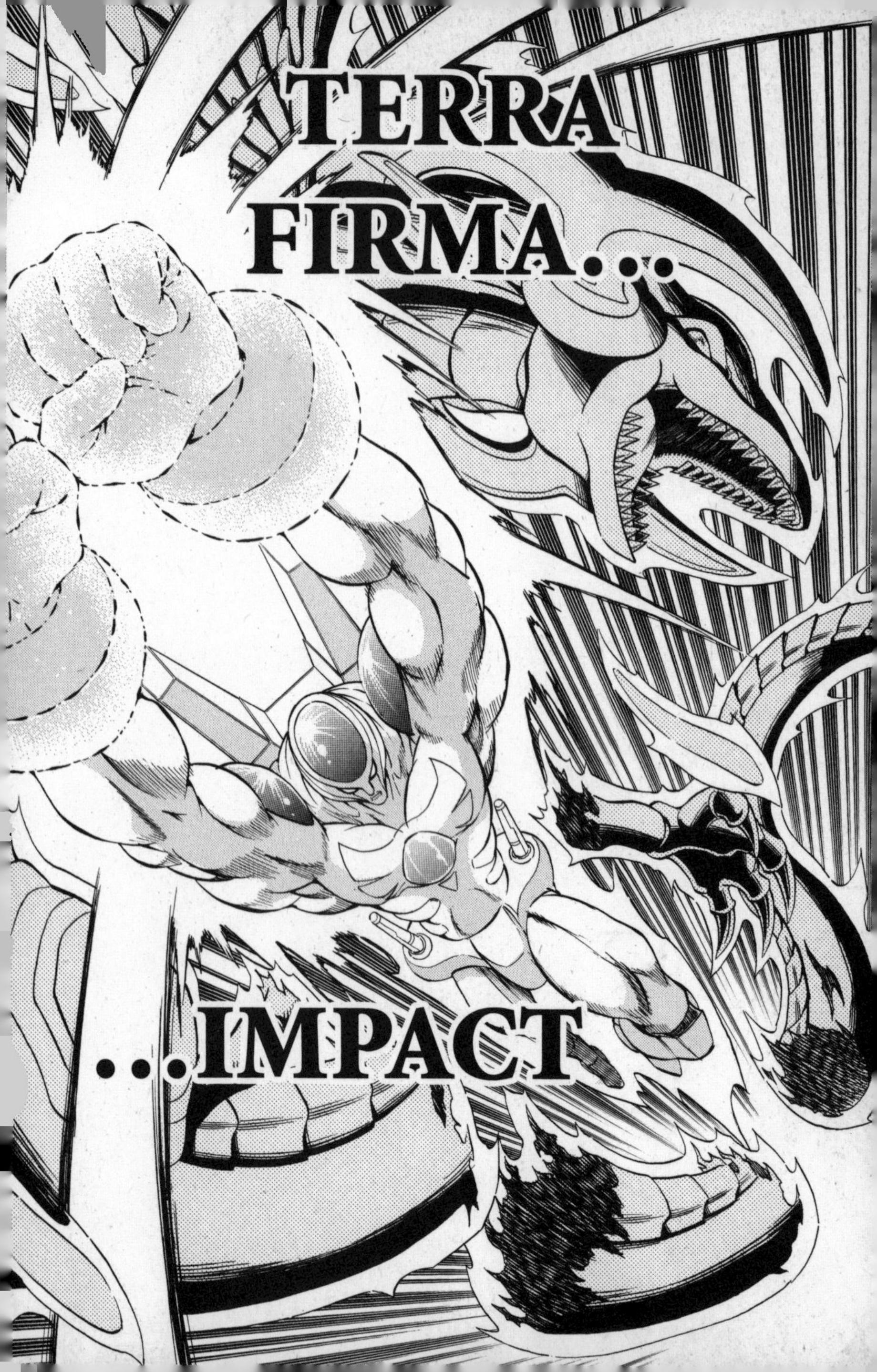
TERRA FIRMA...
...IMPACT

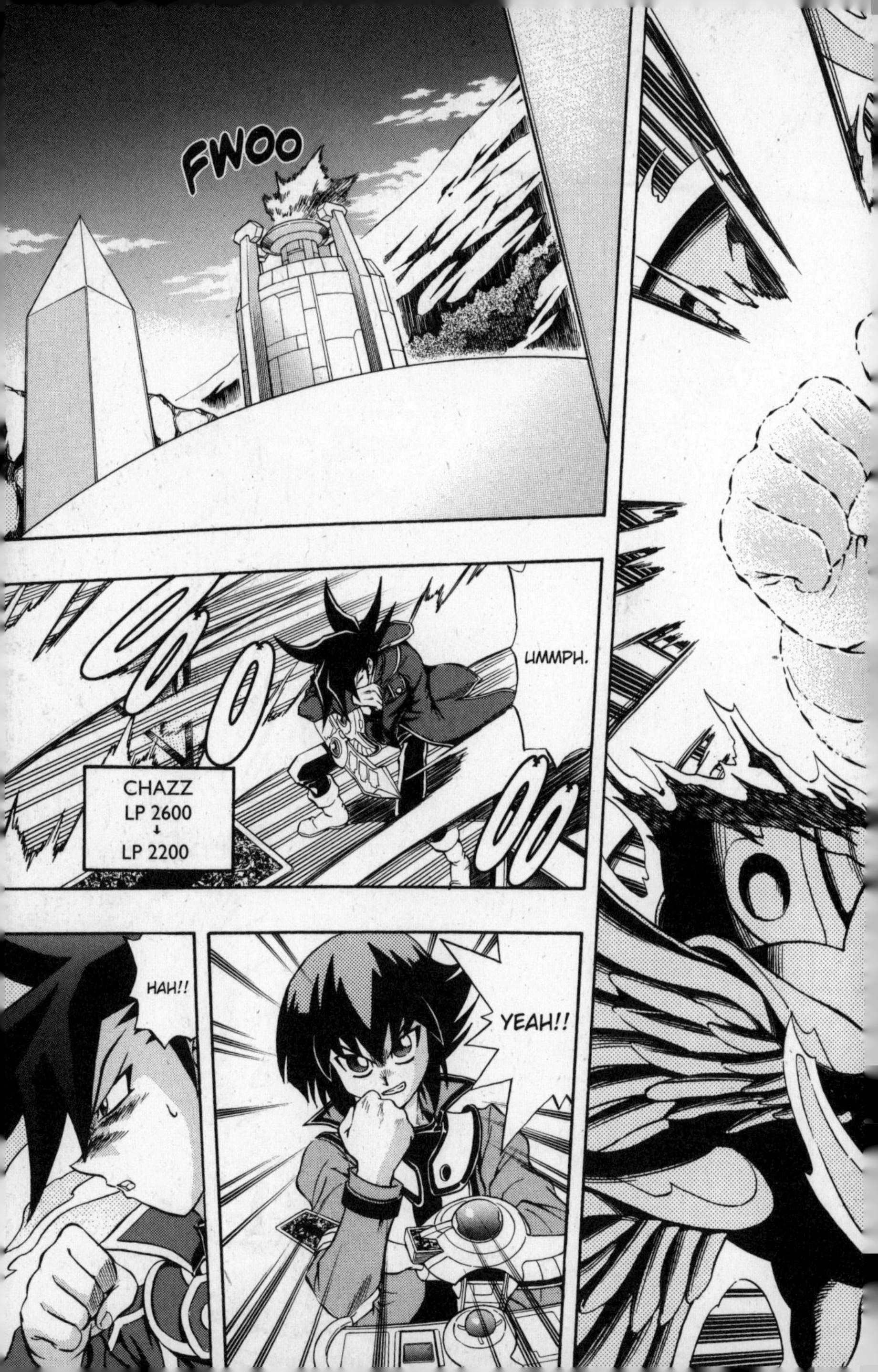
FWOO
UMMPH.
CHAZZ
LP 2600
↓
LP 2200
YEAH!!
HAH!!

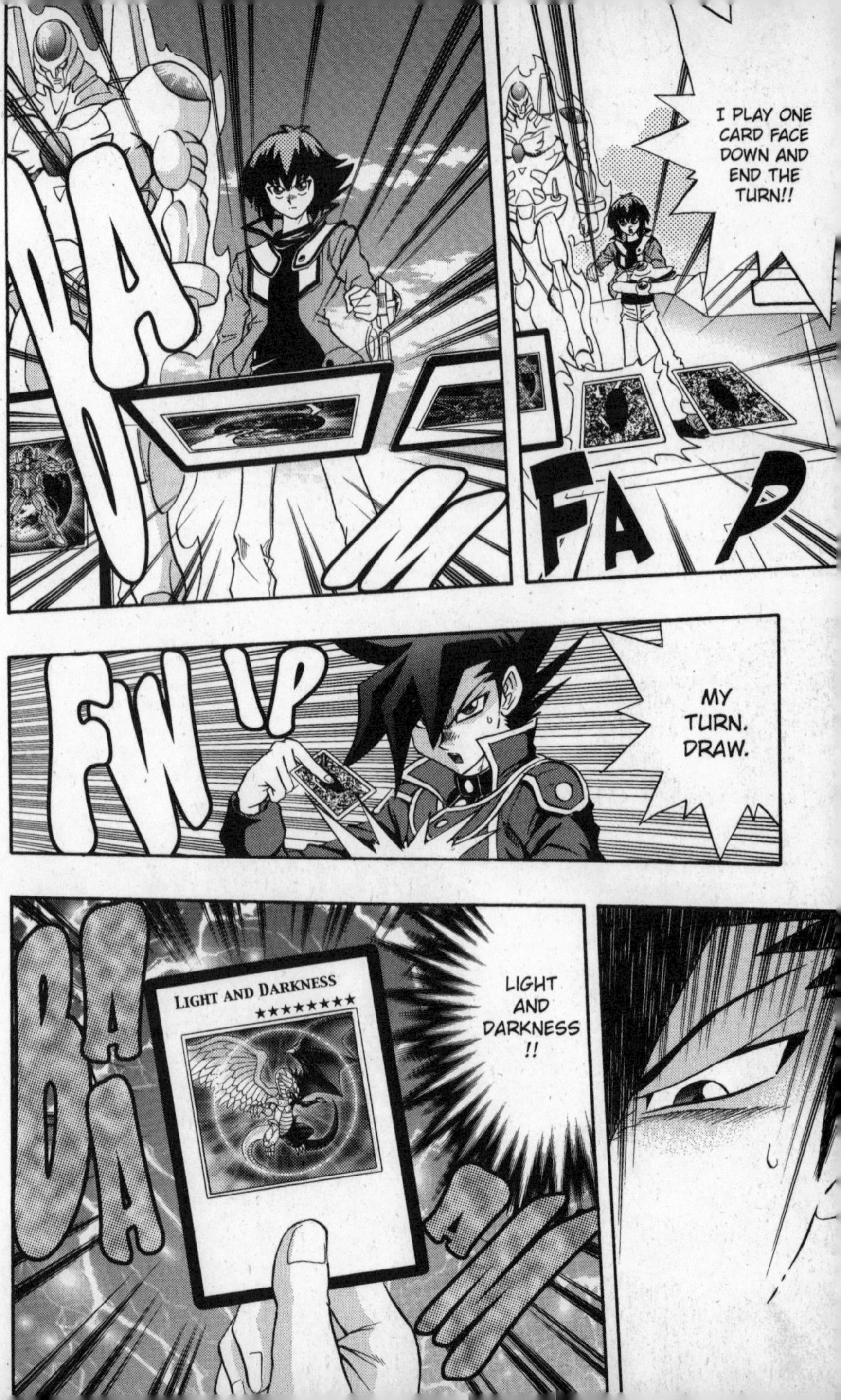
I PLAY ONE CARD FACE DOWN AND END THE TURN!!
FAP
MY TURN. DRAW.
LIGHT AND DARKNESS !!
LIGHT AND DARKNESS

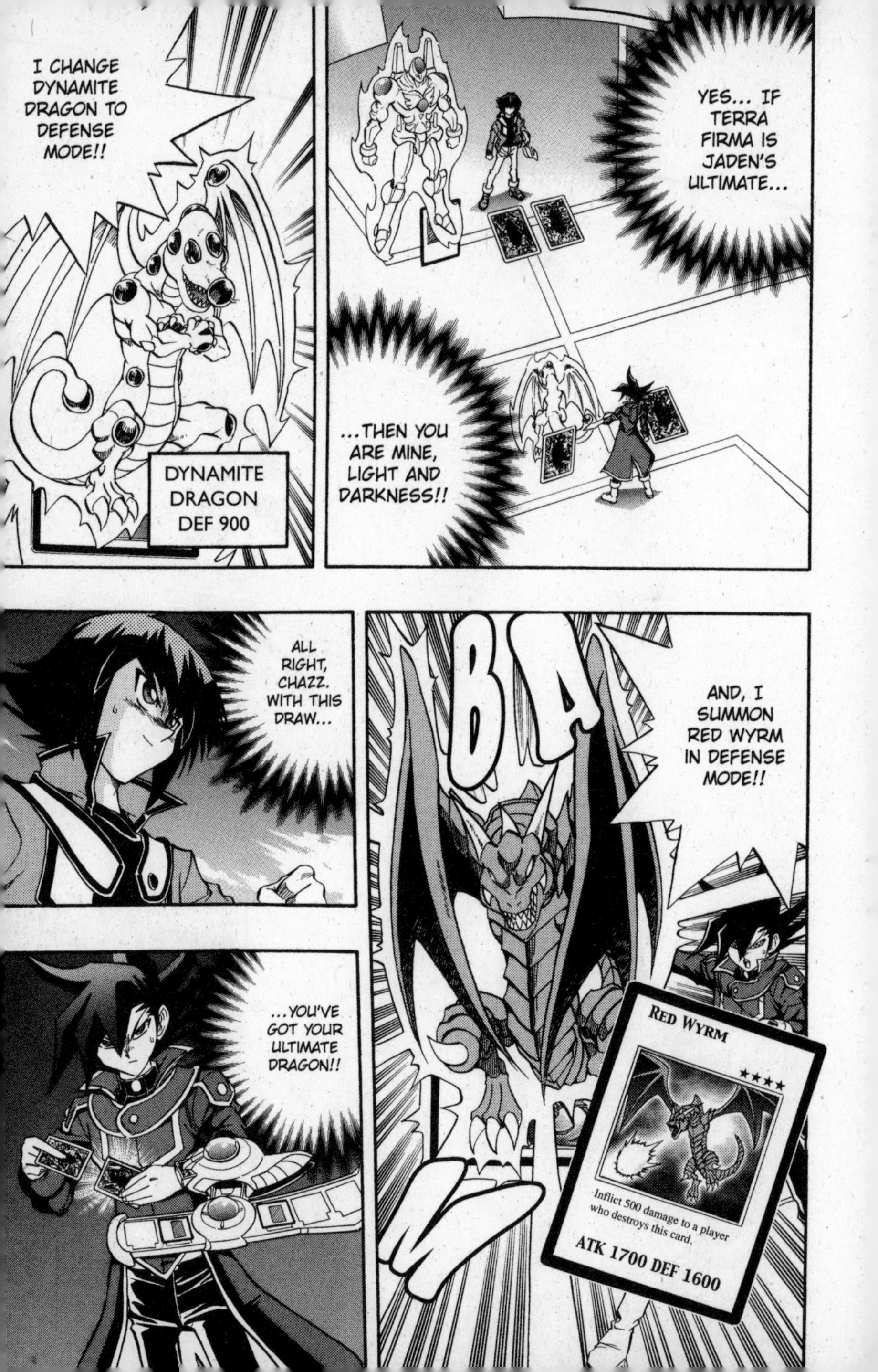
YES... IF TERRA FIRMA IS JADEN'S ULTIMATE...
...THEN YOU ARE MINE, LIGHT AND DARKNESS!!
I CHANGE DYNAMITE DRAGON TO DEFENSE MODE!!
DYNAMITE DRAGON DEF 900
BAM
AND, I SUMMON RED WYRM IN DEFENSE MODE!!
RED WYRM
Inflict 500 damage to a player who destroys this card.
ATK 1700 DEF 1600
ALL RIGHT, CHAZZ. WITH THIS DRAW...
...YOU'VE GOT YOUR ULTIMATE DRAGON!!

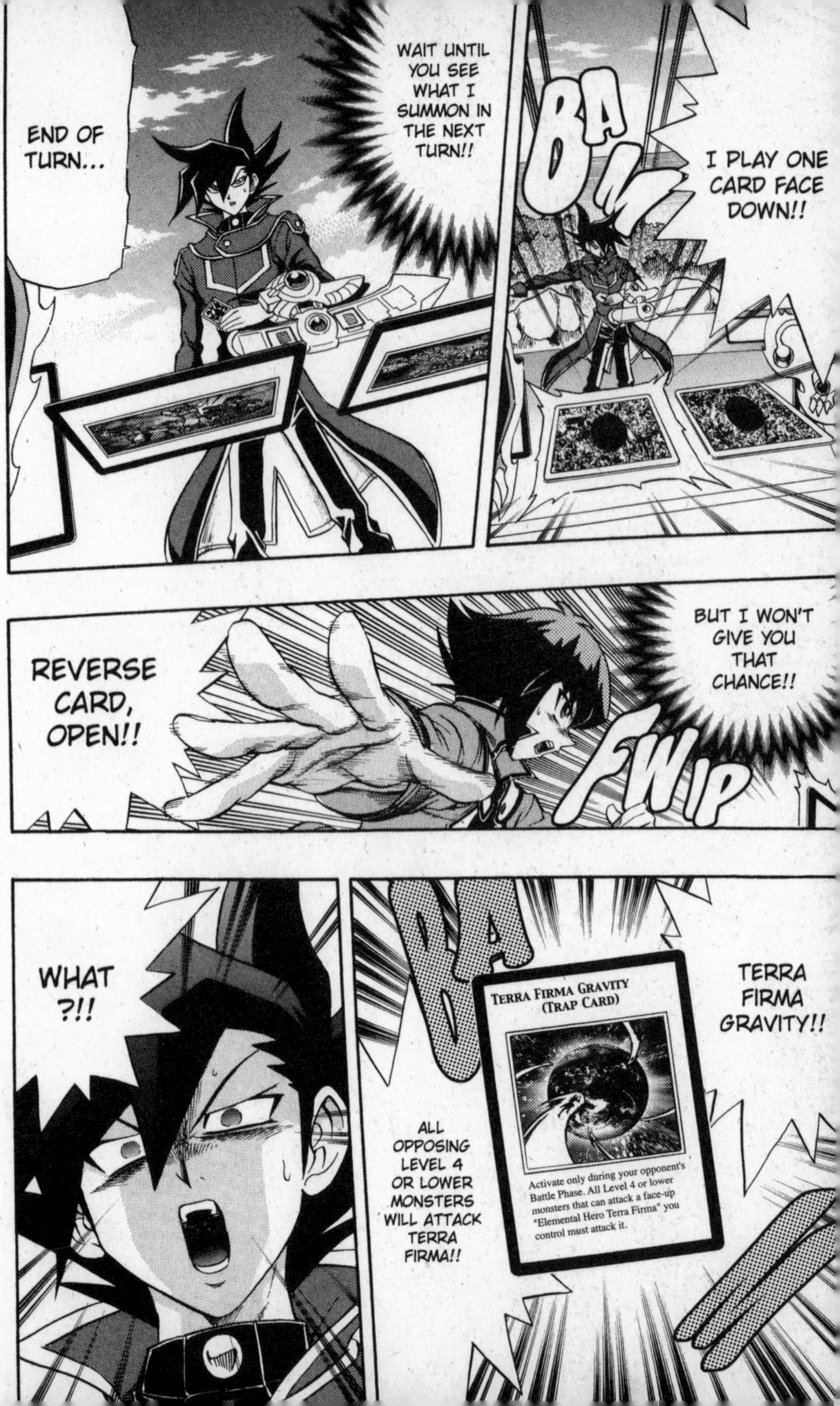
I PLAY ONE CARD FACE DOWN!!
WAIT UNTIL YOU SEE WHAT I SUMMON IN THE NEXT TURN!!
END OF TURN...
BUT I WON'T GIVE YOU THAT CHANCE!!
FWIP
REVERSE CARD, OPEN!!
TERRA FIRMA GRAVITY!!
TERRA FIRMA GRAVITY (TRAP CARD)
Activate only during your opponent's Battle Phase. All Level 4 or lower monsters that can attack a face-up "Elemental Hero Terra Firma" you control must attack it.
ALL OPPOSING LEVEL 4 OR LOWER MONSTERS WILL ATTACK TERRA FIRMA!!
WHAT ?!!

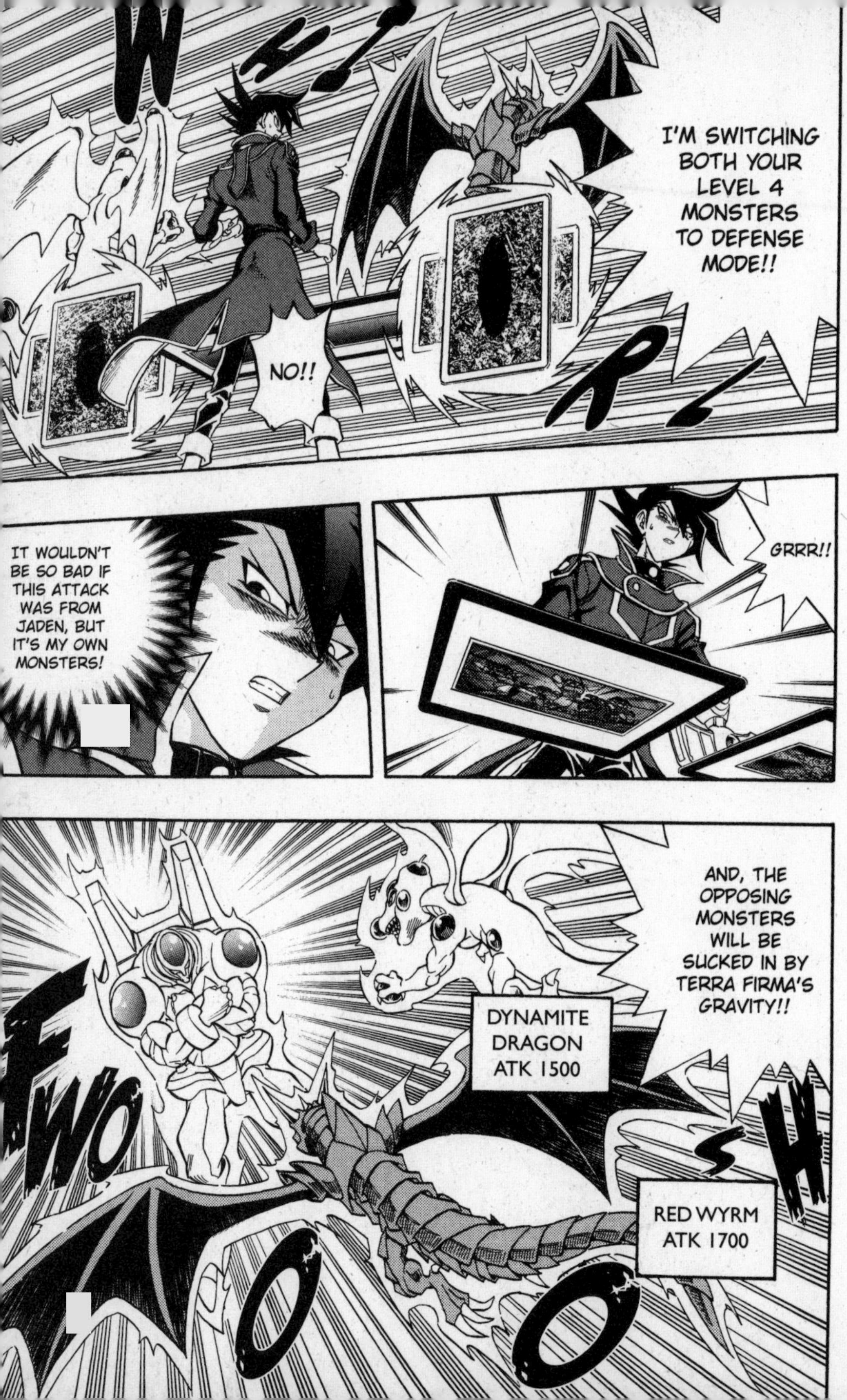
I'M SWITCHING BOTH YOUR LEVEL 4 MONSTERS TO DEFENSE MODE!!
NO!!
GRRR!!
IT WOULDN'T BE SO BAD IF THIS ATTACK WAS FROM JADEN, BUT IT'S MY OWN MONSTERS!
AND, THE OPPOSING MONSTERS WILL BE SUCKED IN BY TERRA FIRMA'S GRAVITY!!
DYNAMITE DRAGON ATK 1500
RED WYRM ATK 1700

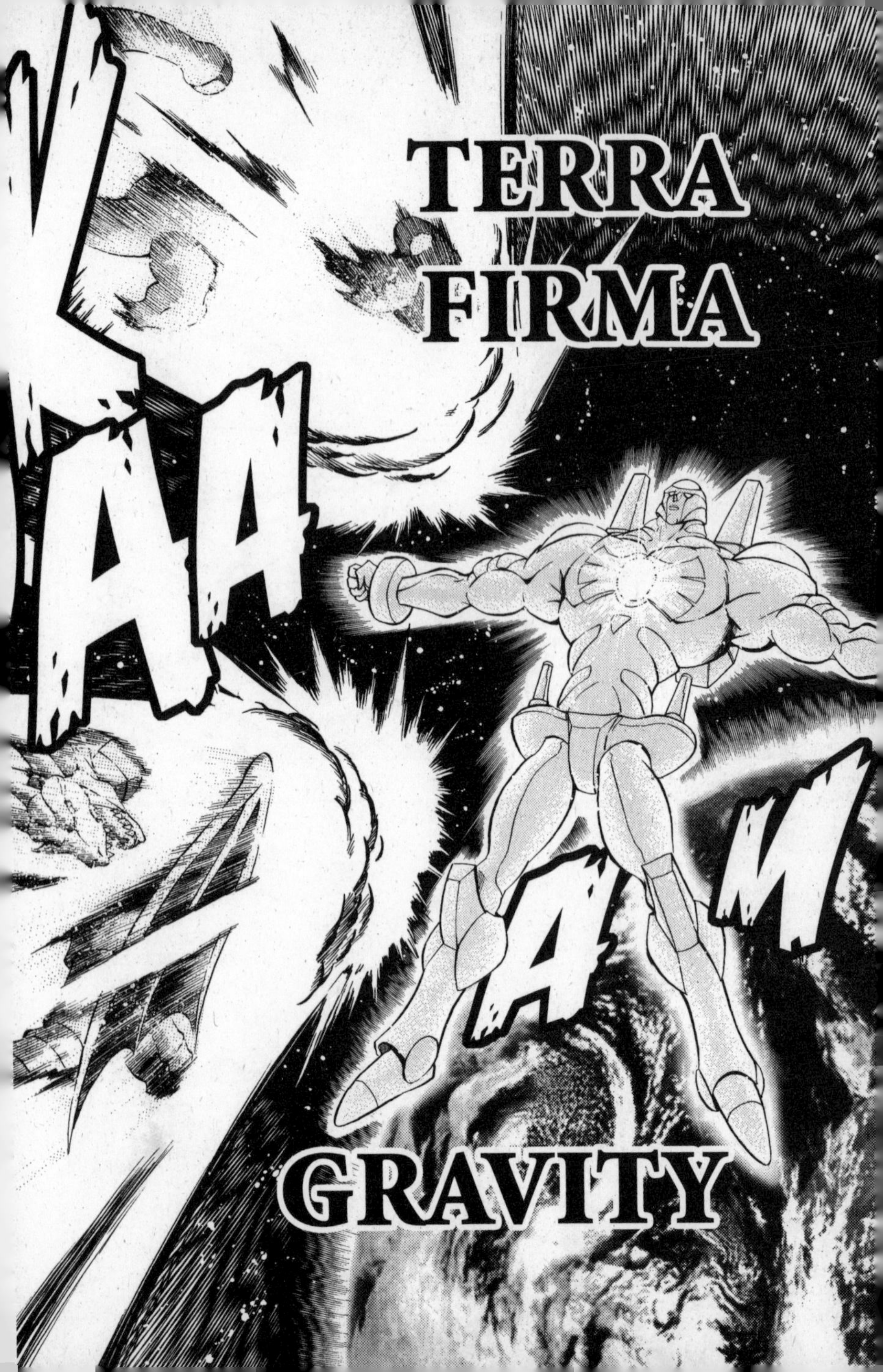
TERRA FIRMA
GRAVITY

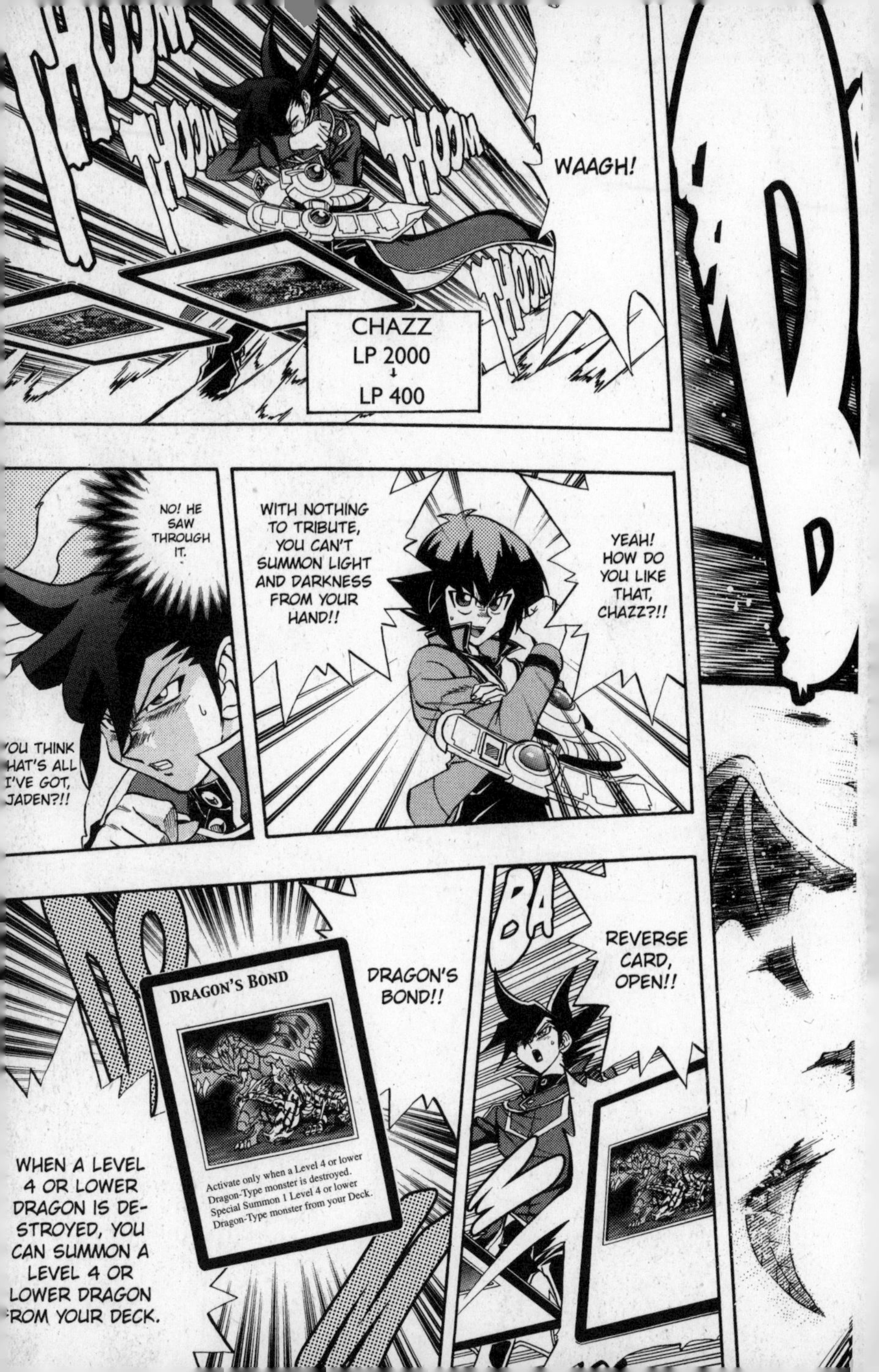
THOOM
THOOM
THOOM
THOOM
WAAGH!
CHAZZ
LP 2000
↓
LP 400
YEAH! HOW DO YOU LIKE THAT, CHAZZ?!!
WITH NOTHING TO TRIBUTE, YOU CAN'T SUMMON LIGHT AND DARKNESS FROM YOUR HAND!!
NO! HE SAW THROUGH IT.
OU THINK HAT'S ALL I'VE GOT, JADEN?!!
BA
REVERSE CARD, OPEN!!
DRAGON'S BOND!!
DRAGON'S BOND
Activate only when a Level 4 or lower Dragon-Type monster is destroyed. Special Summon 1 Level 4 or lower Dragon-Type monster from your Deck.
WHEN A LEVEL 4 OR LOWER DRAGON IS DE-STROYED, YOU CAN SUMMON A LEVEL 4 OR LOWER DRAGON ROM YOUR DECK.

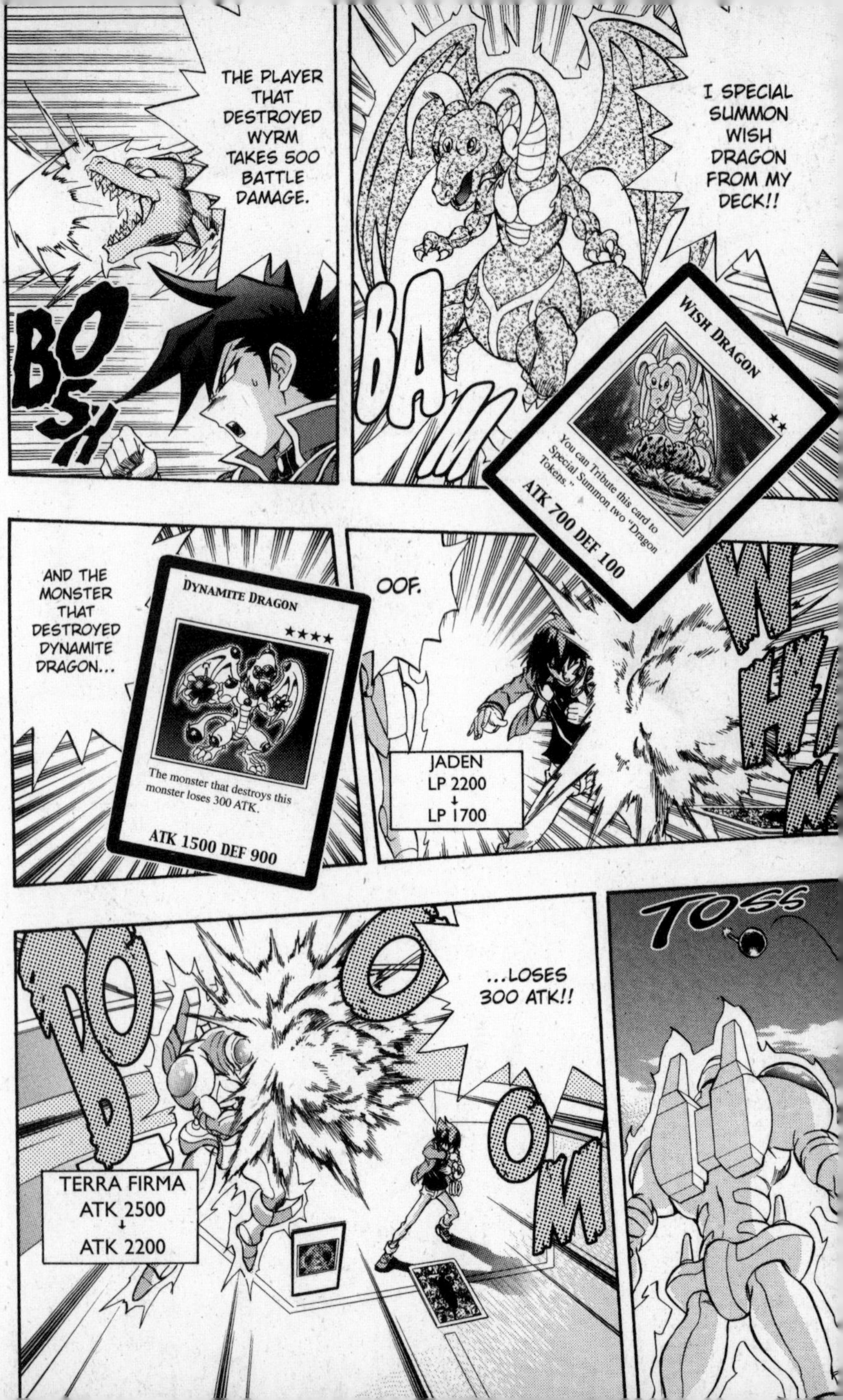
I SPECIAL SUMMON WISH DRAGON FROM MY DECK!!
BAM
WISH DRAGON
You can Tribute this card to Special Summon two "Dragon Tokens."
ATK 700 DEF 100
THE PLAYER THAT DESTROYED WYRM TAKES 500 BATTLE DAMAGE.
BOSH
OOF.
JADEN
LP 2200
↓
LP 1700
AND THE MONSTER THAT DESTROYED DYNAMITE DRAGON...
DYNAMITE DRAGON
The monster that destroys this monster loses 300 ATK.
ATK 1500 DEF 900
TOSS
...LOSES 300 ATK!!
DOOOM
TERRA FIRMA
ATK 2500
↓
ATK 2200

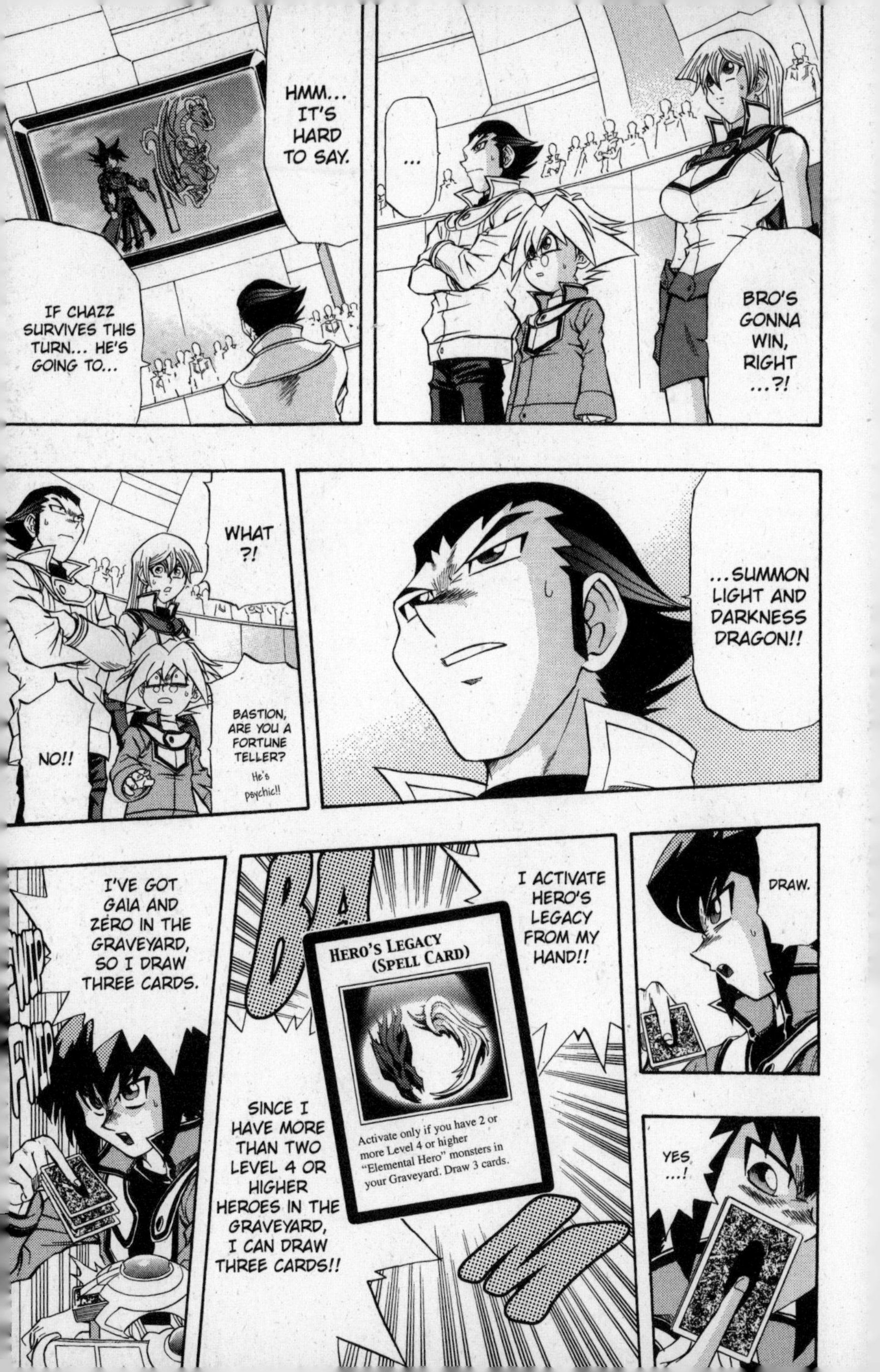
BRO'S GONNA WIN, RIGHT ...?!
...
HMM... IT'S HARD TO SAY.
IF CHAZZ SURVIVES THIS TURN... HE'S GOING TO...
...SUMMON LIGHT AND DARKNESS DRAGON!!
WHAT ?!
BASTION, ARE YOU A FORTUNE TELLER?
He's psychic!!
NO!!
DRAW.
YES ...!
I ACTIVATE HERO'S LEGACY FROM MY HAND!!
HERO'S LEGACY (SPELL CARD)
Activate only if you have 2 or more Level 4 or higher "Elemental Hero" monsters in your Graveyard. Draw 3 cards.
SINCE I HAVE MORE THAN TWO LEVEL 4 OR HIGHER HEROES IN THE GRAVEYARD, I CAN DRAW THREE CARDS!!
I'VE GOT GAIA AND ZERO IN THE GRAVEYARD, SO I DRAW THREE CARDS.

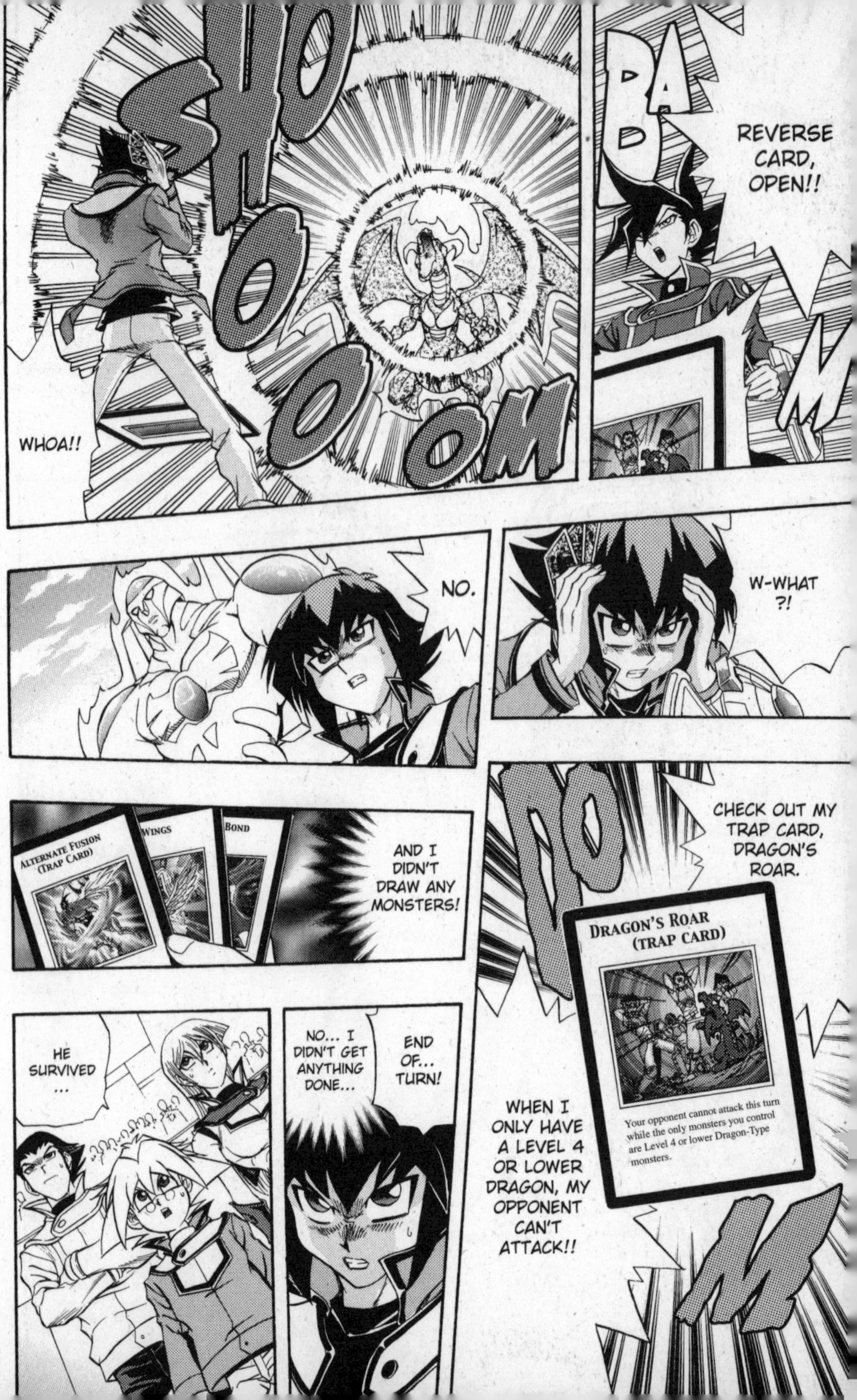
REVERSE CARD, OPEN!!
WHOA!!
W-WHAT ?!
NO.
CHECK OUT MY TRAP CARD, DRAGON'S ROAR.
DRAGON'S ROAR (TRAP CARD)
Your opponent cannot attack this turn while the only monsters you control are Level 4 or lower Dragon-Type monsters.
WHEN I ONLY HAVE A LEVEL 4 OR LOWER DRAGON, MY OPPONENT CAN'T ATTACK!!
ALTERNATE FUSION (TRAP CARD)
WINGS
BOND
AND I DIDN'T DRAW ANY MONSTERS!
END OF... TURN!
NO... I DIDN'T GET ANYTHING DONE...
HE SURVIVED ...

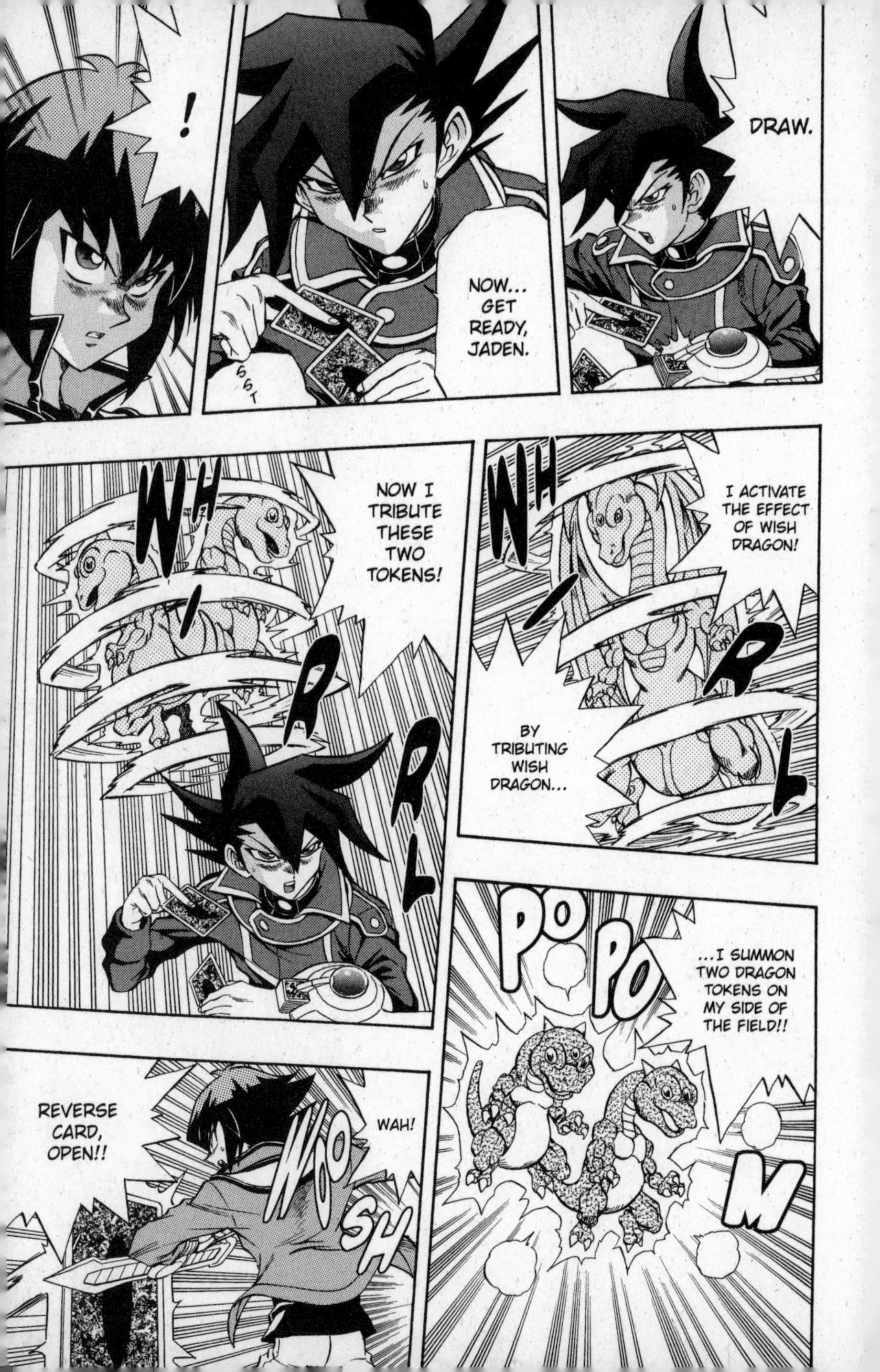
DRAW.
NOW... GET READY, JADEN.
SST
!
I ACTIVATE THE EFFECT OF WISH DRAGON!
WHIRRL
BY TRIBUTING WISH DRAGON...
...I SUMMON TWO DRAGON TOKENS ON MY SIDE OF THE FIELD!!
PO
PO
M
NOW I TRIBUTE THESE TWO TOKENS!
WHIRRL
WAH!
WHOOSH
REVERSE CARD, OPEN!!

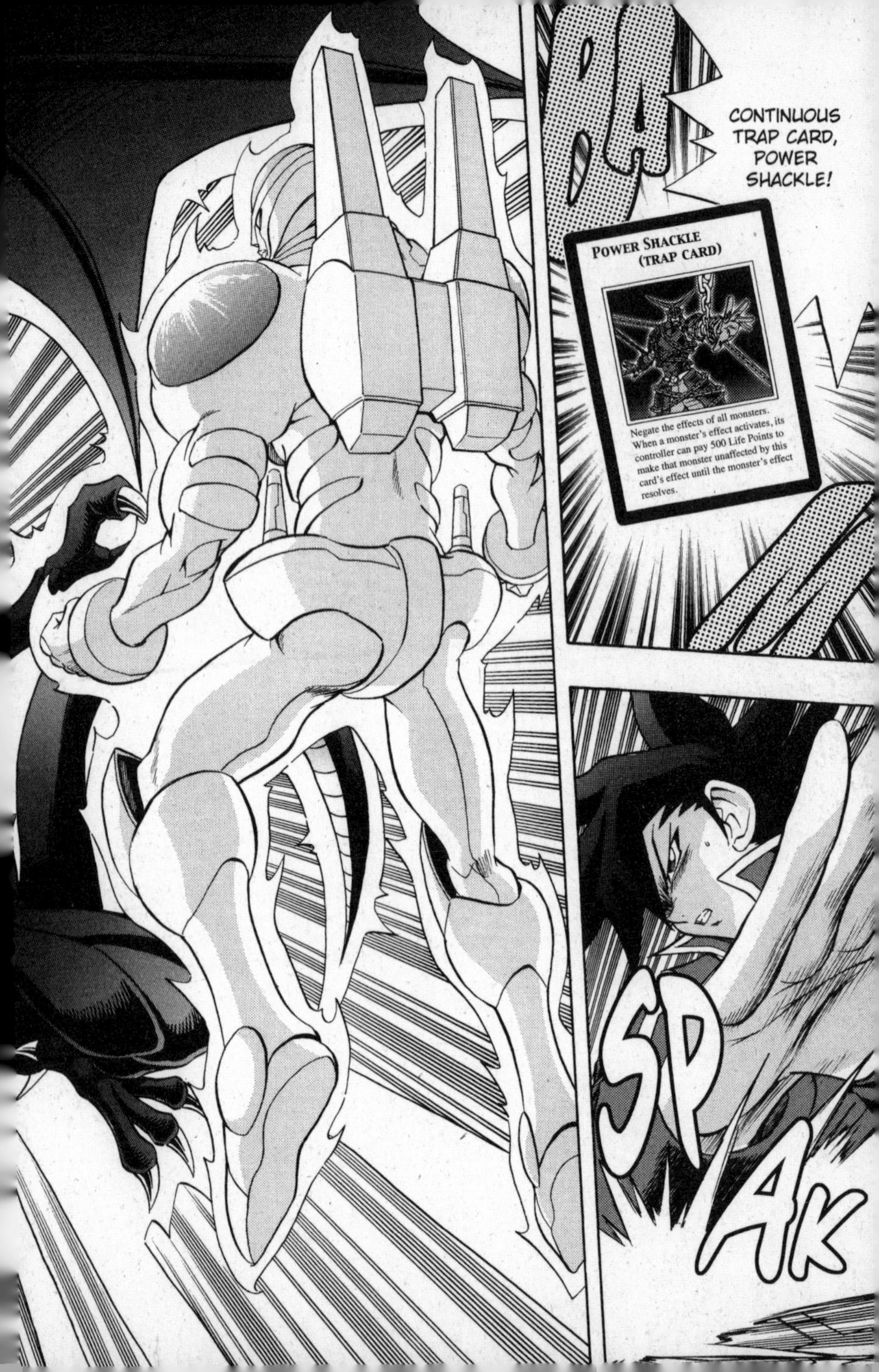
BA
CONTINUOUS TRAP CARD, POWER SHACKLE!
POWER SHACKLE (TRAP CARD)
Negate the effects of all monsters. When a monster's effect activates, its controller can pay 500 Life Points to make that monster unaffected by this card's effect until the monster's effect resolves.
SPAK

I SUMMON LIGHT AND DARKNESS DRAGON!
LIGHT AND DARKNESS DRAGON
★★★★★★★★
This card cannot be Special Summoned. While this card is face-up on the field, its Attribute is also treated as DARK. When a Spell or Trap Card is activated, or the effect of an Effect Monster is activated, that activation is negated and this card loses 500 ATK and DEF. When this card is destroyed and sent to the Graveyard, select 1 monster in your Graveyard. Then destroy all cards you control, and Special Summon that monster.
ATK 2800 DEF 2400
LIGHT AND DARKNESS! GIVE TERRA FIRMA A DARK SHOWER!

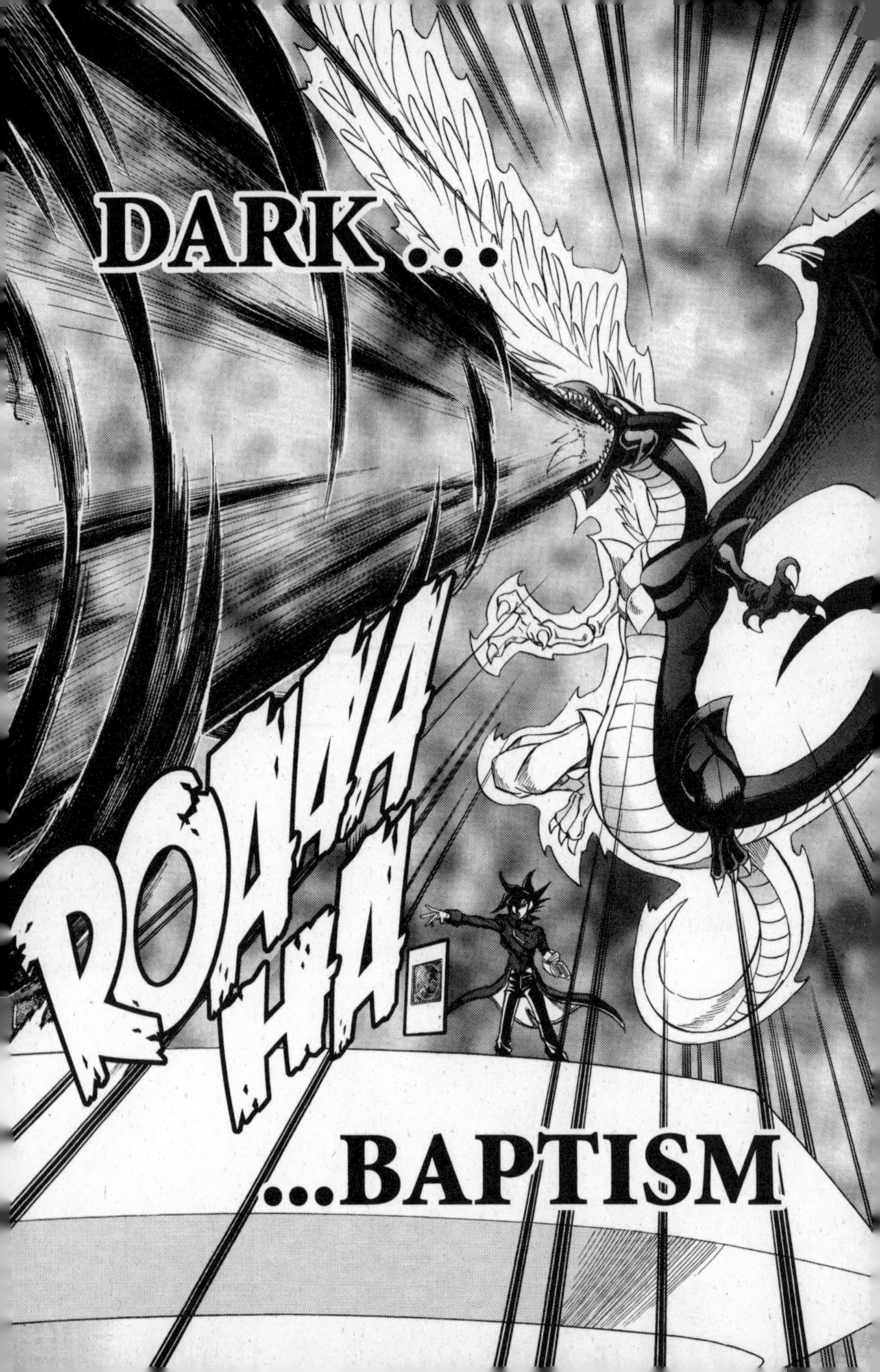
DARK...
ROAAAA
...BAPTISM

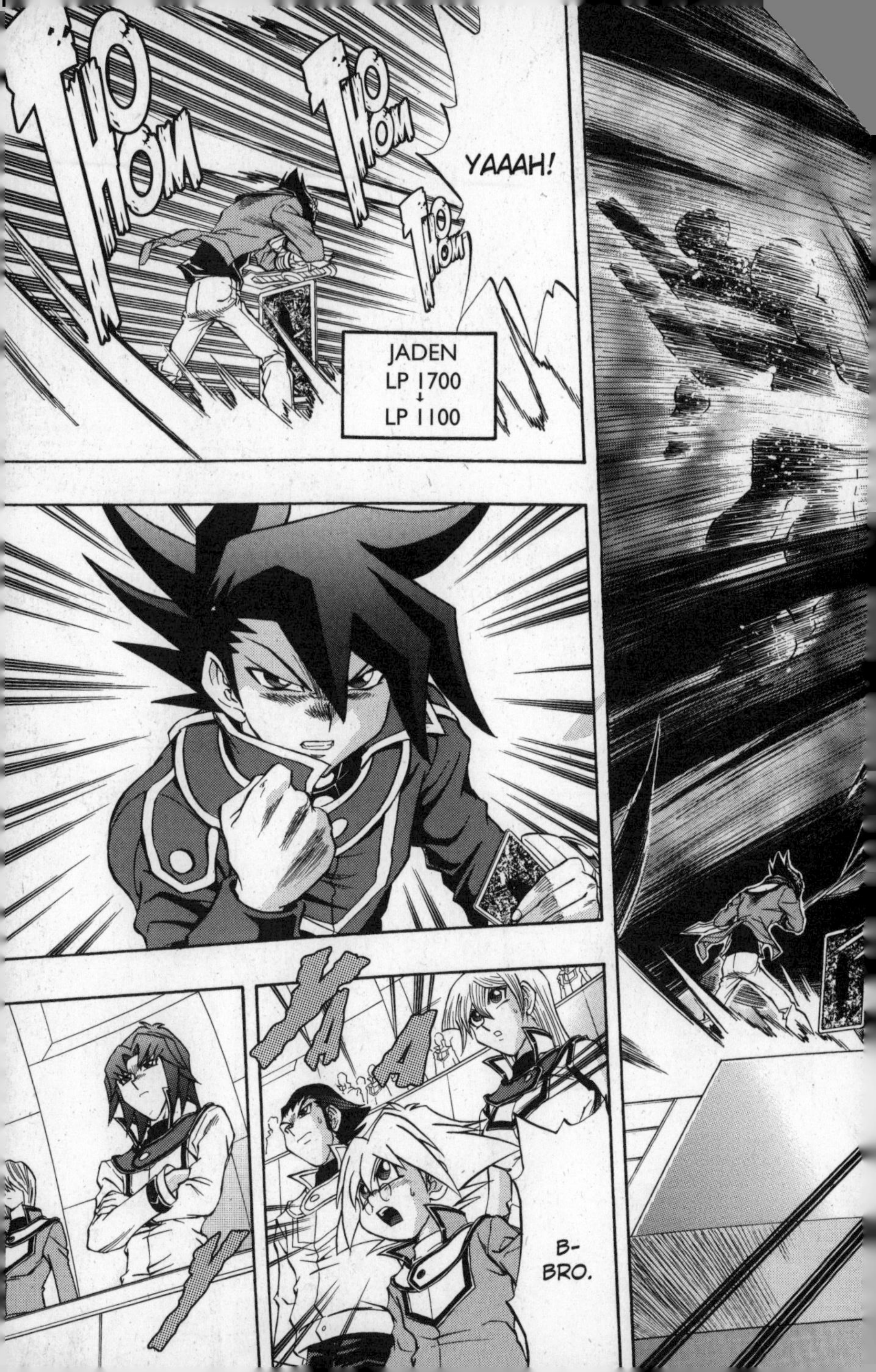
YAAAH!
THOOM
THOOM
THOOM
JADEN
LP 1700
↓
LP 1100
B-
BRO.

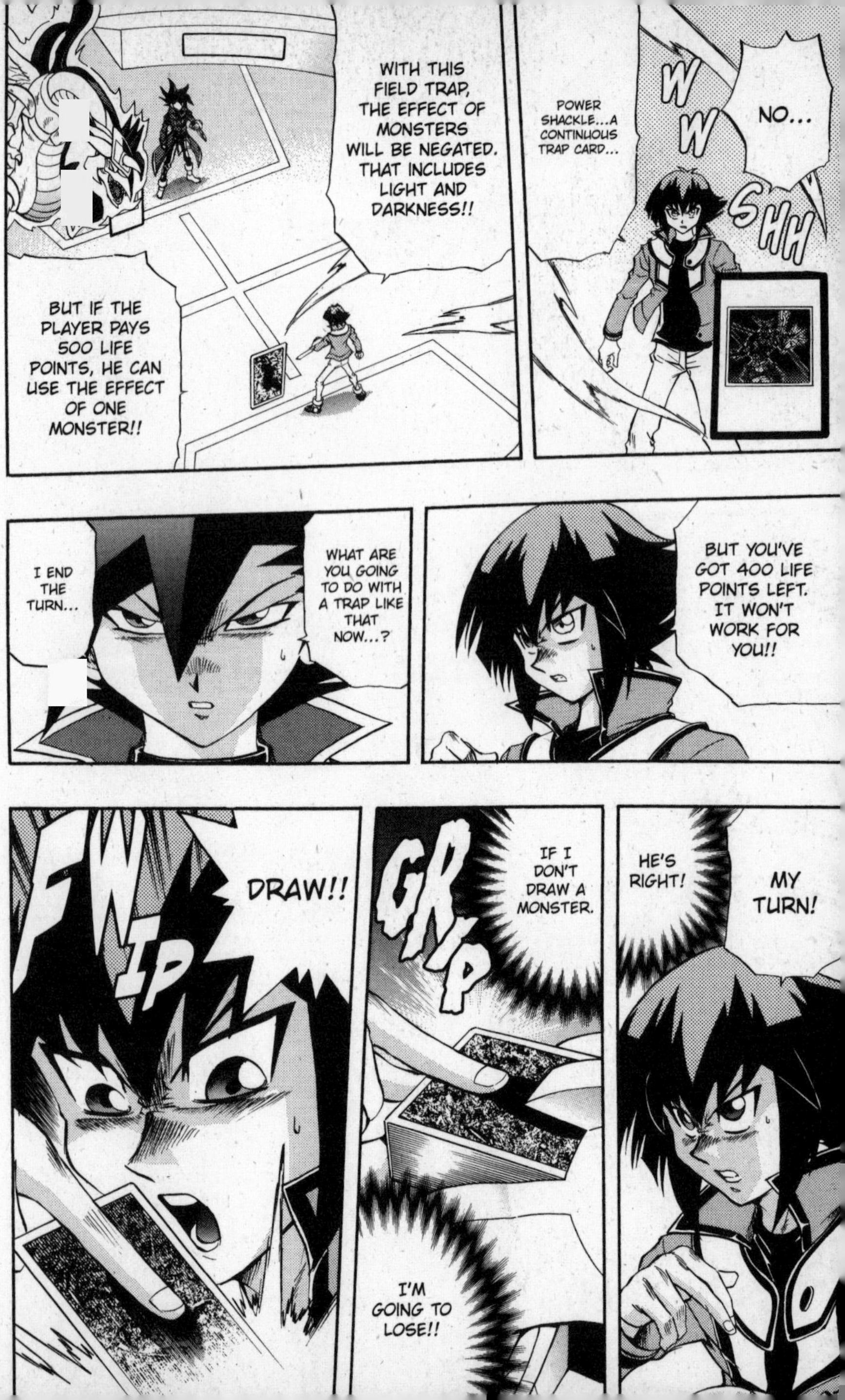
NO...
WWWSHH
POWER SHACKLE...A CONTINUOUS TRAP CARD...
WITH THIS FIELD TRAP, THE EFFECT OF MONSTERS WILL BE NEGATED. THAT INCLUDES LIGHT AND DARKNESS!!
BUT IF THE PLAYER PAYS 500 LIFE POINTS, HE CAN USE THE EFFECT OF ONE MONSTER!!
BUT YOU'VE GOT 400 LIFE POINTS LEFT. IT WON'T WORK FOR YOU!!
WHAT ARE YOU GOING TO DO WITH A TRAP LIKE THAT NOW...?
I END THE TURN...
MY TURN!
HE'S RIGHT!
IF I DON'T DRAW A MONSTER.
GRIP
I'M GOING TO LOSE!!
FWIP
DRAW!!

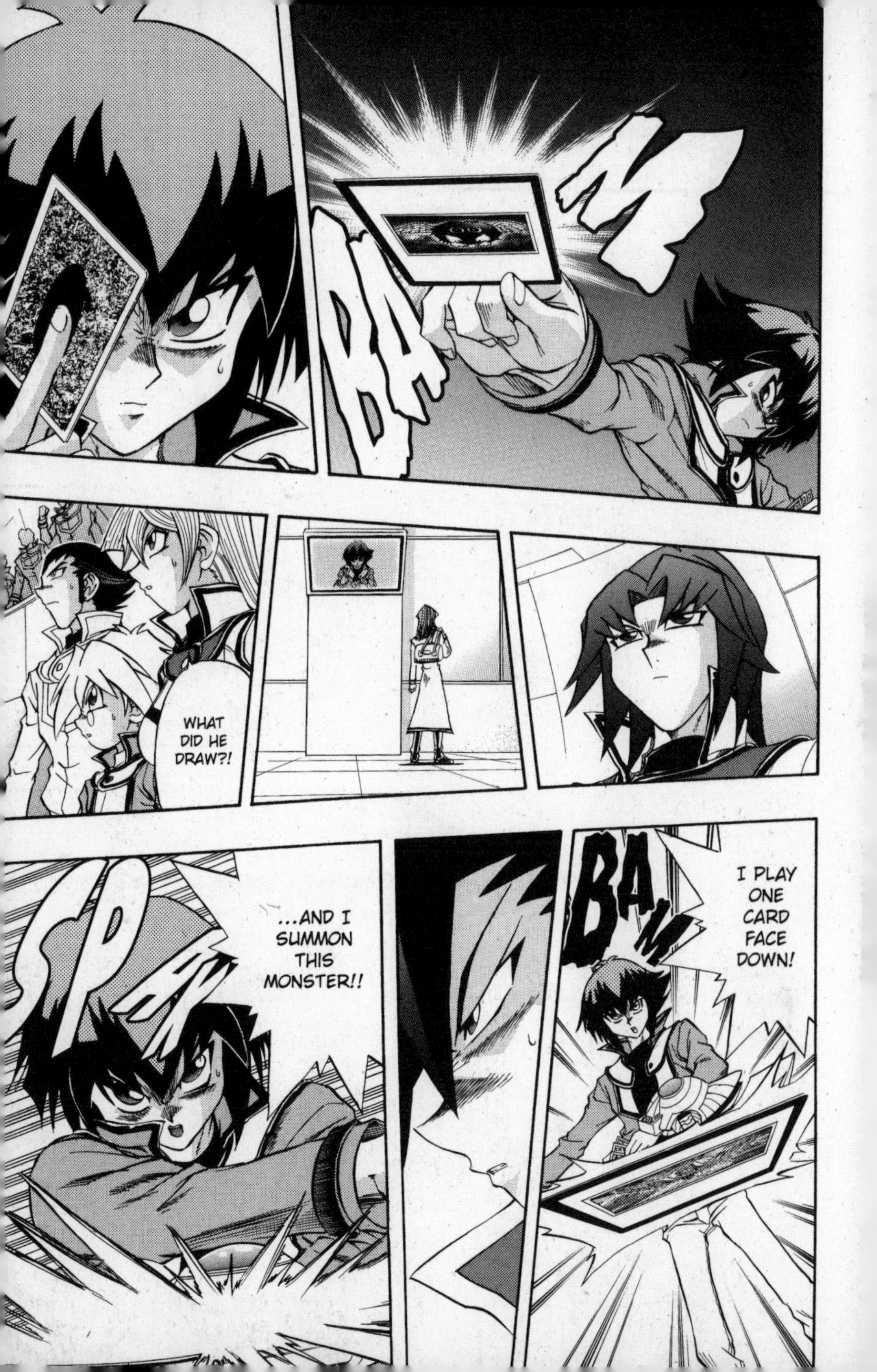
BAM
WHAT DID HE DRAW?!
BAM
I PLAY ONE CARD FACE DOWN!
...AND I SUMMON THIS MONSTER!!

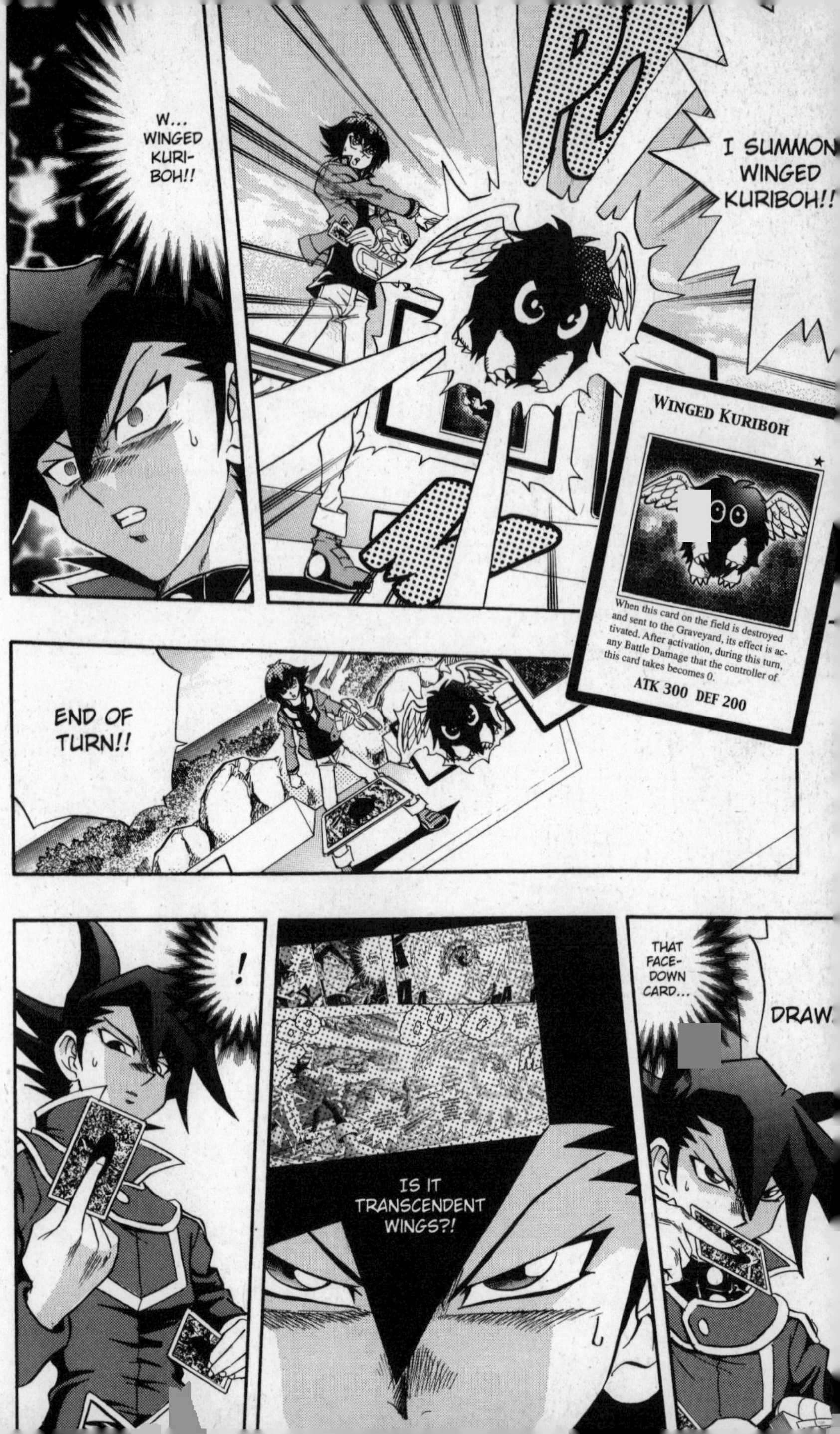
I SUMMON WINGED KURIBOH!!
WINGED KURIBOH
When this card on the field is destroyed and sent to the Graveyard, its effect is activated. After activation, during this turn, any Battle Damage that the controller of this card takes becomes 0.
ATK 300 DEF 200
W... WINGED KURI-BOH!!
END OF TURN!!
DRAW.
THAT FACE-DOWN CARD...
IS IT TRANSCENDENT WINGS?!
!

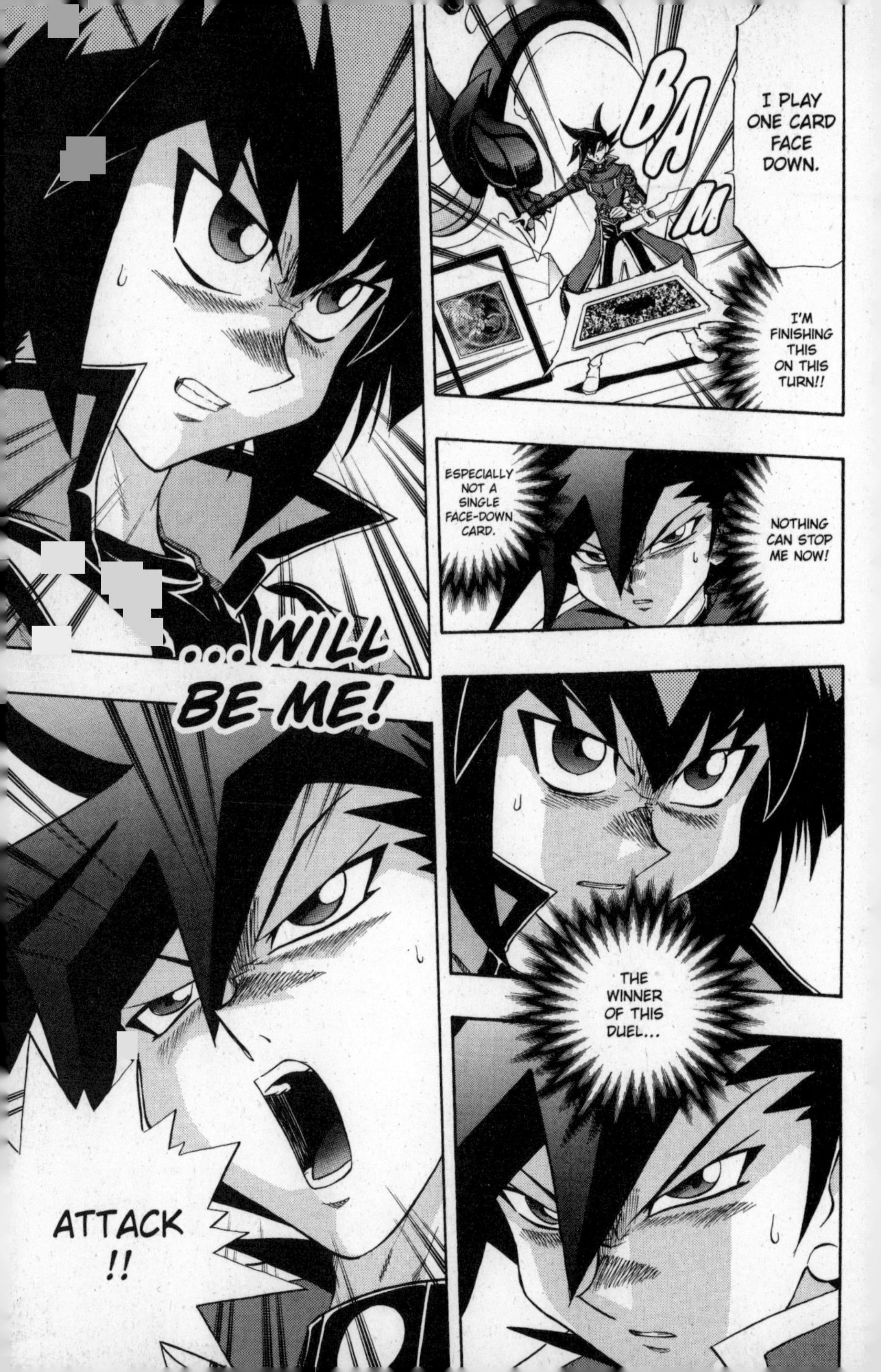
I PLAY ONE CARD FACE DOWN.
BAM
I'M FINISHING THIS ON THIS TURN!!
NOTHING CAN STOP ME NOW!
ESPECIALLY NOT A SINGLE FACE-DOWN CARD.
THE WINNER OF THIS DUEL...
...WILL BE ME!
ATTACK!!

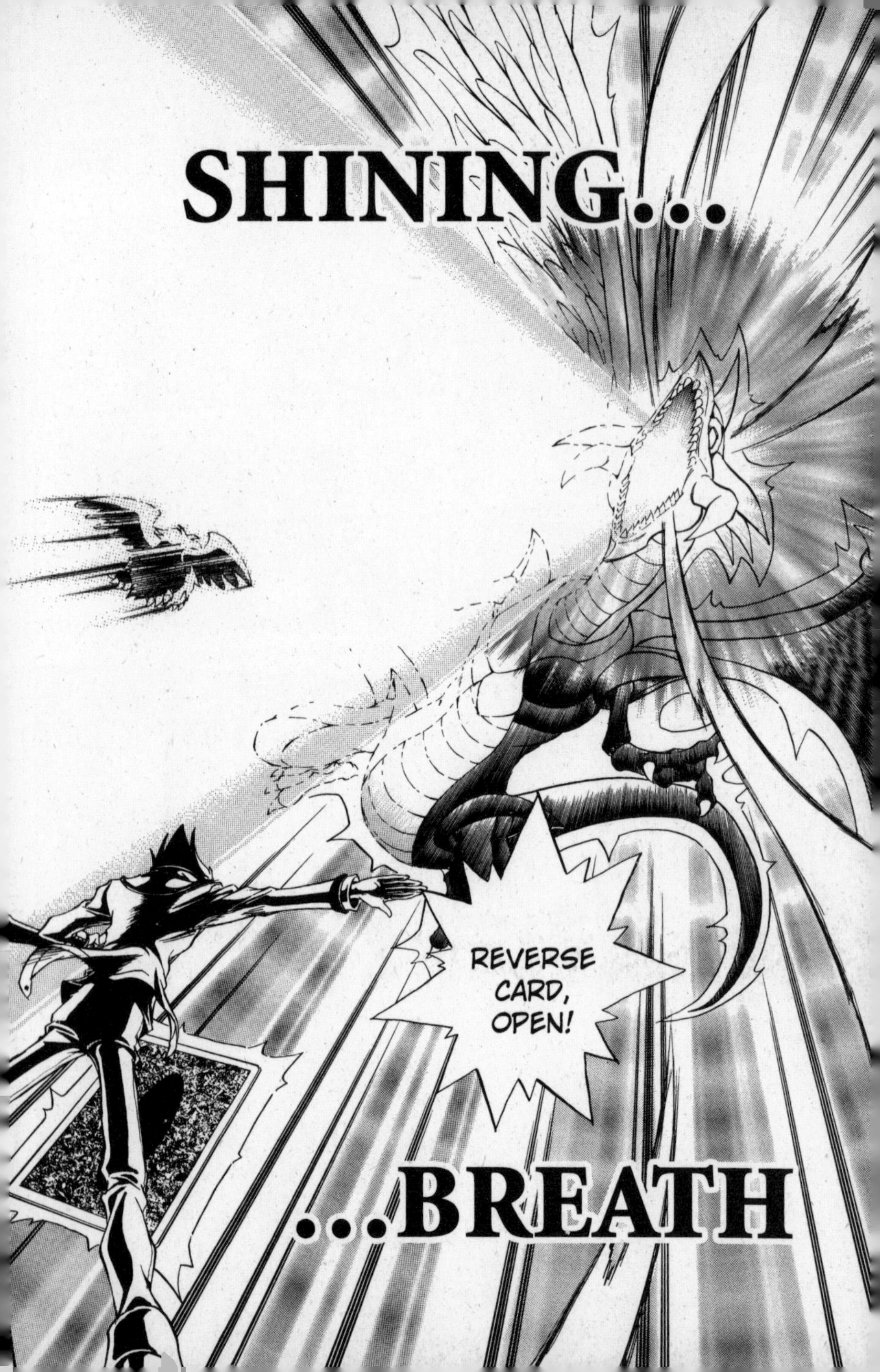
SHINING...
REVERSE CARD, OPEN!
...BREATH

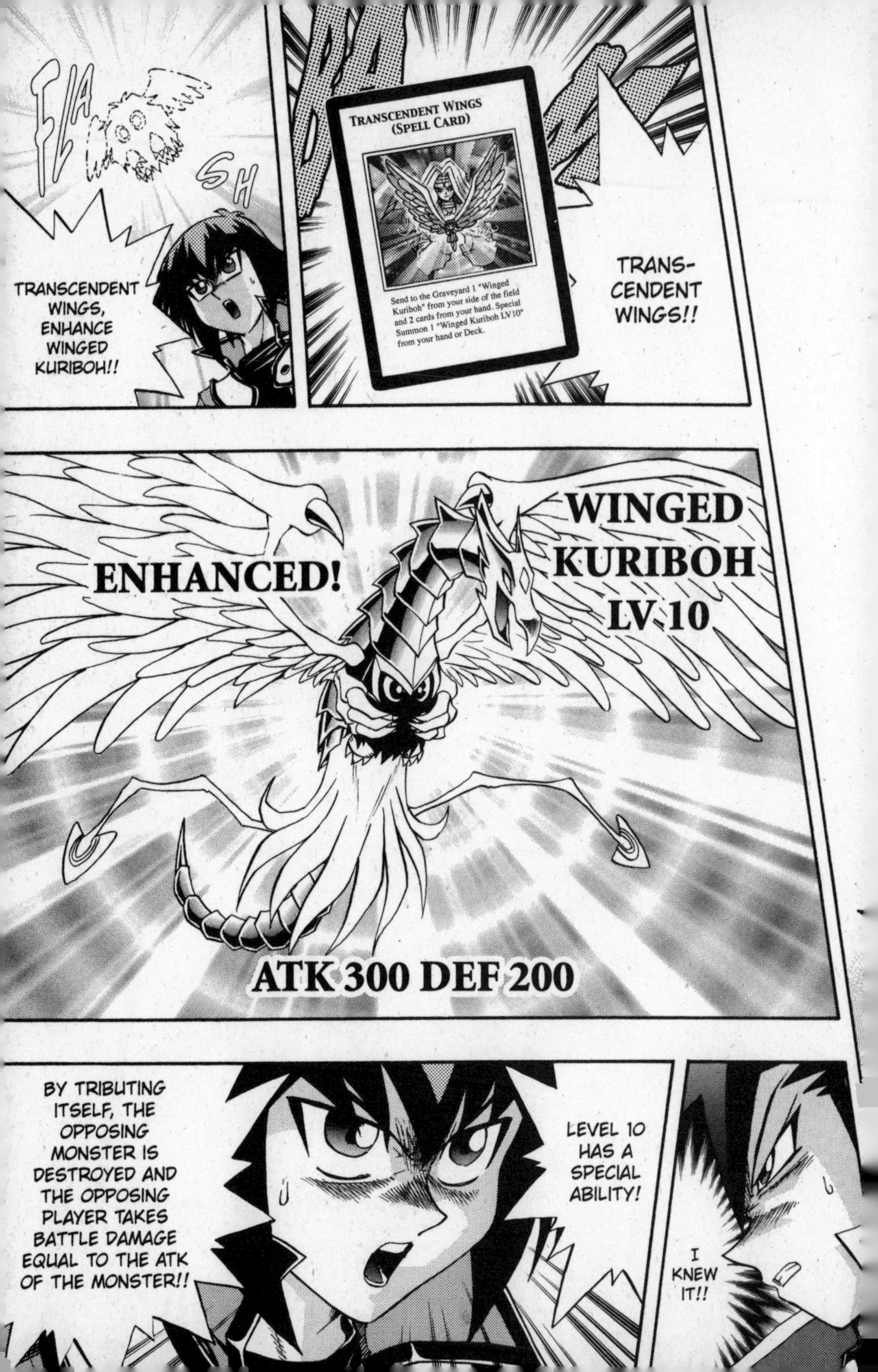
TRANSCENDENT WINGS (SPELL CARD)
Send to the Graveyard 1 "Winged Kuriboh" from your side of the field and 2 cards from your hand. Special Summon 1 "Winged Kuriboh LV10" from your hand or Deck.
TRANS-CENDENT WINGS!!
FLA SH
TRANSCENDENT WINGS, ENHANCE WINGED KURIBOH!!
WINGED KURIBOH LV 10
ENHANCED!
ATK 300 DEF 200
I KNEW IT!!
LEVEL 10 HAS A SPECIAL ABILITY!
BY TRIBUTING ITSELF, THE OPPOSING MONSTER IS DESTROYED AND THE OPPOSING PLAYER TAKES BATTLE DAMAGE EQUAL TO THE ATK OF THE MONSTER!!

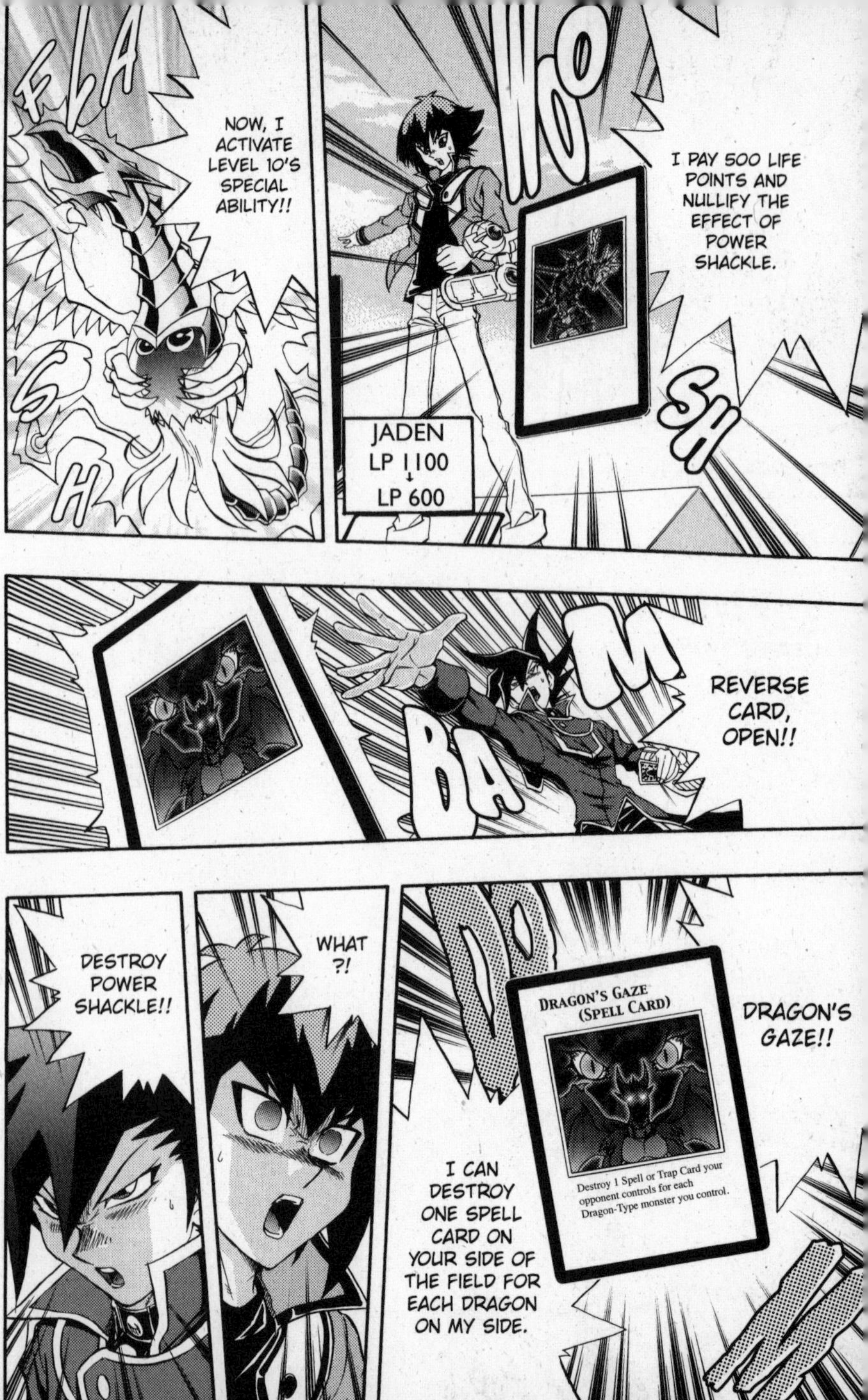
WOO
I PAY 500 LIFE POINTS AND NULLIFY THE EFFECT OF POWER SHACKLE.
SH
JADEN
LP 1100
↓
LP 600
FLA
NOW, I ACTIVATE LEVEL 10'S SPECIAL ABILITY!!
SH
REVERSE CARD, OPEN!!
BAM
DRAGON'S GAZE!!
DRAGON'S GAZE (SPELL CARD)
Destroy 1 Spell or Trap Card your opponent controls for each Dragon-Type monster you control.
I CAN DESTROY ONE SPELL CARD ON YOUR SIDE OF THE FIELD FOR EACH DRAGON ON MY SIDE.
WHAT ?!
DESTROY POWER SHACKLE!!

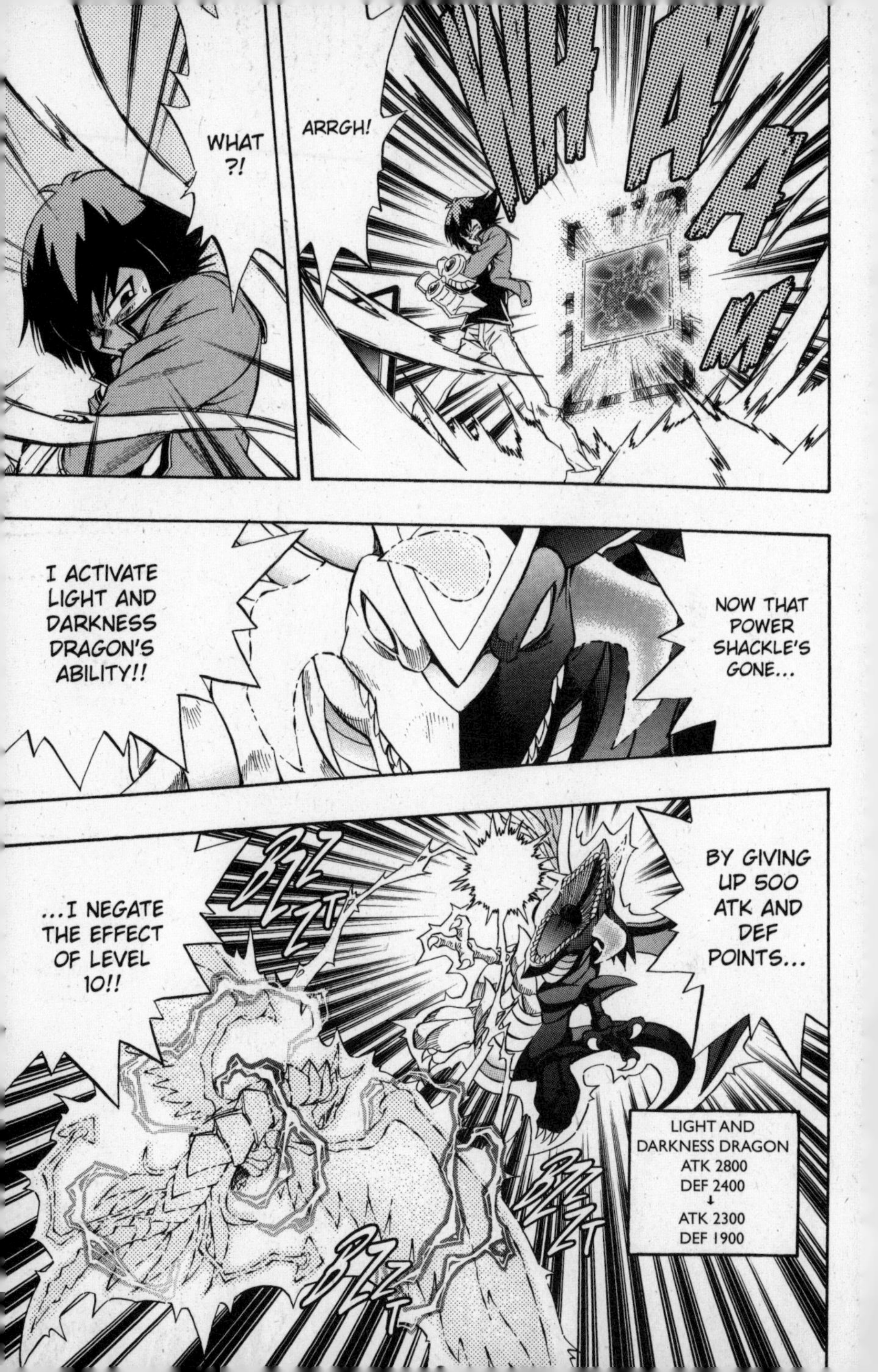
ARRGH!
WHAT ?!
NOW THAT POWER SHACKLE'S GONE...
I ACTIVATE LIGHT AND DARKNESS DRAGON'S ABILITY!!
BY GIVING UP 500 ATK AND DEF POINTS...
...I NEGATE THE EFFECT OF LEVEL 10!!
LIGHT AND DARKNESS DRAGON
ATK 2800
DEF 2400
↓
ATK 2300
DEF 1900

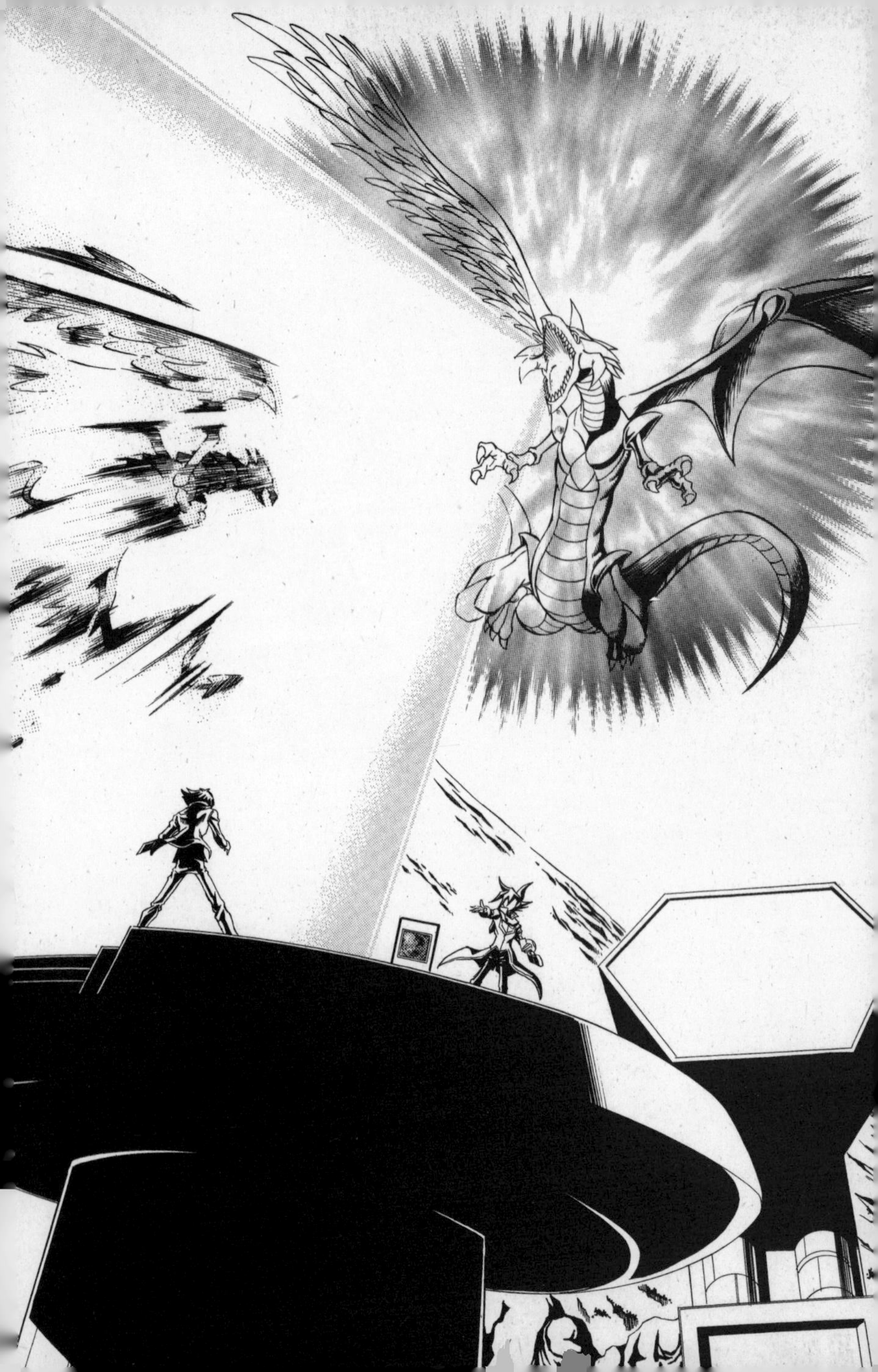

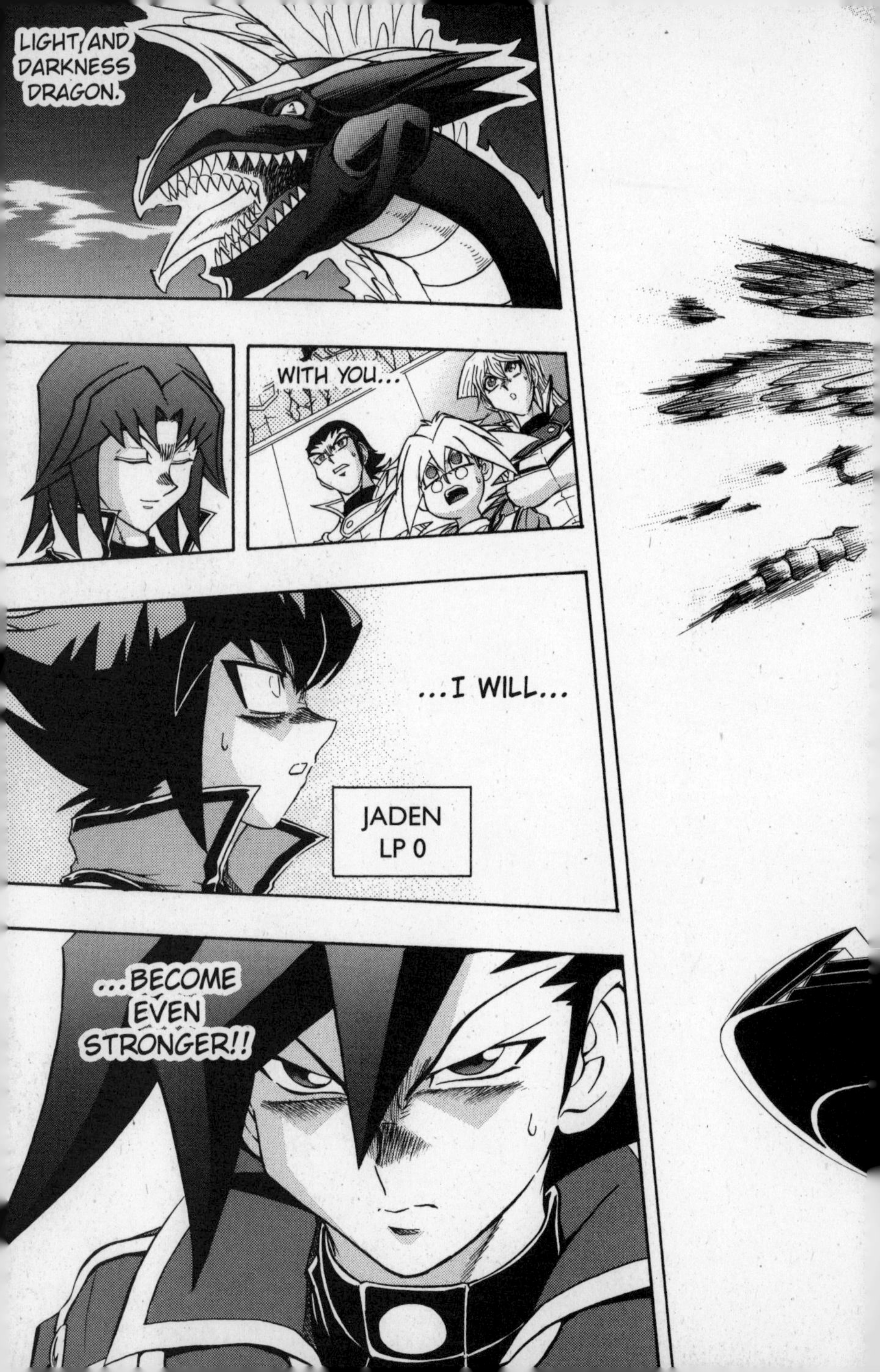
LIGHT AND DARKNESS DRAGON.
WITH YOU...
...I WILL...
JADEN LP 0
...BECOME EVEN STRONGER!!

PSUEDO-MENTAL HERO

WHEN OUR WORK DAY IS OVER...
ALL RIGHT, LET'S CALL IT A DAY!!
EVERY EVENING...
...I DUEL MR. SATO.
DO YOU REALLY THINK YOUR LITTLE MANGA'S "PSEUDO-MENTAL" DECK CAN BEAT MY WARRIOR SYNCHRO DECK?!*
PSEUDO ...?!
SATO
HEY! YOUR SYNCHRO MONSTERS ARE ALMOST ALL DRAGON-TYPES! WHAT'S THIS "WARRIOR" BUSINESS?!!
THE SYNCHRO BIT MAKES THEM WARRIORS. INCLUDING COLOSSAL.
I'VE NEVER EVEN SEEN COLOSSAL IN THERE.

"PSEUDO-MENTAL"! THAT WAS A GOOD ONE!!

*NOTE: IN THE ORIGINAL JAPANESE, THE WORD IS "ESE-MENTAL," A COMBINATION OF "ELEMENTAL" AND "ESE" (FAKE).

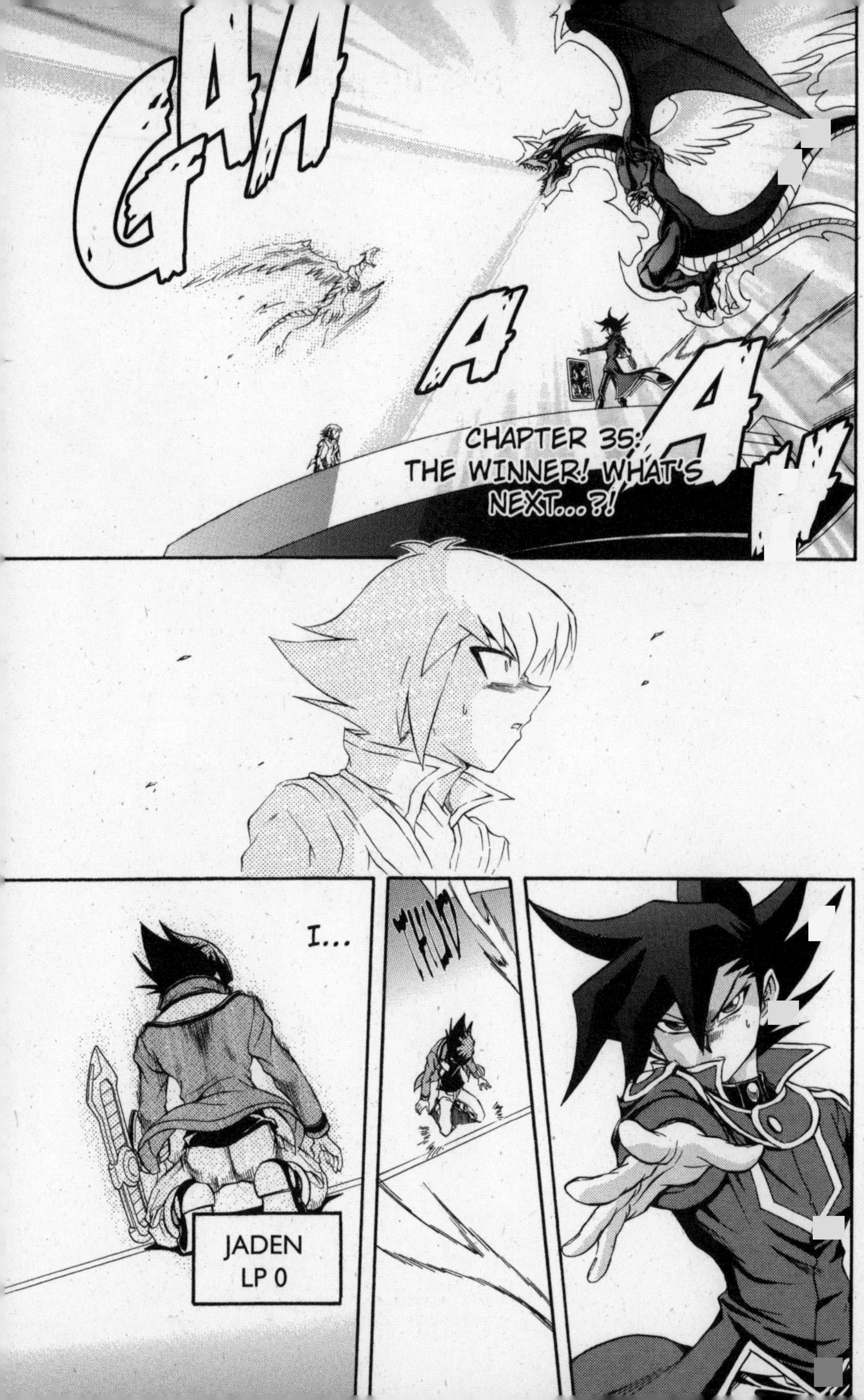
GAAAAH
CHAPTER 35: THE WINNER! WHAT'S NEXT...?!
I...
JADEN
LP 0

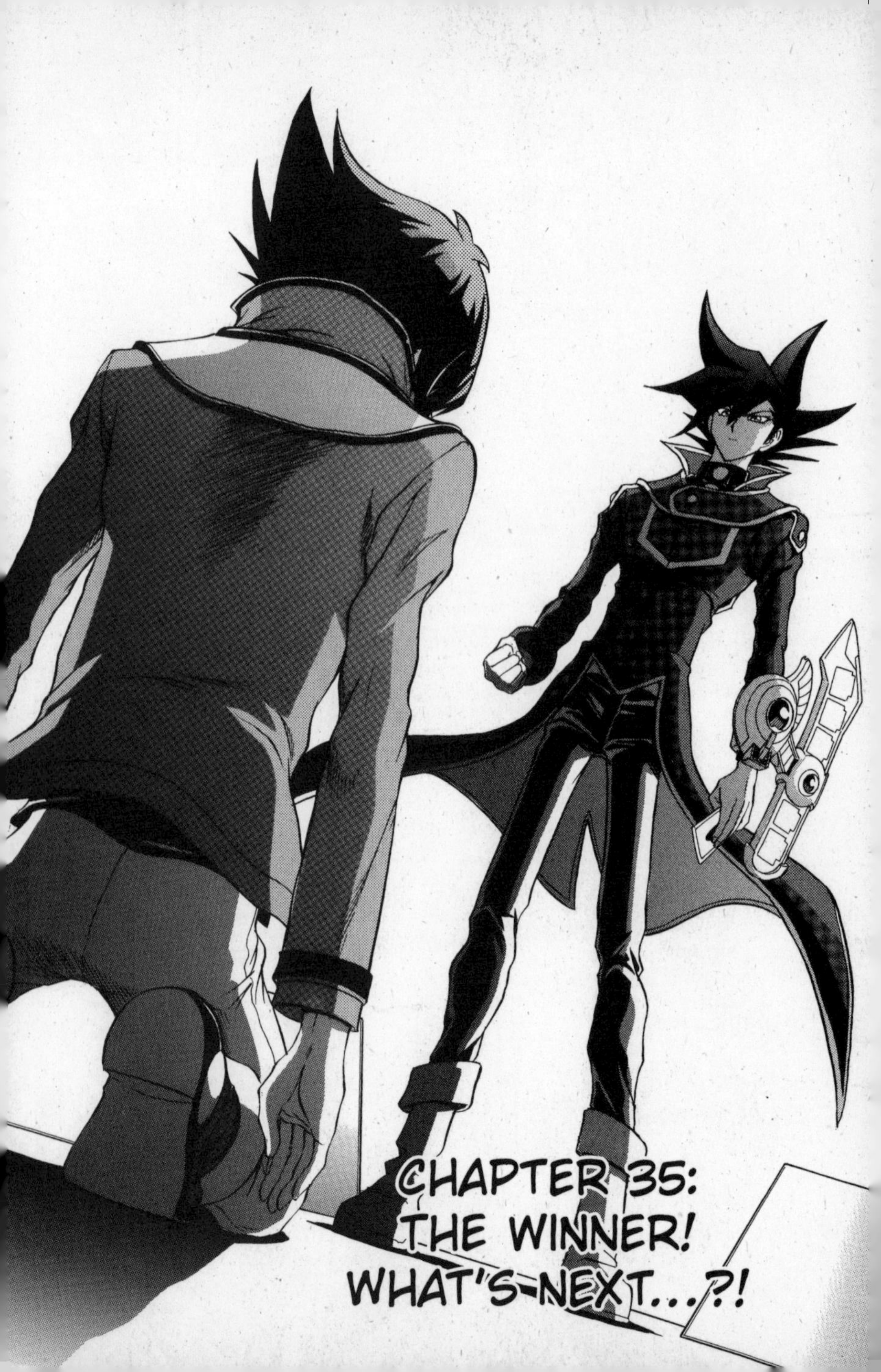
CHAPTER 35:
THE WINNER!
WHAT'S NEXT...?!

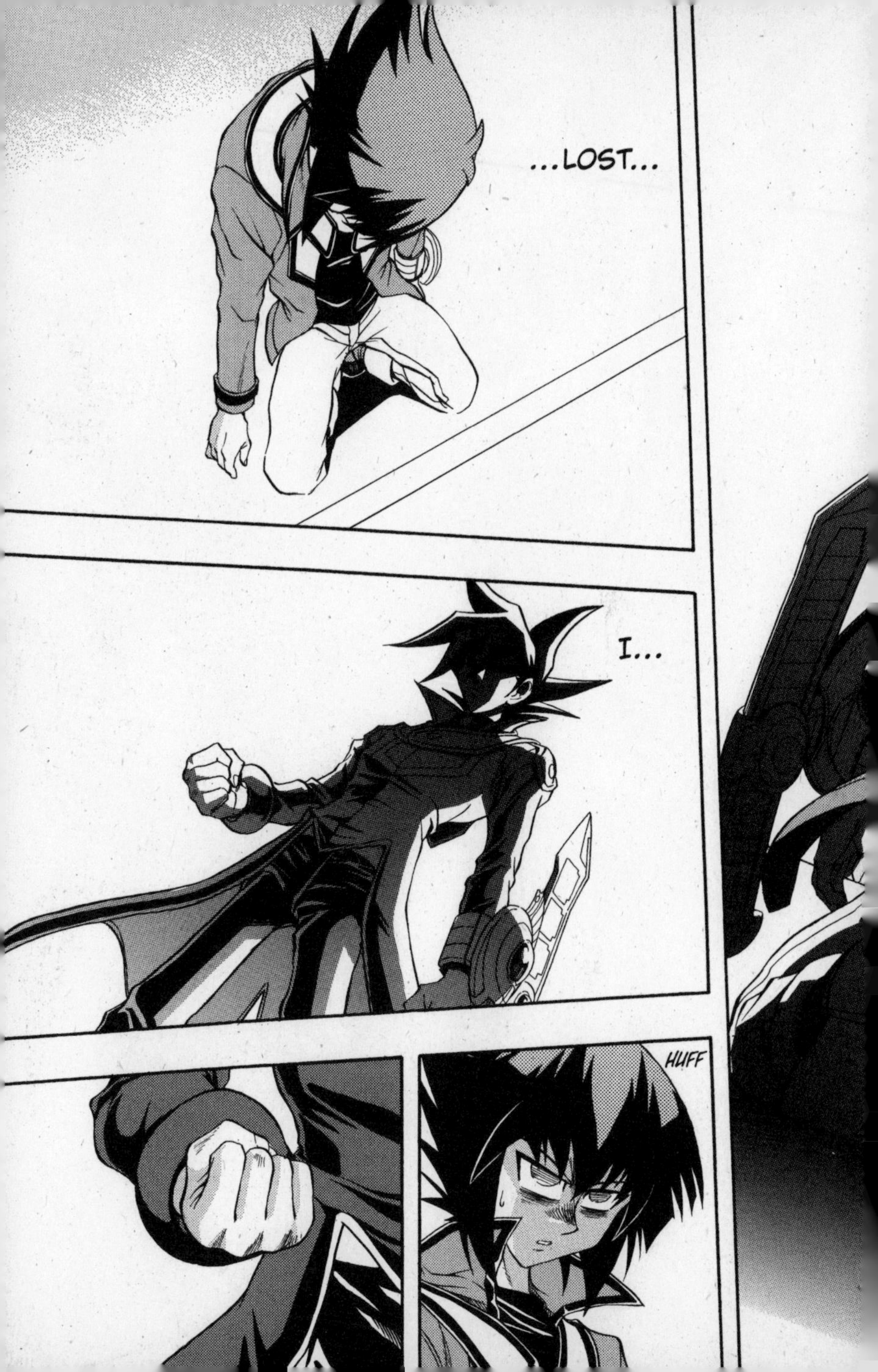
...LOST...
I...
HUFF

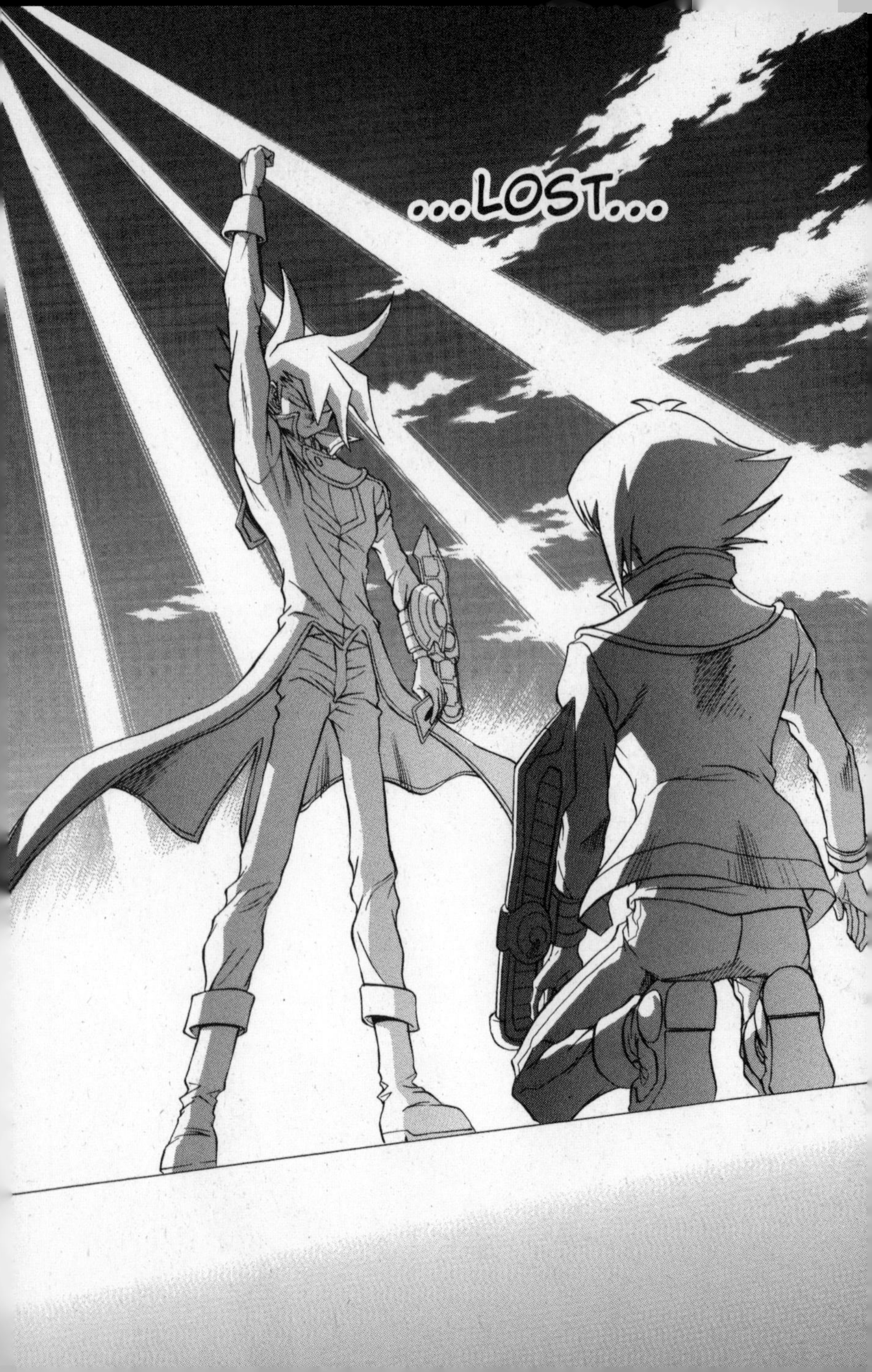
...LOST...

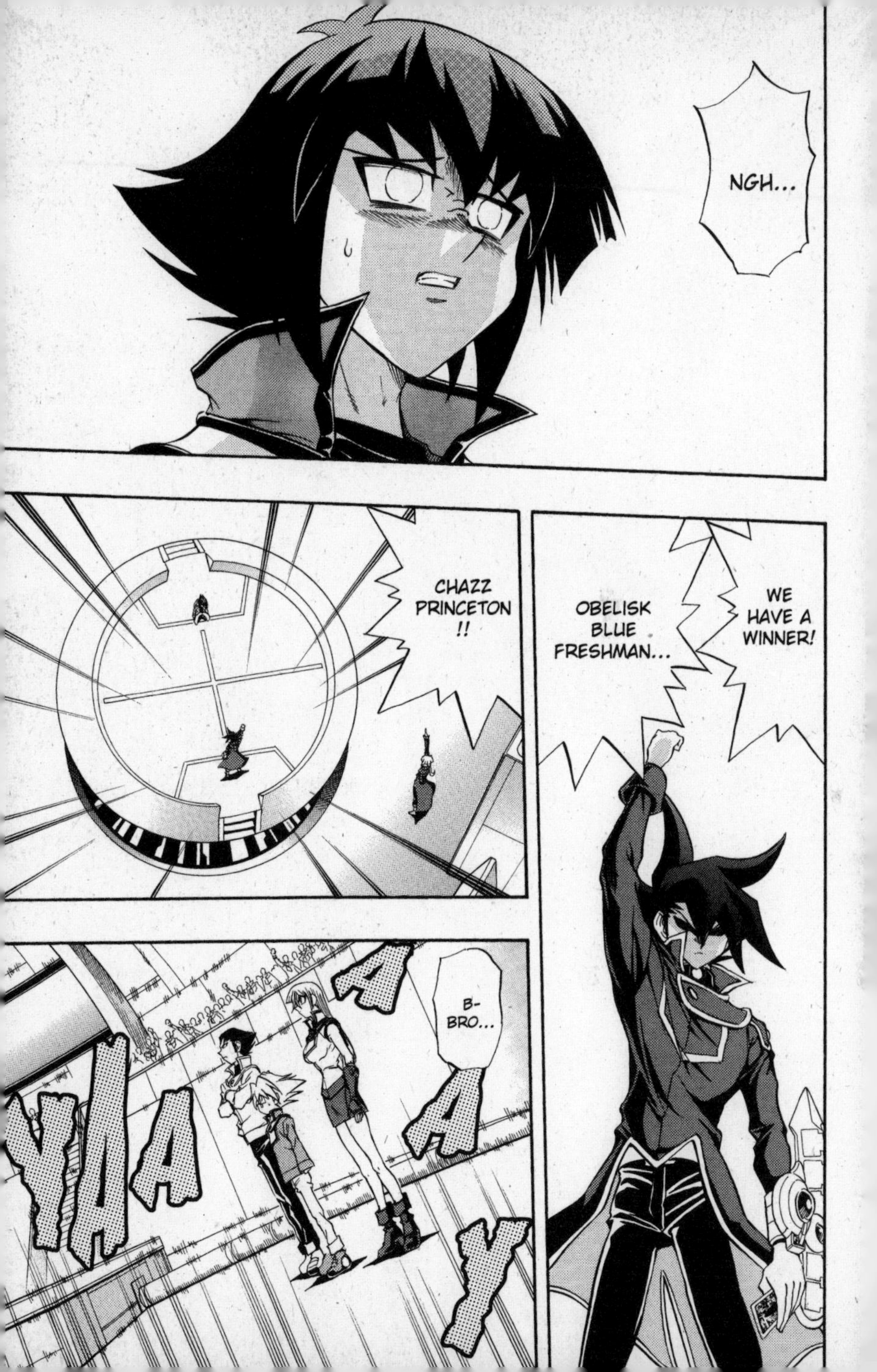
NGH...
WE HAVE A WINNER!
OBELISK BLUE FRESHMAN...
CHAZZ PRINCETON !!
B-BRO...
YAAAAY

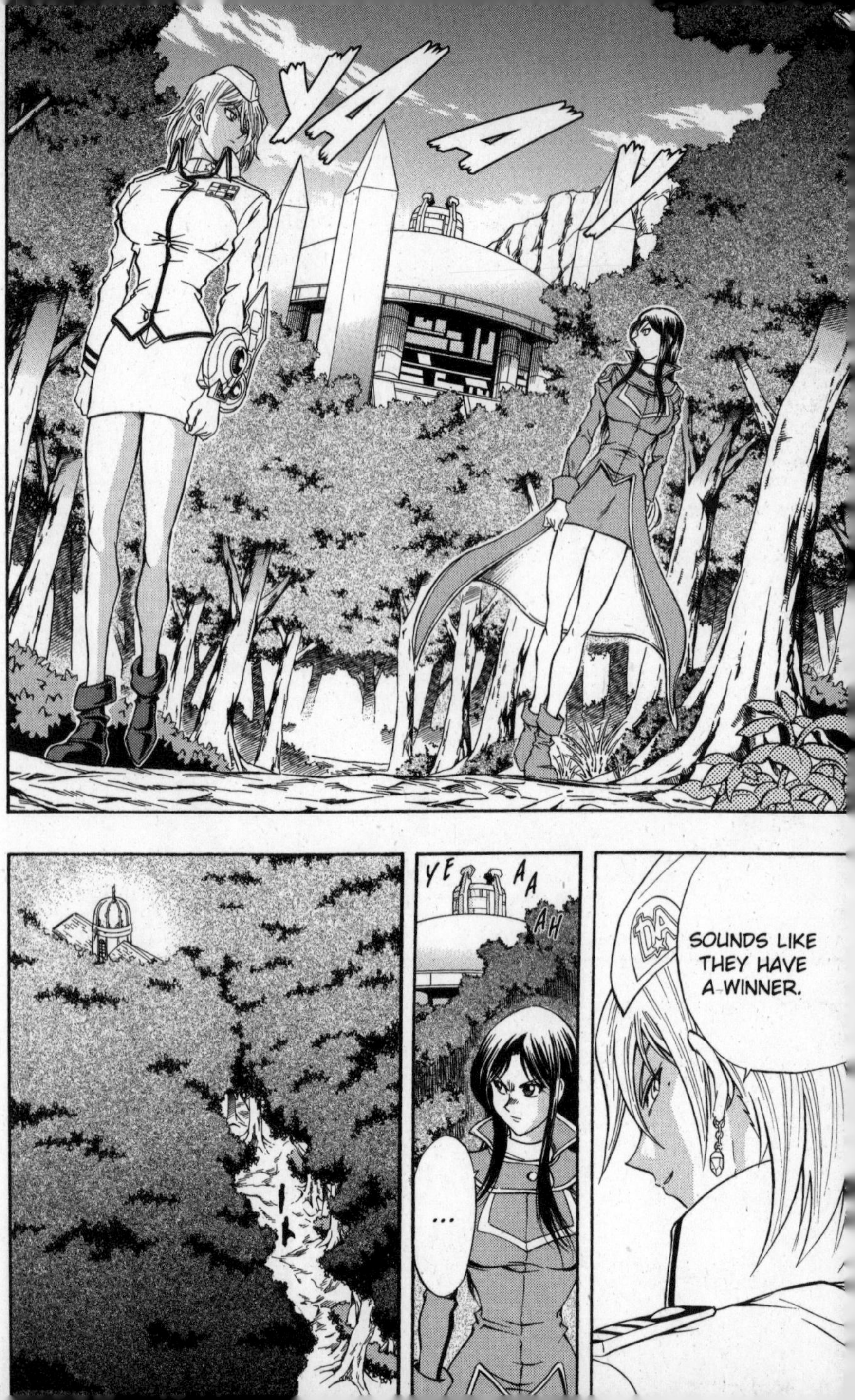
YAAY
SOUNDS LIKE THEY HAVE A WINNER.
YEAAAH
...

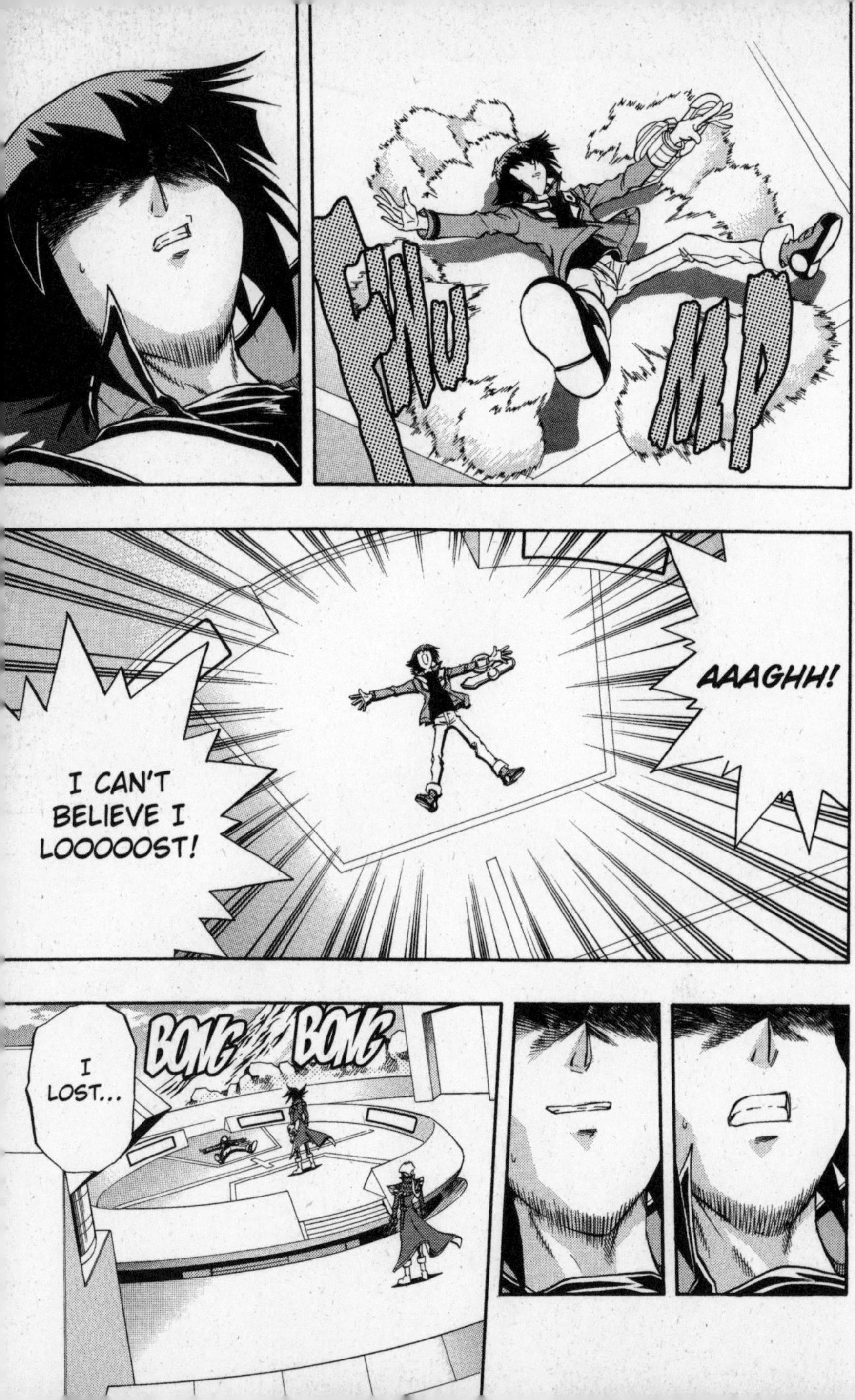
CHUMP
AAAGHH!
I CAN'T BELIEVE I LOOOOOST!
BONG BONG
I LOST...

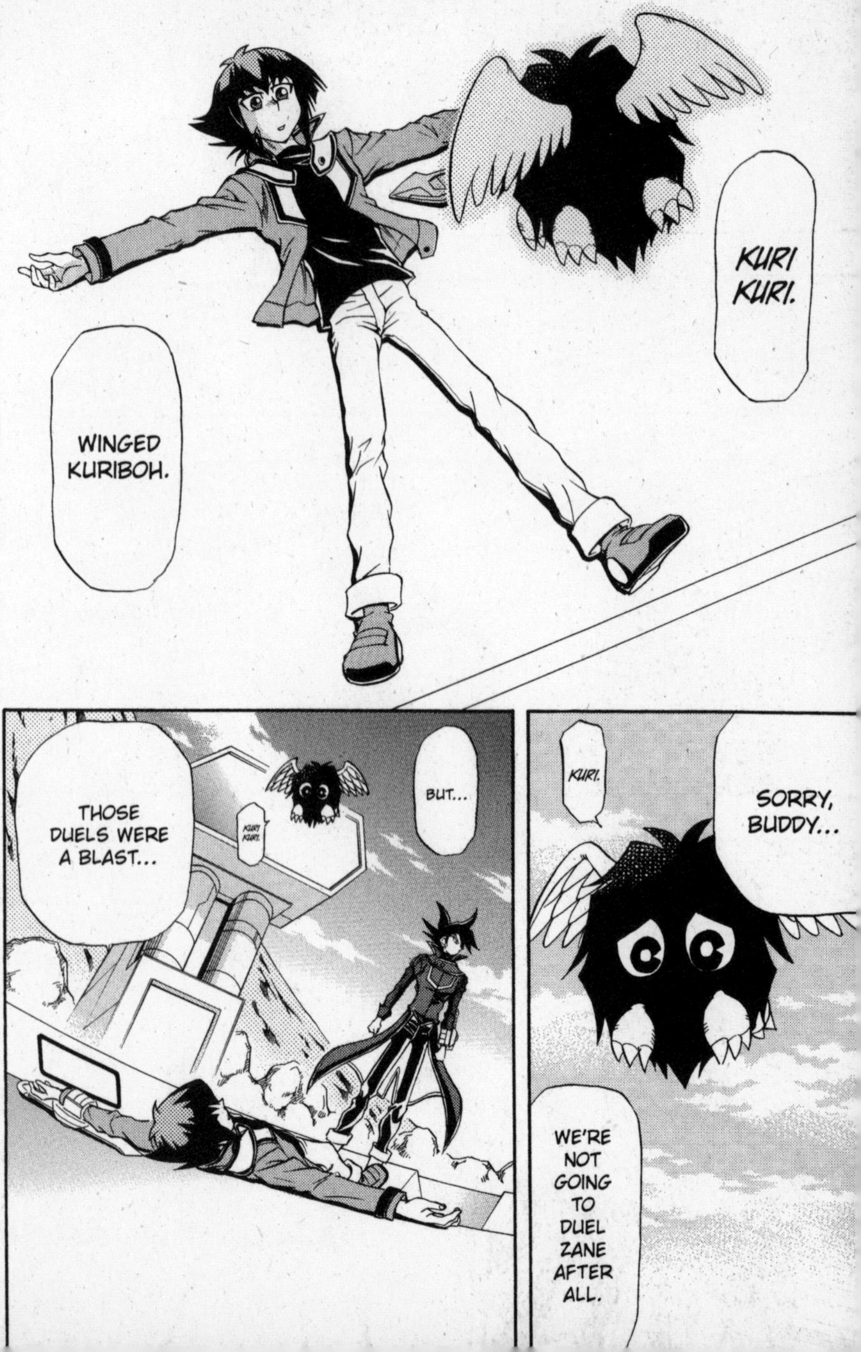
KURI KURI.
WINGED KURIBOH.
SORRY, BUDDY...
KURI.
WE'RE NOT GOING TO DUEL ZANE AFTER ALL.
BUT...
KURI KURI.
THOSE DUELS WERE A BLAST...

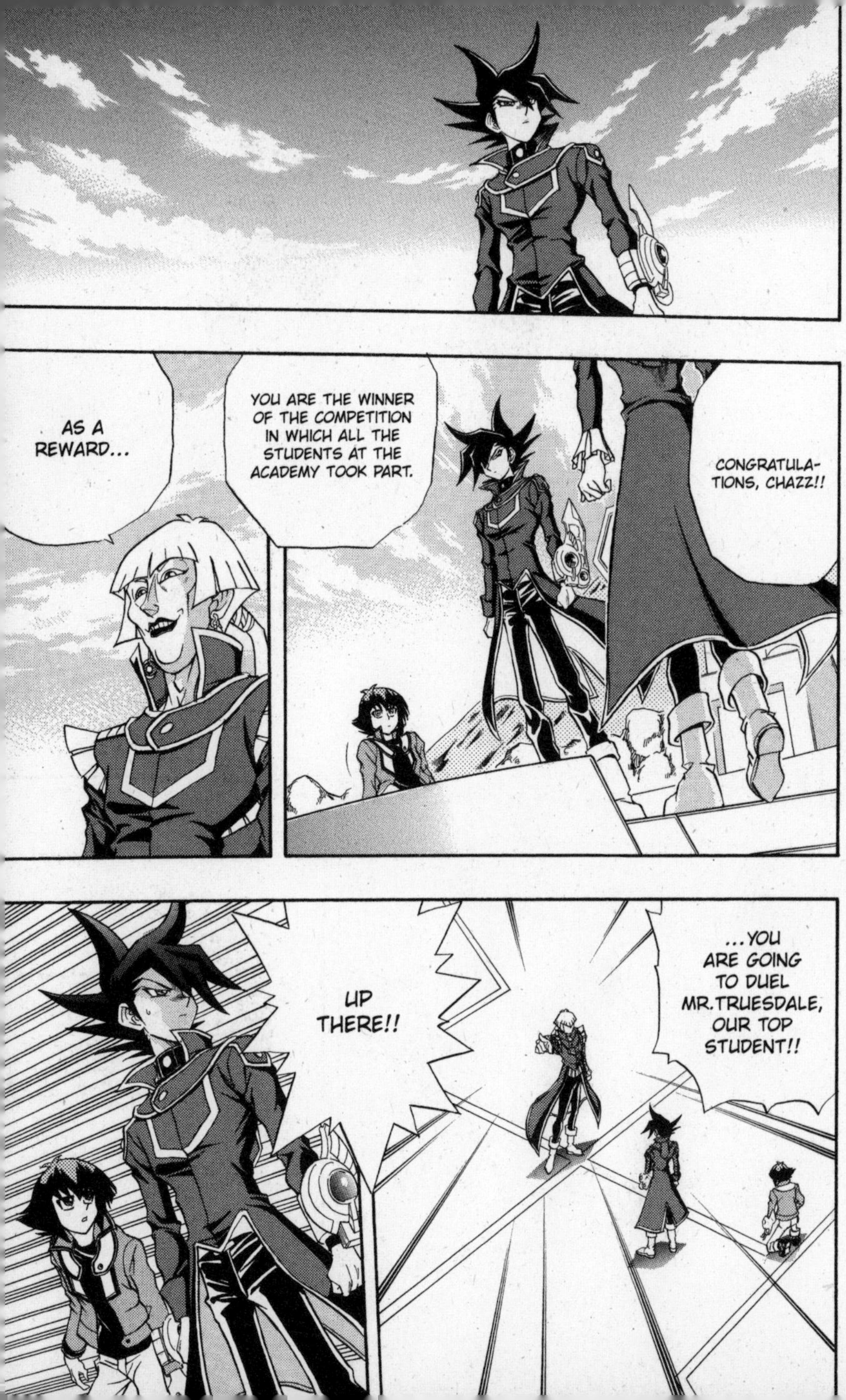
CONGRATULATIONS, CHAZZ!!
YOU ARE THE WINNER OF THE COMPETITION IN WHICH ALL THE STUDENTS AT THE ACADEMY TOOK PART.
AS A REWARD...
...YOU ARE GOING TO DUEL MR.TRUESDALE, OUR TOP STUDENT!!
UP THERE!!

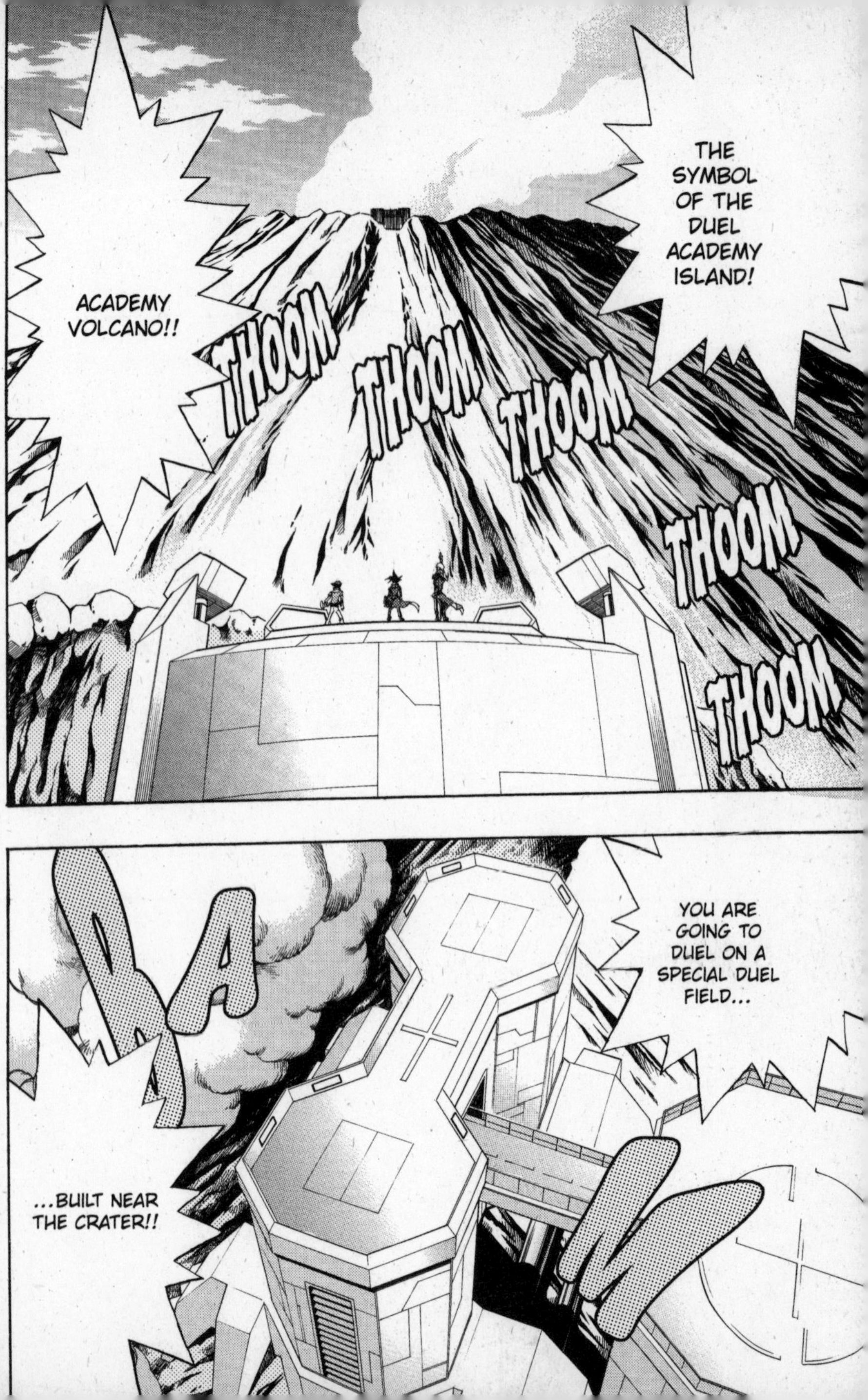
THE SYMBOL OF THE DUEL ACADEMY ISLAND!
ACADEMY VOLCANO!!
THOOM
THOOM
THOOM
THOOM
THOOM
YOU ARE GOING TO DUEL ON A SPECIAL DUEL FIELD...
...BUILT NEAR THE CRATER!!
BAM

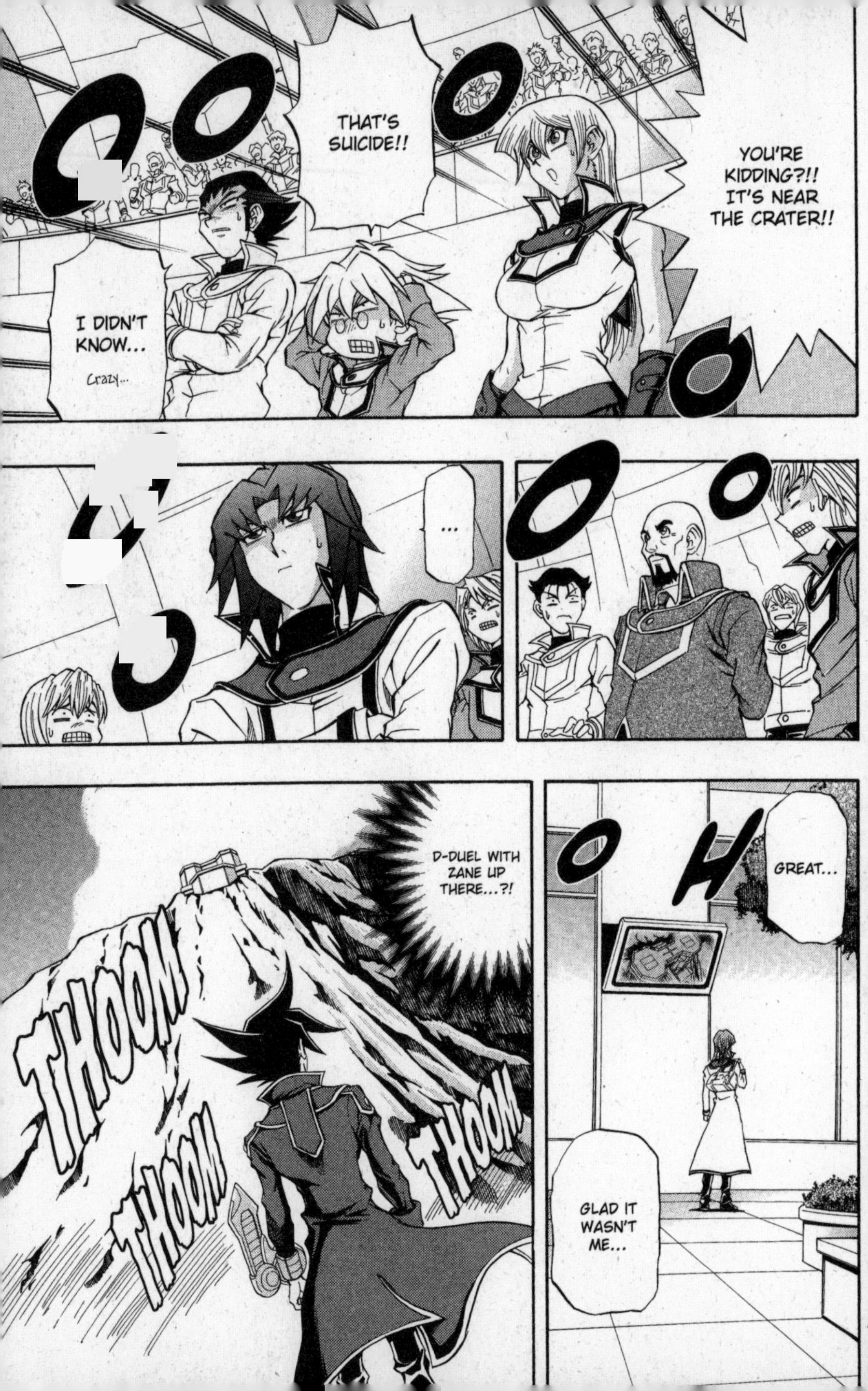

YOU'RE KIDDING?!! IT'S NEAR THE CRATER!!
THAT'S SUICIDE!!
I DIDN'T KNOW...
Crazy...
...
GREAT...
OH
GLAD IT WASN'T ME...
D-DUEL WITH ZANE UP THERE...?!
THOOM
THOOM
THOOM

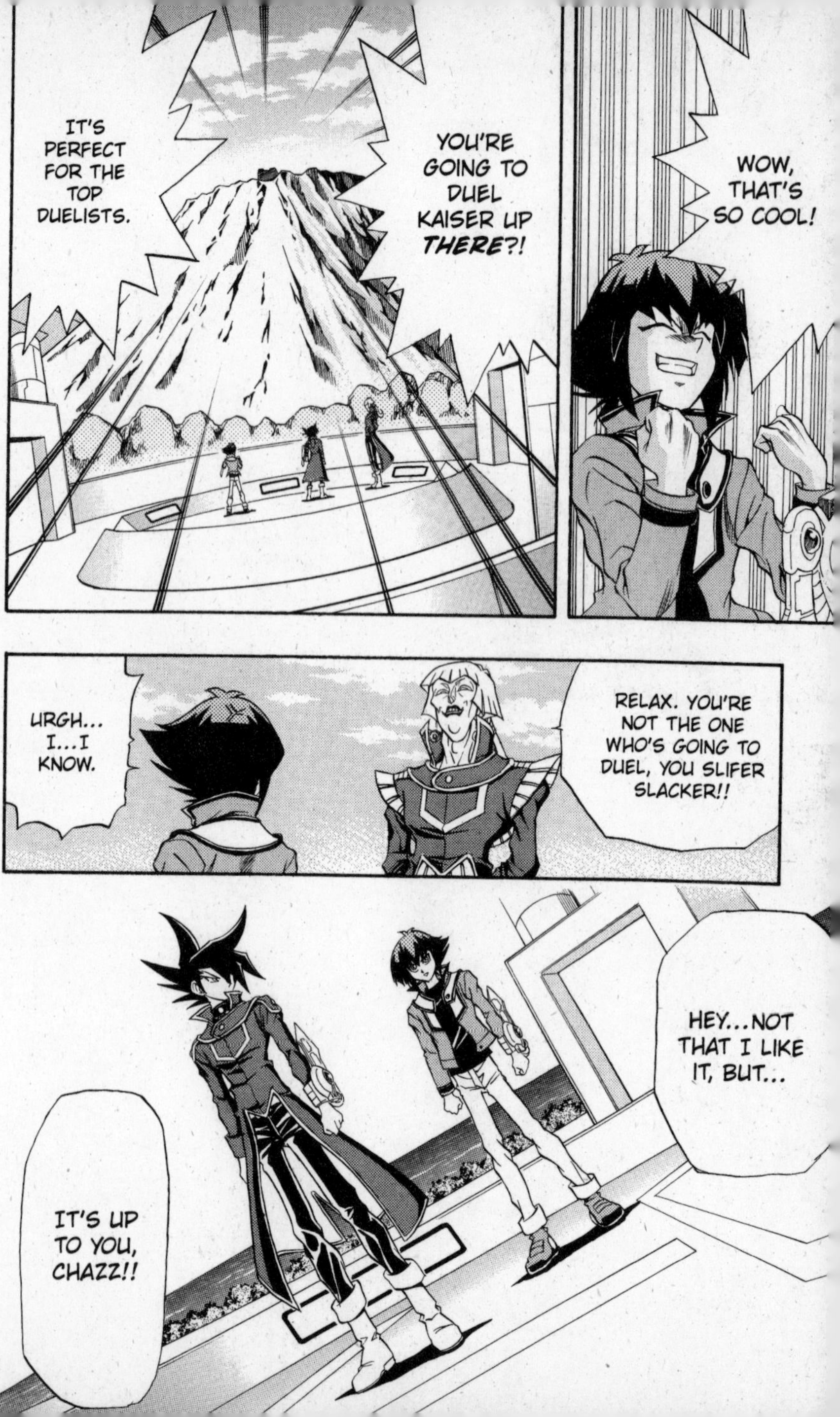
WOW, THAT'S SO COOL!
YOU'RE GOING TO DUEL KAISER UP *THERE*?!
IT'S PERFECT FOR THE TOP DUELISTS.
RELAX. YOU'RE NOT THE ONE WHO'S GOING TO DUEL, YOU SLIFER SLACKER!!
URGH... I...I KNOW.
HEY...NOT THAT I LIKE IT, BUT...
IT'S UP TO YOU, CHAZZ!!

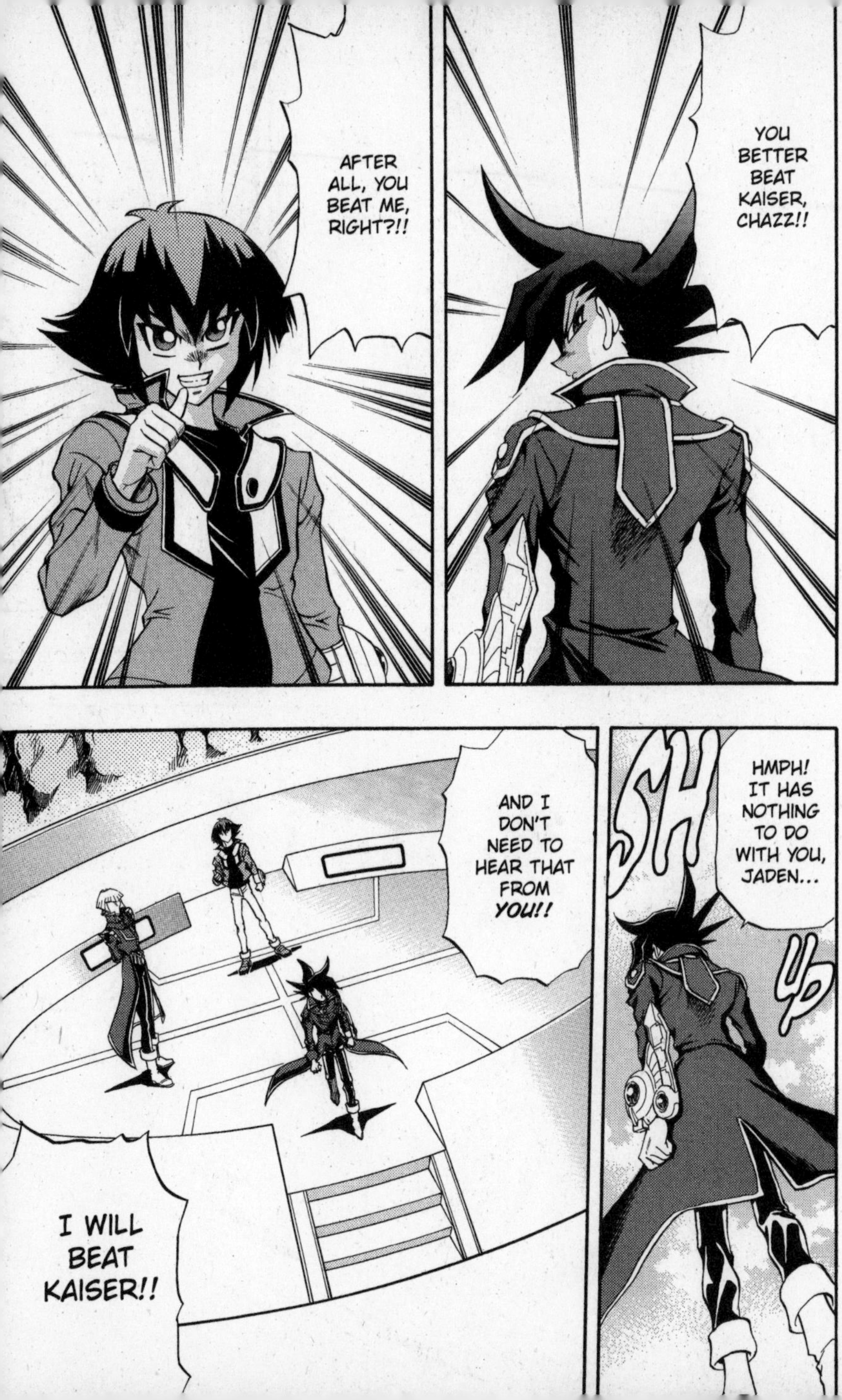
YOU BETTER BEAT KAISER, CHAZZ!!
AFTER ALL, YOU BEAT ME, RIGHT?!!
SH
HMPH! IT HAS NOTHING TO DO WITH YOU, JADEN...
UP
AND I DON'T NEED TO HEAR THAT FROM *YOU!!*
I WILL BEAT KAISER!!

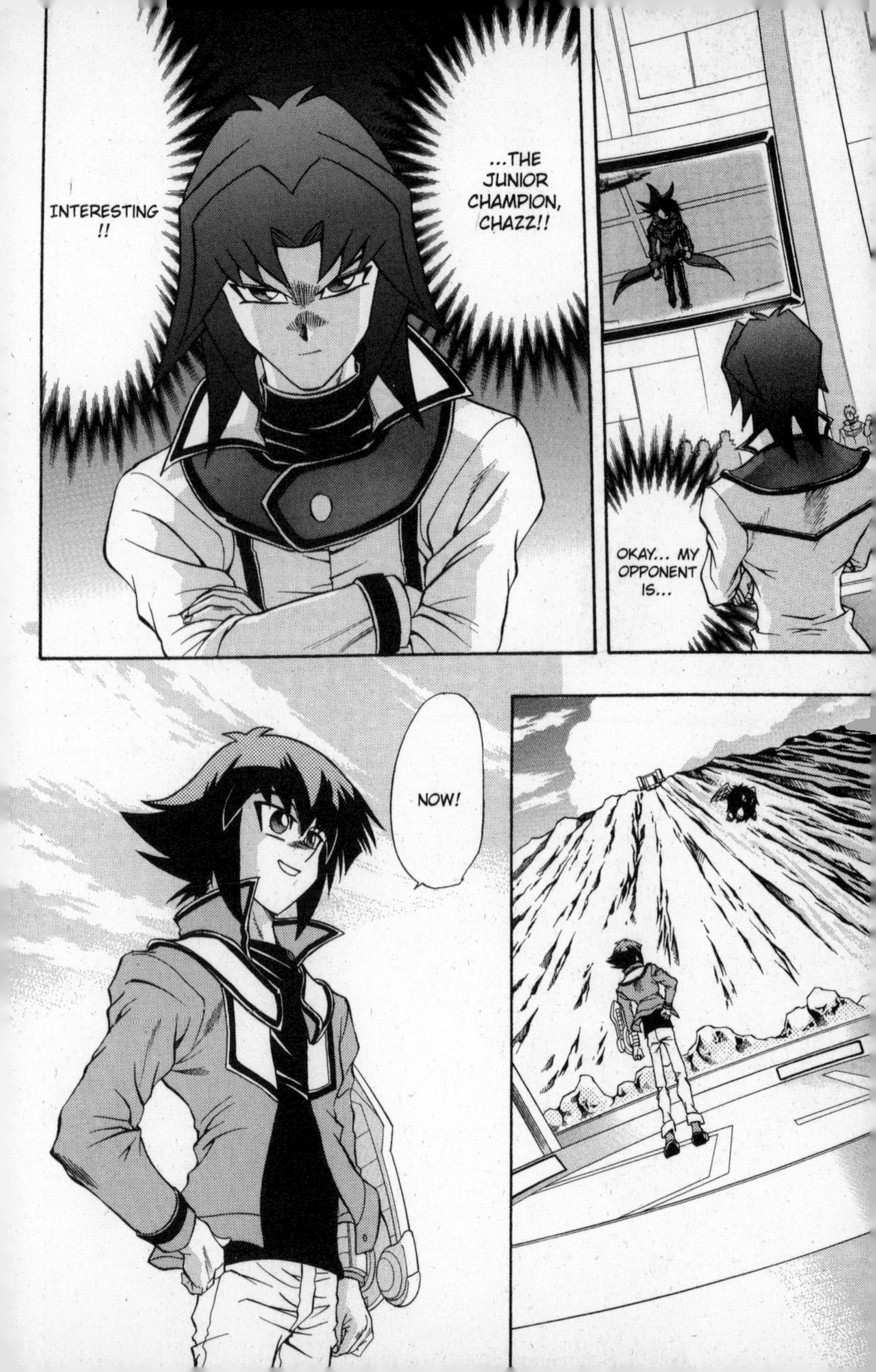
OKAY... MY OPPONENT IS...
...THE JUNIOR CHAMPION, CHAZZ!!
INTERESTING !!
NOW!

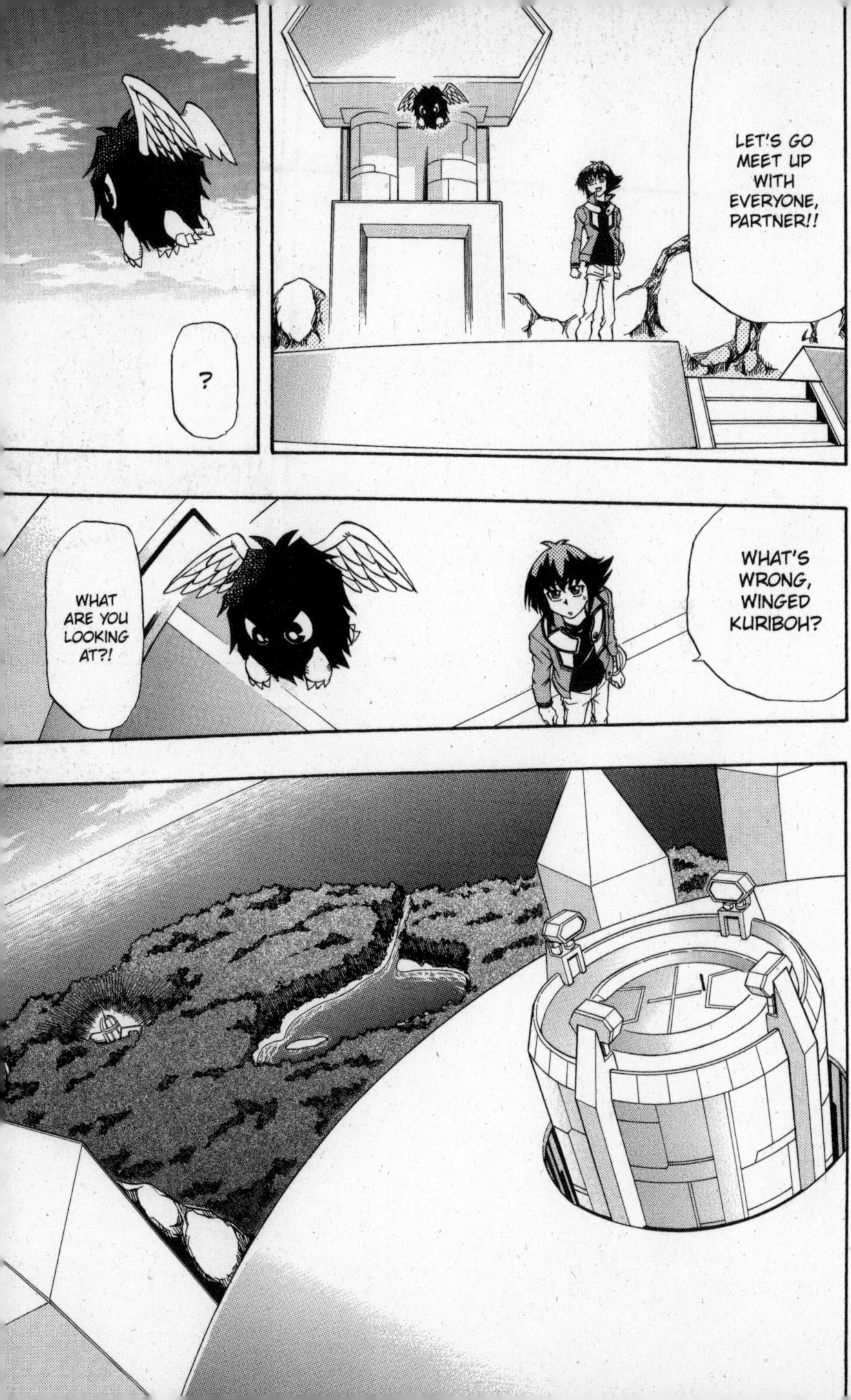
LET'S GO MEET UP WITH EVERYONE, PARTNER!!
?
WHAT'S WRONG, WINGED KURIBOH?
WHAT ARE YOU LOOKING AT?!

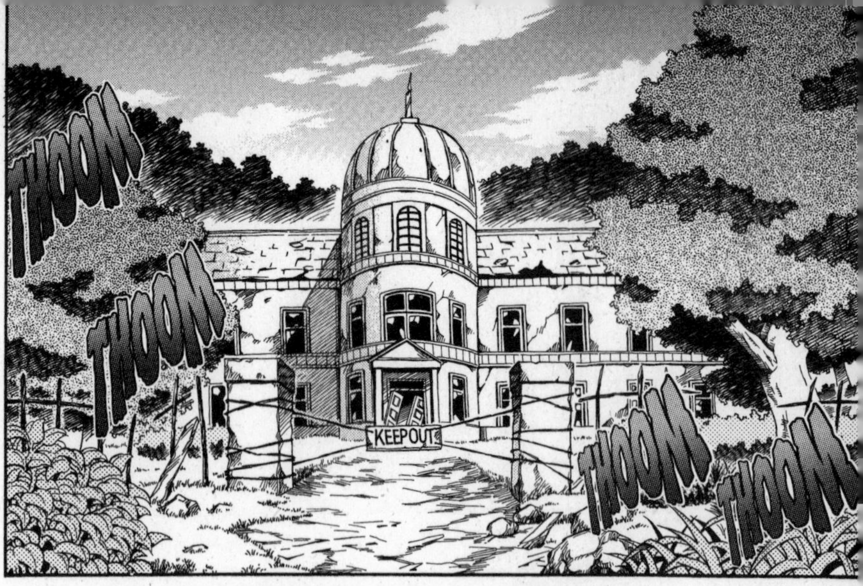
THOOM
THOOM
KEEP OUT
THOOM
THOOM
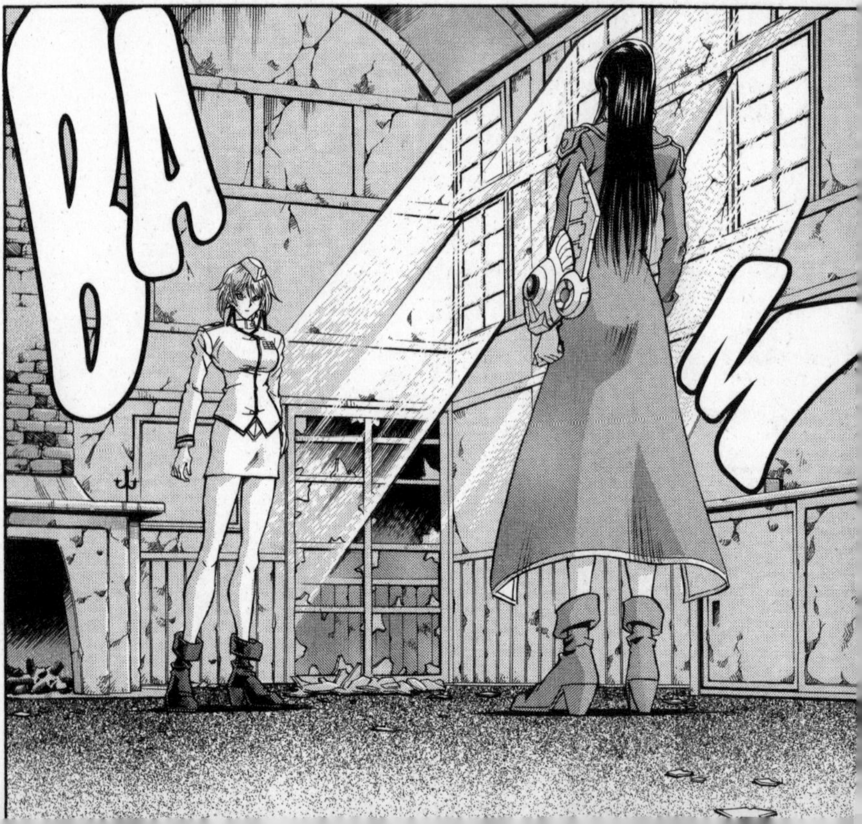
BA
M

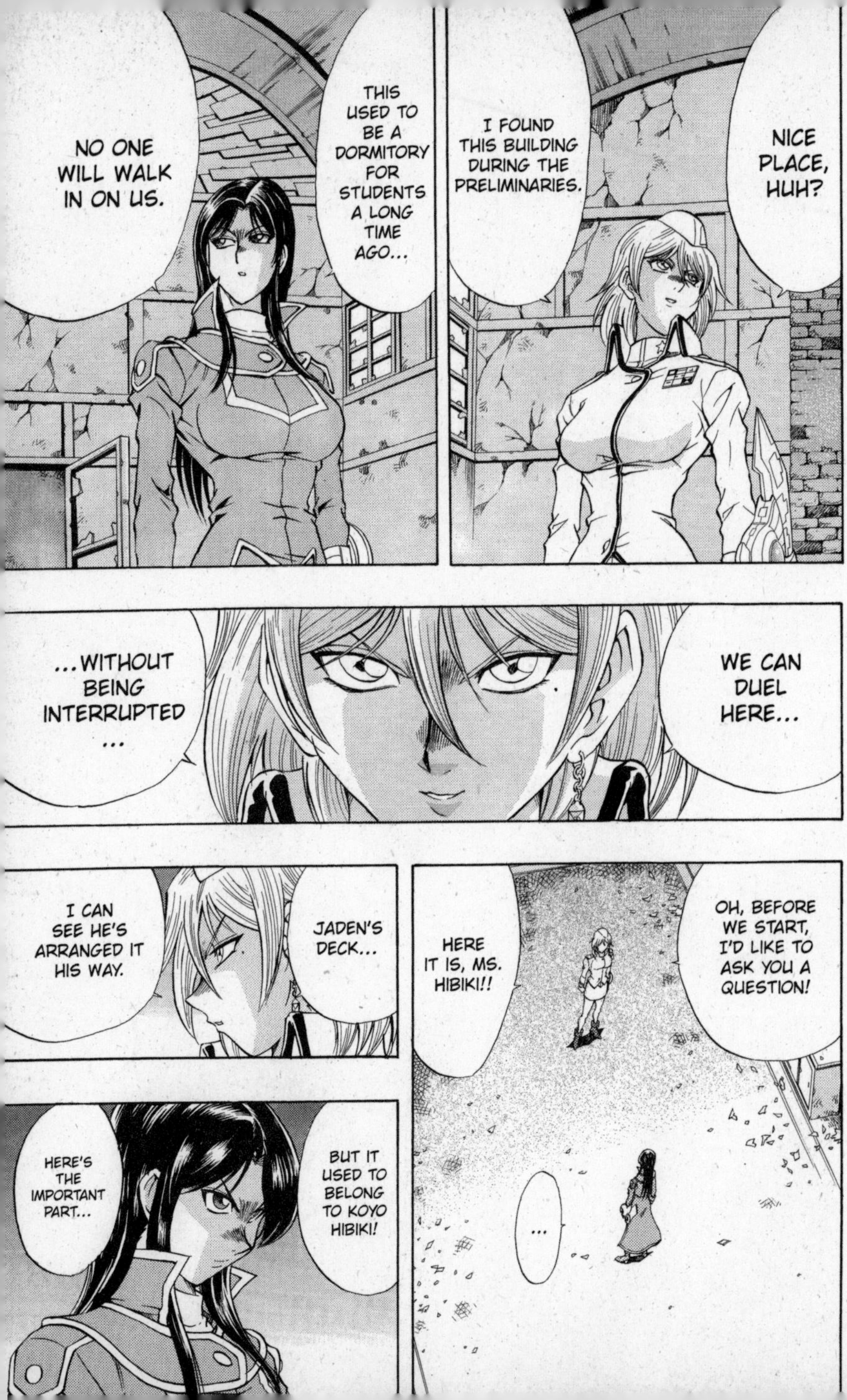
NICE PLACE, HUH?
I FOUND THIS BUILDING DURING THE PRELIMINARIES.
THIS USED TO BE A DORMITORY FOR STUDENTS A LONG TIME AGO...
NO ONE WILL WALK IN ON US.
WE CAN DUEL HERE...
...WITHOUT BEING INTERRUPTED...
OH, BEFORE WE START, I'D LIKE TO ASK YOU A QUESTION!
HERE IT IS, MS. HIBIKI!!
...
JADEN'S DECK...
I CAN SEE HE'S ARRANGED IT HIS WAY.
BUT IT USED TO BELONG TO KOYO HIBIKI!
HERE'S THE IMPORTANT PART...

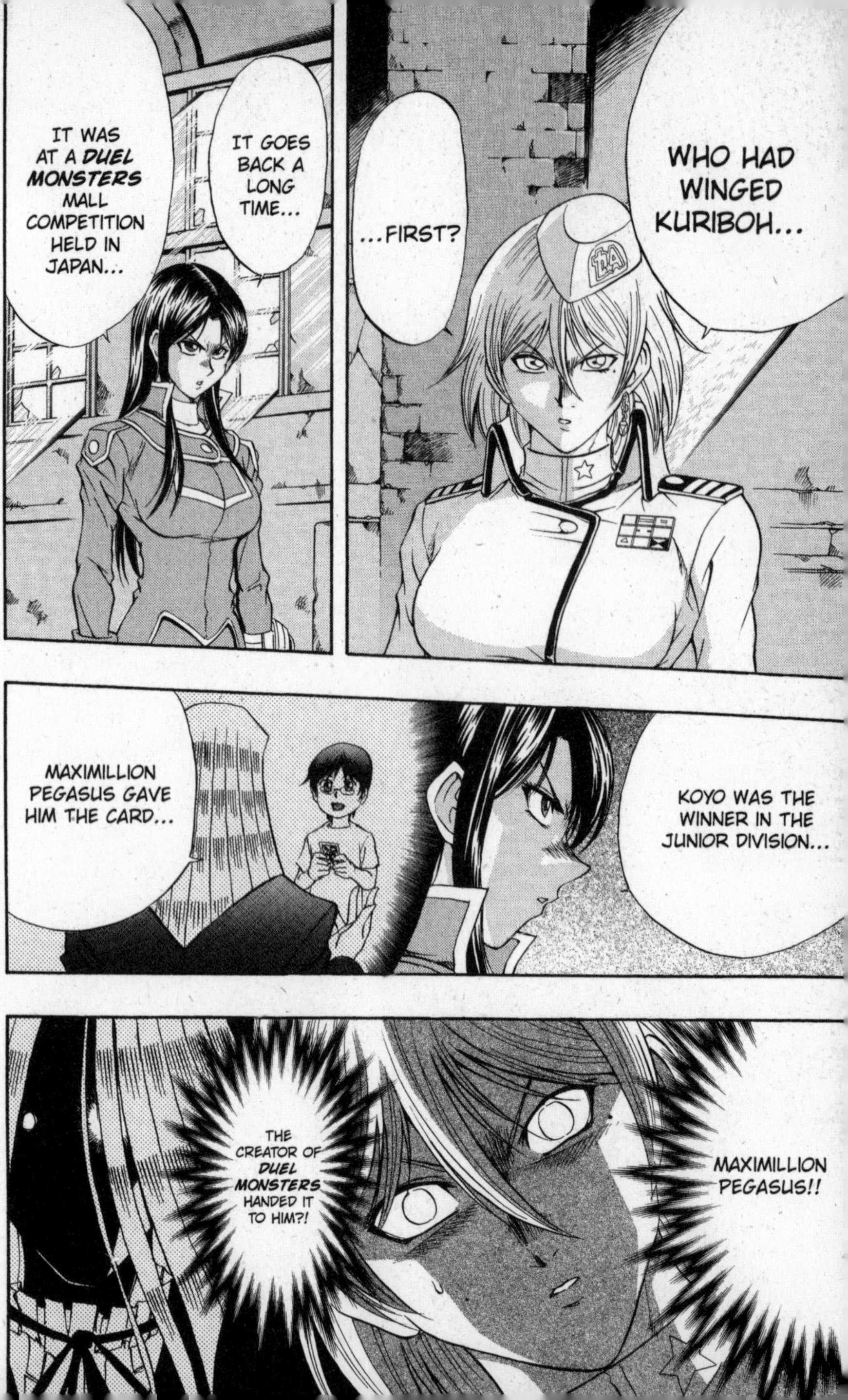
WHO HAD WINGED KURIBOH...
...FIRST?
IT GOES BACK A LONG TIME...
IT WAS AT A DUEL MONSTERS MALL COMPETITION HELD IN JAPAN...
KOYO WAS THE WINNER IN THE JUNIOR DIVISION...
MAXIMILLION PEGASUS GAVE HIM THE CARD...
MAXIMILLION PEGASUS!!
THE CREATOR OF DUEL MONSTERS HANDED IT TO HIM?!

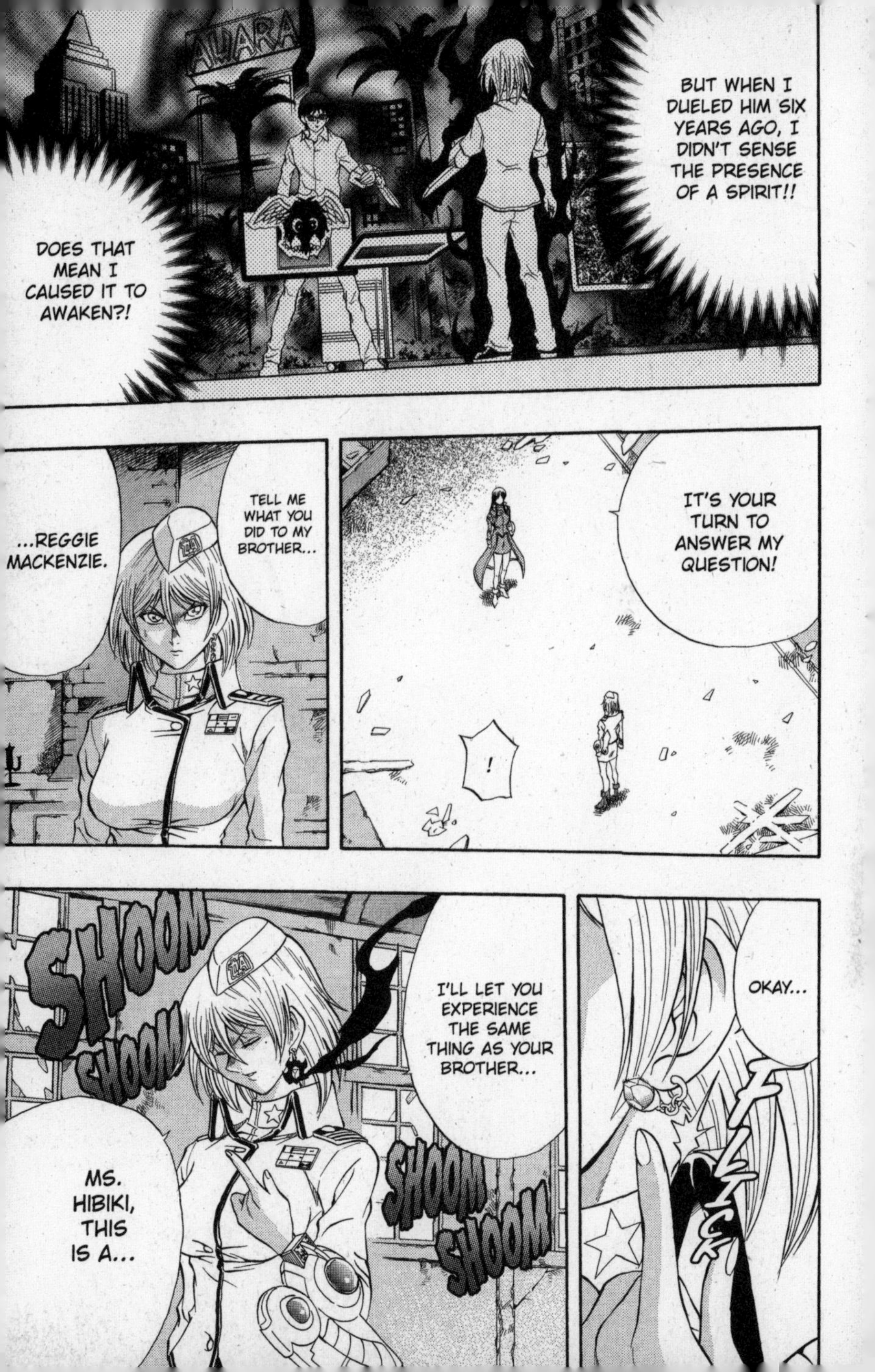
BUT WHEN I DUELED HIM SIX YEARS AGO, I DIDN'T SENSE THE PRESENCE OF A SPIRIT!!
DOES THAT MEAN I CAUSED IT TO AWAKEN?!
IT'S YOUR TURN TO ANSWER MY QUESTION!
!
TELL ME WHAT YOU DID TO MY BROTHER...
...REGGIE MACKENZIE.
OKAY...
FLICK
I'LL LET YOU EXPERIENCE THE SAME THING AS YOUR BROTHER...
SHOOM SHOOM
SHOOM SHOOM
MS. HIBIKI, THIS IS A...

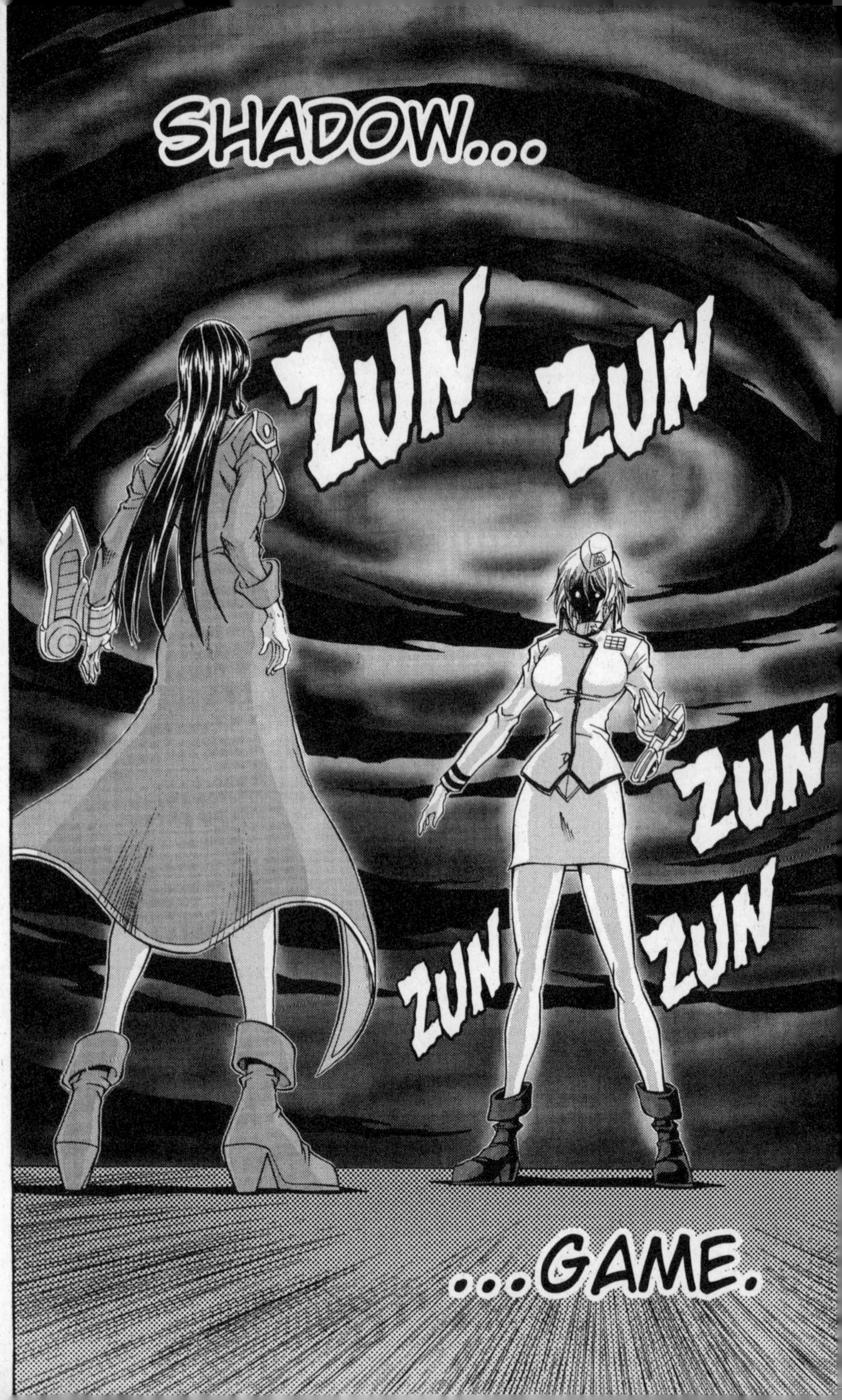
SHADOW...
ZUN
ZUN
ZUN
ZUN
ZUN
...GAME.

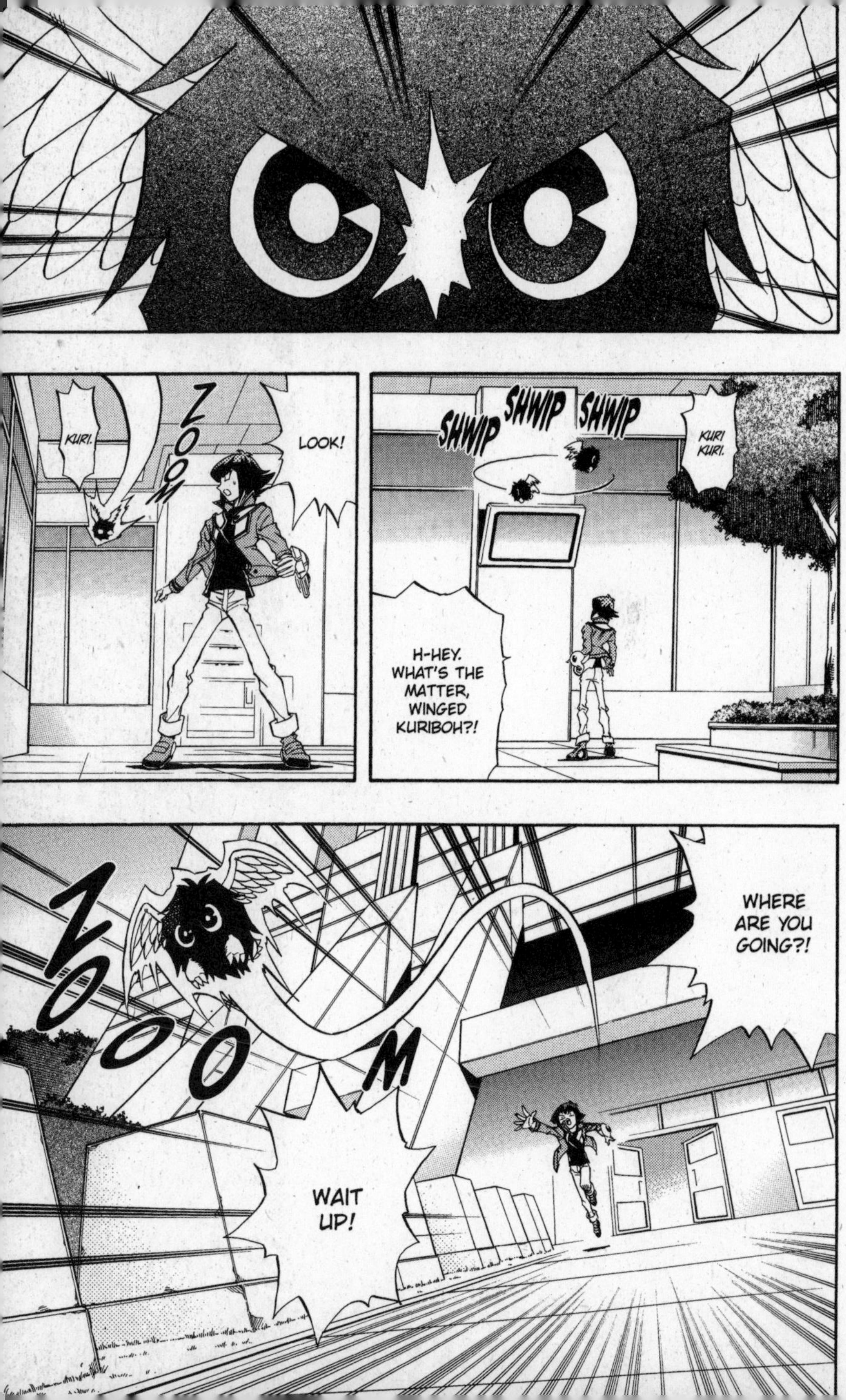
KURI! KURI!
SHWIP SHWIP SHWIP
H-HEY. WHAT'S THE MATTER, WINGED KURIBOH?!
LOOK!
ZOOM
KURI!
WHERE ARE YOU GOING?!
ZOOOOM
WAIT UP!

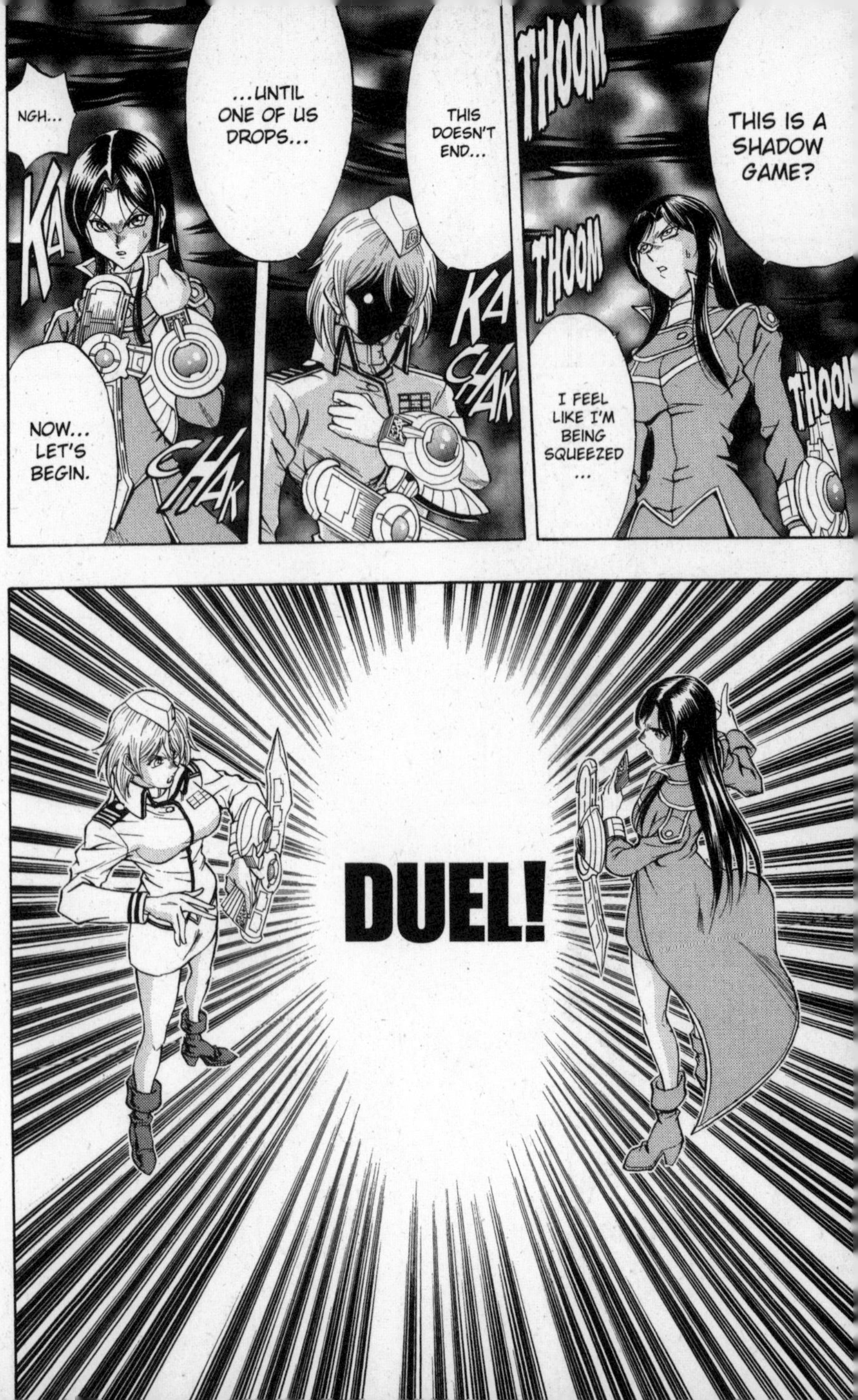
THIS IS A SHADOW GAME?
THOOM
THOOM
I FEEL LIKE I'M BEING SQUEEZED ...
THIS DOESN'T END...
...UNTIL ONE OF US DROPS...
KA CHAK
NGH...
KA
NOW... LET'S BEGIN.
CHAK
DUEL!

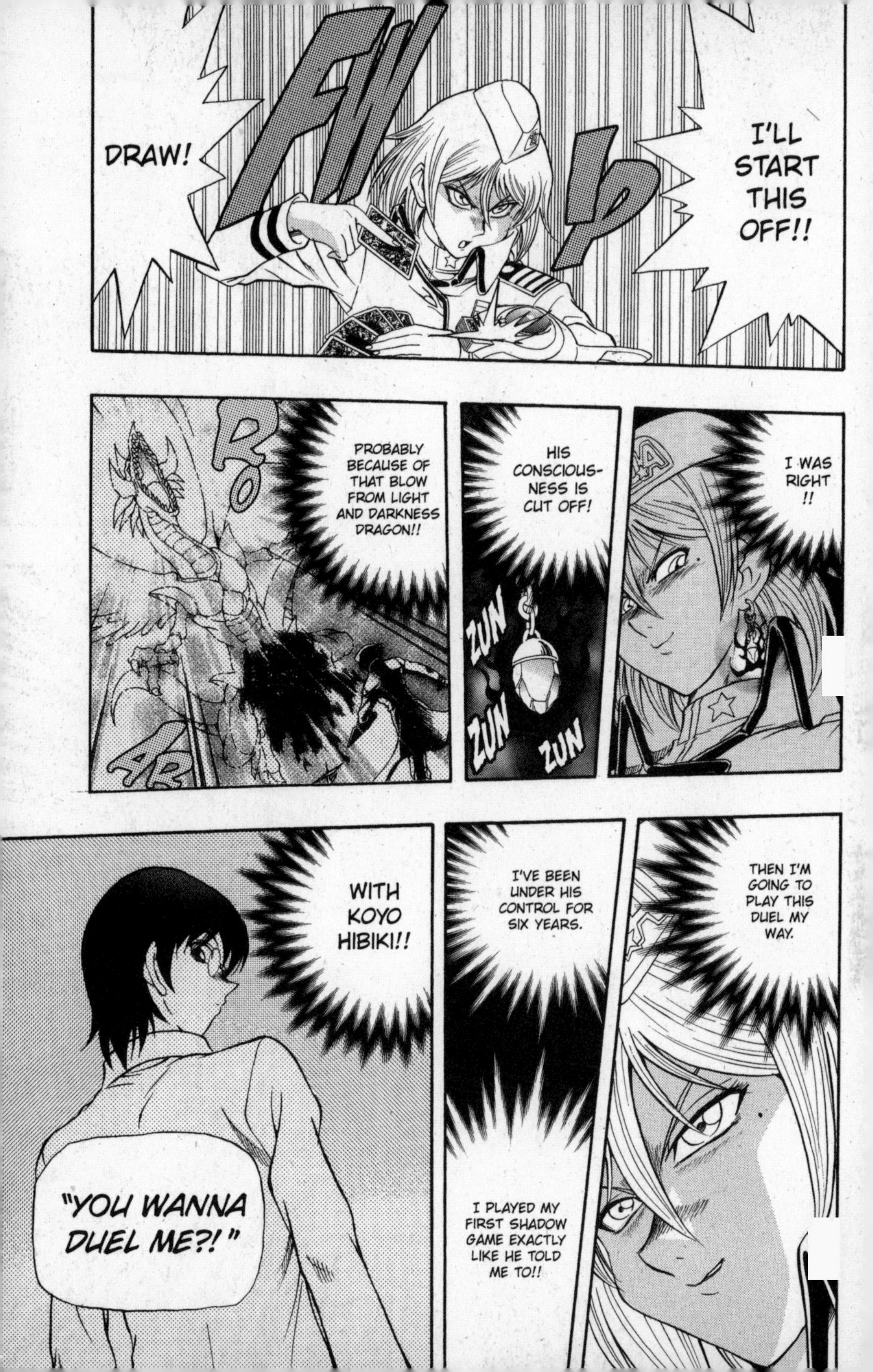
I'LL START THIS OFF!!
FLIP
DRAW!
I WAS RIGHT !!
HIS CONSCIOUS-NESS IS CUT OFF!
ZUN ZUN ZUN
PROBABLY BECAUSE OF THAT BLOW FROM LIGHT AND DARKNESS DRAGON!!
ROAR
THEN I'M GOING TO PLAY THIS DUEL MY WAY.
I'VE BEEN UNDER HIS CONTROL FOR SIX YEARS.
I PLAYED MY FIRST SHADOW GAME EXACTLY LIKE HE TOLD ME TO!!
WITH KOYO HIBIKI!!
"YOU WANNA DUEL ME?!"

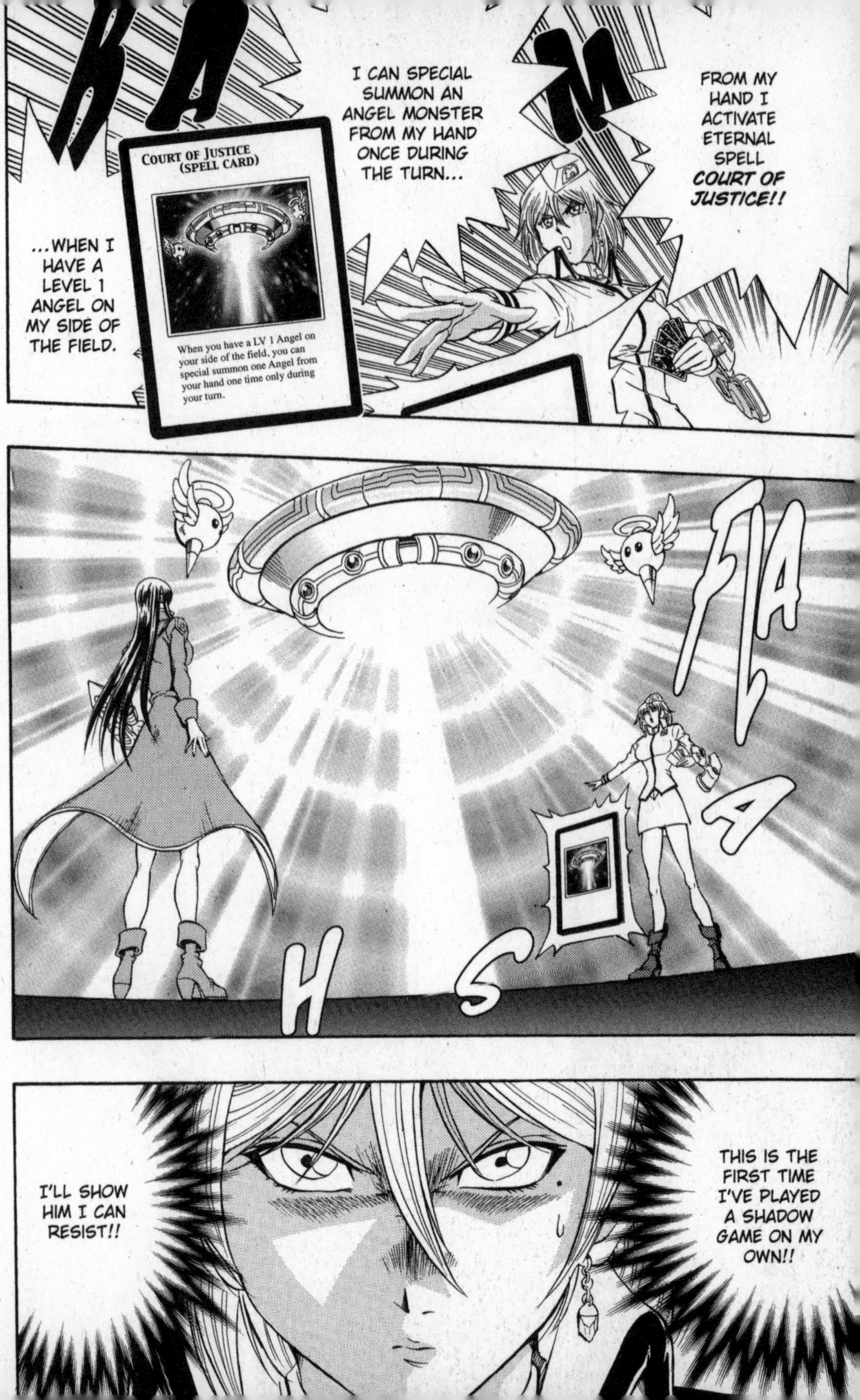
FROM MY HAND I ACTIVATE ETERNAL SPELL COURT OF JUSTICE!!
I CAN SPECIAL SUMMON AN ANGEL MONSTER FROM MY HAND ONCE DURING THE TURN...
...WHEN I HAVE A LEVEL 1 ANGEL ON MY SIDE OF THE FIELD.
COURT OF JUSTICE (SPELL CARD)
When you have a LV 1 Angel on your side of the field, you can special summon one Angel from your hand one time only during your turn.
FLA
A
S
H
THIS IS THE FIRST TIME I'VE PLAYED A SHADOW GAME ON MY OWN!!
I'LL SHOW HIM I CAN RESIST!!

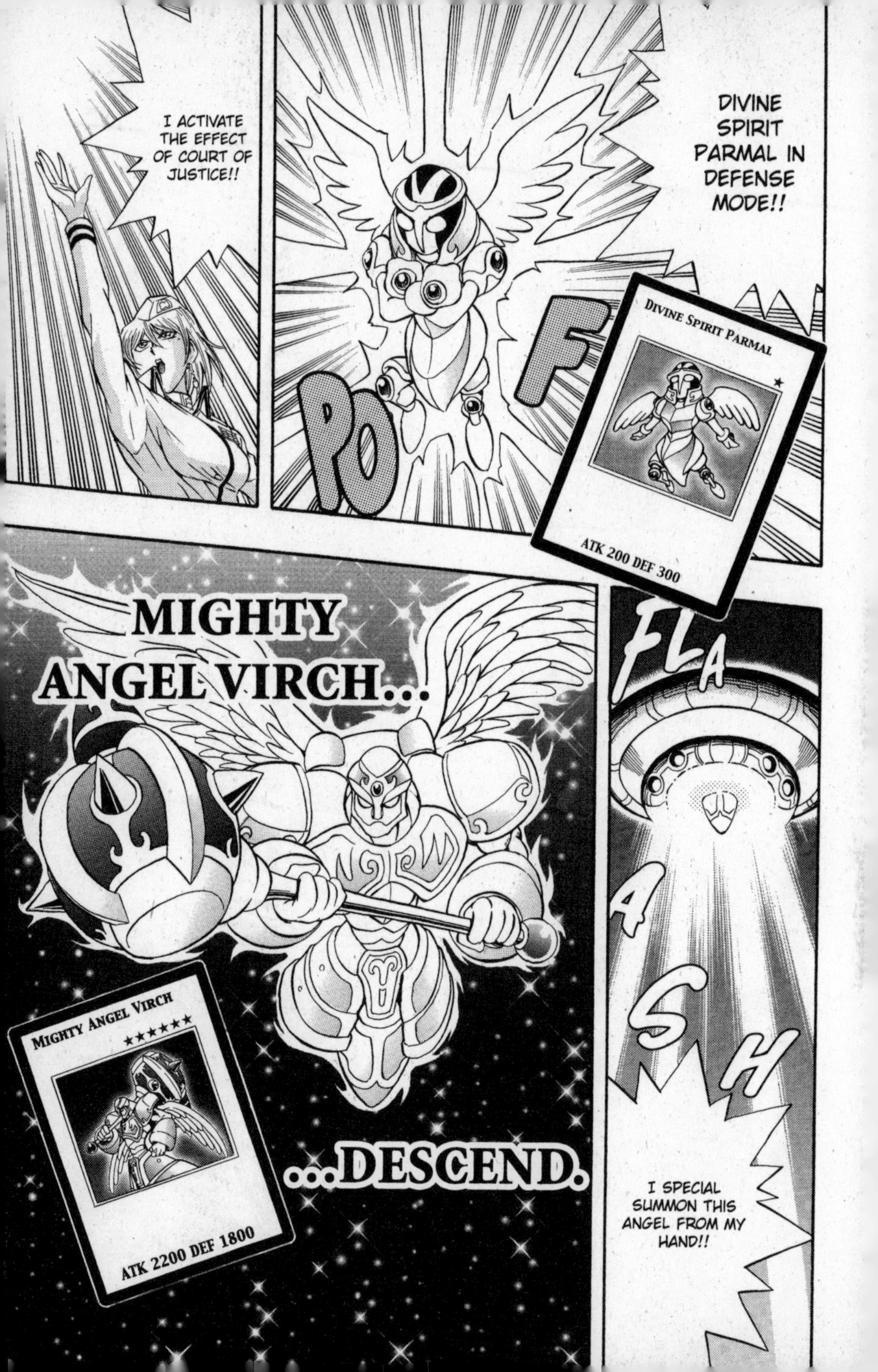

DIVINE SPIRIT PARMAL IN DEFENSE MODE!!
DIVINE SPIRIT PARMAL
ATK 200 DEF 300
POF
I ACTIVATE THE EFFECT OF COURT OF JUSTICE!!
FLASH
I SPECIAL SUMMON THIS ANGEL FROM MY HAND!!
MIGHTY ANGEL VIRCH...
...DESCEND.
MIGHTY ANGEL VIRCH
ATK 2200 DEF 1800

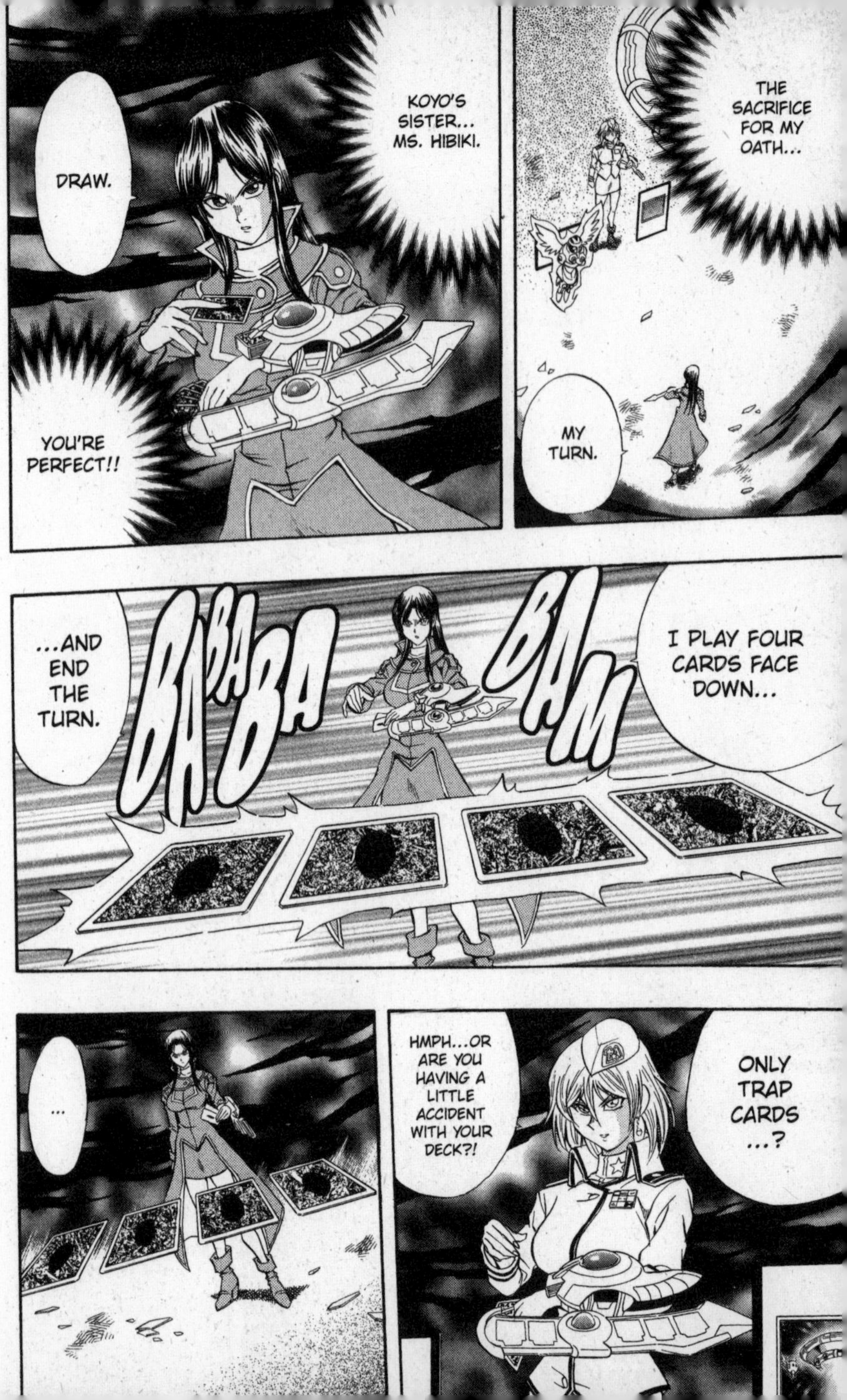
THE SACRIFICE FOR MY OATH...
MY TURN.
KOYO'S SISTER... MS. HIBIKI.
DRAW.
YOU'RE PERFECT!!
I PLAY FOUR CARDS FACE DOWN...
BAM
BABABA
...AND END THE TURN.
ONLY TRAP CARDS ...?
HMPH...OR ARE YOU HAVING A LITTLE ACCIDENT WITH YOUR DECK?!
...

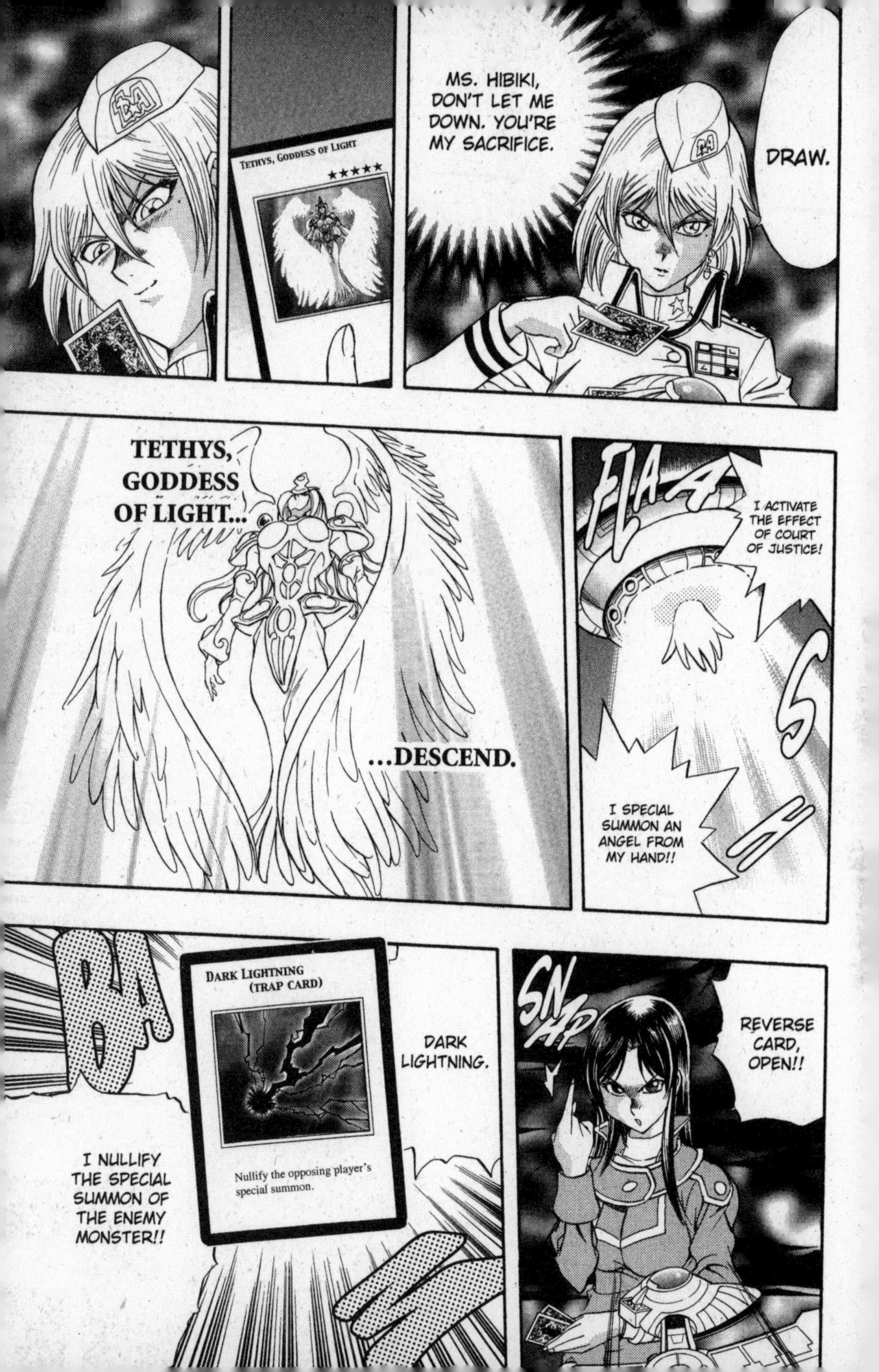
DRAW.
MS. HIBIKI, DON'T LET ME DOWN. YOU'RE MY SACRIFICE.
TETHYS, GODDESS OF LIGHT ★★★★★
FLAASH
I ACTIVATE THE EFFECT OF COURT OF JUSTICE!
I SPECIAL SUMMON AN ANGEL FROM MY HAND!!
TETHYS, GODDESS OF LIGHT...
...DESCEND.
SNAP
REVERSE CARD, OPEN!!
DARK LIGHTNING.
DARK LIGHTNING (TRAP CARD)
Nullify the opposing player's special summon.
I NULLIFY THE SPECIAL SUMMON OF THE ENEMY MONSTER!!
BA

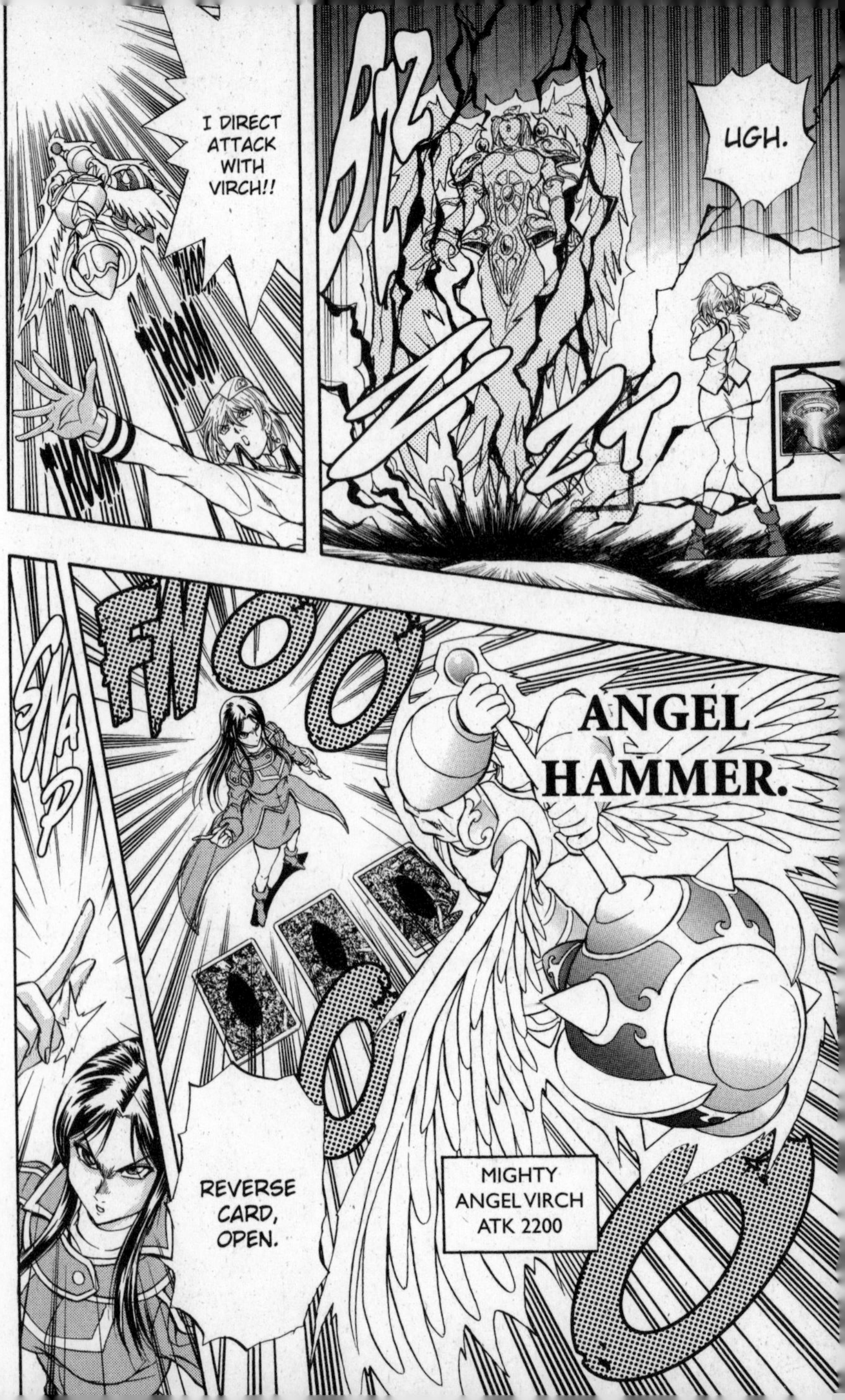
BZZ
UGH.
I DIRECT ATTACK WITH VIRCH!!
THOOM
THOOM
THOOM
ANGEL HAMMER.
FWOO
MIGHTY ANGEL VIRCH ATK 2200
SNAP
REVERSE CARD, OPEN.

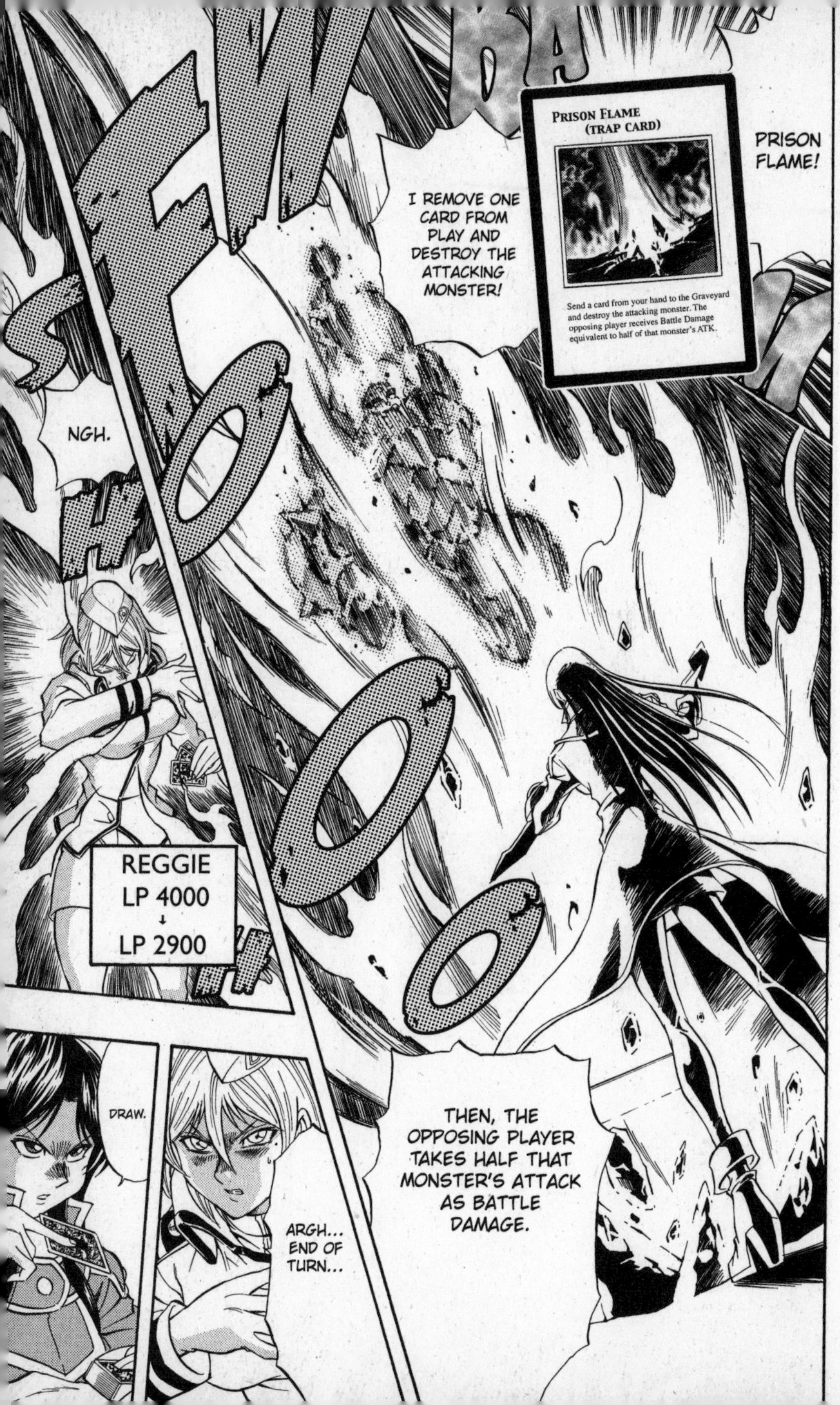
PRISON FLAME!
PRISON FLAME
(TRAP CARD)
Send a card from your hand to the Graveyard and destroy the attacking monster. The opposing player receives Battle Damage equivalent to half of that monster's ATK.
I REMOVE ONE CARD FROM PLAY AND DESTROY THE ATTACKING MONSTER!
NGH.
REGGIE LP 4000 ↓ LP 2900
THEN, THE OPPOSING PLAYER TAKES HALF THAT MONSTER'S ATTACK AS BATTLE DAMAGE.
ARGH... END OF TURN...
DRAW.

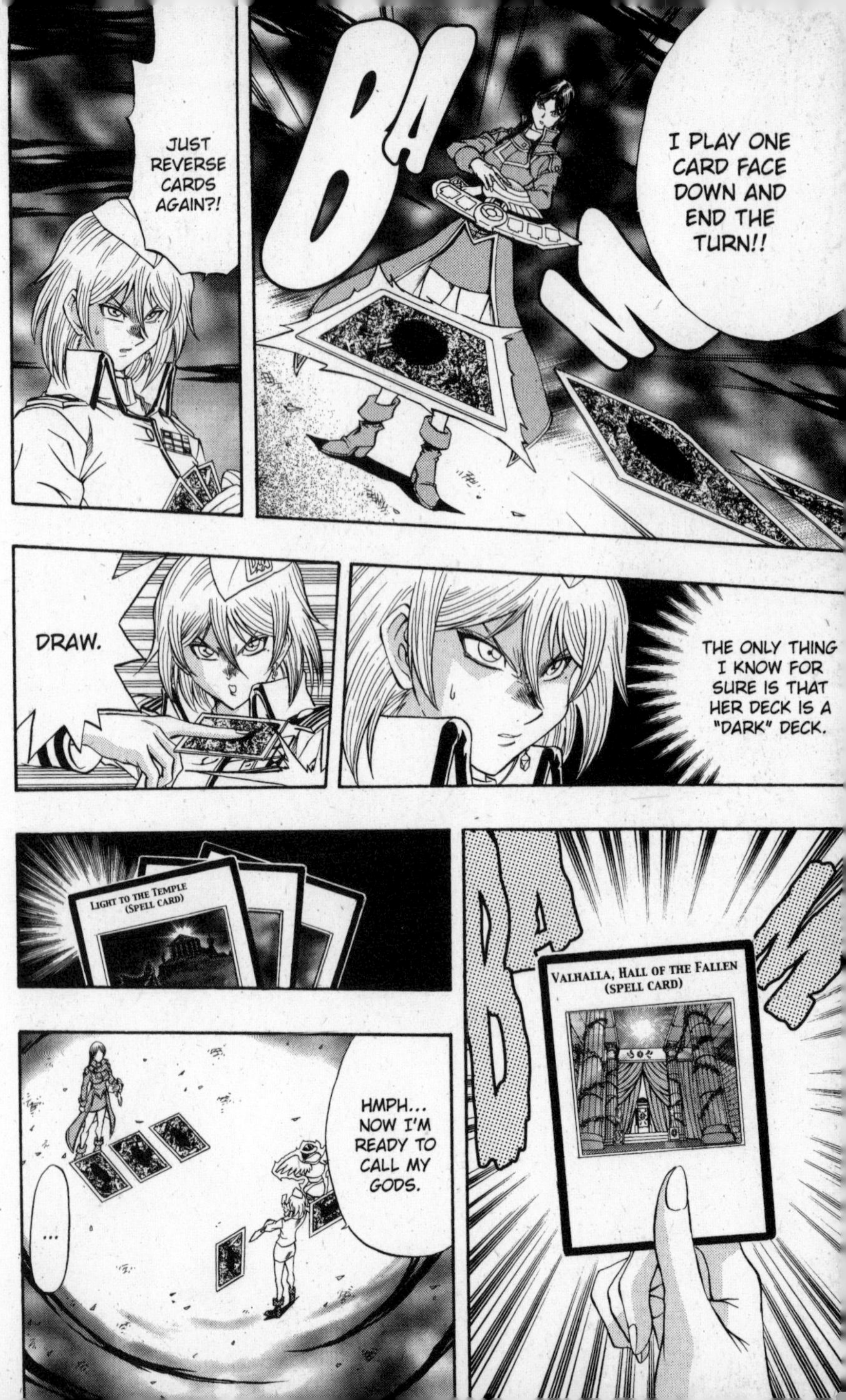
BAM
I PLAY ONE CARD FACE DOWN AND END THE TURN!!
JUST REVERSE CARDS AGAIN?!
THE ONLY THING I KNOW FOR SURE IS THAT HER DECK IS A "DARK" DECK.
DRAW.
BAM
VALHALLA, HALL OF THE FALLEN
(SPELL CARD)
LIGHT TO THE TEMPLE
(SPELL CARD)
HMPH... NOW I'M READY TO CALL MY GODS.
...

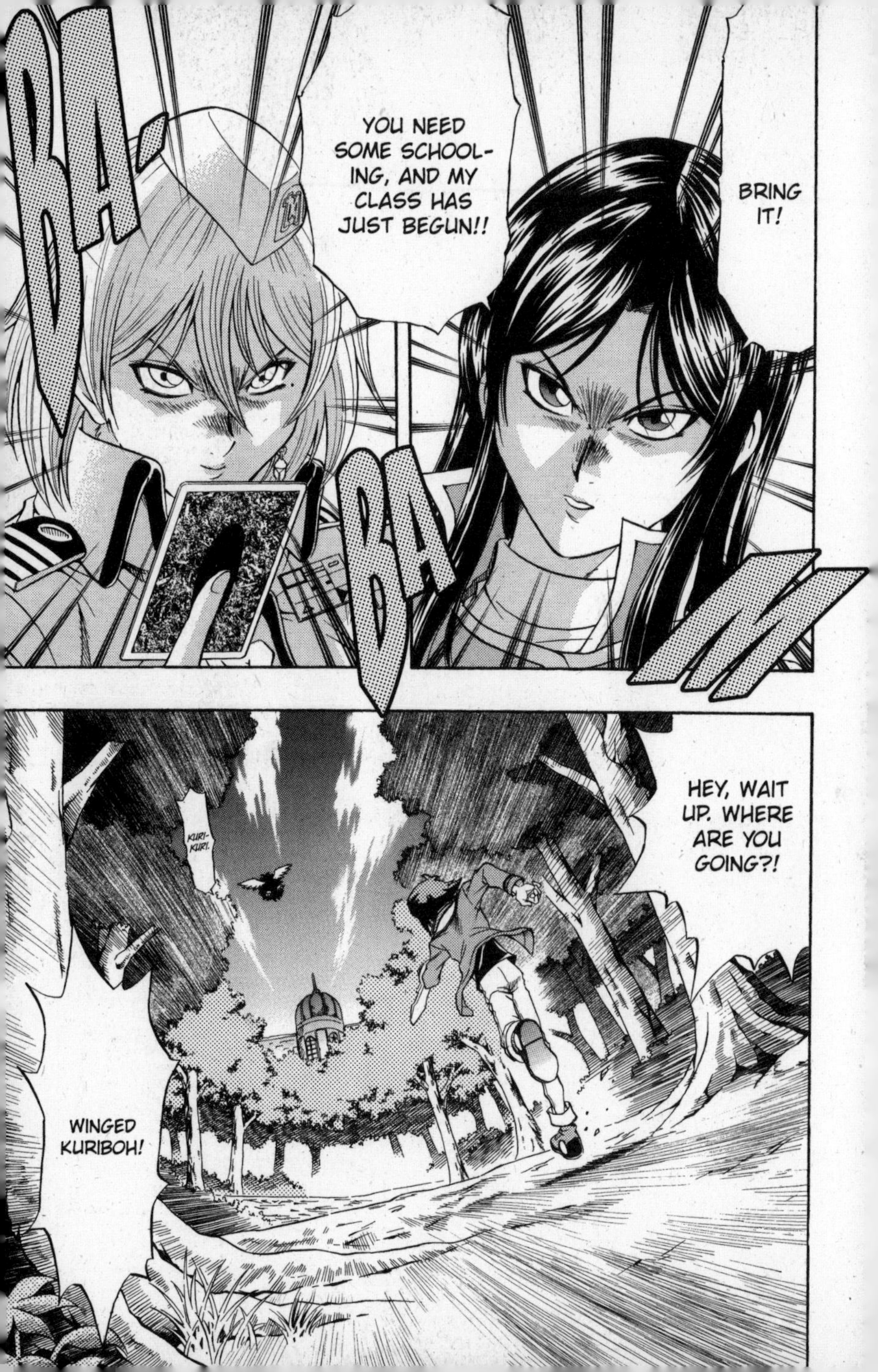
YOU NEED SOME SCHOOLING, AND MY CLASS HAS JUST BEGUN!!
BRING IT!
BA-
BAM
HEY, WAIT UP. WHERE ARE YOU GOING?!
KURI-KURI.
WINGED KURIBOH!

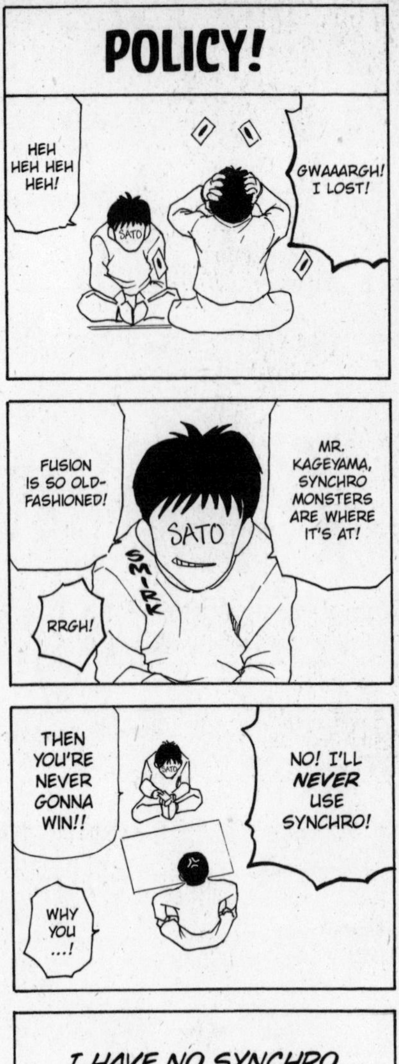
POLICY!
GWAAARGH! I LOST!
HEH HEH HEH HEH!
SATO
MR. KAGEYAMA, SYNCHRO MONSTERS ARE WHERE IT'S AT!
FUSION IS SO OLD-FASHIONED!
SATO
SMIRK
RRGH!
NO! I'LL ***NEVER*** USE SYNCHRO!
THEN YOU'RE NEVER GONNA WIN!!
SATO
WHY YOU ...!
I HAVE NO SYNCHRO CARDS IN MY DECK! I DON'T HAVE ANY OF AKIRA ITO'S MONSTERS, EITHER! I USE SPELL AND TRAP CARDS!*

*AKIRA ITO IS KAZUKI TAKAHASHI'S EX-ASSISTANT AND THE AUTHOR OF YU-GI-OH! R.

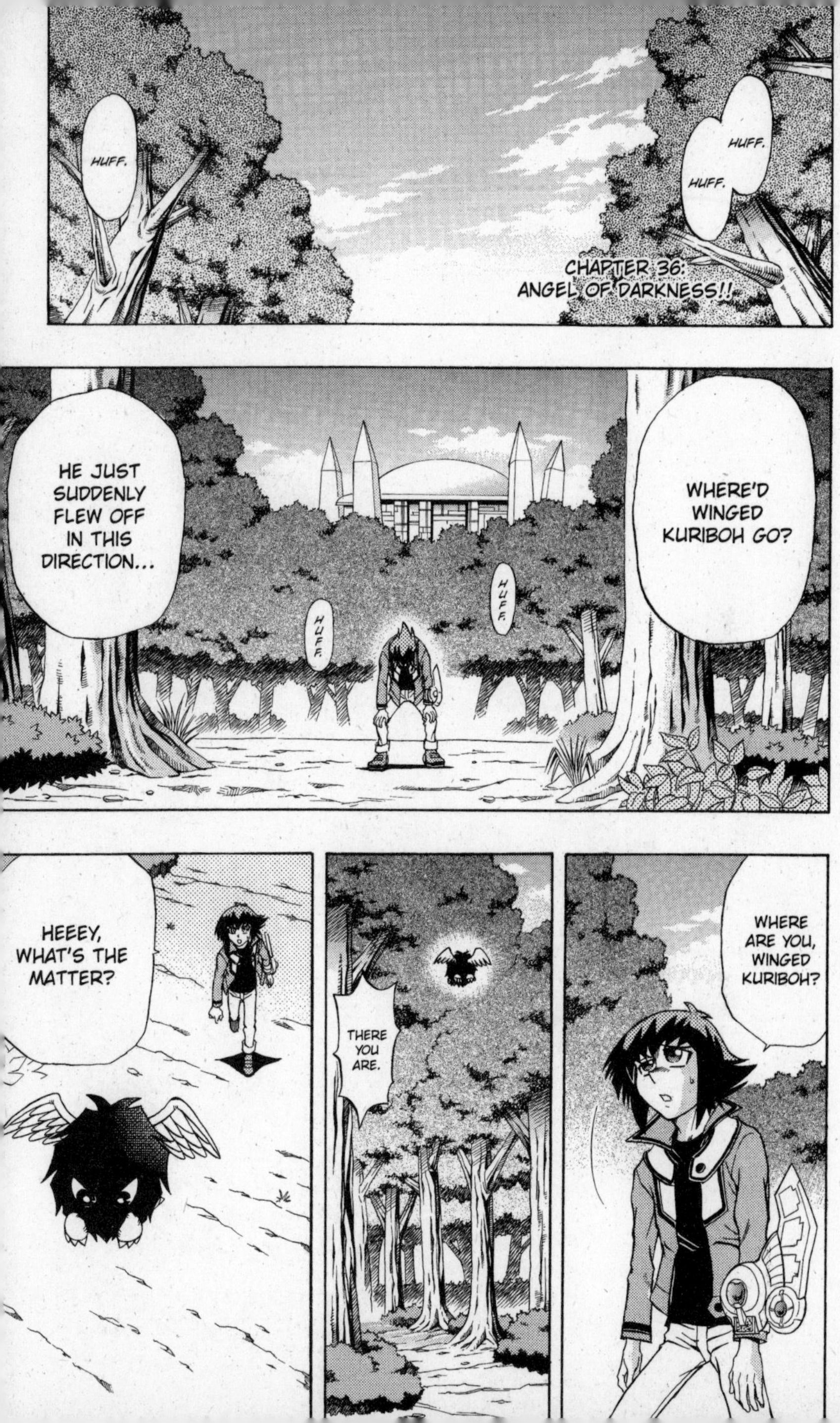
HUFF.
HUFF.
CHAPTER 36: ANGEL OF DARKNESS!!
HUFF.
WHERE'D WINGED KURIBOH GO?
HUFF.
HUFF.
HE JUST SUDDENLY FLEW OFF IN THIS DIRECTION...
WHERE ARE YOU, WINGED KURIBOH?
THERE YOU ARE.
HEEEY, WHAT'S THE MATTER?

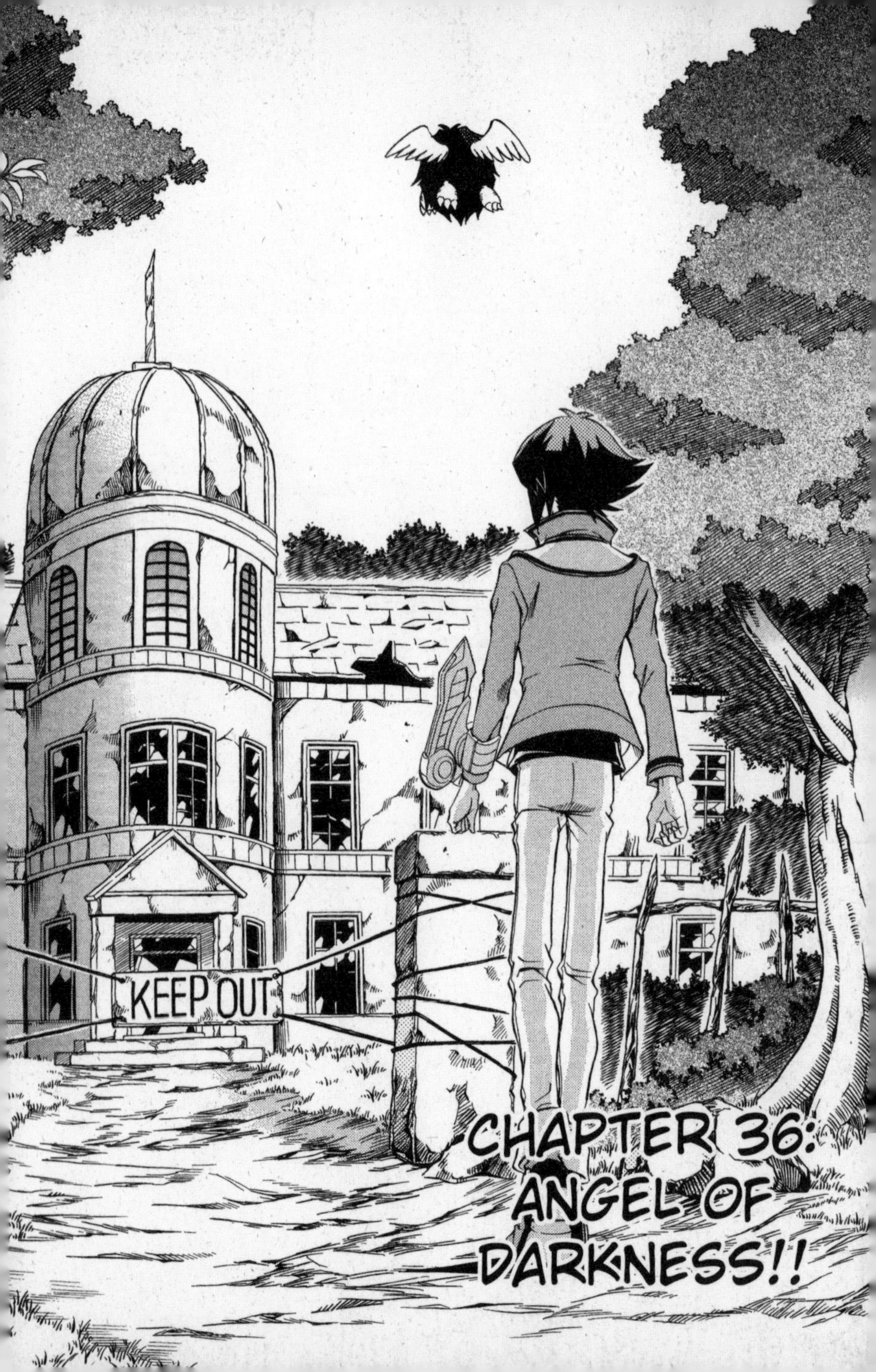
KEEP OUT
CHAPTER 36:
ANGEL OF
DARKNESS!!

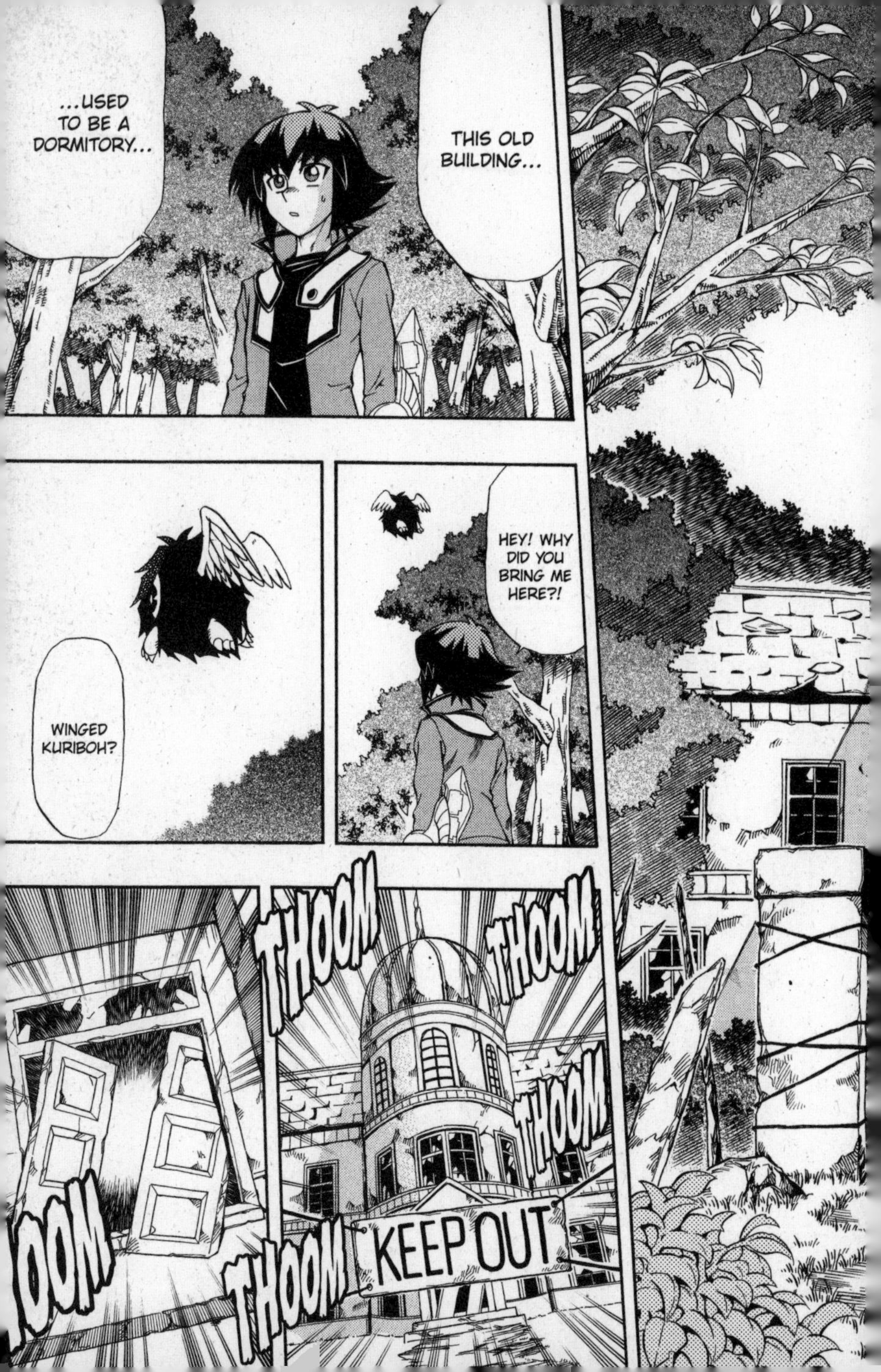
THIS OLD BUILDING...
...USED TO BE A DORMITORY...
HEY! WHY DID YOU BRING ME HERE?!
WINGED KURIBOH?
THOOM
THOOM
THOOM
THOOM
KEEP OUT
THOOM
OOM

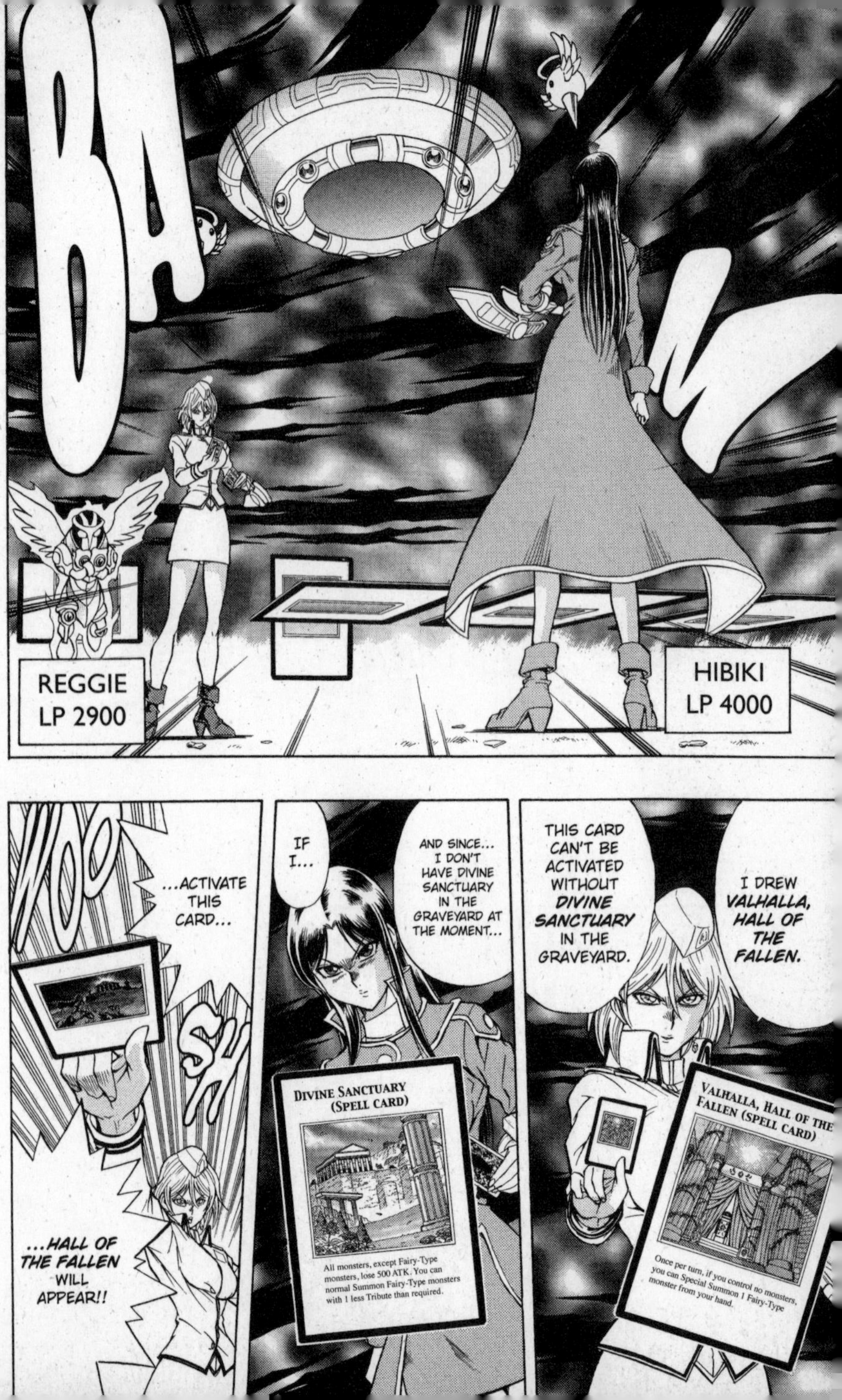
BAM
REGGIE
LP 2900
HIBIKI
LP 4000
I DREW VALHALLA, HALL OF THE FALLEN.
THIS CARD CAN'T BE ACTIVATED WITHOUT DIVINE SANCTUARY IN THE GRAVEYARD.
Valhalla, Hall of the Fallen (Spell Card)
Once per turn, if you control no monsters, you can Special Summon 1 Fairy-Type monster from your hand.
AND SINCE... I DON'T HAVE DIVINE SANCTUARY IN THE GRAVEYARD AT THE MOMENT...
IF I...
Divine Sanctuary (Spell Card)
All monsters, except Fairy-Type monsters, lose 500 ATK. You can normal Summon Fairy-Type monsters with 1 less Tribute than required.
WOO
...ACTIVATE THIS CARD...
SH
...HALL OF THE FALLEN WILL APPEAR!!

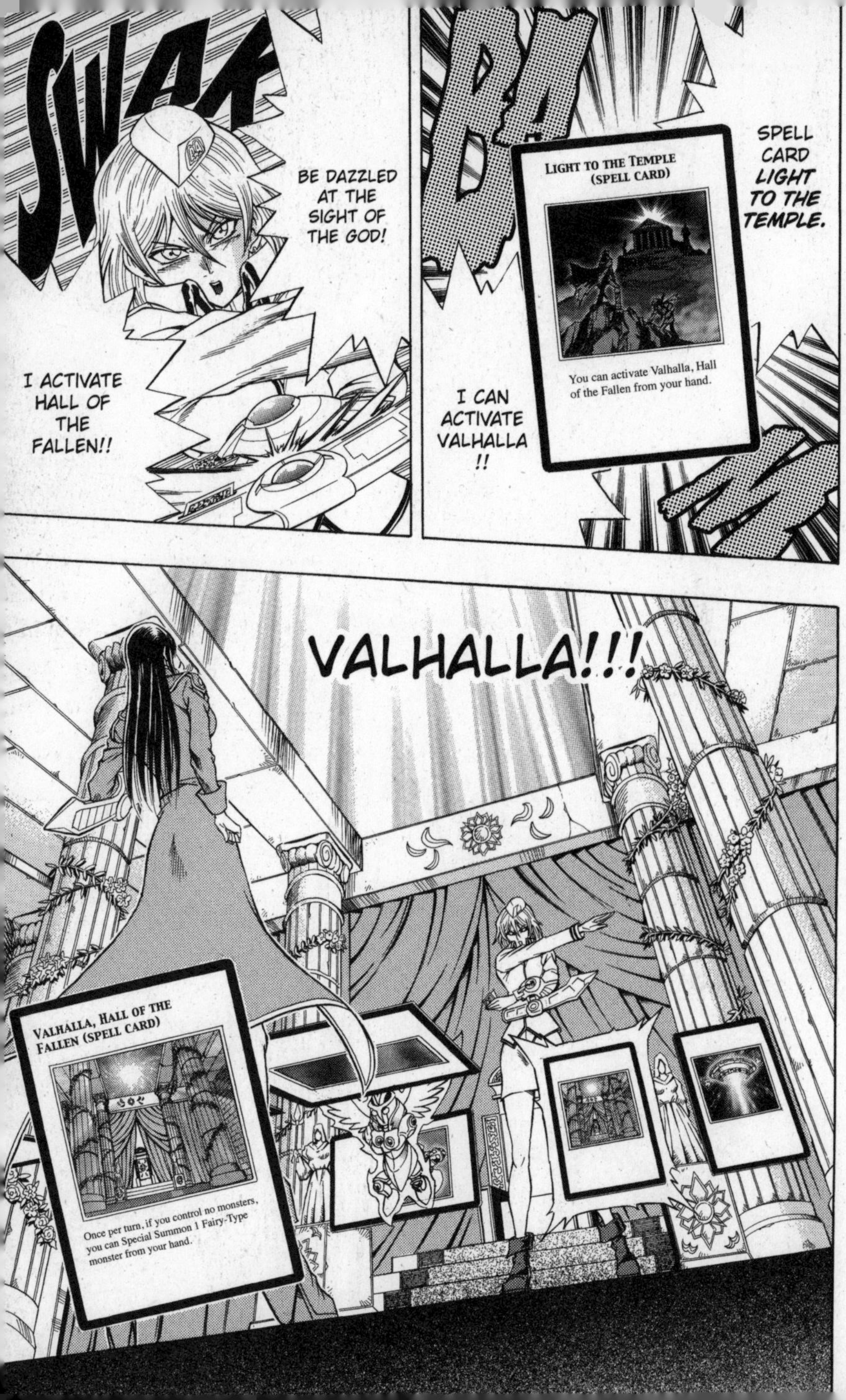

SPELL CARD LIGHT TO THE TEMPLE.
BA
LIGHT TO THE TEMPLE (SPELL CARD)
You can activate Valhalla, Hall of the Fallen from your hand.
I CAN ACTIVATE VALHALLA !!
SWAK
BE DAZZLED AT THE SIGHT OF THE GOD!
I ACTIVATE HALL OF THE FALLEN!!
VALHALLA!!!
VALHALLA, HALL OF THE FALLEN (SPELL CARD)
Once per turn, if you control no monsters, you can Special Summon 1 Fairy-Type monster from your hand.

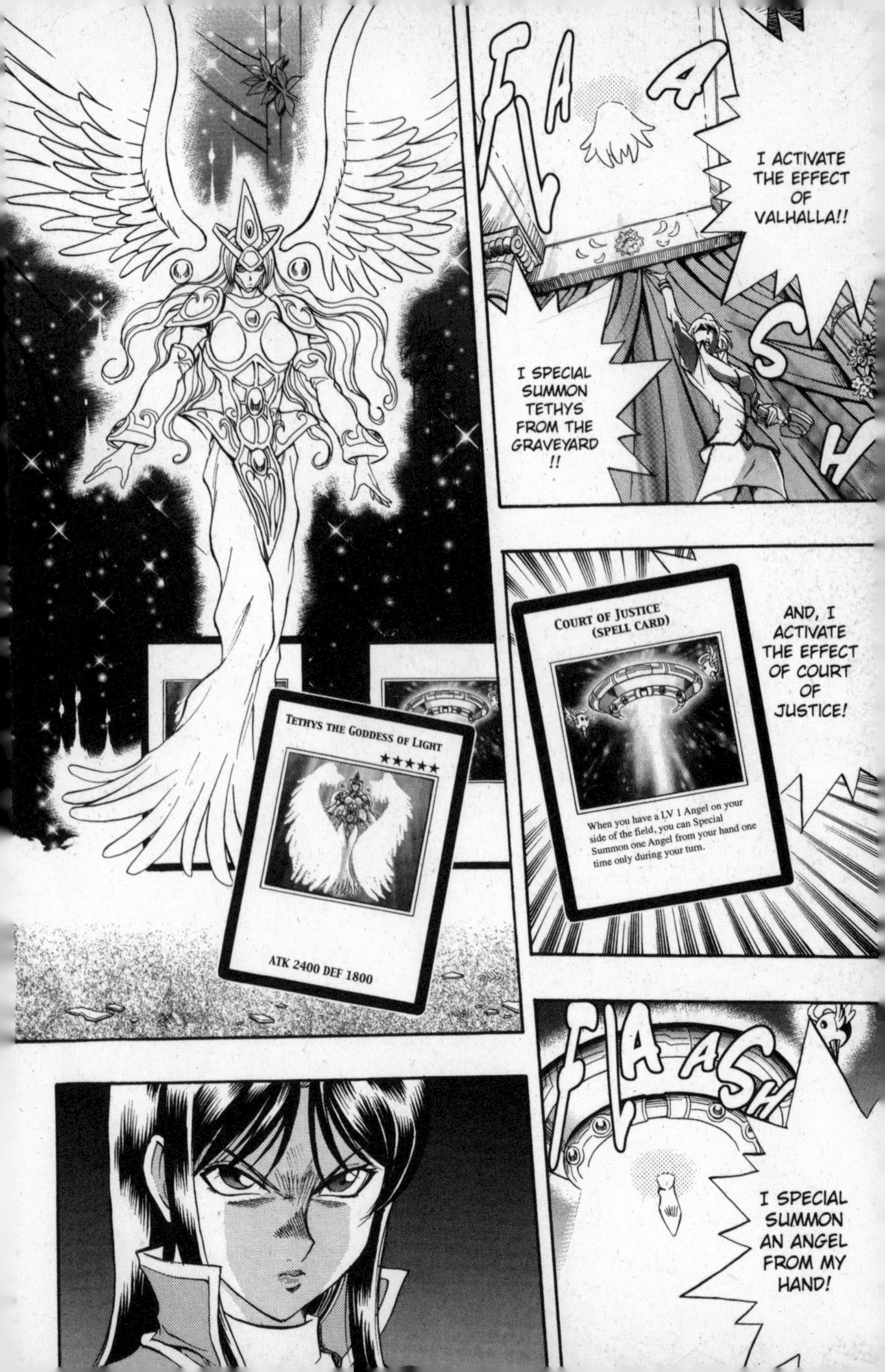

FLAASH
I ACTIVATE THE EFFECT OF VALHALLA!!
I SPECIAL SUMMON TETHYS FROM THE GRAVEYARD!!
TETHYS THE GODDESS OF LIGHT
★★★★★
ATK 2400 DEF 1800
COURT OF JUSTICE (SPELL CARD)
When you have a LV 1 Angel on your side of the field, you can Special Summon one Angel from your hand one time only during your turn.
AND, I ACTIVATE THE EFFECT OF COURT OF JUSTICE!
FLAASH
I SPECIAL SUMMON AN ANGEL FROM MY HAND!

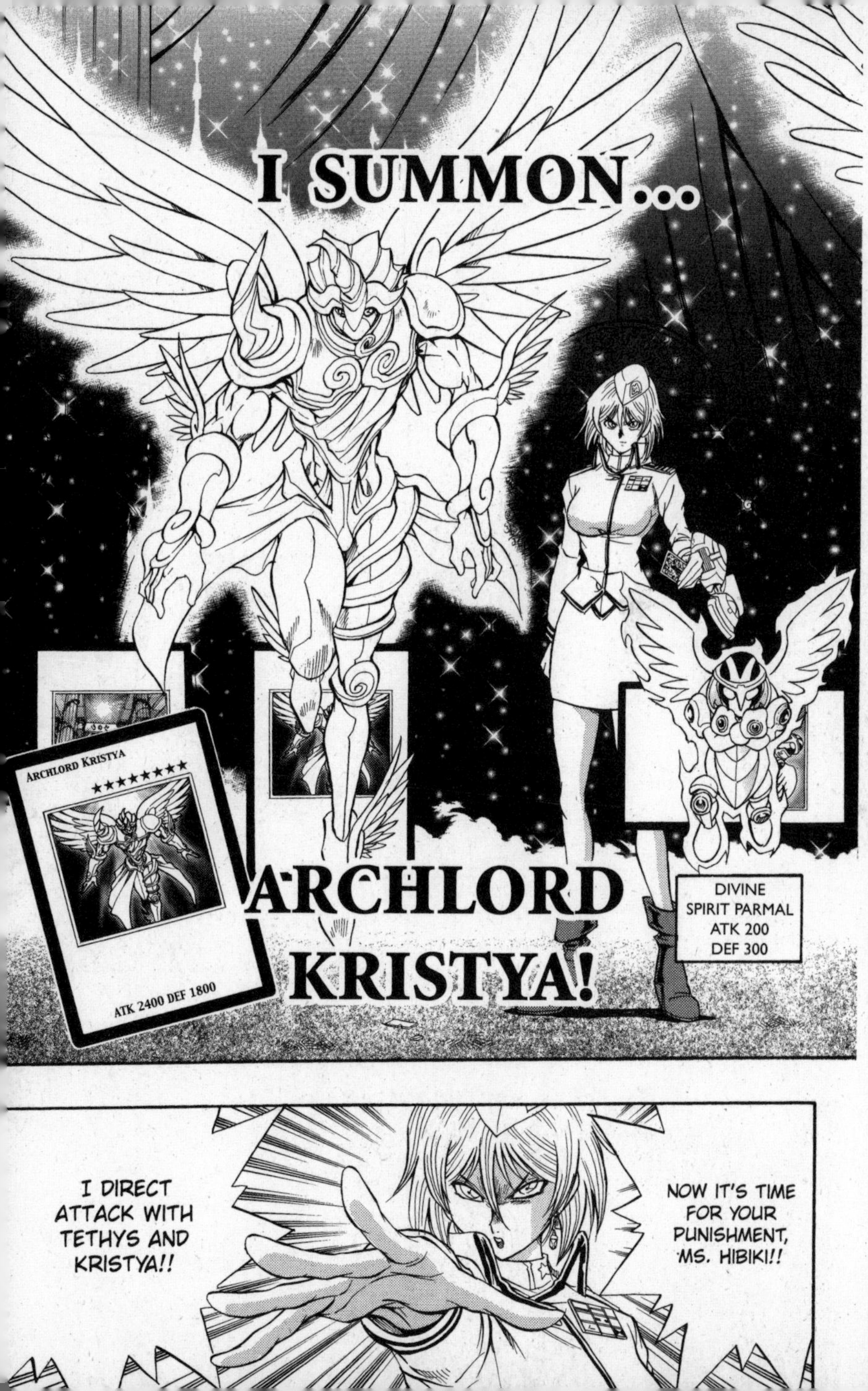
I SUMMON...
ARCHLORD KRISTYA!
ARCHLORD KRISTYA
ATK 2400 DEF 1800
DIVINE SPIRIT PARMAL ATK 200 DEF 300
NOW IT'S TIME FOR YOUR PUNISHMENT, MS. HIBIKI!!
I DIRECT ATTACK WITH TETHYS AND KRISTYA!!

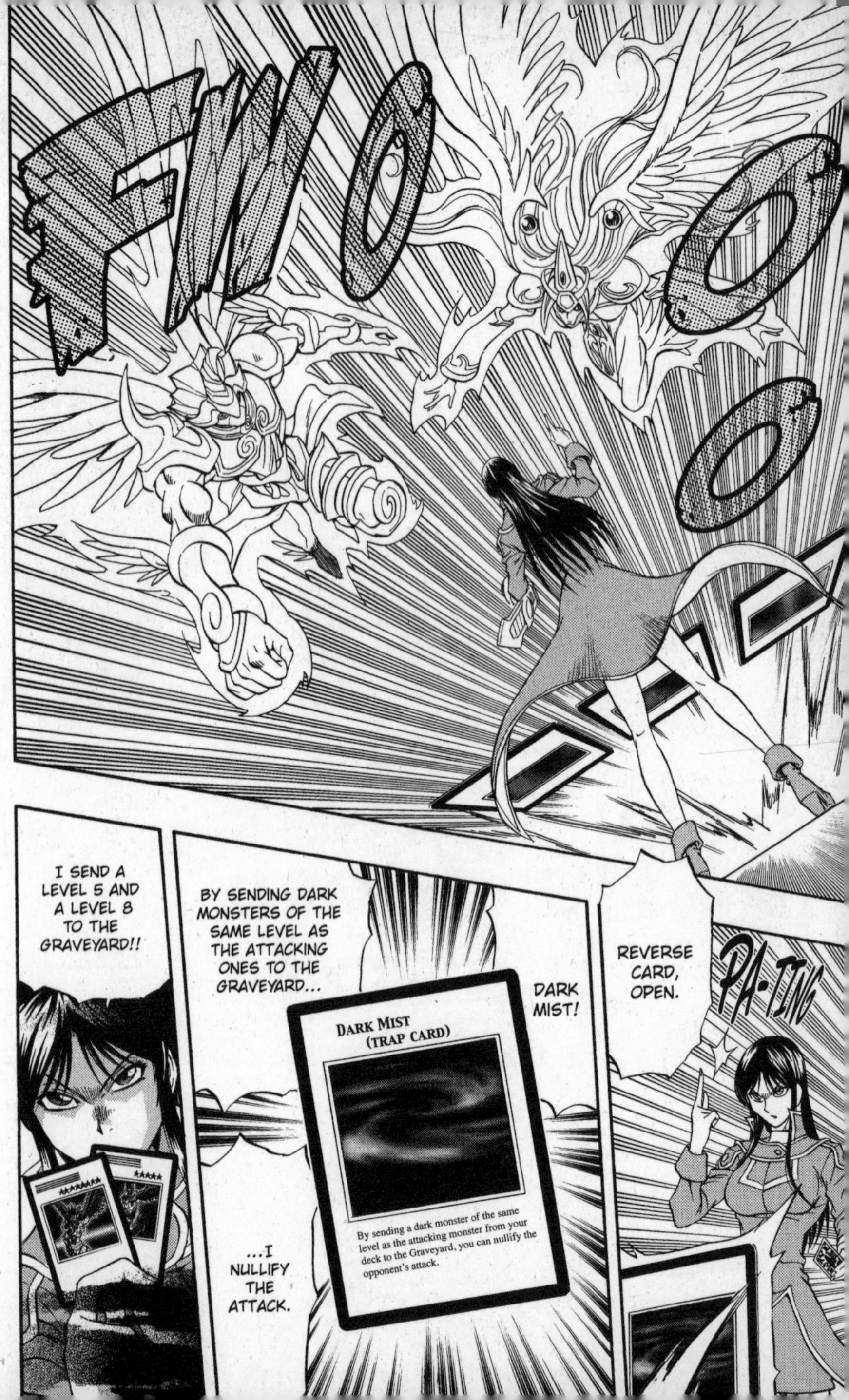
FWOOO
REVERSE CARD, OPEN.
PA-TING
DARK MIST!
DARK MIST (TRAP CARD)
By sending a dark monster of the same level as the attacking monster from your deck to the Graveyard, you can nullify the opponent's attack.
BY SENDING DARK MONSTERS OF THE SAME LEVEL AS THE ATTACKING ONES TO THE GRAVEYARD...
...I NULLIFY THE ATTACK.
I SEND A LEVEL 5 AND A LEVEL 8 TO THE GRAVEYARD!!

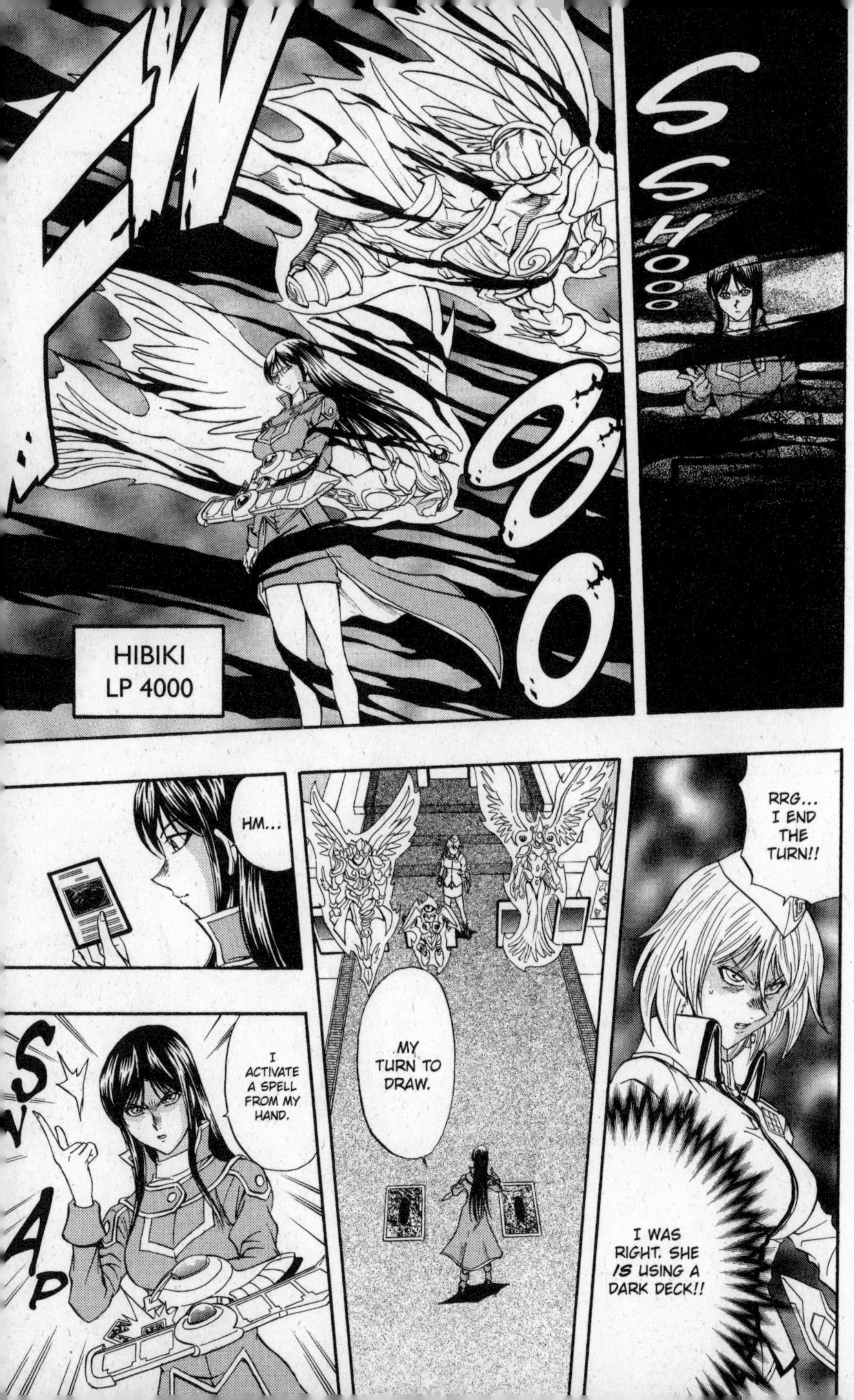
SSHOOOO
OOO
HIBIKI
LP 4000
RRG... I END THE TURN!!
I WAS RIGHT. SHE *IS* USING A DARK DECK!!
MY TURN TO DRAW.
HM...
I ACTIVATE A SPELL FROM MY HAND.
SNAP

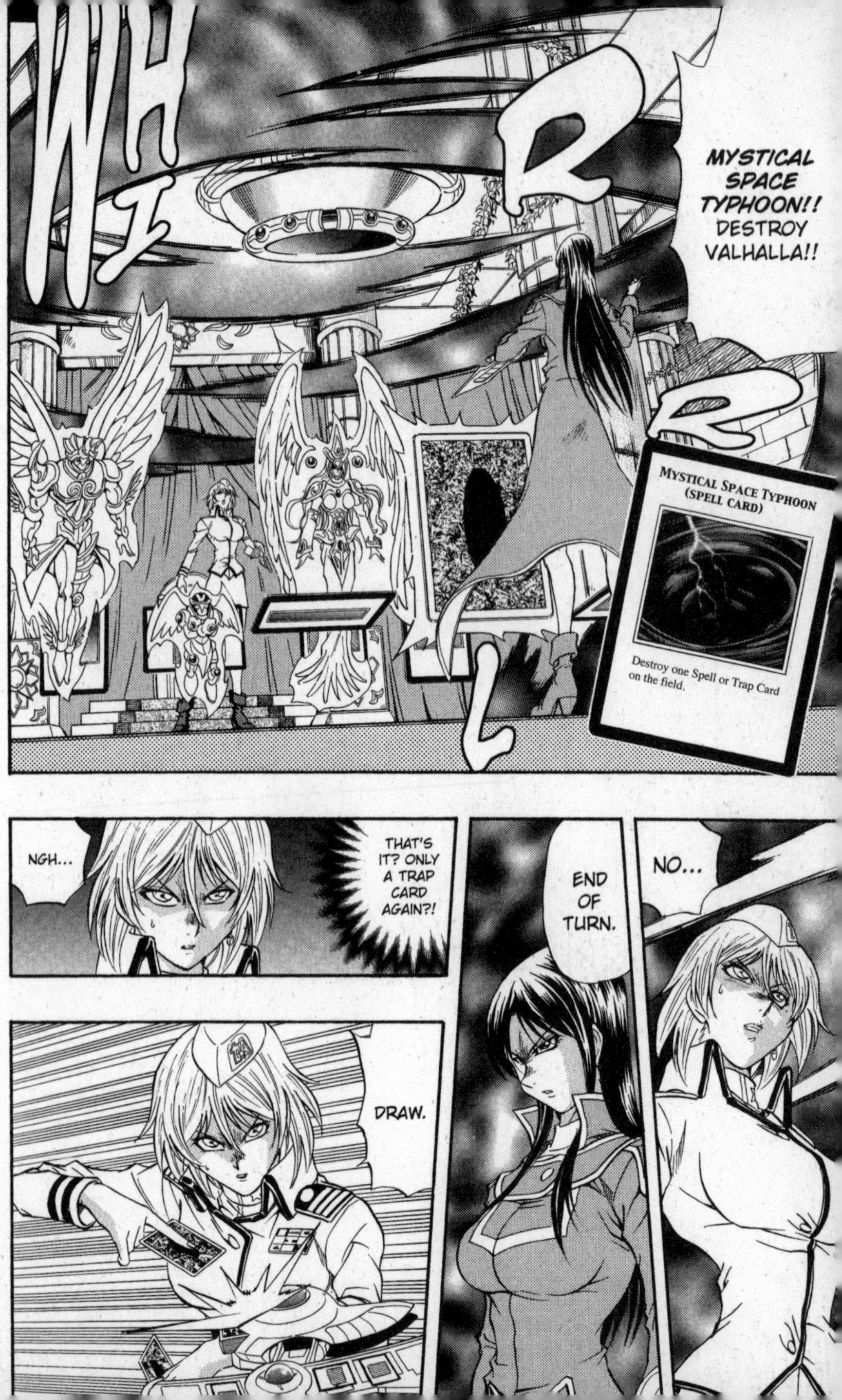
WHIRR
MYSTICAL SPACE TYPHOON!! DESTROY VALHALLA!!
MYSTICAL SPACE TYPHOON
(SPELL CARD)
Destroy one Spell or Trap Card on the field.
NO...
END OF TURN.
THAT'S IT? ONLY A TRAP CARD AGAIN?!
NGH...
DRAW.

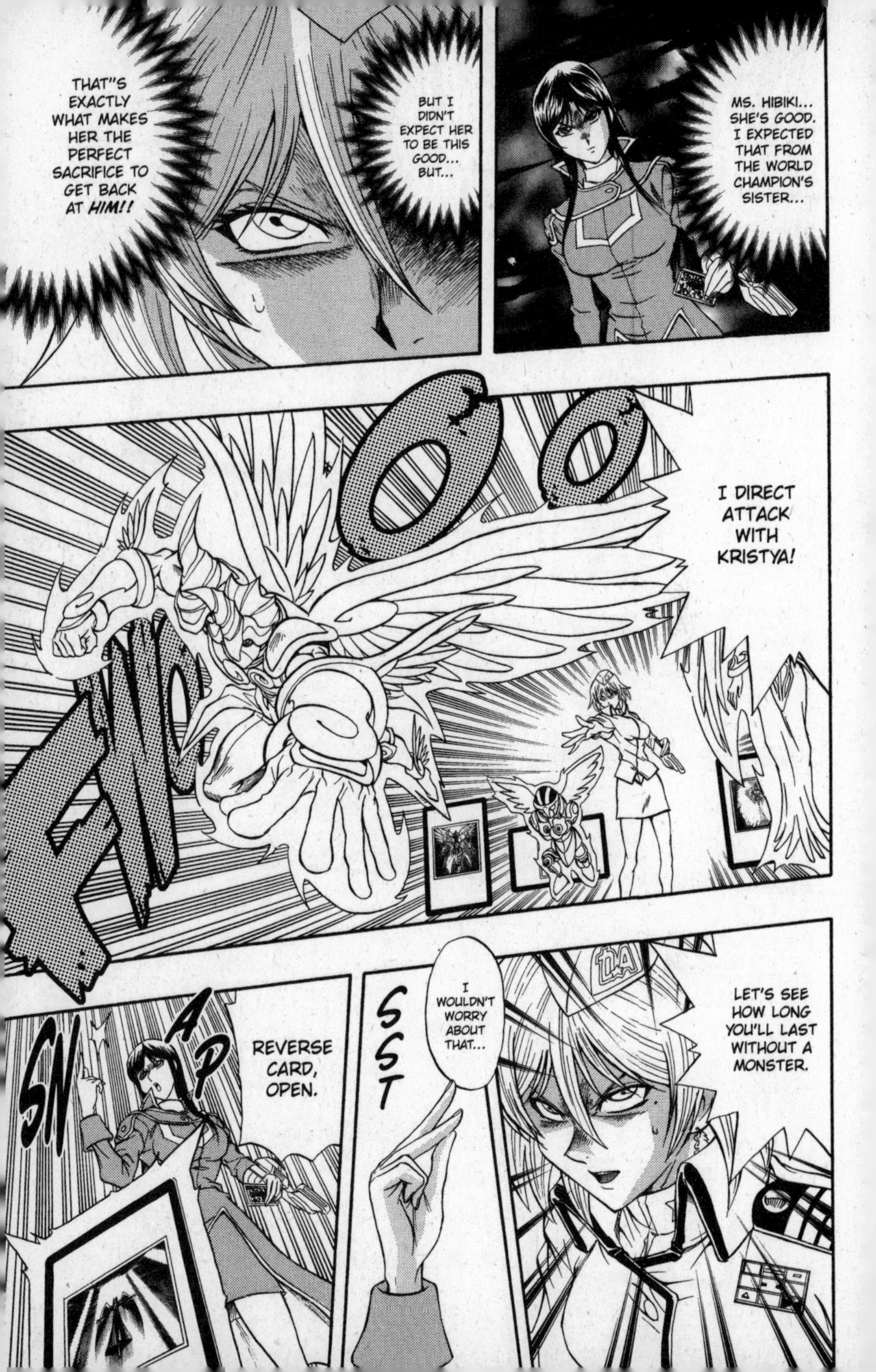
MS. HIBIKI... SHE'S GOOD. I EXPECTED THAT FROM THE WORLD CHAMPION'S SISTER...
BUT I DIDN'T EXPECT HER TO BE THIS GOOD... BUT...
THAT''S EXACTLY WHAT MAKES HER THE PERFECT SACRIFICE TO GET BACK AT *HIM!!*
I DIRECT ATTACK WITH KRISTYA!
LET'S SEE HOW LONG YOU'LL LAST WITHOUT A MONSTER.
I WOULDN'T WORRY ABOUT THAT...
SST
REVERSE CARD, OPEN.
SNAP

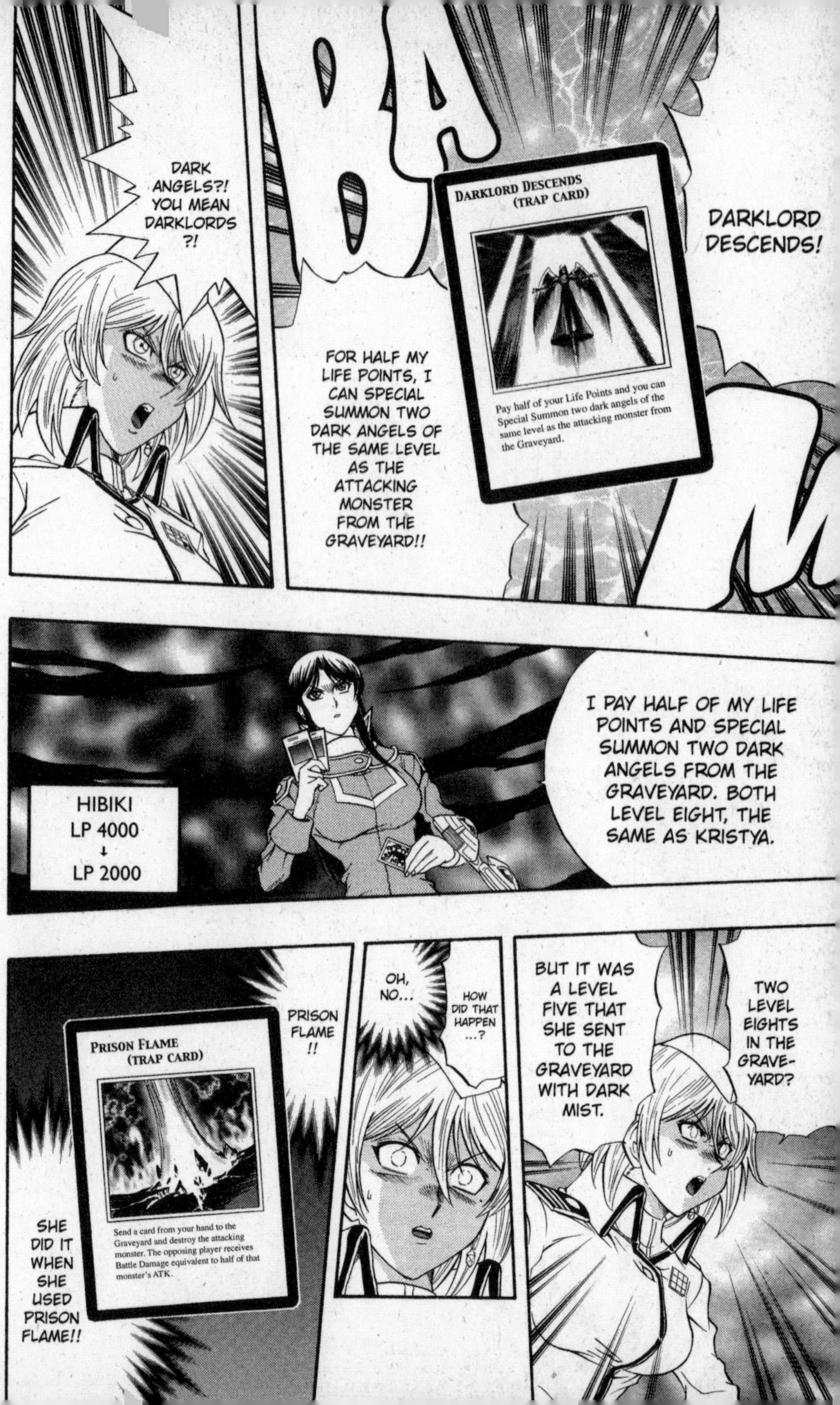
DARKLORD DESCENDS!
DARKLORD DESCENDS (TRAP CARD)
Pay half of your Life Points and you can Special Summon two dark angels of the same level as the attacking monster from the Graveyard.
FOR HALF MY LIFE POINTS, I CAN SPECIAL SUMMON TWO DARK ANGELS OF THE SAME LEVEL AS THE ATTACKING MONSTER FROM THE GRAVEYARD!!
DARK ANGELS?! YOU MEAN DARKLORDS?!
I PAY HALF OF MY LIFE POINTS AND SPECIAL SUMMON TWO DARK ANGELS FROM THE GRAVEYARD. BOTH LEVEL EIGHT, THE SAME AS KRISTYA.
HIBIKI LP 4000 ↓ LP 2000
TWO LEVEL EIGHTS IN THE GRAVE-YARD?
BUT IT WAS A LEVEL FIVE THAT SHE SENT TO THE GRAVEYARD WITH DARK MIST.
OH, NO...
HOW DID THAT HAPPEN ...?
PRISON FLAME!!
PRISON FLAME (TRAP CARD)
Send a card from your hand to the Graveyard and destroy the attacking monster. The opposing player receives Battle Damage equivalent to half of that monster's ATK.
SHE DID IT WHEN SHE USED PRISON FLAME!!

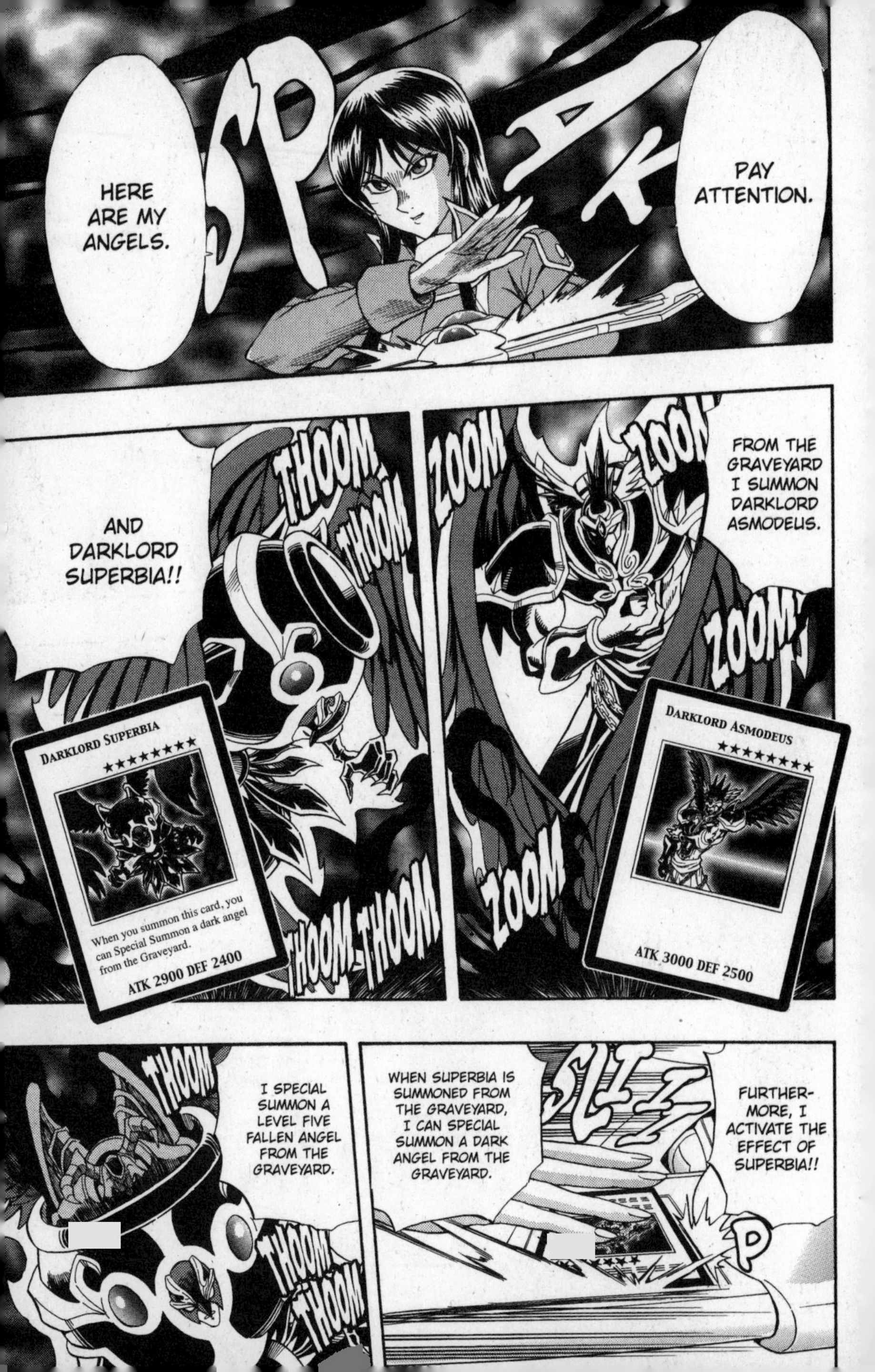
PAY ATTENTION.
SPAK
HERE ARE MY ANGELS.
FROM THE GRAVEYARD I SUMMON DARKLORD ASMODEUS.
ZOOM ZOOM ZOOM ZOOM
Darklord Asmodeus
ATK 3000 DEF 2500
AND DARKLORD SUPERBIA!!
THOOM THOOM THOOM THOOM
Darklord Superbia
When you summon this card, you can Special Summon a dark angel from the Graveyard.
ATK 2900 DEF 2400
FURTHER-MORE, I ACTIVATE THE EFFECT OF SUPERBIA!!
WHEN SUPERBIA IS SUMMONED FROM THE GRAVEYARD, I CAN SPECIAL SUMMON A DARK ANGEL FROM THE GRAVEYARD.
SLIIIP
I SPECIAL SUMMON A LEVEL FIVE FALLEN ANGEL FROM THE GRAVEYARD.
THOOM THOOM THOOM

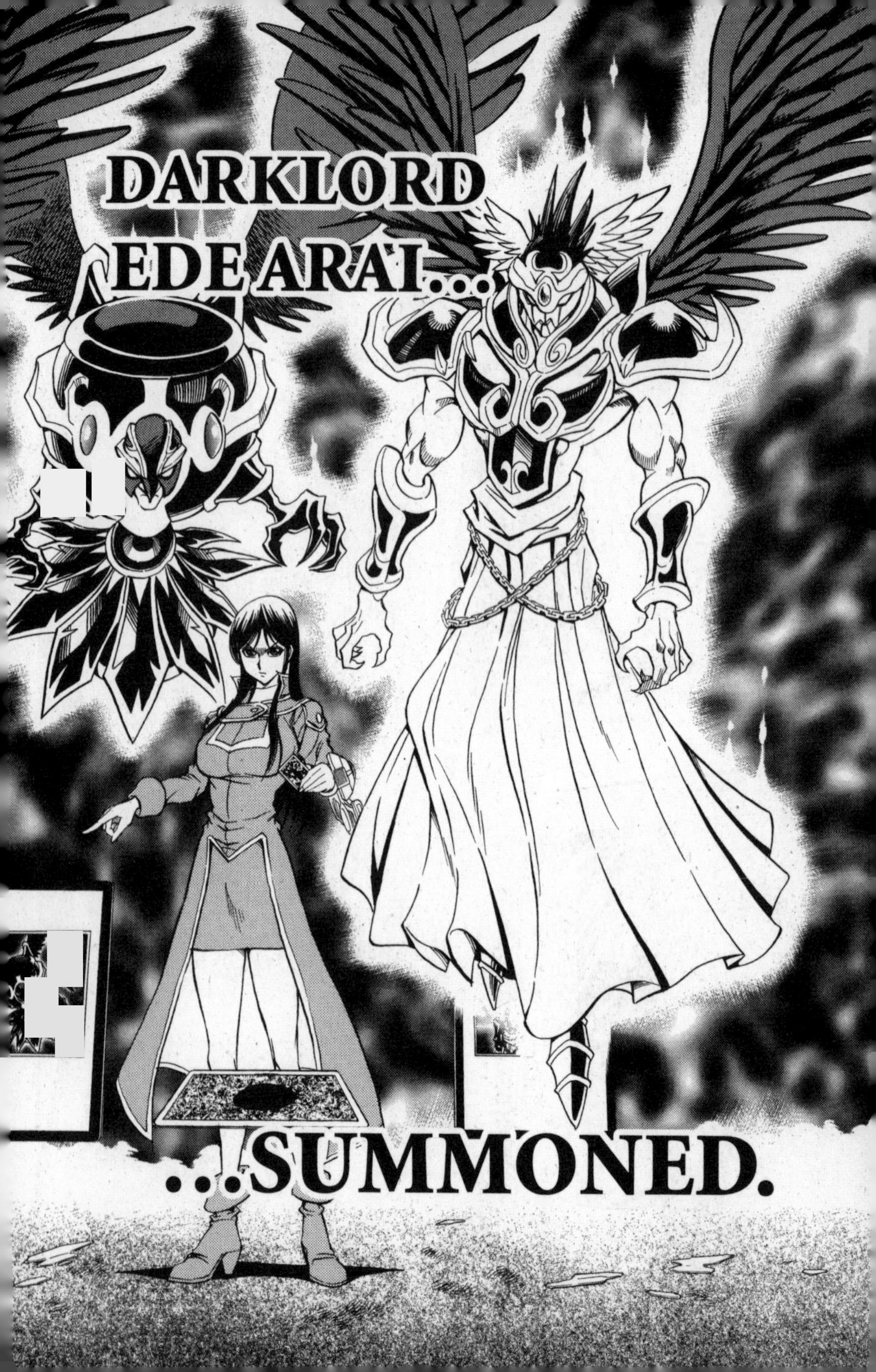

DARKLORD EDE ARAI...
...SUMMONED.

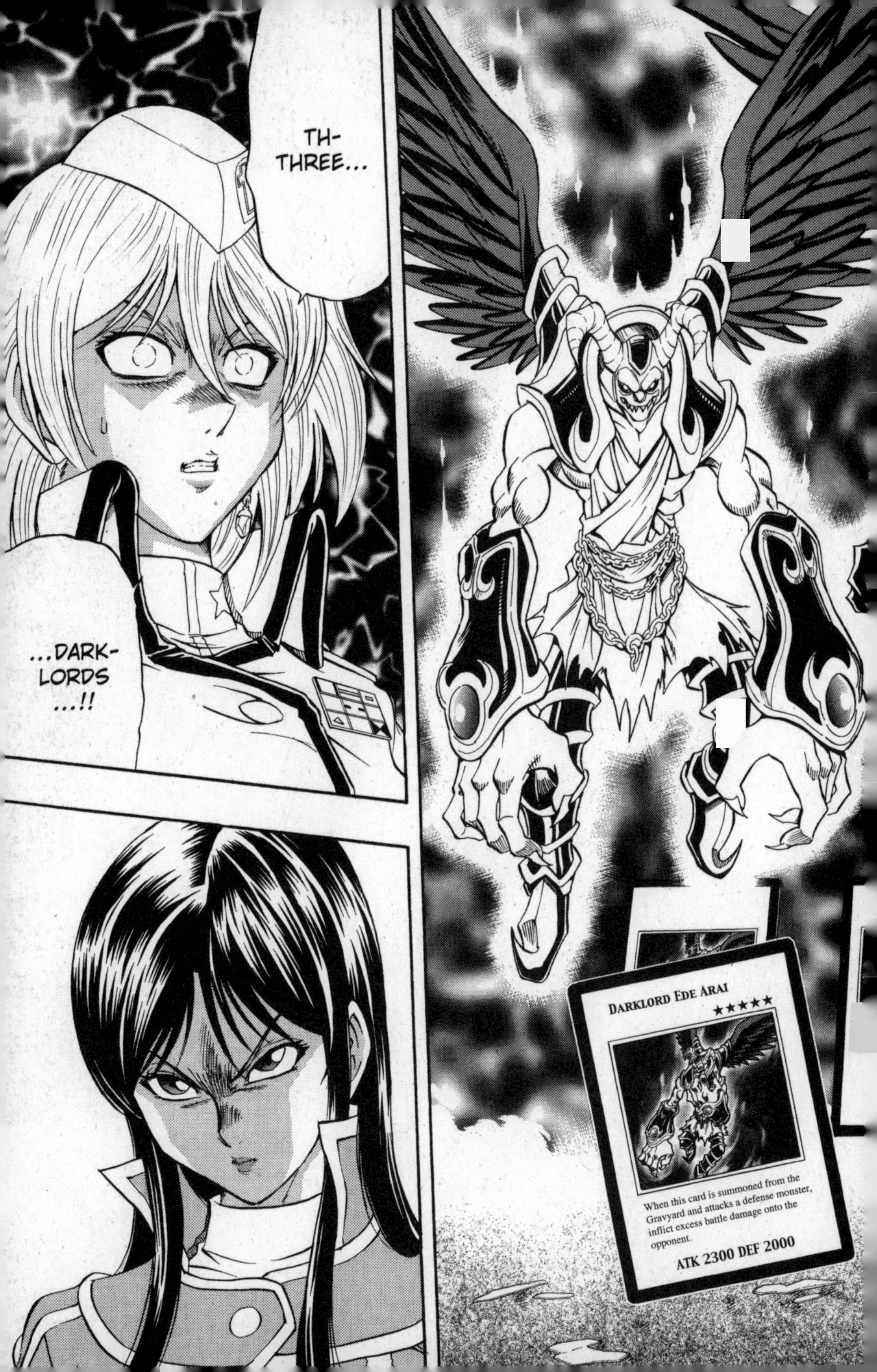
DARKLORD EDE ARAI
When this card is summoned from the Gravyard and attacks a defense monster, inflict excess battle damage onto the opponent.
ATK 2300 DEF 2000
TH- THREE...
...DARK- LORDS ...!!

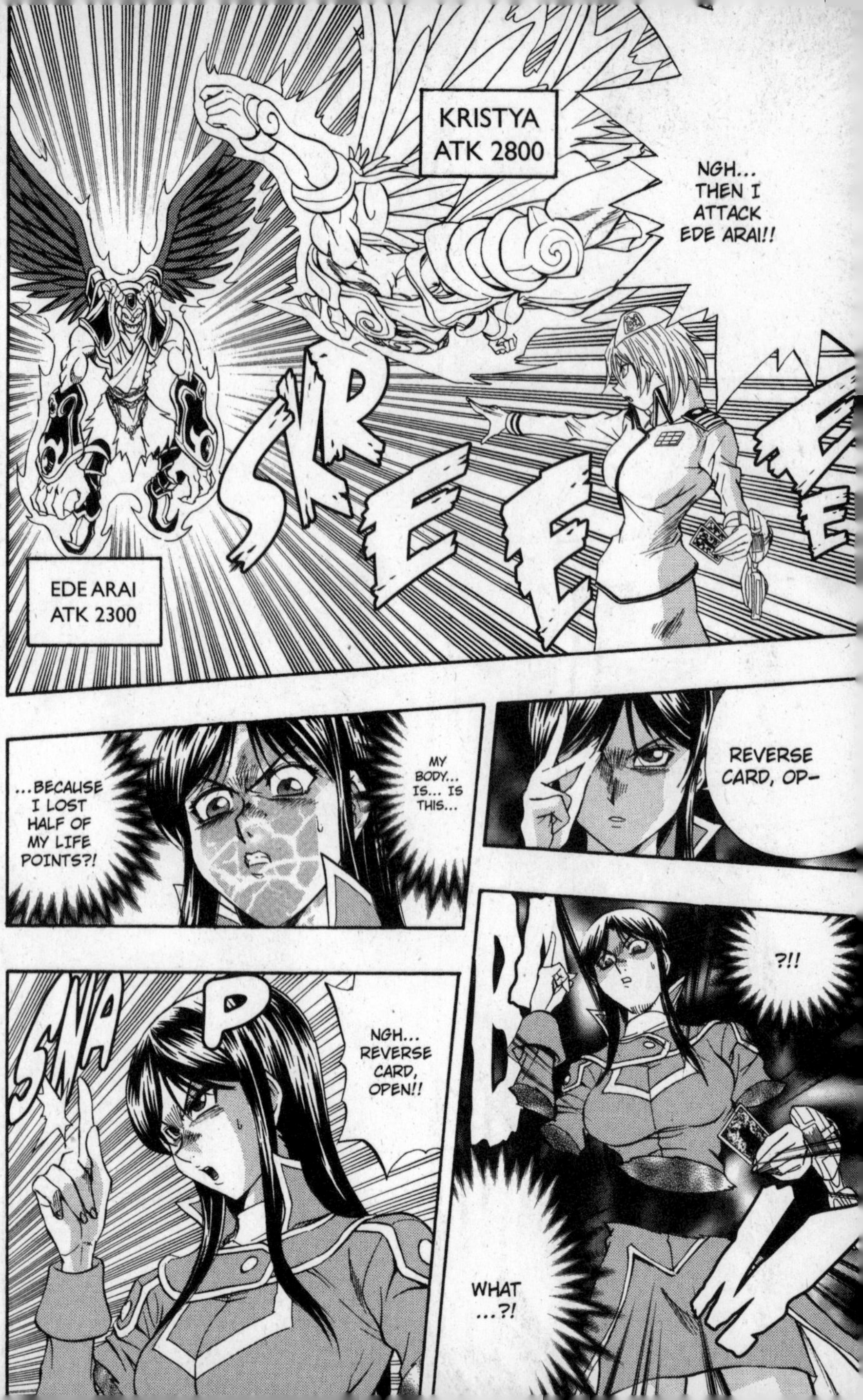
NGH... THEN I ATTACK EDE ARAI!!
KRISTYA ATK 2800
SKREEEE
EDE ARAI ATK 2300
REVERSE CARD, OP-
MY BODY... IS... IS THIS...
...BECAUSE I LOST HALF OF MY LIFE POINTS?!
?!!
WHAT ...?!
SNAP
NGH... REVERSE CARD, OPEN!!

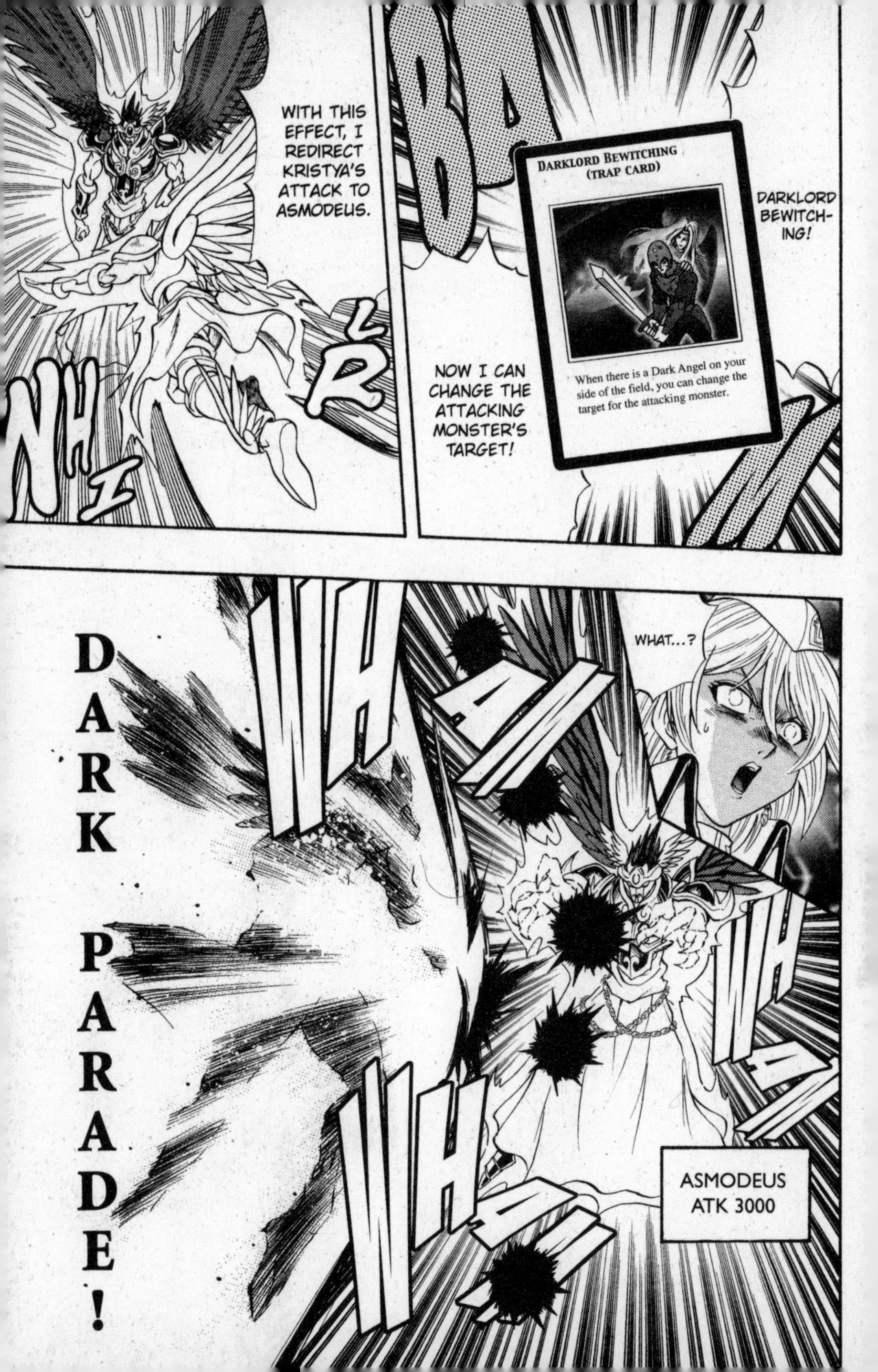
DARKLORD BEWITCHING!
Darklord Bewitching
(Trap Card)
When there is a Dark Angel on your side of the field, you can change the target for the attacking monster.
NOW I CAN CHANGE THE ATTACKING MONSTER'S TARGET!
WITH THIS EFFECT, I REDIRECT KRISTYA'S ATTACK TO ASMODEUS.
WHAT...?
DARK PARADE!
ASMODEUS ATK 3000

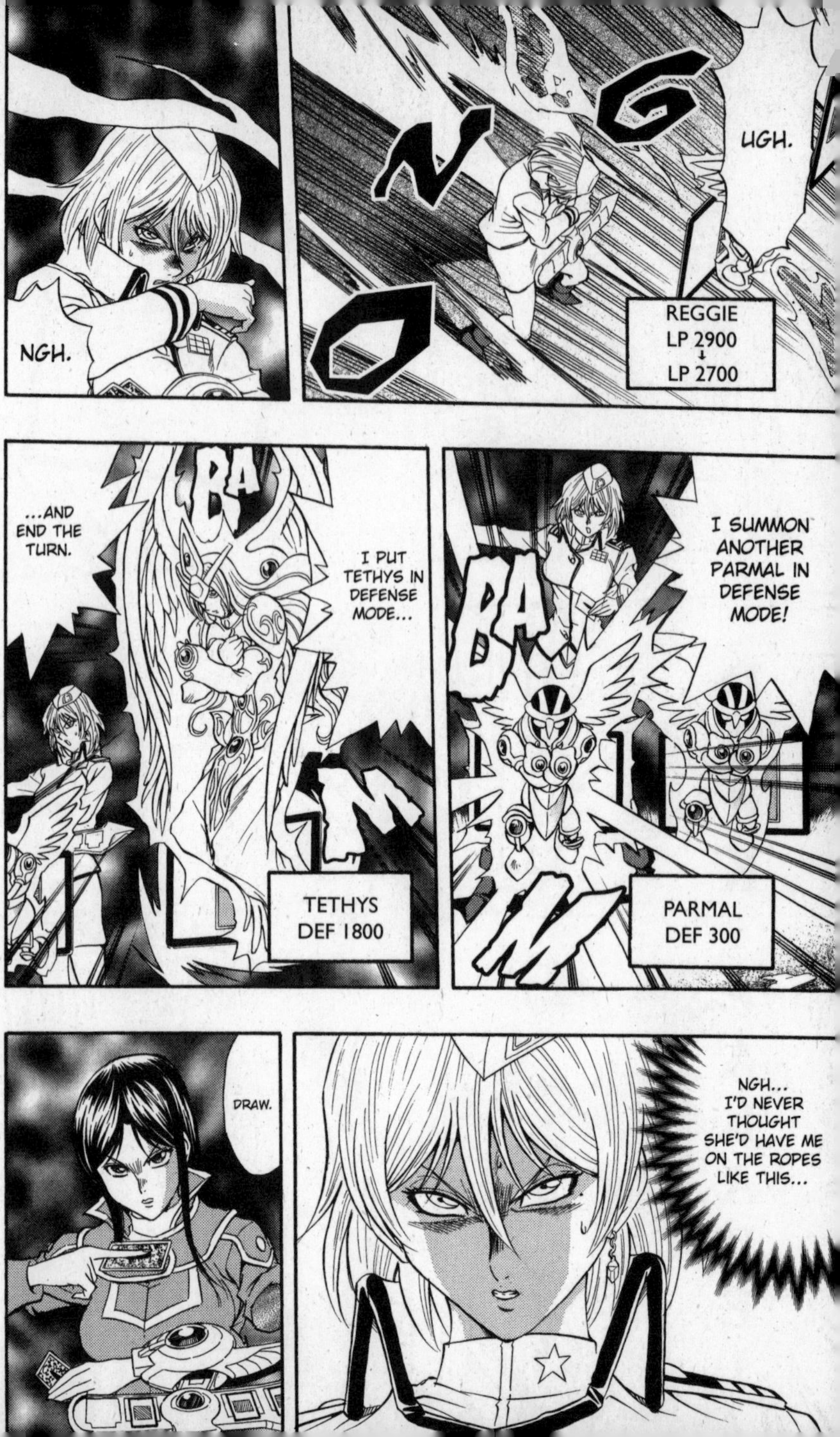
UGH.
REGGIE LP 2900 ↓ LP 2700
NGH.
I SUMMON ANOTHER PARMAL IN DEFENSE MODE!
BAM
PARMAL DEF 300
I PUT TETHYS IN DEFENSE MODE...
...AND END THE TURN.
BAM
TETHYS DEF 1800
NGH... I'D NEVER THOUGHT SHE'D HAVE ME ON THE ROPES LIKE THIS...
DRAW.

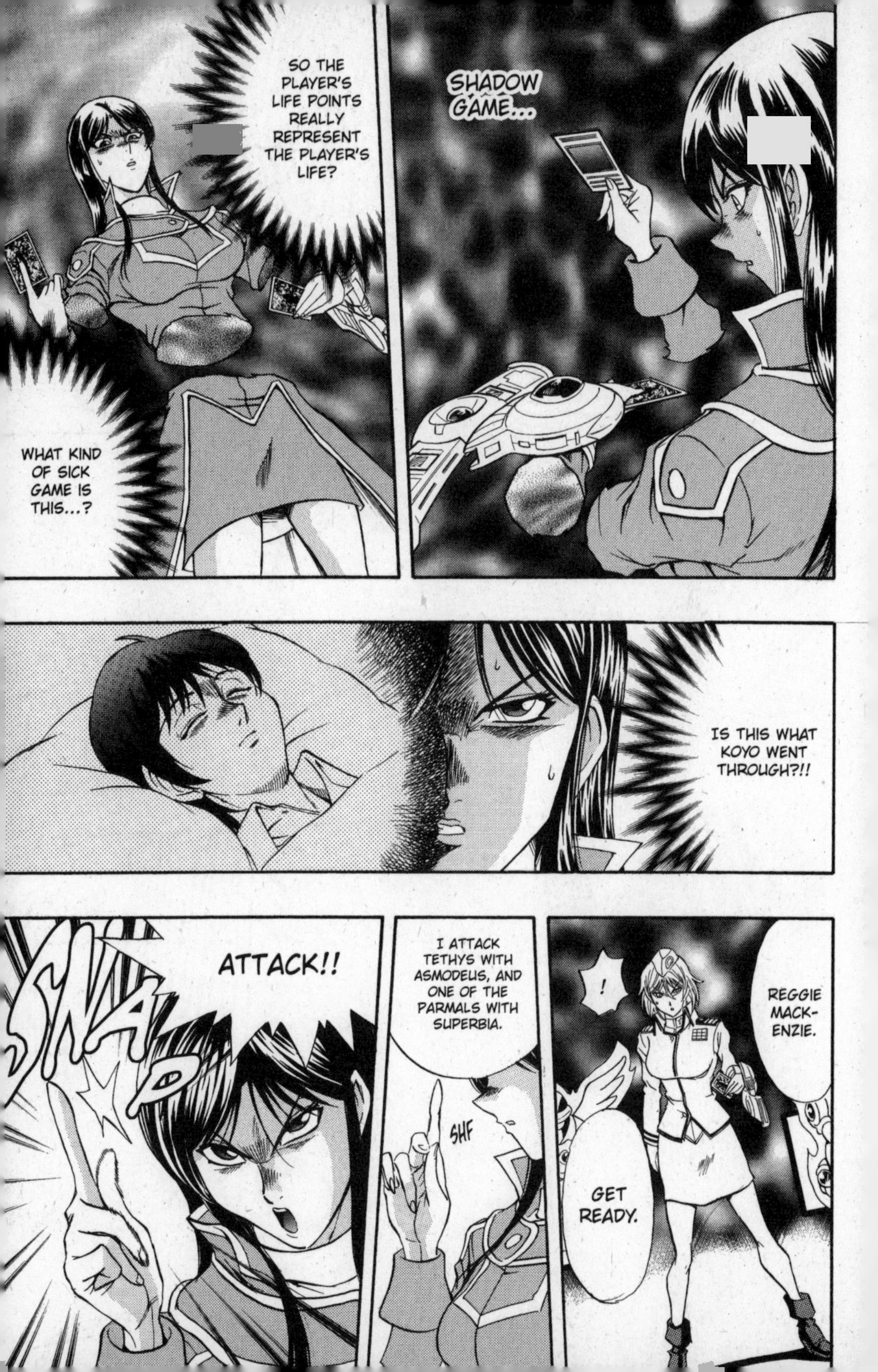
SHADOW GAME...
SO THE PLAYER'S LIFE POINTS REALLY REPRESENT THE PLAYER'S LIFE?
WHAT KIND OF SICK GAME IS THIS...?
IS THIS WHAT KOYO WENT THROUGH?!!
REGGIE MACK-ENZIE.
!
GET READY.
I ATTACK TETHYS WITH ASMODEUS, AND ONE OF THE PARMALS WITH SUPERBIA.
SHF
ATTACK!!
SNAP

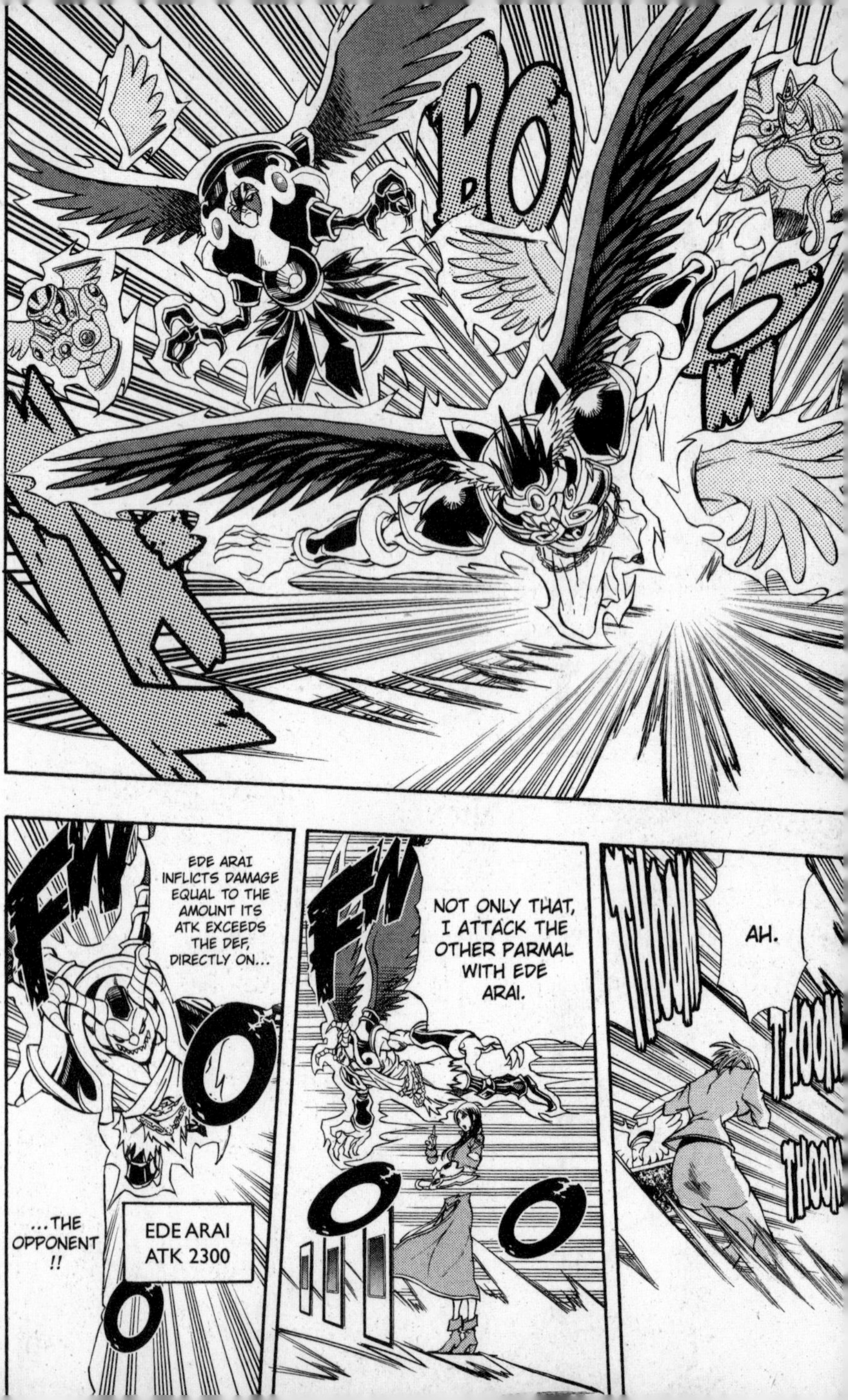
THOOM
AH.
THOOM
THOOM
NOT ONLY THAT, I ATTACK THE OTHER PARMAL WITH EDE ARAI.
EDE ARAI INFLICTS DAMAGE EQUAL TO THE AMOUNT ITS ATK EXCEEDS THE DEF, DIRECTLY ON...
EDE ARAI ATK 2300
...THE OPPONENT!!

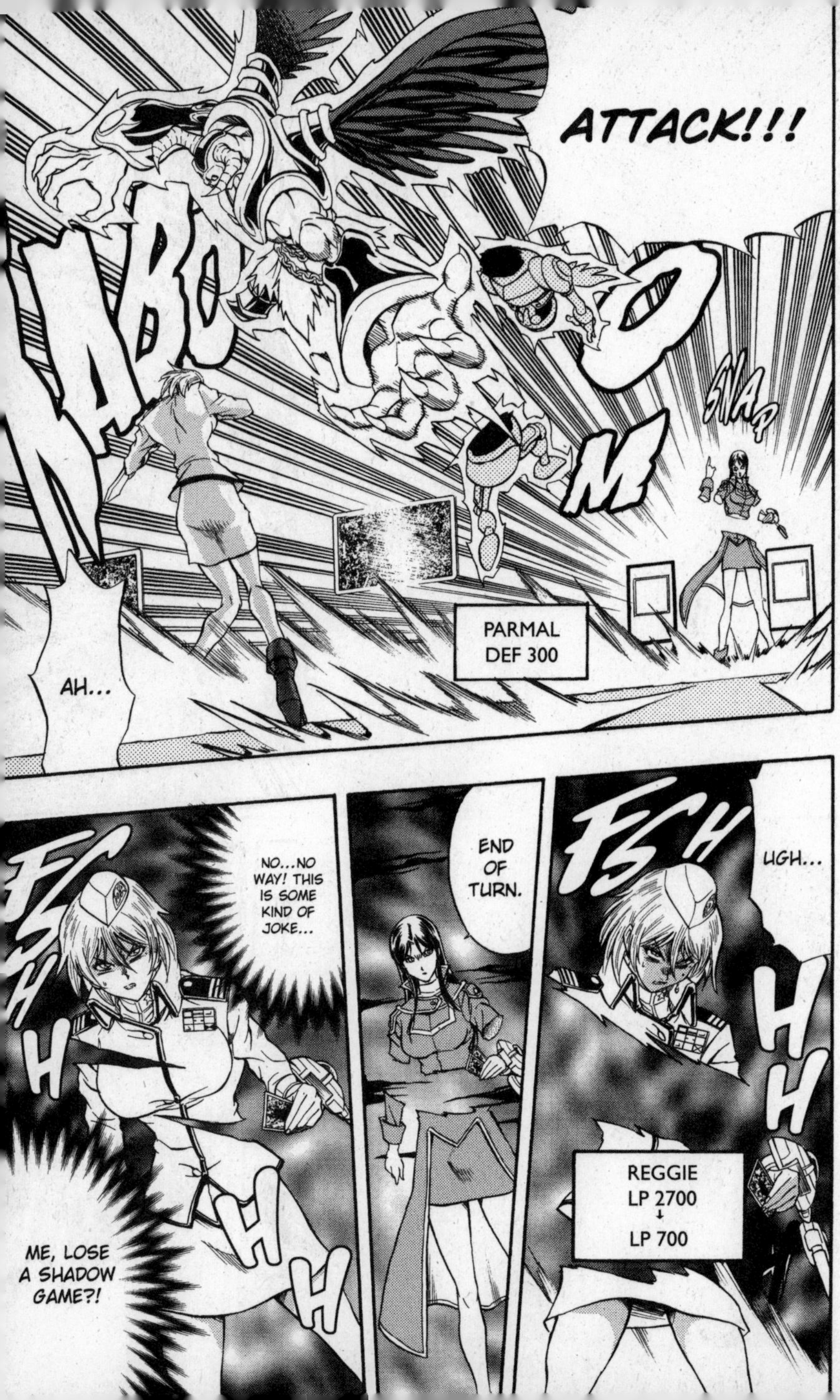
ATTACK!!!
SNAP
PARMAL
DEF 300
AH...
UGH...
REGGIE
LP 2700
↓
LP 700
END OF TURN.
NO...NO WAY! THIS IS SOME KIND OF JOKE...
ME, LOSE A SHADOW GAME?!

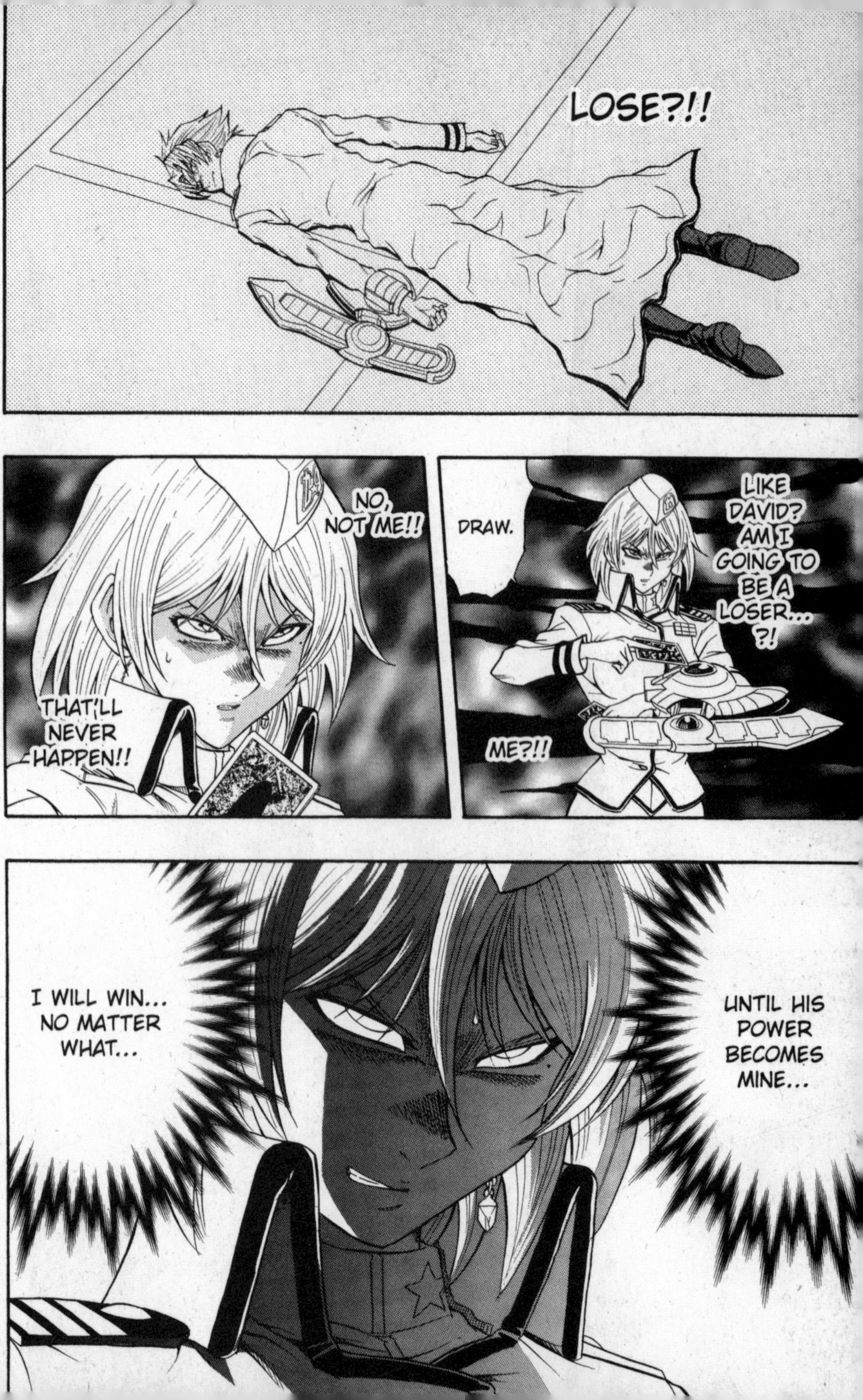
LOSE?!!
LIKE DAVID? AM I GOING TO BE A LOSER...?!
DRAW.
ME?!!
NO, NOT ME!!
THAT'LL NEVER HAPPEN!!
UNTIL HIS POWER BECOMES MINE...
I WILL WIN... NO MATTER WHAT...

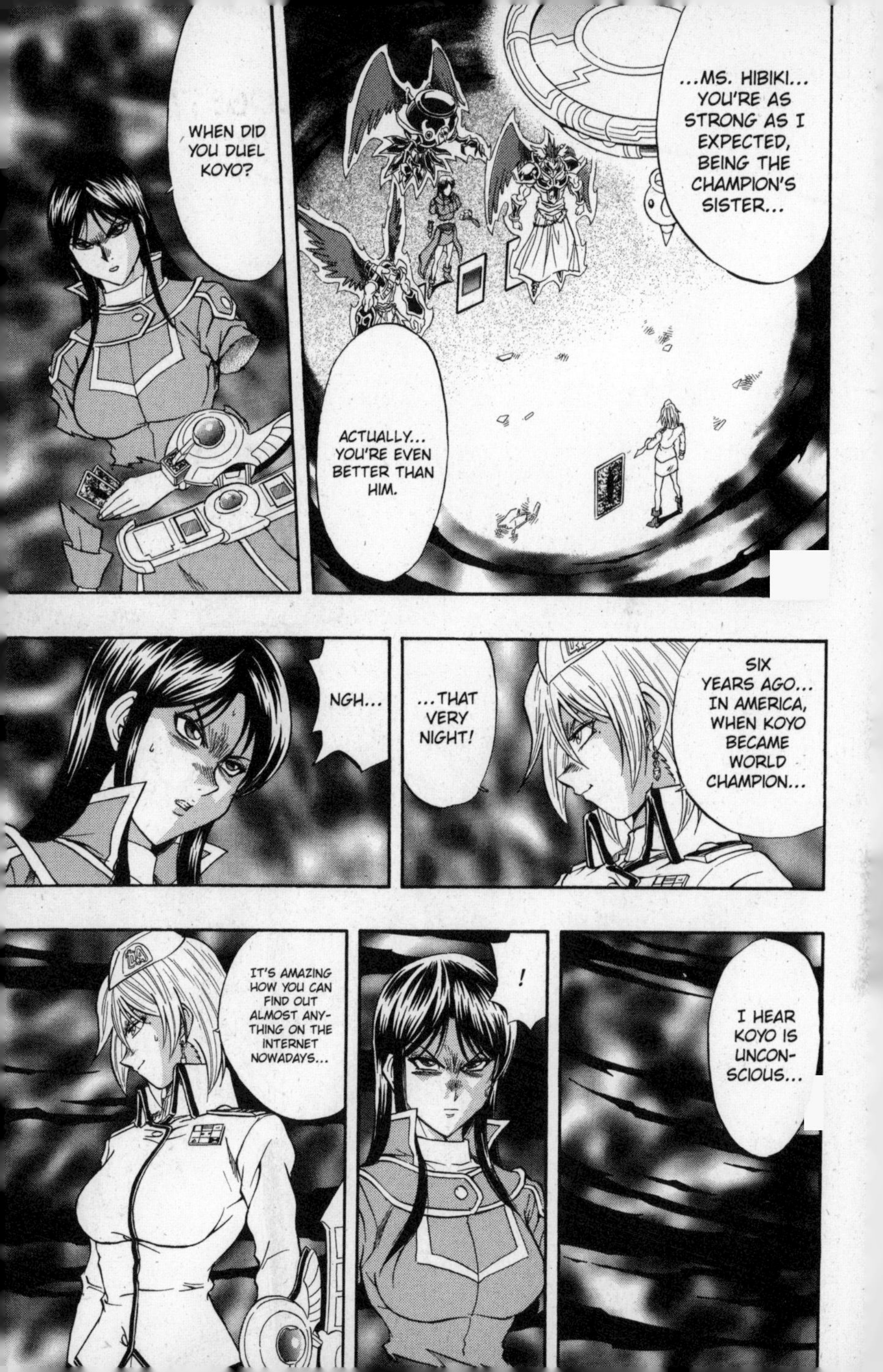
...MS. HIBIKI... YOU'RE AS STRONG AS I EXPECTED, BEING THE CHAMPION'S SISTER...
ACTUALLY... YOU'RE EVEN BETTER THAN HIM.
WHEN DID YOU DUEL KOYO?
SIX YEARS AGO... IN AMERICA, WHEN KOYO BECAME WORLD CHAMPION...
...THAT VERY NIGHT!
NGH...
I HEAR KOYO IS UNCONSCIOUS...
!
IT'S AMAZING HOW YOU CAN FIND OUT ALMOST ANYTHING ON THE INTERNET NOWADAYS...

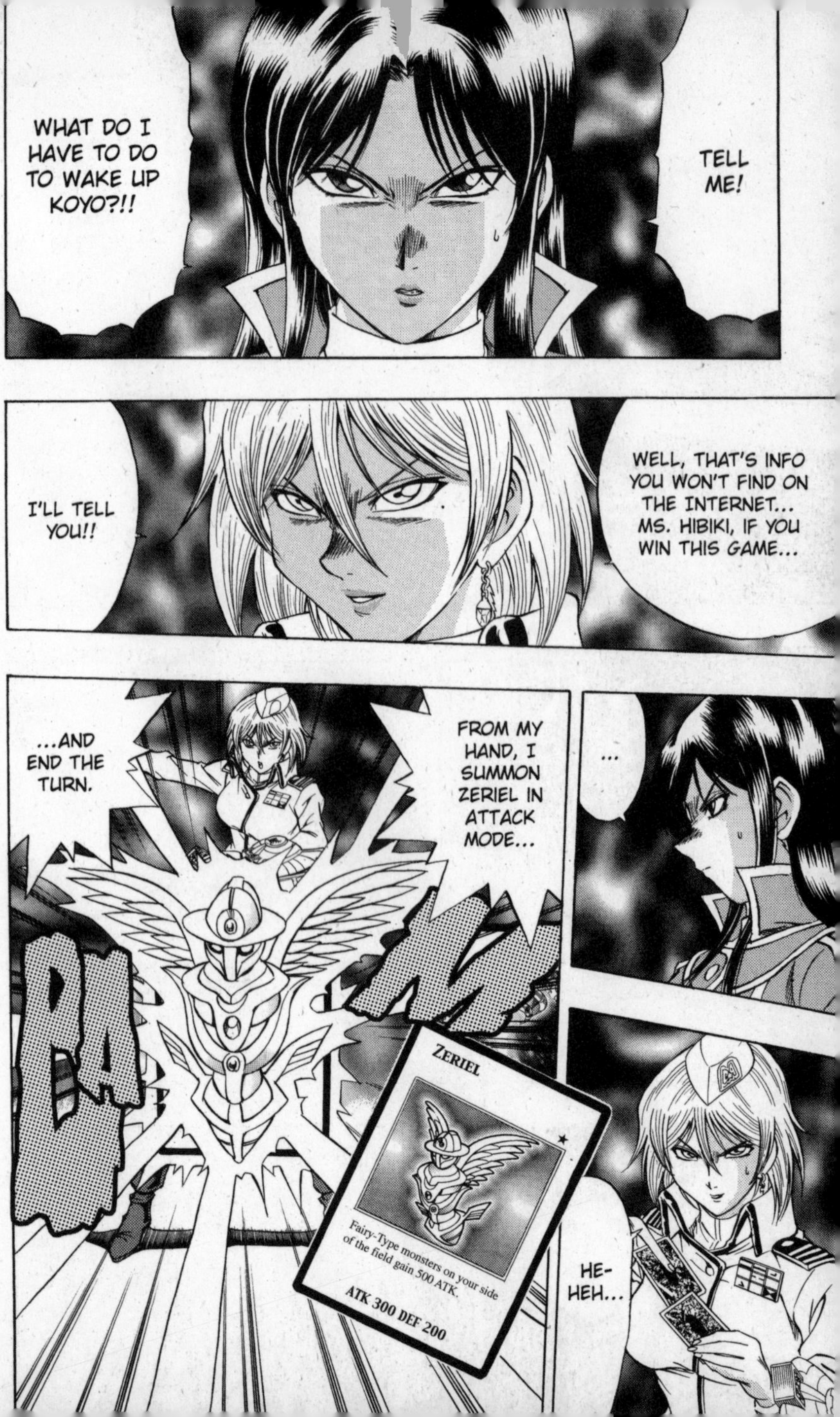

WHAT DO I HAVE TO DO TO WAKE UP KOYO?!!
TELL ME!
WELL, THAT'S INFO YOU WON'T FIND ON THE INTERNET... MS. HIBIKI, IF YOU WIN THIS GAME...
I'LL TELL YOU!!
...
HE-HEH...
FROM MY HAND, I SUMMON ZERIEL IN ATTACK MODE...
...AND END THE TURN.
ZERIEL
Fairy-Type monsters on your side of the field gain 500 ATK.
ATK 300 DEF 200

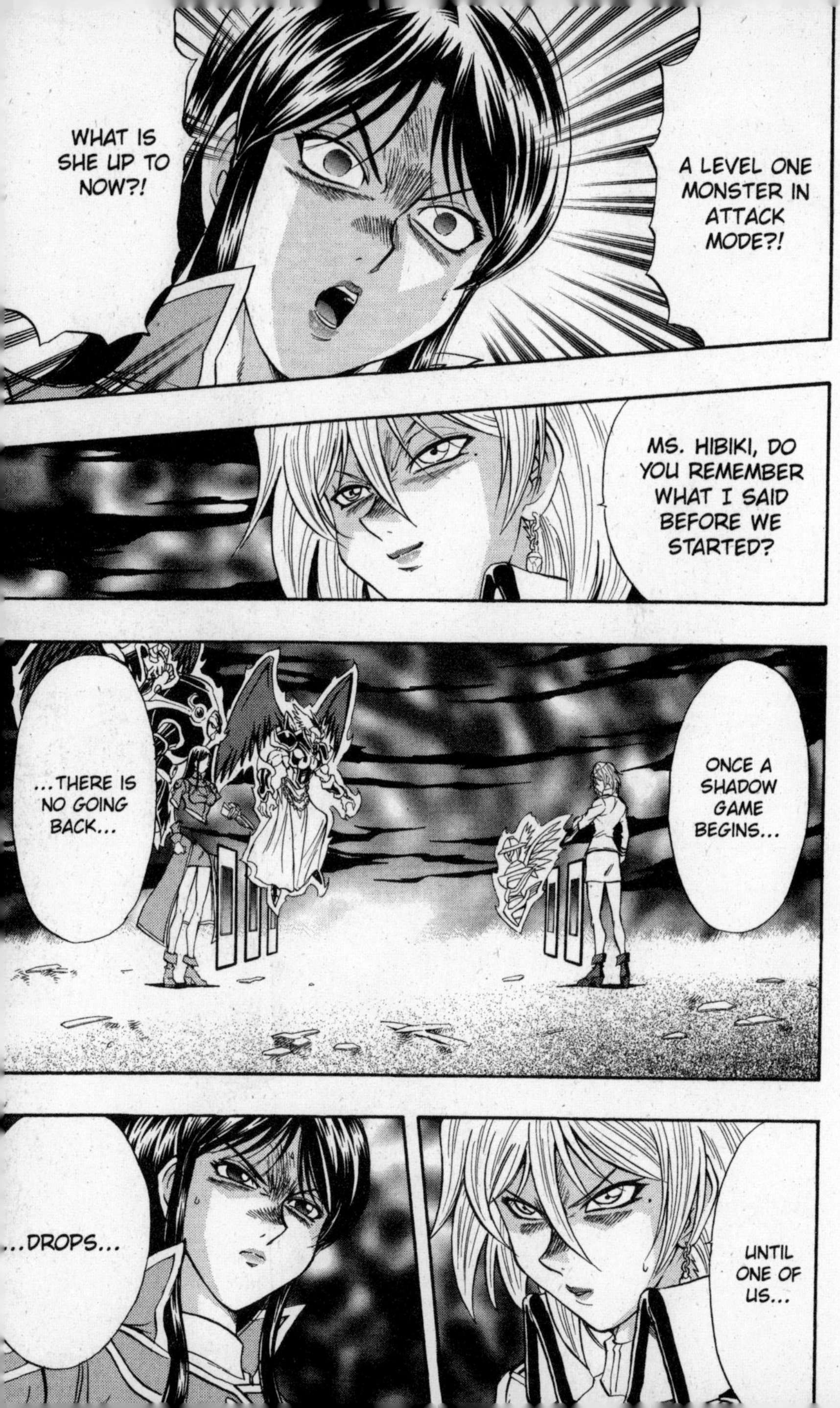
A LEVEL ONE MONSTER IN ATTACK MODE?!
WHAT IS SHE UP TO NOW?!
MS. HIBIKI, DO YOU REMEMBER WHAT I SAID BEFORE WE STARTED?
ONCE A SHADOW GAME BEGINS...
...THERE IS NO GOING BACK...
UNTIL ONE OF US...
...DROPS...

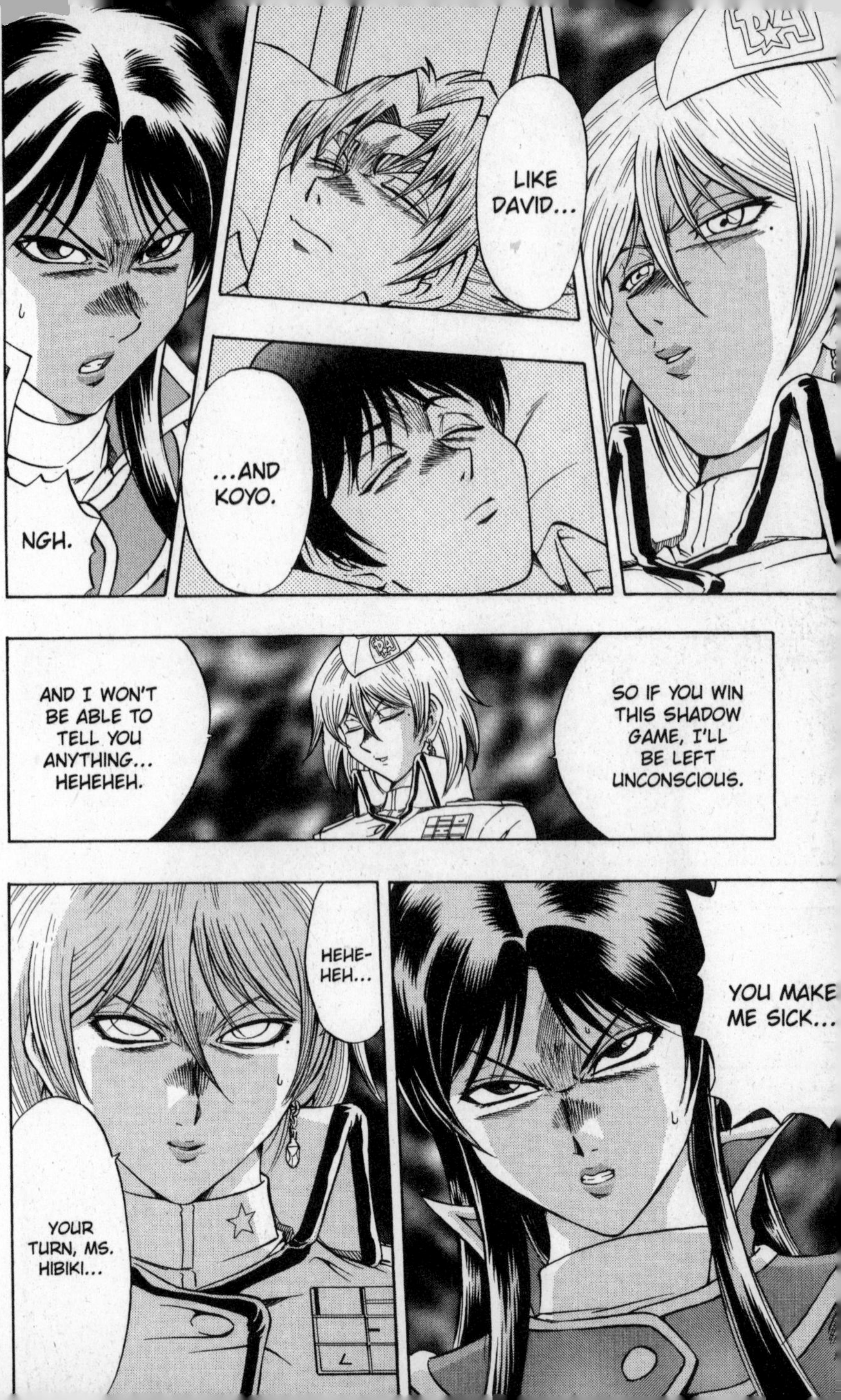
LIKE DAVID...
...AND KOYO.
NGH.
SO IF YOU WIN THIS SHADOW GAME, I'LL BE LEFT UNCONSCIOUS.
AND I WON'T BE ABLE TO TELL YOU ANYTHING... HEHEHEH.
YOU MAKE ME SICK...
HEHE-HEH...
YOUR TURN, MS. HIBIKI...

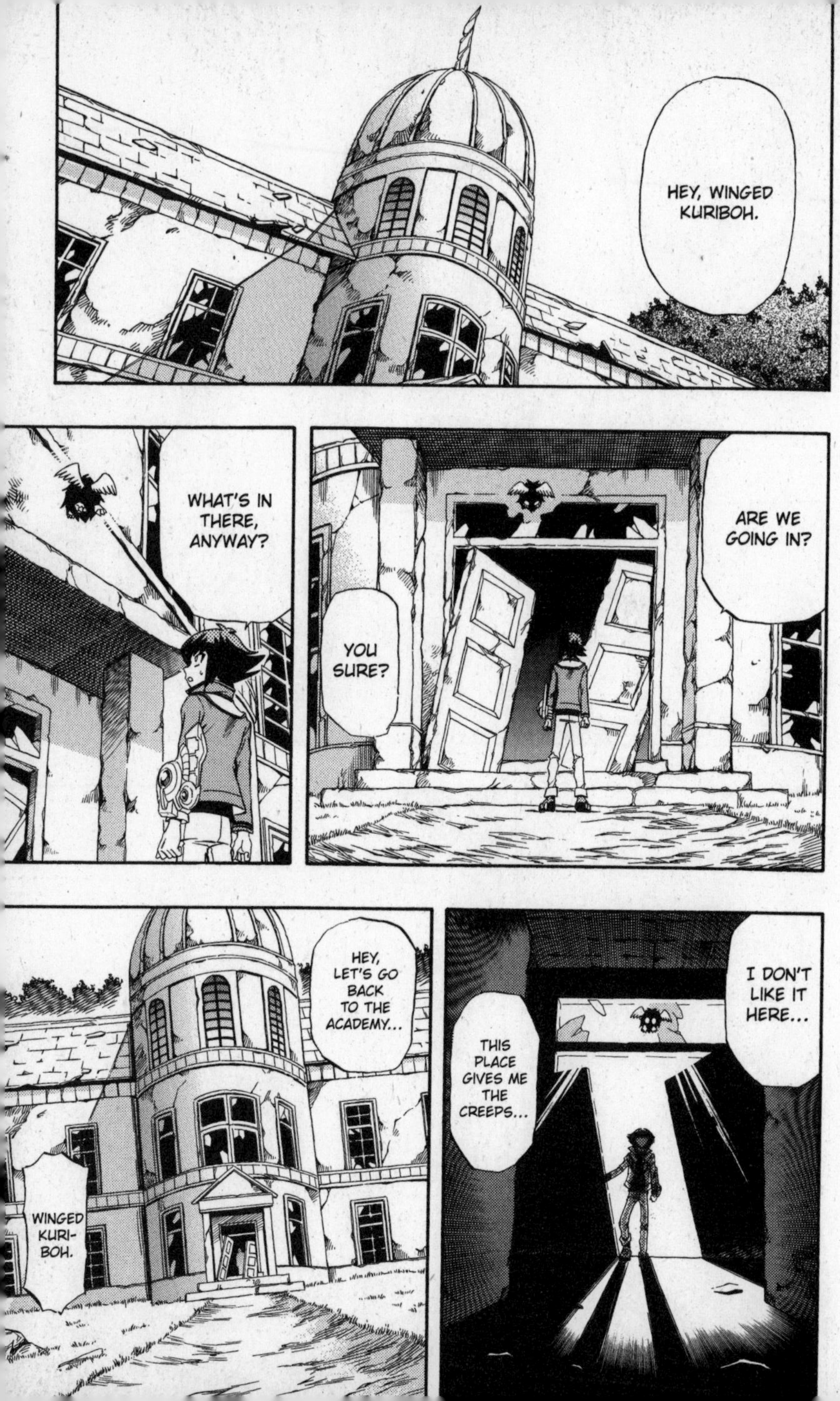
HEY, WINGED KURIBOH.
ARE WE GOING IN?
YOU SURE?
WHAT'S IN THERE, ANYWAY?
I DON'T LIKE IT HERE...
THIS PLACE GIVES ME THE CREEPS...
HEY, LET'S GO BACK TO THE ACADEMY...
WINGED KURI-BOH.

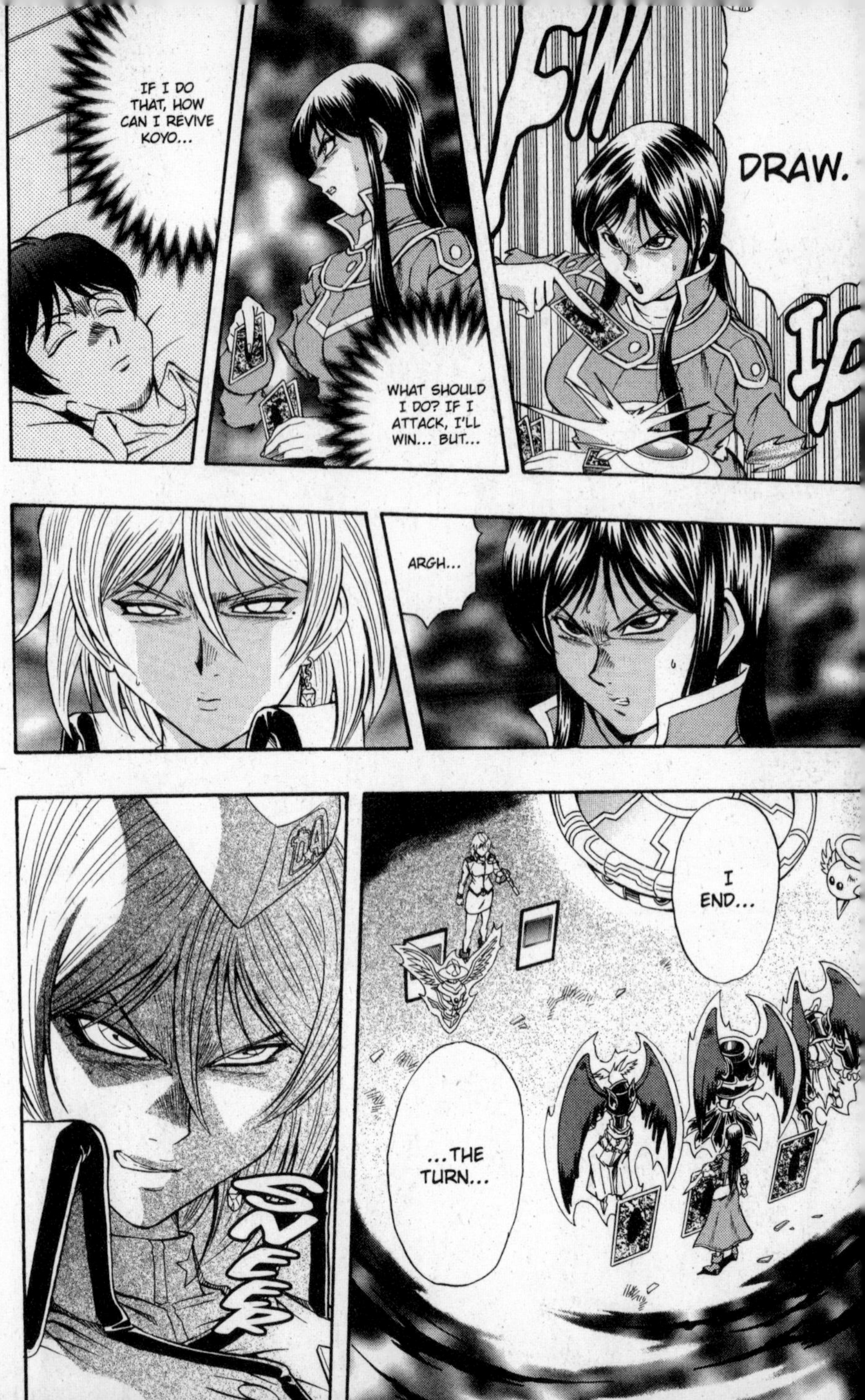
FW
DRAW.
WHAT SHOULD I DO? IF I ATTACK, I'LL WIN... BUT...
IF I DO THAT, HOW CAN I REVIVE KOYO...
ARGH...
I END...
...THE TURN...

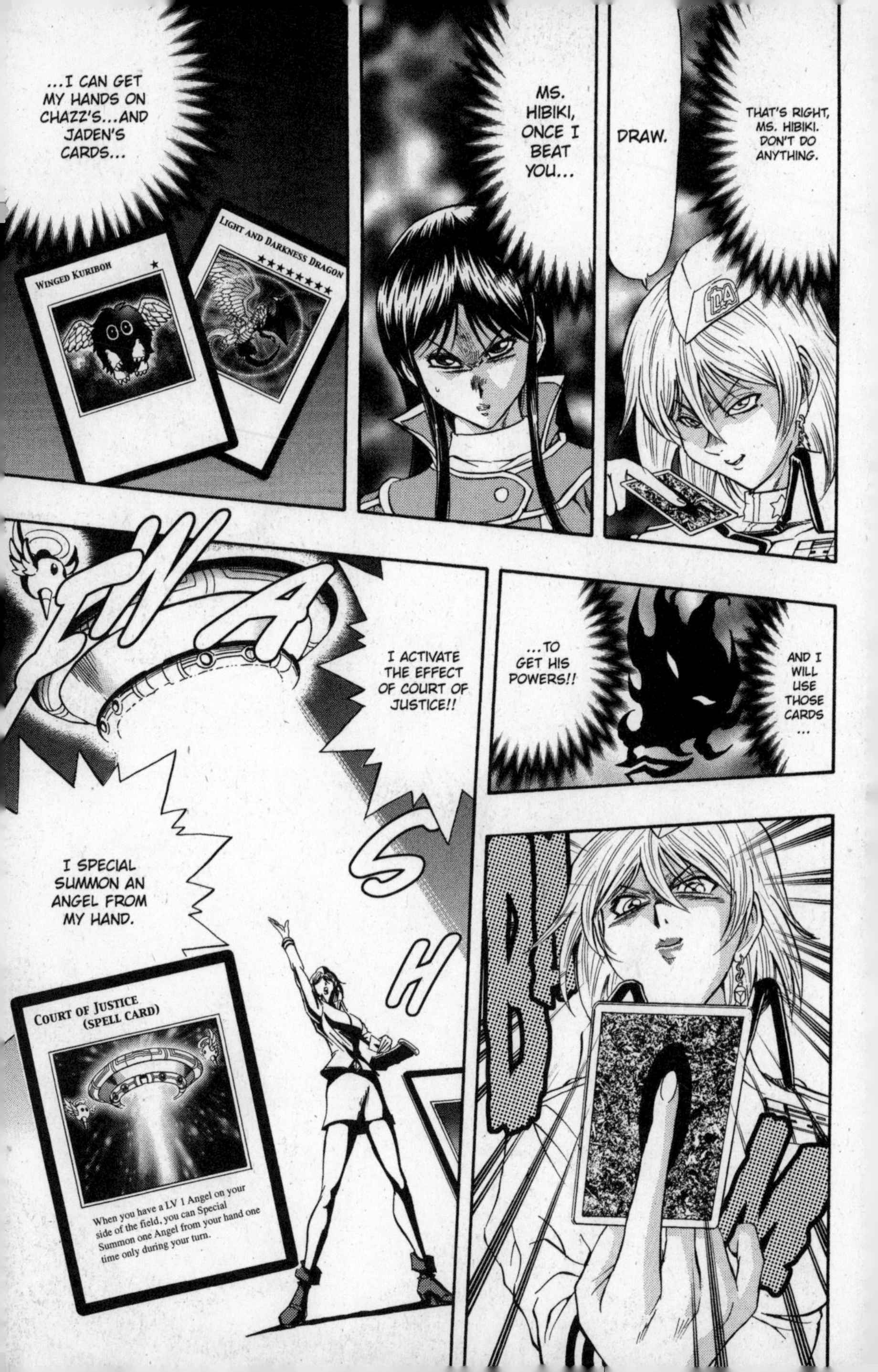

THAT'S RIGHT, MS. HIBIKI. DON'T DO ANYTHING.
DRAW.
MS. HIBIKI, ONCE I BEAT YOU...
...I CAN GET MY HANDS ON CHAZZ'S...AND JADEN'S CARDS...
LIGHT AND DARKNESS DRAGON
WINGED KURIBOH
AND I WILL USE THOSE CARDS ...
...TO GET HIS POWERS!!
FLASH
I ACTIVATE THE EFFECT OF COURT OF JUSTICE!!
I SPECIAL SUMMON AN ANGEL FROM MY HAND.
COURT OF JUSTICE (SPELL CARD)
When you have a LV 1 Angel on your side of the field, you can Special Summon one Angel from your hand one time only during your turn.

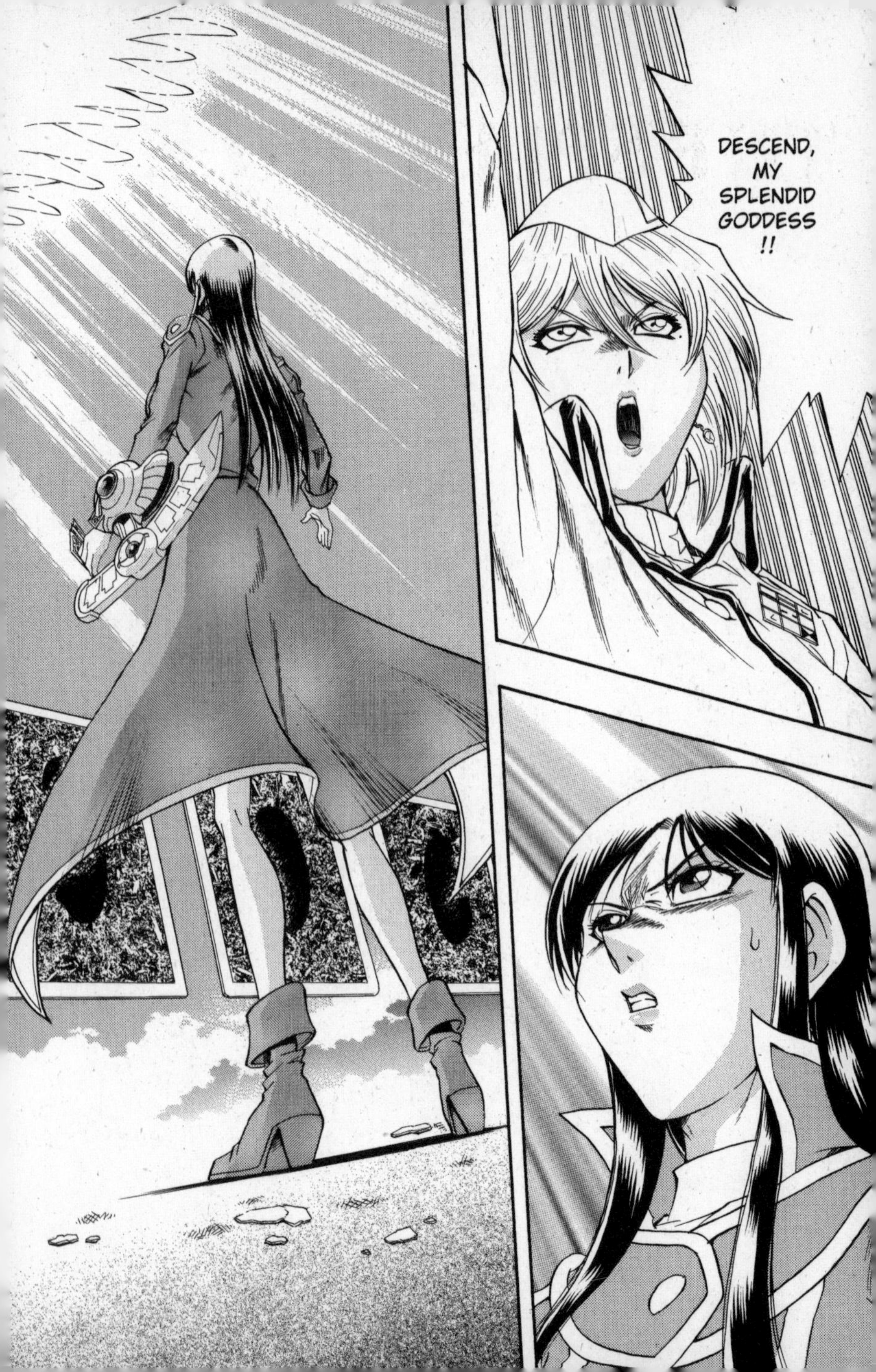
DESCEND, MY SPLENDID GODDESS !!

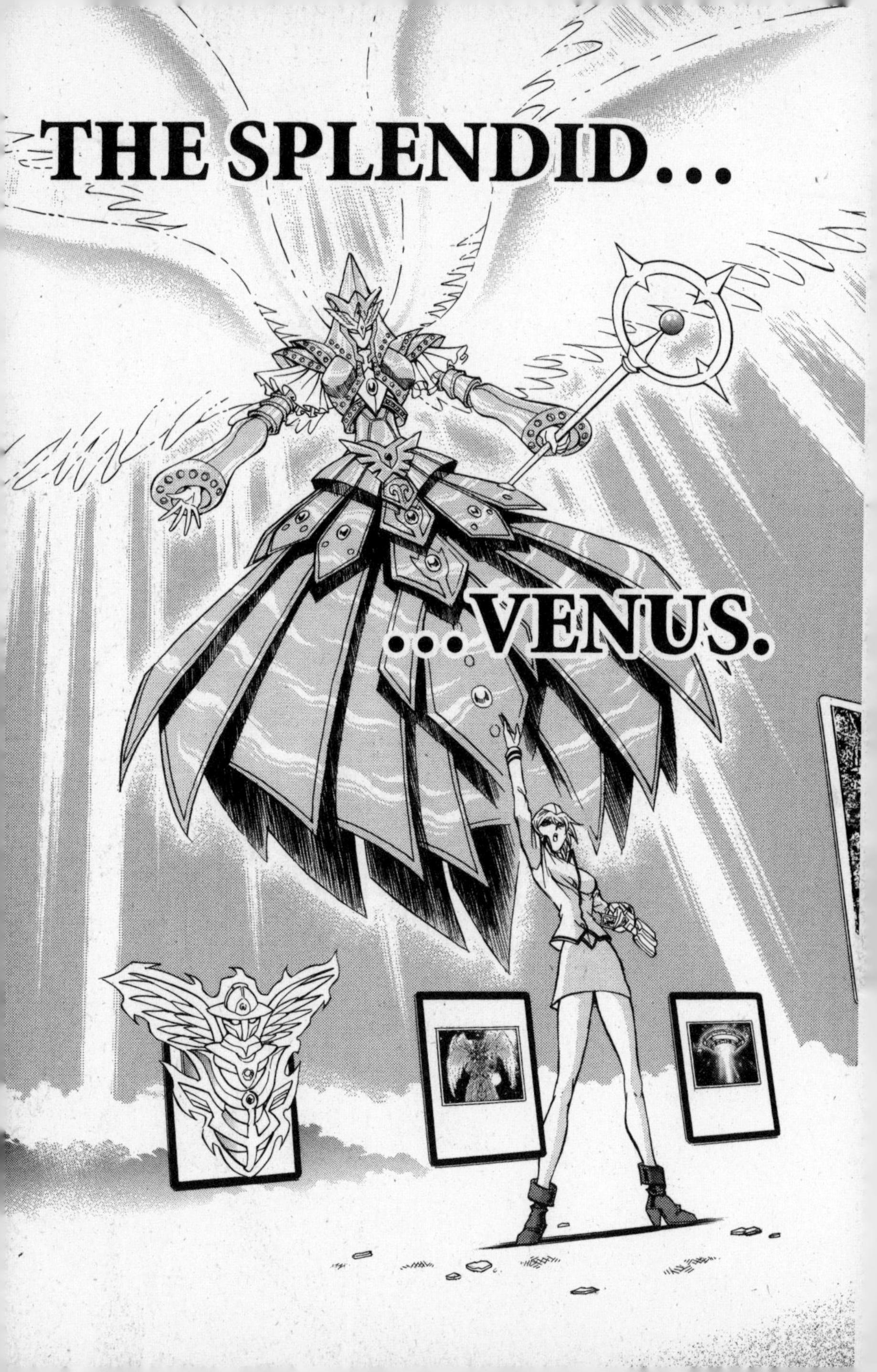
THE SPLENDID...
...VENUS.

AT THE 2008 JUMP FESTA...

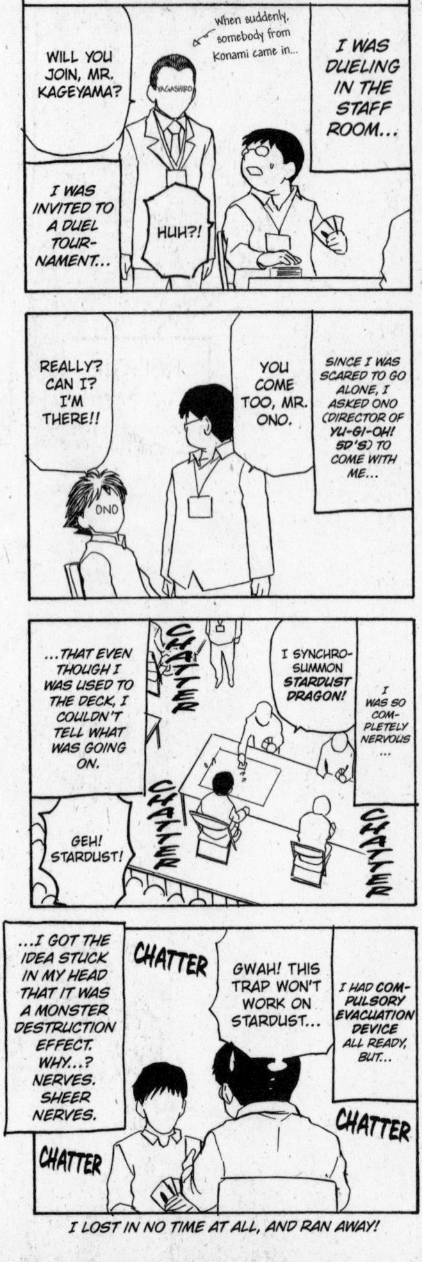
I WAS DUELING IN THE STAFF ROOM...
When suddenly, somebody from Konami came in...
YAGASHIRO
WILL YOU JOIN, MR. KAGEYAMA?
HUH?!
I WAS INVITED TO A DUEL TOUR-NAMENT...
SINCE I WAS SCARED TO GO ALONE, I ASKED ONO (DIRECTOR OF YU-GI-OH! 5D'S) TO COME WITH ME...
YOU COME TOO, MR. ONO.
ONO
REALLY? CAN I? I'M THERE!!
I WAS SO COM-PLETELY NERVOUS...
I SYNCHRO-SUMMON STARDUST DRAGON!
CHATTER
...THAT EVEN THOUGH I WAS USED TO THE DECK, I COULDN'T TELL WHAT WAS GOING ON.
CHATTER
CHATTER
GEH! STARDUST!
I HAD COM-PULSORY EVACUATION DEVICE ALL READY, BUT...
GWAH! THIS TRAP WON'T WORK ON STARDUST...
CHATTER
...I GOT THE IDEA STUCK IN MY HEAD THAT IT WAS A MONSTER DESTRUCTION EFFECT. WHY...? NERVES. SHEER NERVES.
CHATTER
CHATTER

I LOST IN NO TIME AT ALL, AND RAN AWAY!

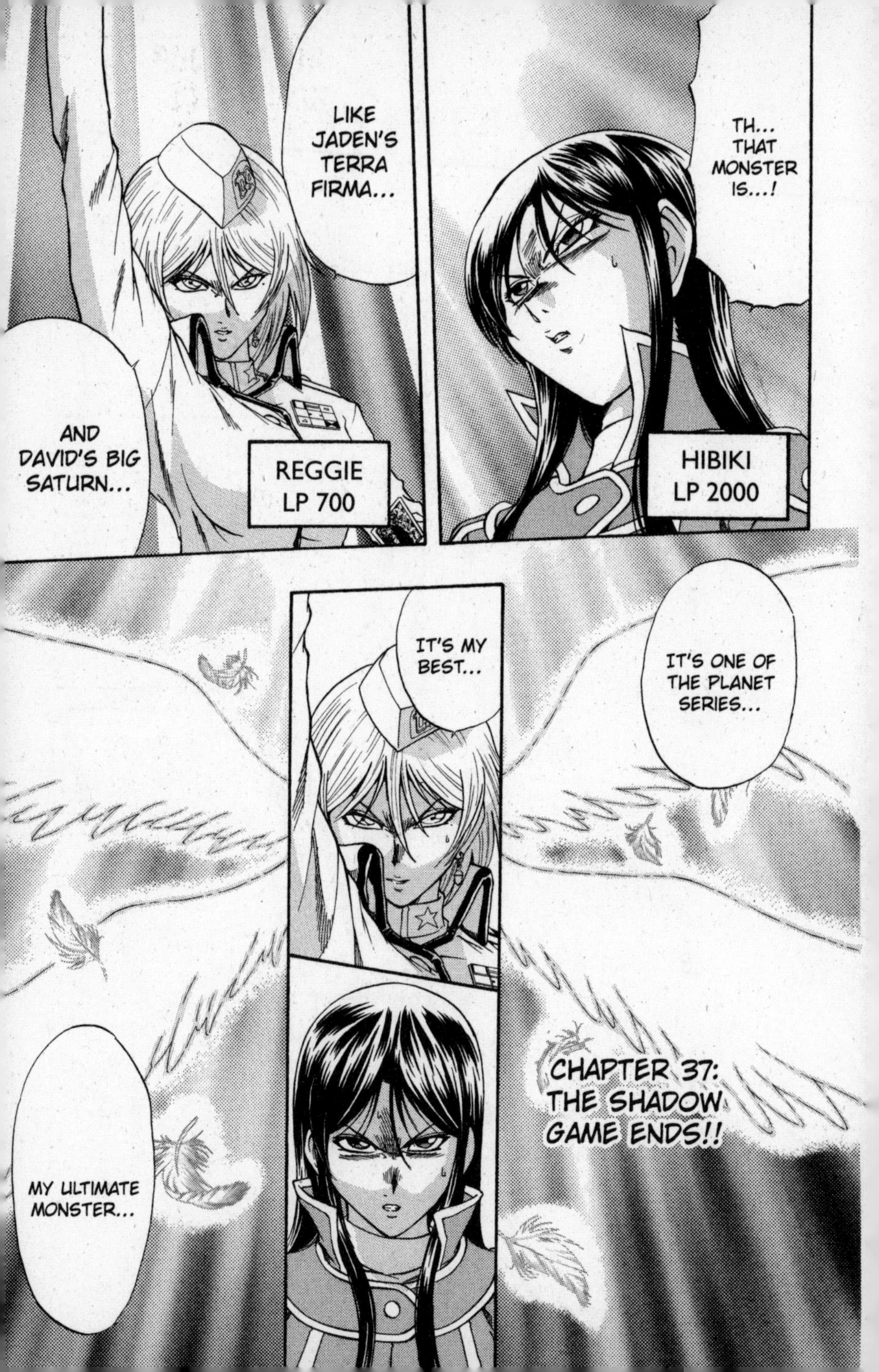
TH... THAT MONSTER IS...!
HIBIKI LP 2000
LIKE JADEN'S TERRA FIRMA...
AND DAVID'S BIG SATURN...
REGGIE LP 700
IT'S ONE OF THE PLANET SERIES...
IT'S MY BEST...
MY ULTIMATE MONSTER...
CHAPTER 37: THE SHADOW GAME ENDS!!

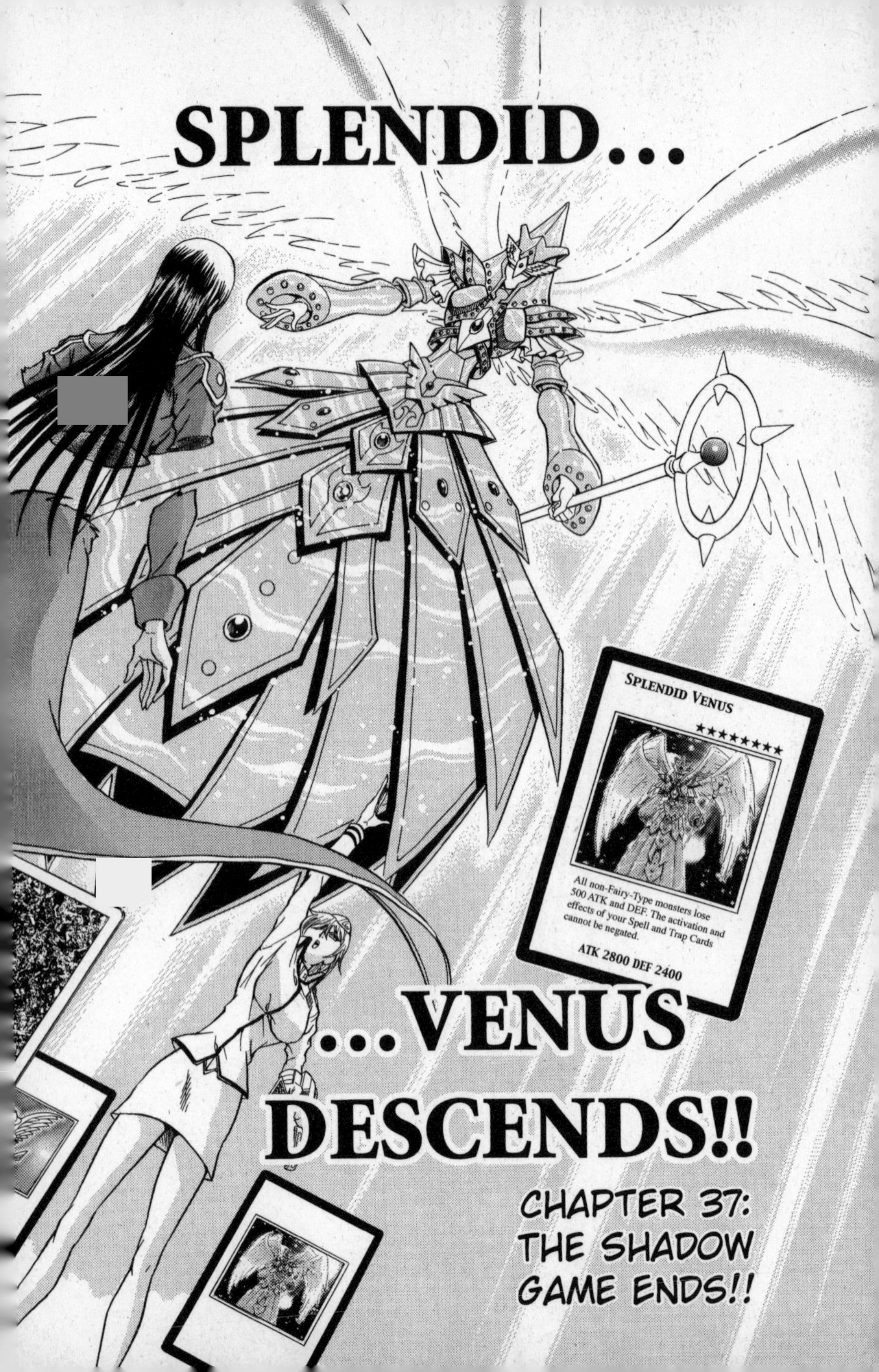
SPLENDID...
SPLENDID VENUS
All non-Fairy-Type monsters lose 500 ATK and DEF. The activation and effects of your Spell and Trap Cards cannot be negated.
ATK 2800 DEF 2400
...VENUS DESCENDS!!
CHAPTER 37: THE SHADOW GAME ENDS!!

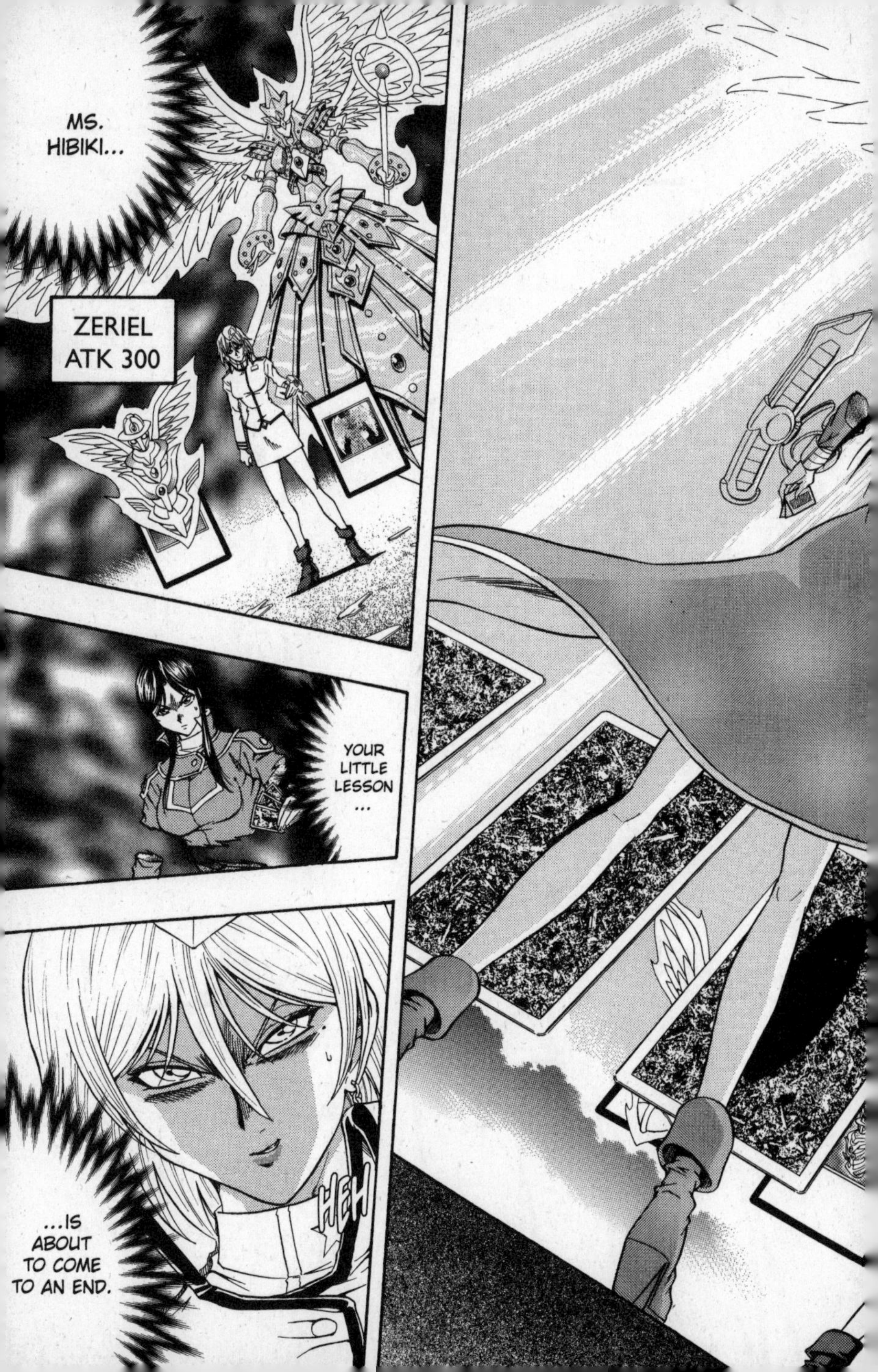
MS. HIBIKI...
ZERIEL ATK 300
YOUR LITTLE LESSON ...
HEH
...IS ABOUT TO COME TO AN END.

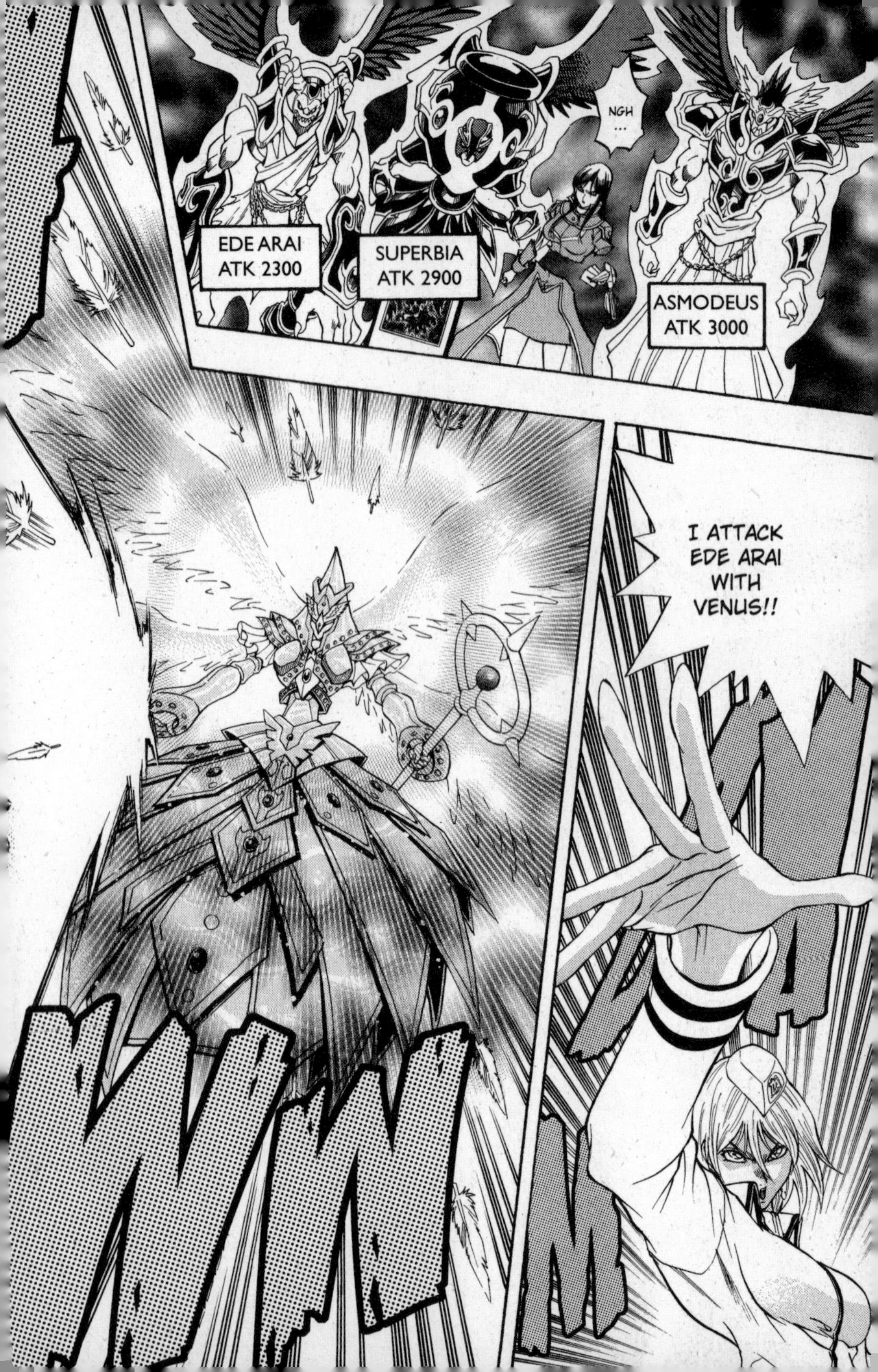
NGH ...
ASMODEUS ATK 3000
SUPERBIA ATK 2900
EDE ARAI ATK 2300
I ATTACK EDE ARAI WITH VENUS!!

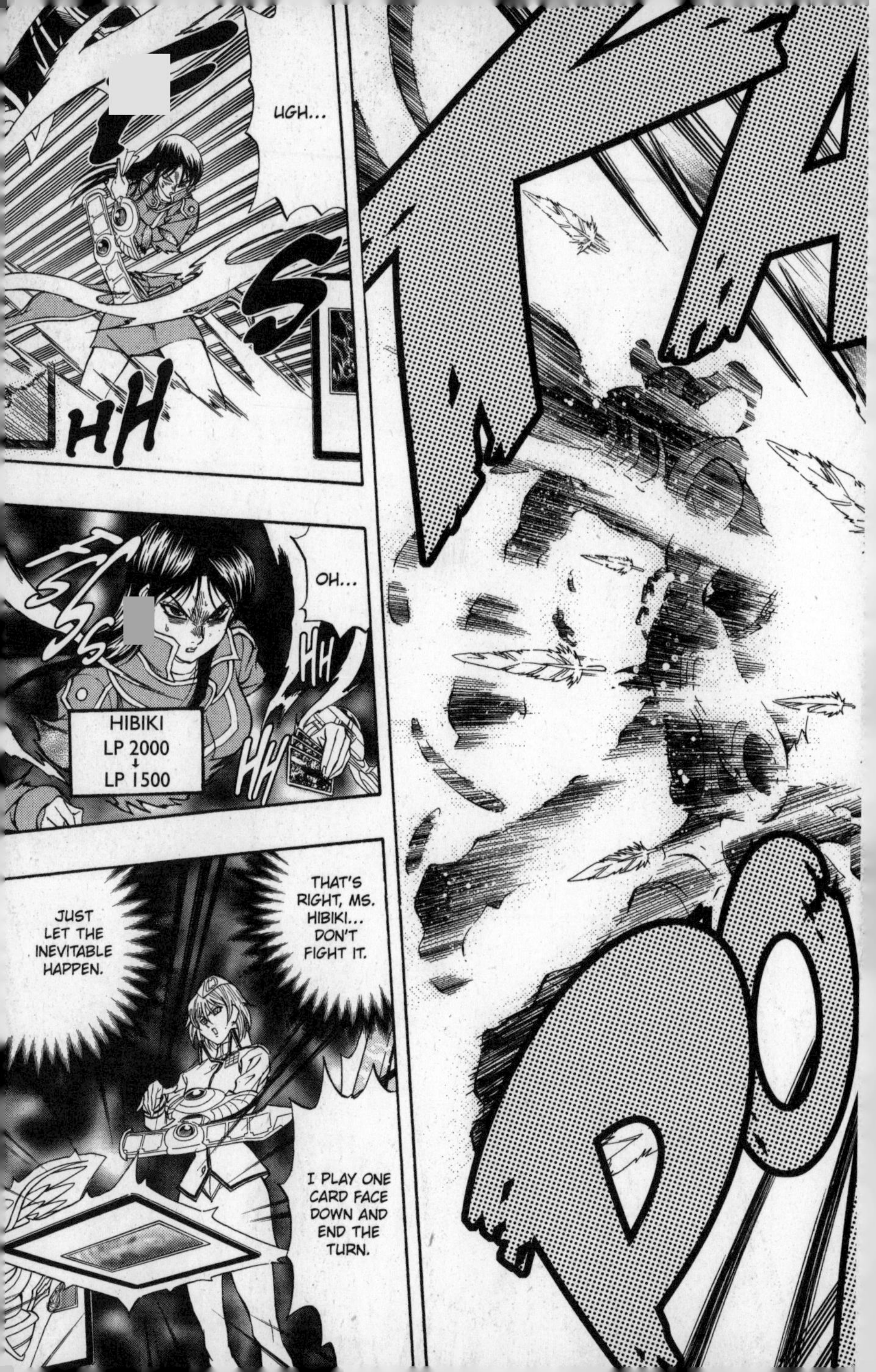
UGH...
OH...
HIBIKI
LP 2000
LP 1500
THAT'S RIGHT, MS. HIBIKI... DON'T FIGHT IT.
JUST LET THE INEVITABLE HAPPEN.
I PLAY ONE CARD FACE DOWN AND END THE TURN.

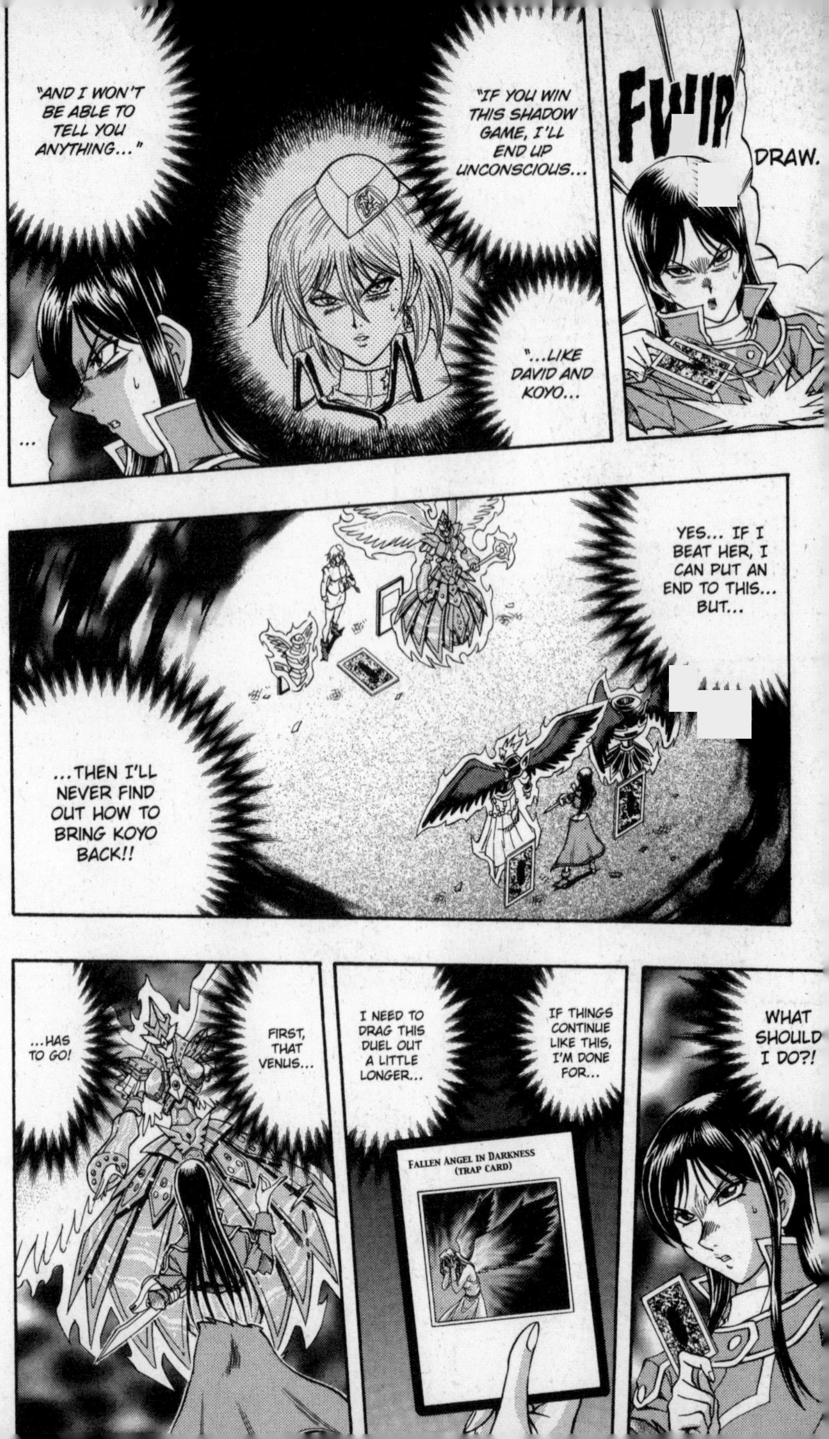
FWIP
DRAW.
"IF YOU WIN THIS SHADOW GAME, I'LL END UP UNCONSCIOUS...
"...LIKE DAVID AND KOYO...
"AND I WON'T BE ABLE TO TELL YOU ANYTHING..."
...
YES... IF I BEAT HER, I CAN PUT AN END TO THIS... BUT...
...THEN I'LL NEVER FIND OUT HOW TO BRING KOYO BACK!!
WHAT SHOULD I DO?!
IF THINGS CONTINUE LIKE THIS, I'M DONE FOR...
I NEED TO DRAG THIS DUEL OUT A LITTLE LONGER...
FALLEN ANGEL IN DARKNESS
(TRAP CARD)
FIRST, THAT VENUS...
...HAS TO GO!

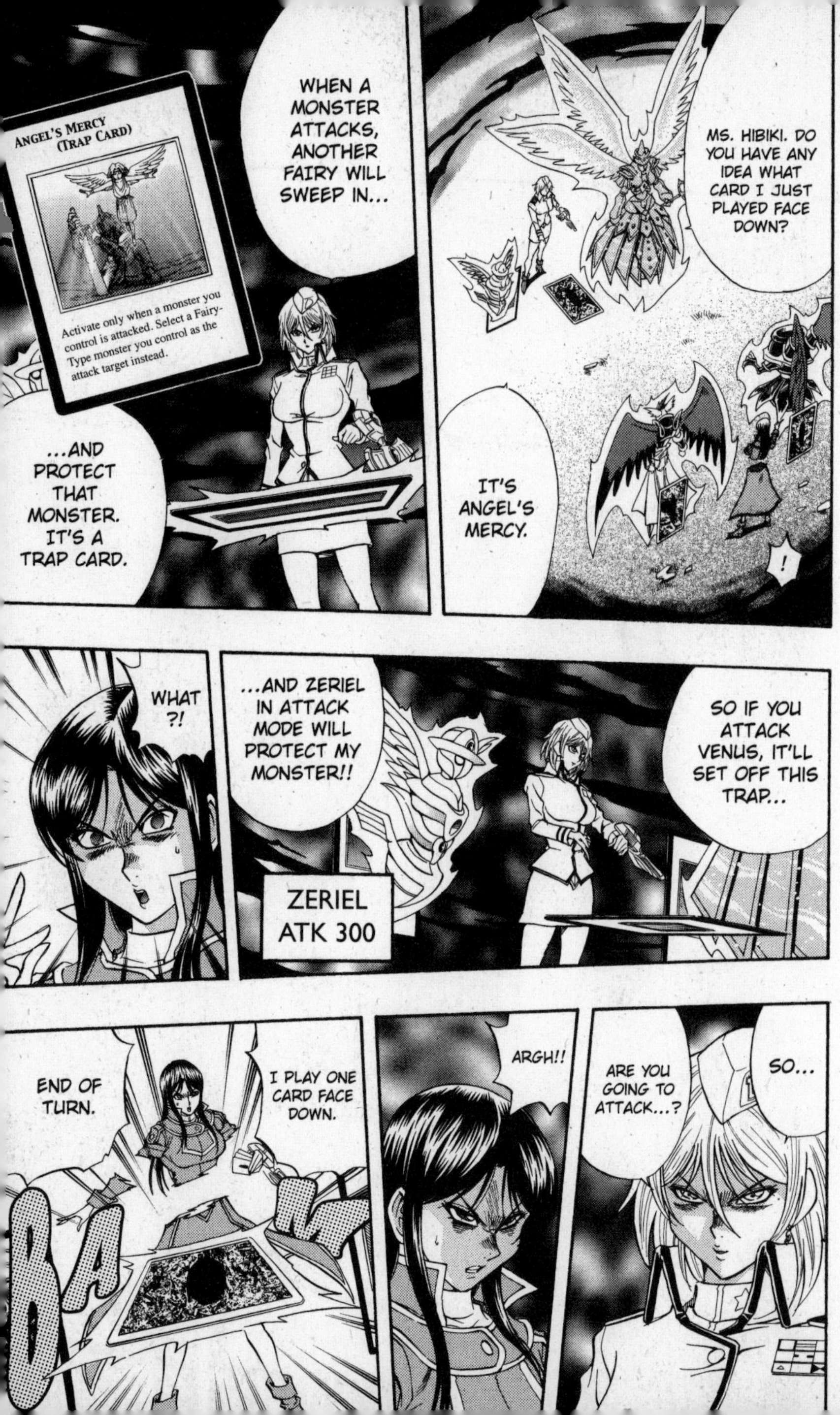
MS. HIBIKI. DO YOU HAVE ANY IDEA WHAT CARD I JUST PLAYED FACE DOWN?
IT'S ANGEL'S MERCY.
!
WHEN A MONSTER ATTACKS, ANOTHER FAIRY WILL SWEEP IN...
ANGEL'S MERCY (TRAP CARD)
Activate only when a monster you control is attacked. Select a Fairy-Type monster you control as the attack target instead.
...AND PROTECT THAT MONSTER. IT'S A TRAP CARD.
SO IF YOU ATTACK VENUS, IT'LL SET OFF THIS TRAP...
...AND ZERIEL IN ATTACK MODE WILL PROTECT MY MONSTER!!
ZERIEL ATK 300
WHAT ?!
SO...
ARE YOU GOING TO ATTACK...?
ARGH!!
I PLAY ONE CARD FACE DOWN.
END OF TURN.
BAM

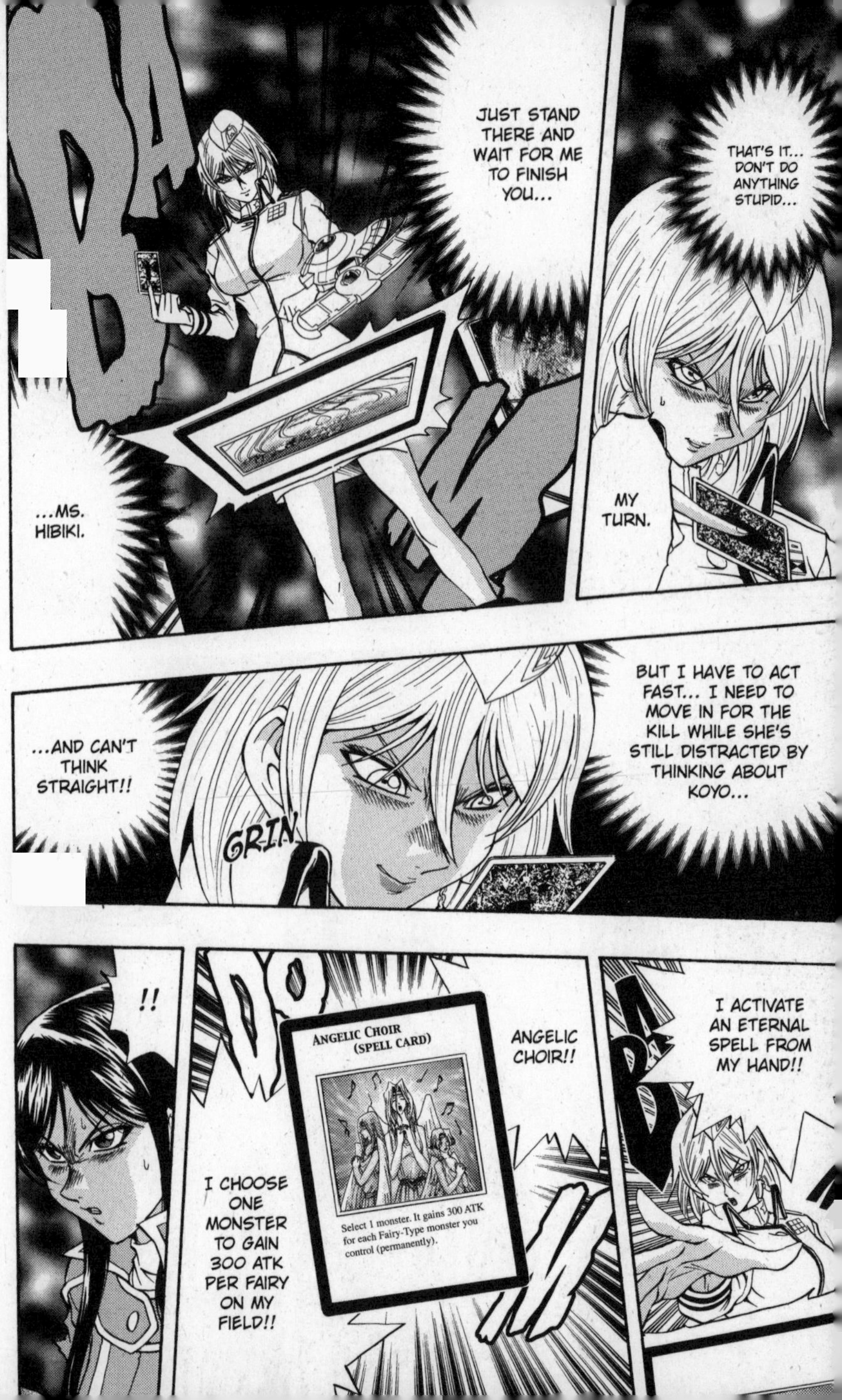
THAT'S IT... DON'T DO ANYTHING STUPID...
MY TURN.
JUST STAND THERE AND WAIT FOR ME TO FINISH YOU...
...MS. HIBIKI.
BUT I HAVE TO ACT FAST... I NEED TO MOVE IN FOR THE KILL WHILE SHE'S STILL DISTRACTED BY THINKING ABOUT KOYO...
GRIN
...AND CAN'T THINK STRAIGHT!!
I ACTIVATE AN ETERNAL SPELL FROM MY HAND!!
ANGELIC CHOIR!!
ANGELIC CHOIR (SPELL CARD)
Select 1 monster. It gains 300 ATK for each Fairy-Type monster you control (permanently).
I CHOOSE ONE MONSTER TO GAIN 300 ATK PER FAIRY ON MY FIELD!!
!!

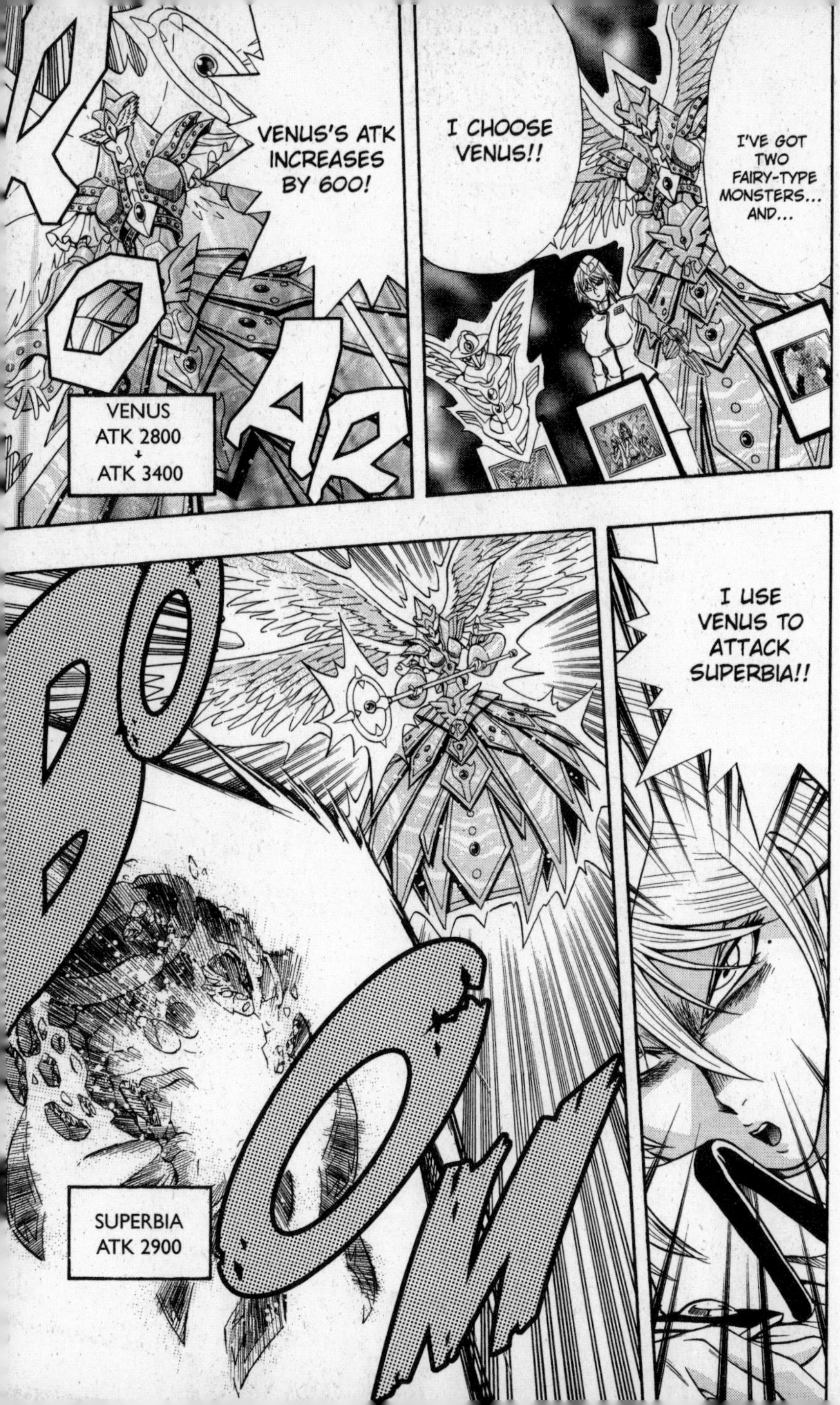

I'VE GOT TWO FAIRY-TYPE MONSTERS... AND...
I CHOOSE VENUS!!
VENUS'S ATK INCREASES BY 600!
VENUS
ATK 2800
→
ATK 3400
I USE VENUS TO ATTACK SUPERBIA!!
SUPERBIA
ATK 2900

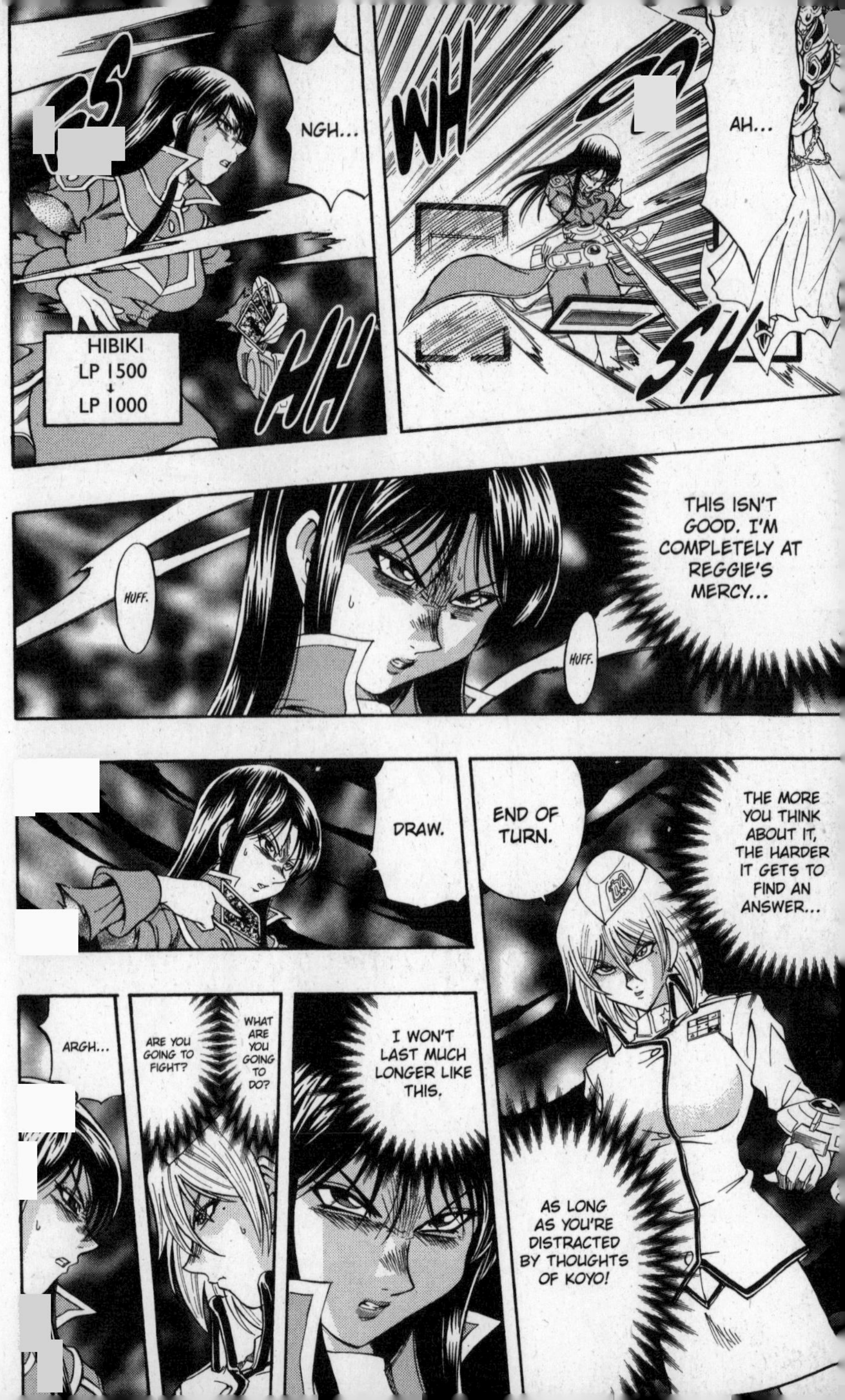
AH...
WH
SH
NGH...
HIBIKI
LP 1500
↓
LP 1000
THIS ISN'T GOOD. I'M COMPLETELY AT REGGIE'S MERCY...
HUFF.
HUFF.
THE MORE YOU THINK ABOUT IT, THE HARDER IT GETS TO FIND AN ANSWER...
END OF TURN.
AS LONG AS YOU'RE DISTRACTED BY THOUGHTS OF KOYO!
DRAW.
I WON'T LAST MUCH LONGER LIKE THIS.
WHAT ARE YOU GOING TO DO?
ARE YOU GOING TO FIGHT?
ARGH...

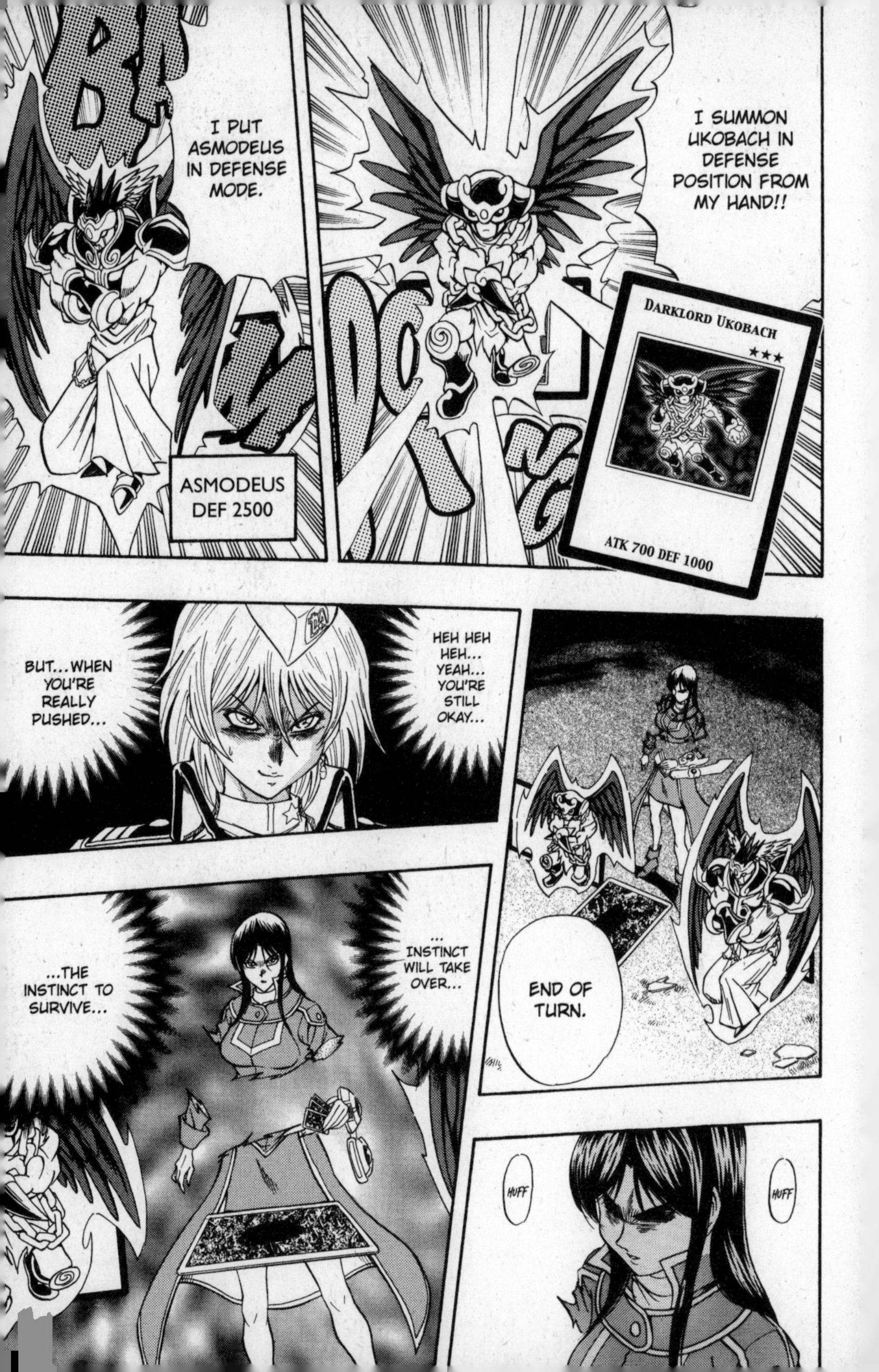
I SUMMON UKOBACH IN DEFENSE POSITION FROM MY HAND!!
DARKLORD UKOBACH
ATK 700 DEF 1000
I PUT ASMODEUS IN DEFENSE MODE.
ASMODEUS DEF 2500
END OF TURN.
HEH HEH HEH... YEAH... YOU'RE STILL OKAY...
BUT...WHEN YOU'RE REALLY PUSHED...
...INSTINCT WILL TAKE OVER...
...THE INSTINCT TO SURVIVE...
HUFF
HUFF

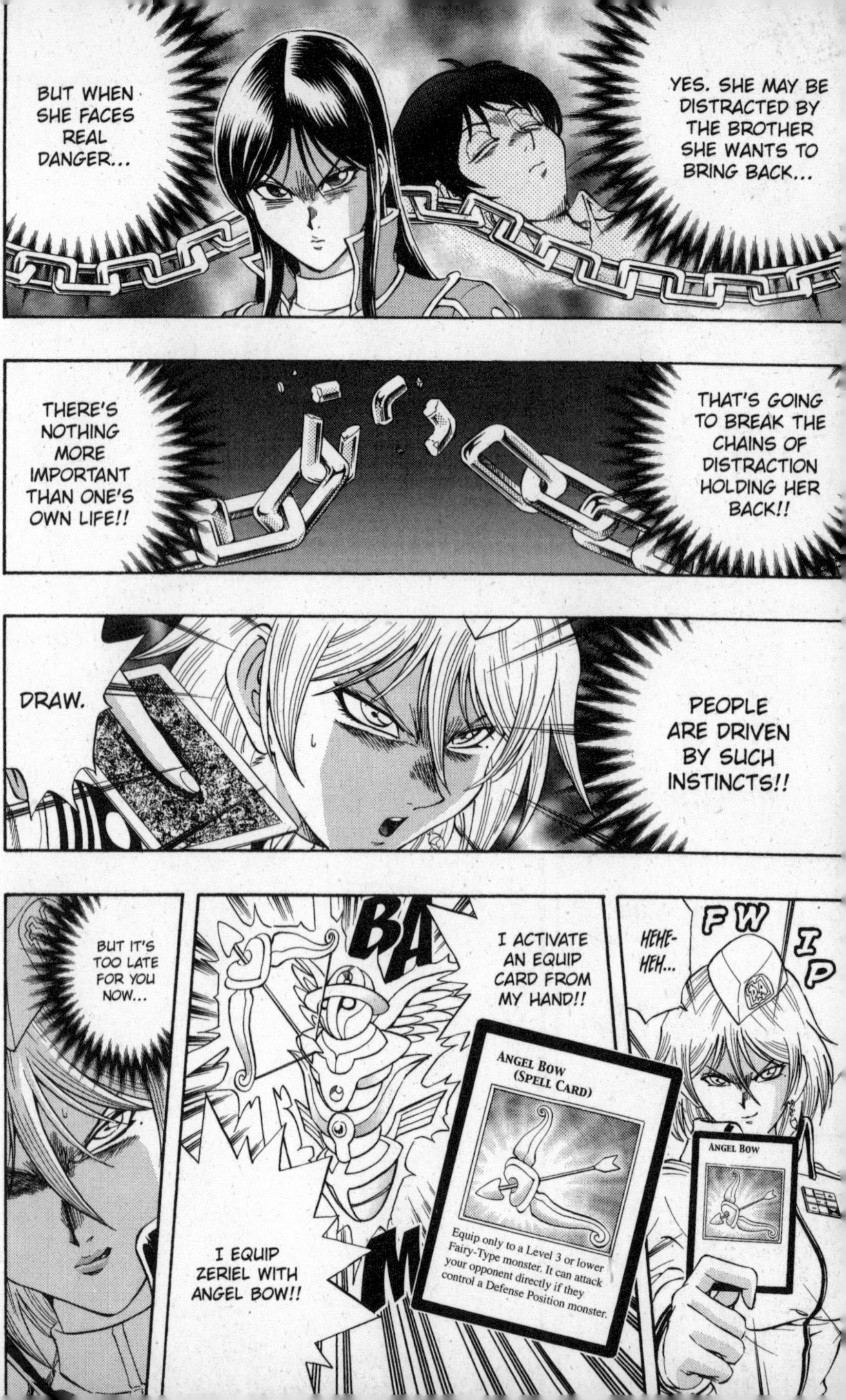
YES. SHE MAY BE DISTRACTED BY THE BROTHER SHE WANTS TO BRING BACK...
BUT WHEN SHE FACES REAL DANGER...
THAT'S GOING TO BREAK THE CHAINS OF DISTRACTION HOLDING HER BACK!!
THERE'S NOTHING MORE IMPORTANT THAN ONE'S OWN LIFE!!
PEOPLE ARE DRIVEN BY SUCH INSTINCTS!!
DRAW.
FWIP
HEHE-HEH...
ANGEL BOW
BAM
I ACTIVATE AN EQUIP CARD FROM MY HAND!!
ANGEL BOW (SPELL CARD)
Equip only to a Level 3 or lower Fairy-Type monster. It can attack your opponent directly if they control a Defense Position monster.
I EQUIP ZERIEL WITH ANGEL BOW!!
BUT IT'S TOO LATE FOR YOU NOW...

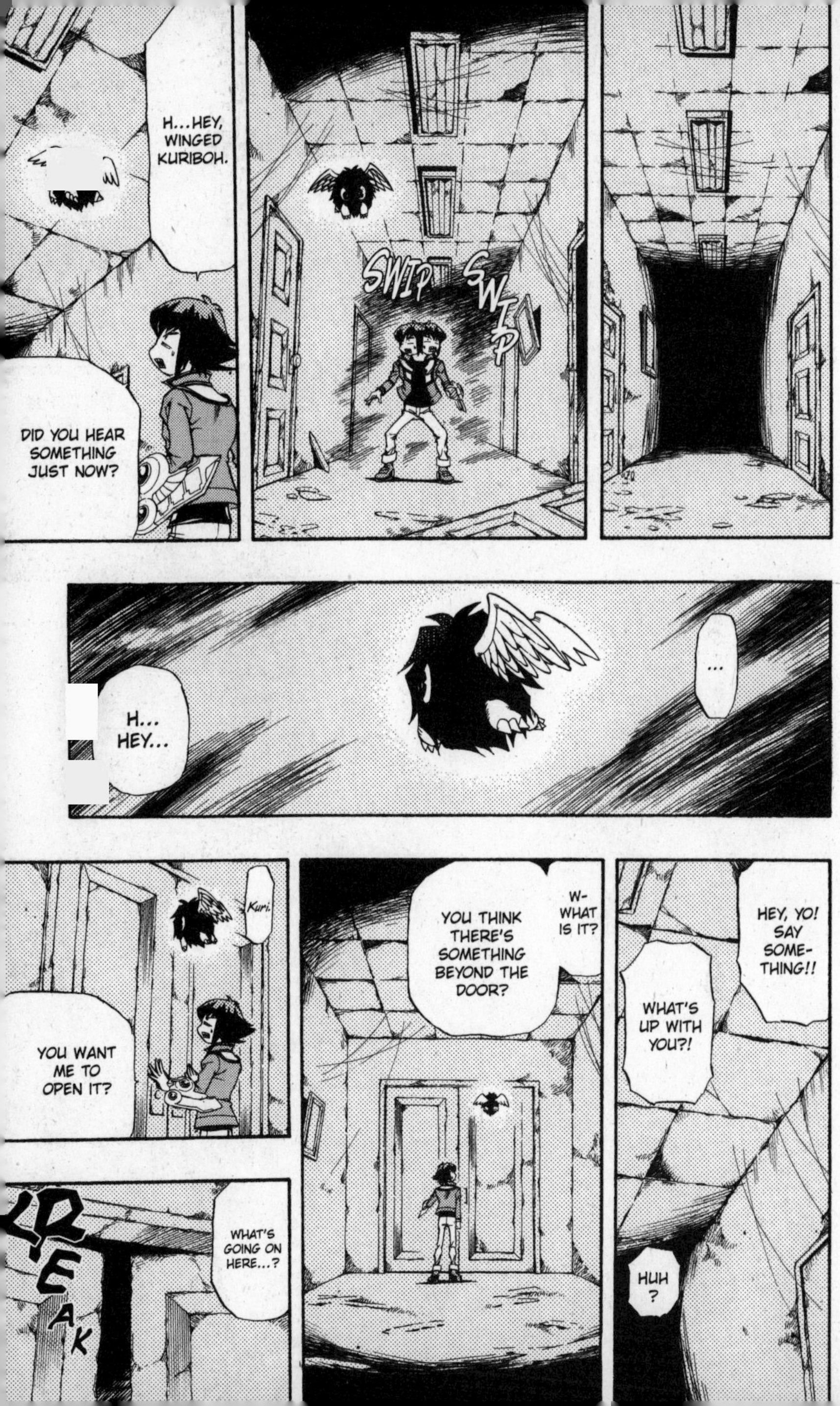
SWIP SWIP
H...HEY, WINGED KURIBOH.
DID YOU HEAR SOMETHING JUST NOW?
...
H... HEY...
HEY, YO! SAY SOME-THING!!
WHAT'S UP WITH YOU?!
HUH?
W-WHAT IS IT?
YOU THINK THERE'S SOMETHING BEYOND THE DOOR?
Kuri.
YOU WANT ME TO OPEN IT?
WHAT'S GOING ON HERE...?
CREAK

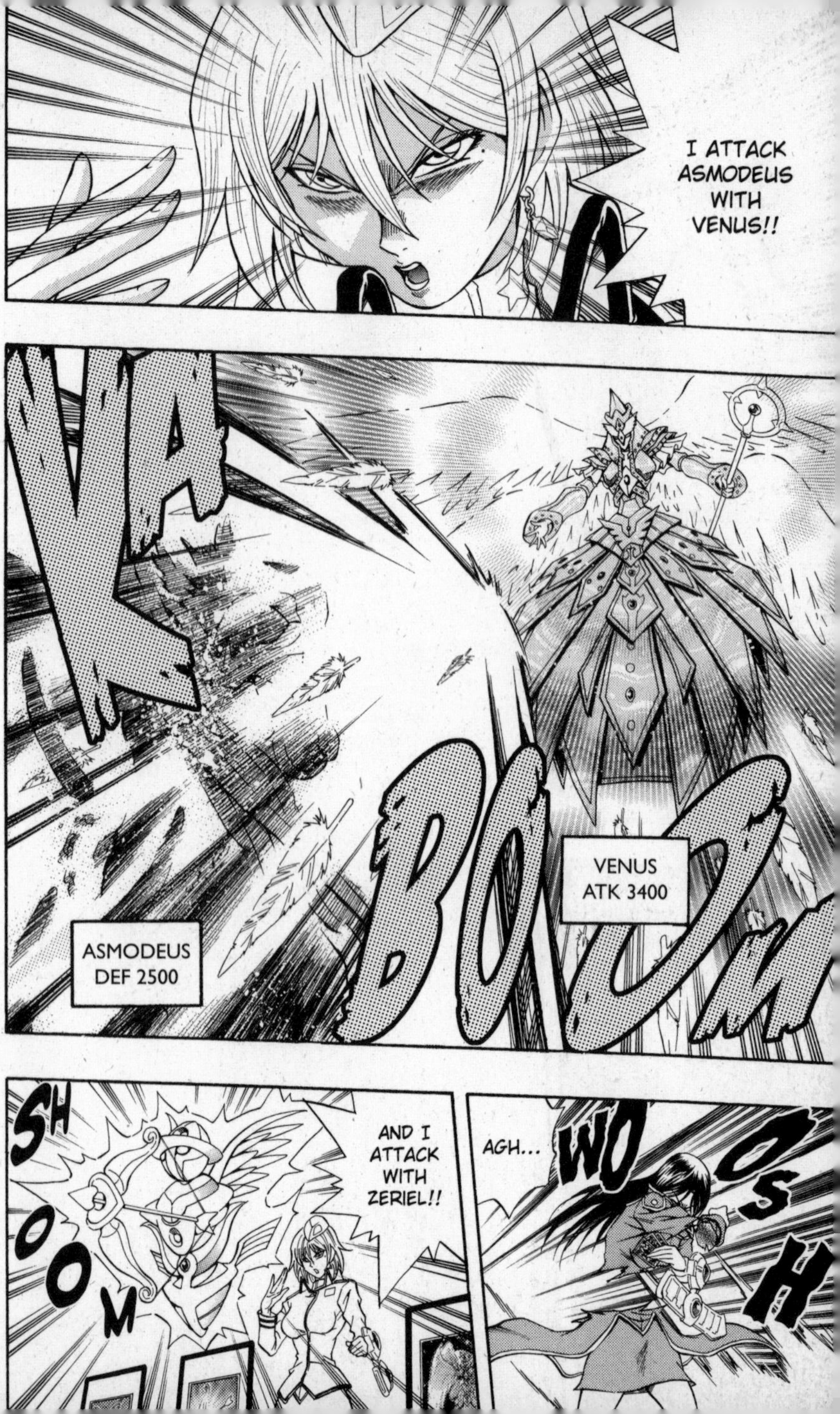
I ATTACK ASMODEUS WITH VENUS!!
VENUS ATK 3400
ASMODEUS DEF 2500
AGH...
WOOSH
AND I ATTACK WITH ZERIEL!!
SHOOM

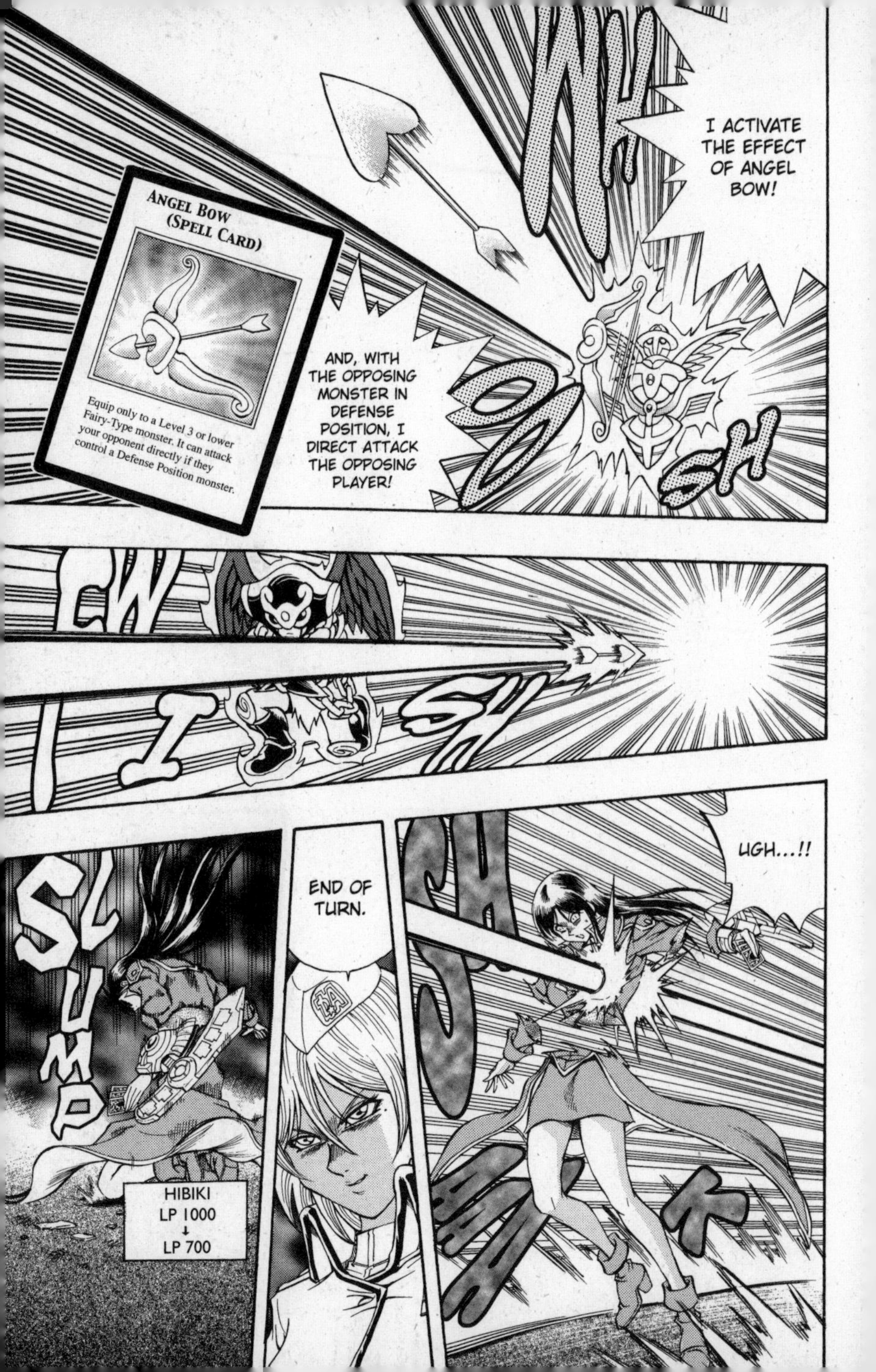
I ACTIVATE THE EFFECT OF ANGEL BOW!
AND, WITH THE OPPOSING MONSTER IN DEFENSE POSITION, I DIRECT ATTACK THE OPPOSING PLAYER!
ANGEL BOW (SPELL CARD)
Equip only to a Level 3 or lower Fairy-Type monster. It can attack your opponent directly if they control a Defense Position monster.
UGH...!!
END OF TURN.
SLUMP
HIBIKI
LP 1000
↓
LP 700

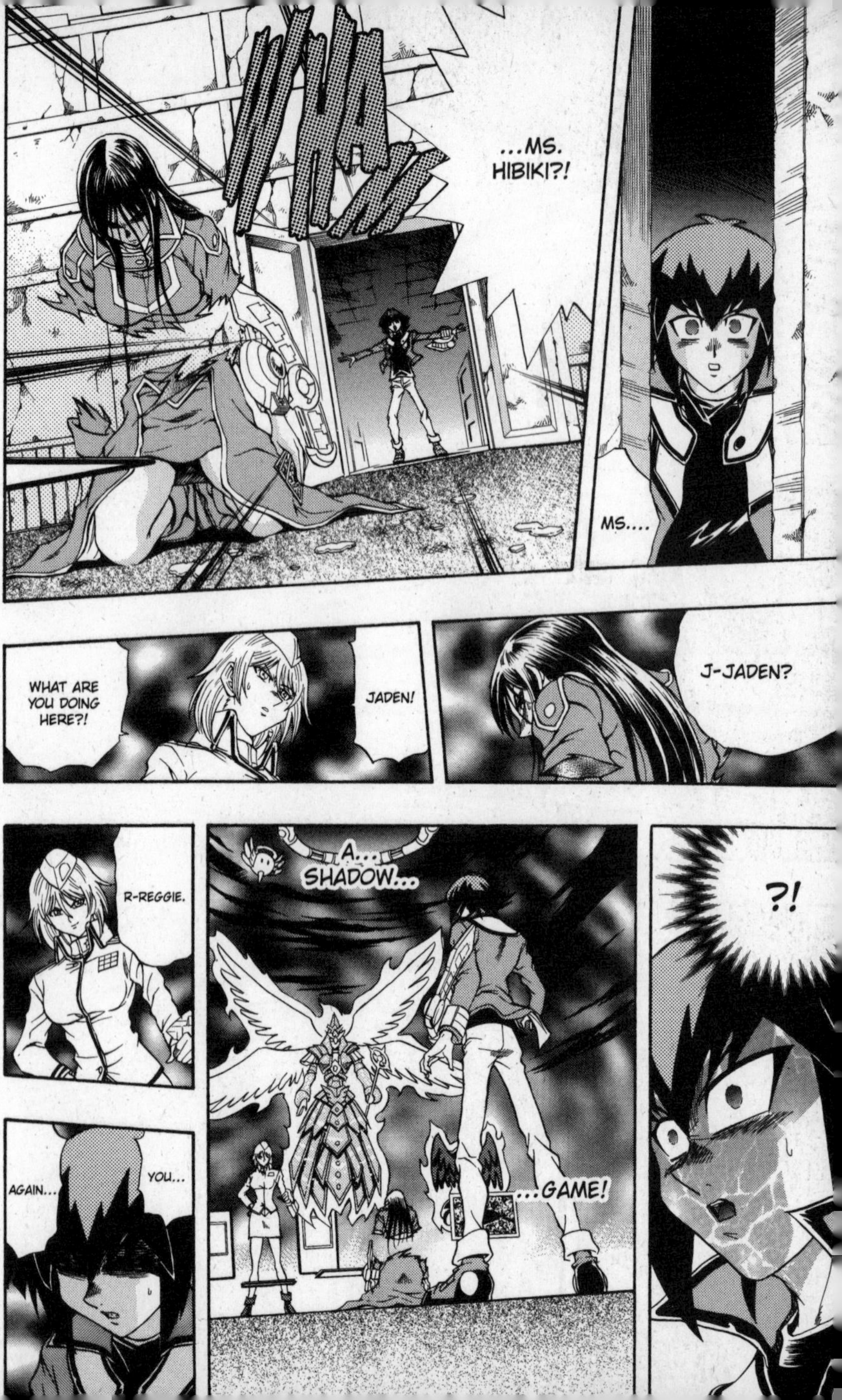
MS....
...MS. HIBIKI?!
J-JADEN?
JADEN!
WHAT ARE YOU DOING HERE?!
?!
A... SHADOW...
...GAME!
R-REGGIE.
YOU...
AGAIN...

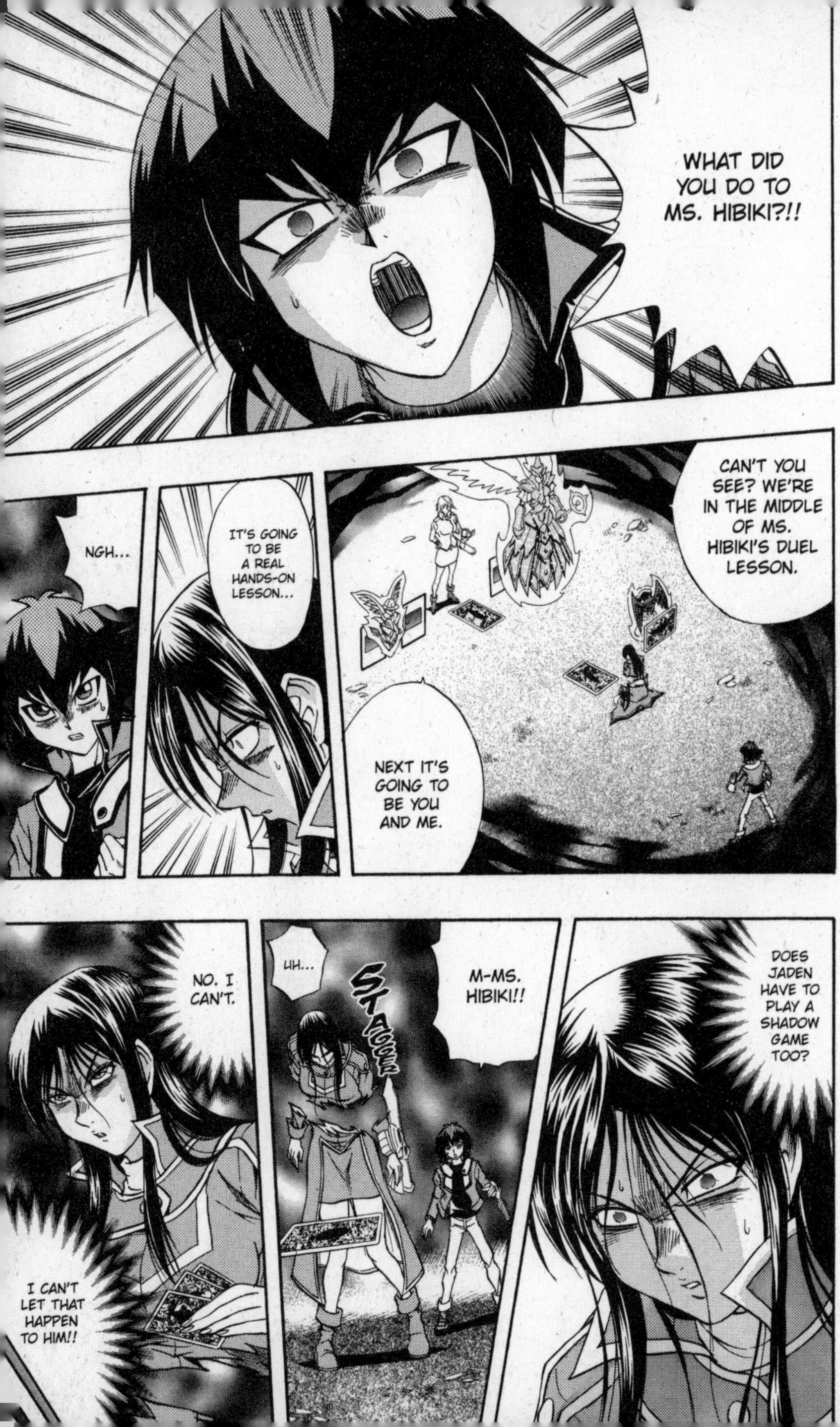
WHAT DID YOU DO TO MS. HIBIKI?!!
CAN'T YOU SEE? WE'RE IN THE MIDDLE OF MS. HIBIKI'S DUEL LESSON.
NEXT IT'S GOING TO BE YOU AND ME.
IT'S GOING TO BE A REAL HANDS-ON LESSON...
NGH...
DOES JADEN HAVE TO PLAY A SHADOW GAME TOO?
M-MS. HIBIKI!!
UH...
STAGGER
NO. I CAN'T.
I CAN'T LET THAT HAPPEN TO HIM!!

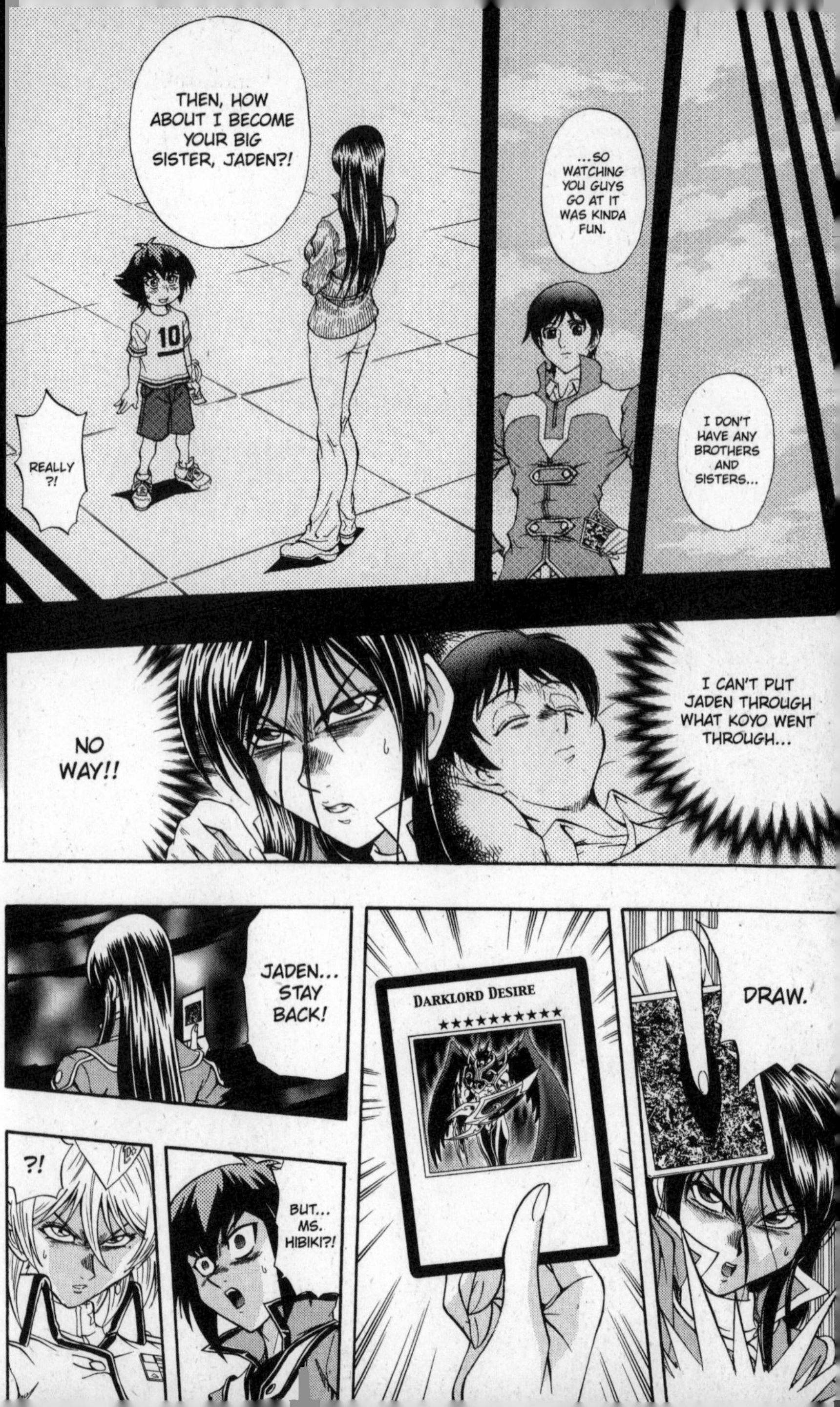
I DON'T HAVE ANY BROTHERS AND SISTERS...
...SO WATCHING YOU GUYS GO AT IT WAS KINDA FUN.
THEN, HOW ABOUT I BECOME YOUR BIG SISTER, JADEN?!
REALLY ?!
I CAN'T PUT JADEN THROUGH WHAT KOYO WENT THROUGH...
NO WAY!!
DRAW.
DARKLORD DESIRE
JADEN... STAY BACK!
BUT... MS. HIBIKI?!
?!

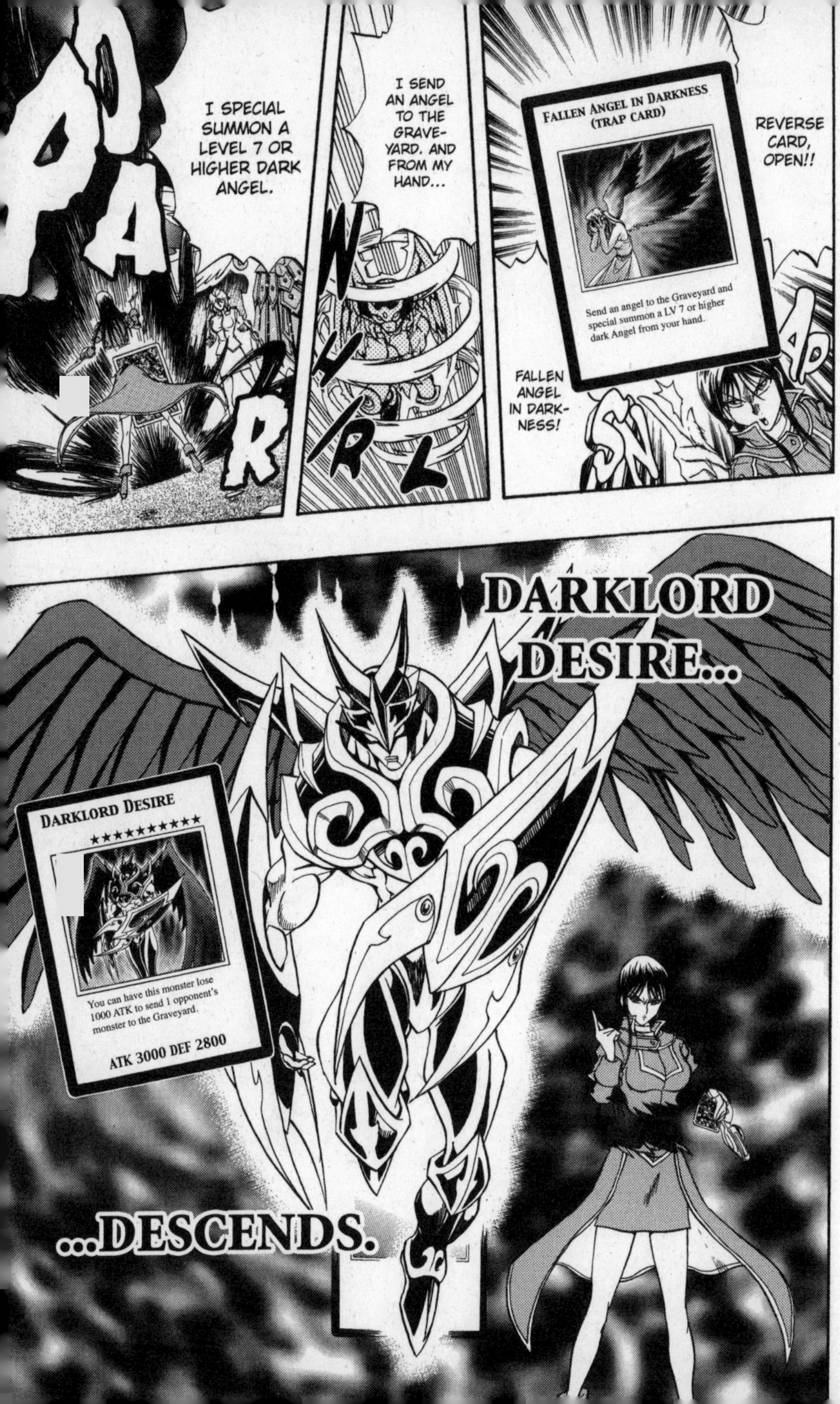
REVERSE CARD, OPEN!!
FALLEN ANGEL IN DARKNESS
(TRAP CARD)
Send an angel to the Graveyard and special summon a LV 7 or higher dark Angel from your hand.
FALLEN ANGEL IN DARKNESS!
I SEND AN ANGEL TO THE GRAVEYARD. AND FROM MY HAND...
WHIRL
I SPECIAL SUMMON A LEVEL 7 OR HIGHER DARK ANGEL.
DARKLORD DESIRE...
DARKLORD DESIRE
★★★★★★★★★★
You can have this monster lose 1000 ATK to send 1 opponent's monster to the Graveyard.
ATK 3000 DEF 2800
...DESCENDS.

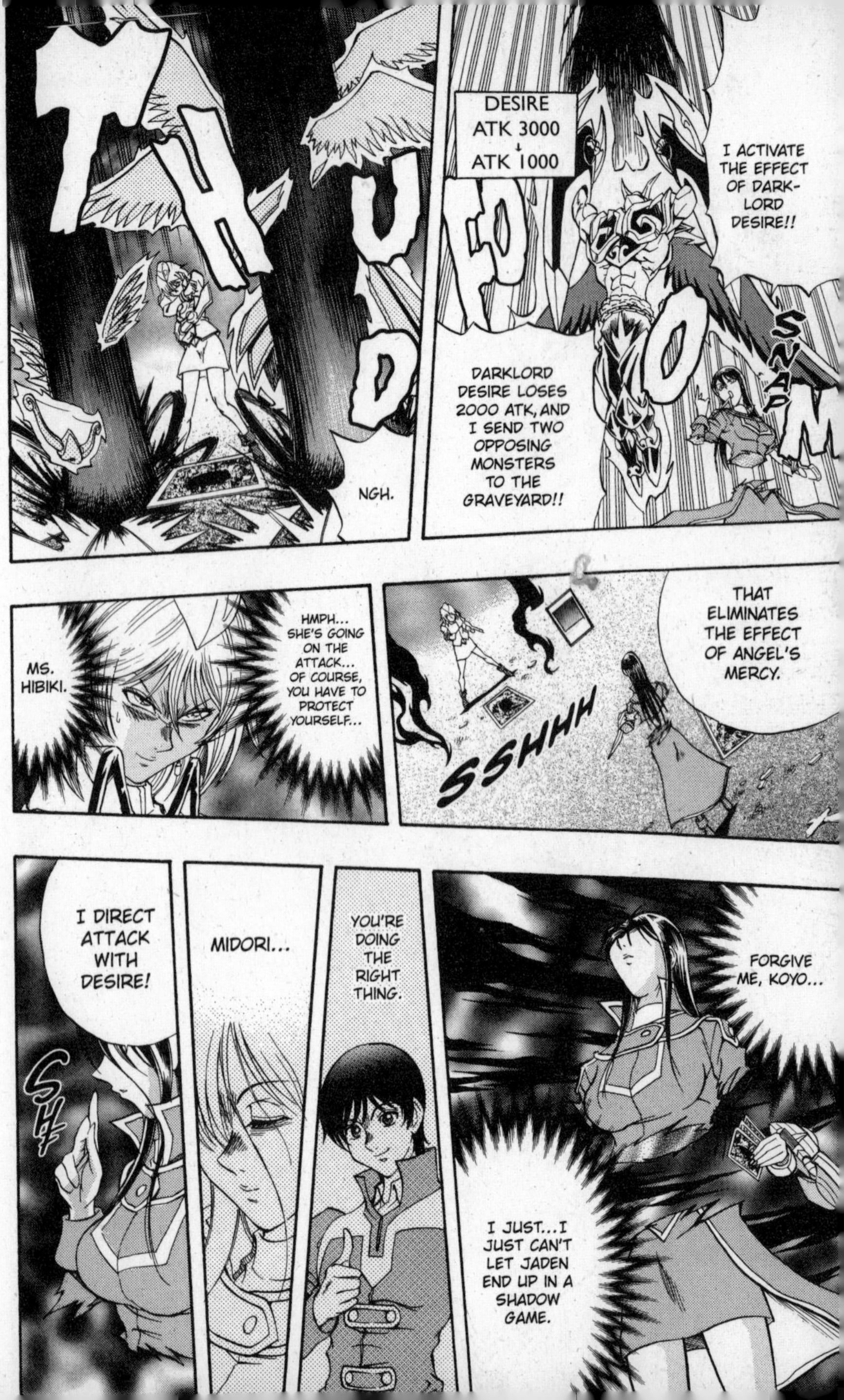
DESIRE
ATK 3000
↓
ATK 1000
I ACTIVATE THE EFFECT OF DARK-LORD DESIRE!!
SNAP
DARKLORD DESIRE LOSES 2000 ATK, AND I SEND TWO OPPOSING MONSTERS TO THE GRAVEYARD!!
THUD
NGH.
THAT ELIMINATES THE EFFECT OF ANGEL'S MERCY.
SSHHH
HMPH... SHE'S GOING ON THE ATTACK... OF COURSE, YOU HAVE TO PROTECT YOURSELF...
MS. HIBIKI.
FORGIVE ME, KOYO...
I JUST...I JUST CAN'T LET JADEN END UP IN A SHADOW GAME.
YOU'RE DOING THE RIGHT THING.
MIDORI...
I DIRECT ATTACK WITH DESIRE!

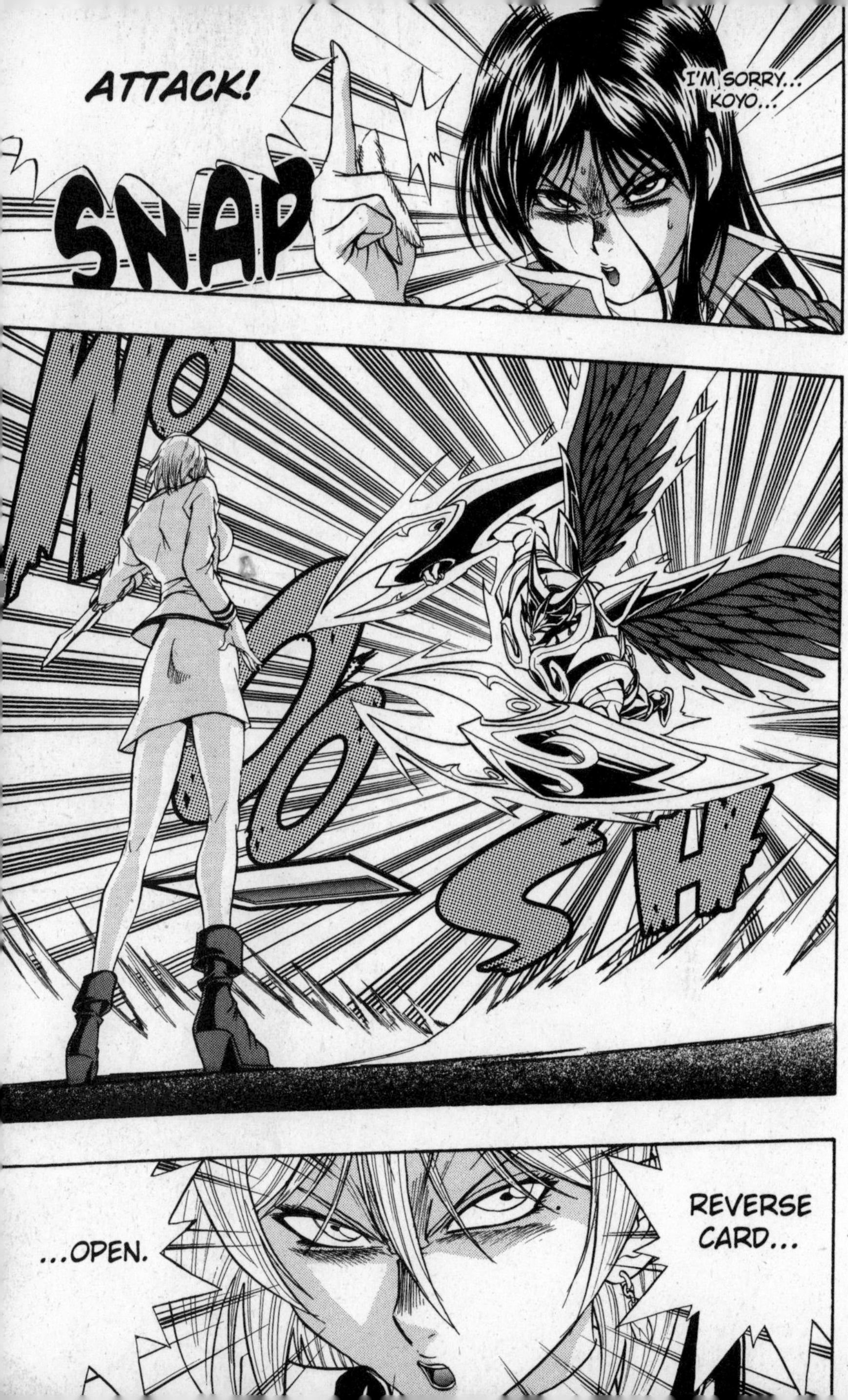
I'M SORRY... KOYO...!
ATTACK!
SNAP
WOOOSH
REVERSE CARD...
...OPEN.

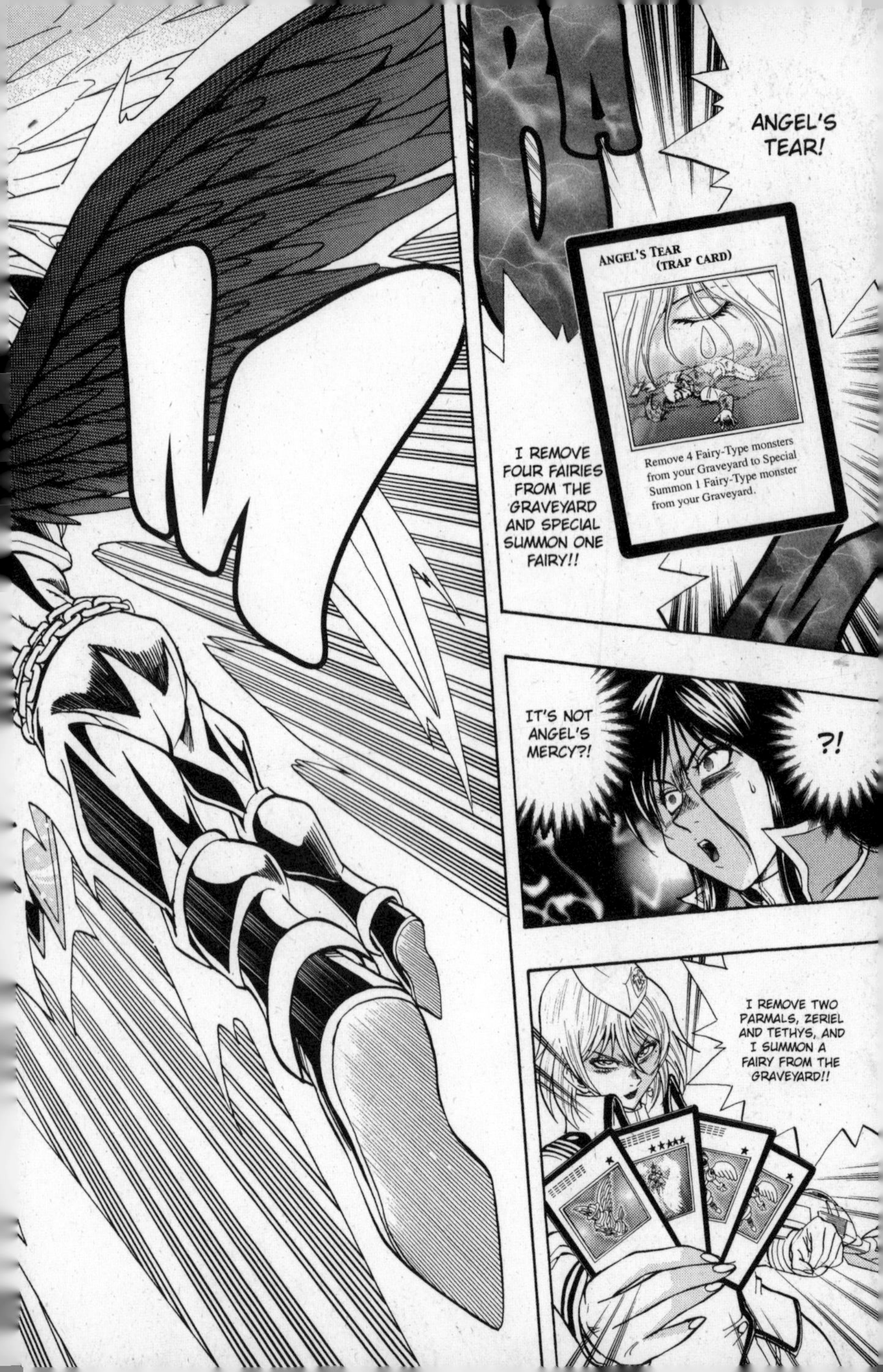
ANGEL'S TEAR!
ANGEL'S TEAR (TRAP CARD)
Remove 4 Fairy-Type monsters from your Graveyard to Special Summon 1 Fairy-Type monster from your Graveyard.
I REMOVE FOUR FAIRIES FROM THE GRAVEYARD AND SPECIAL SUMMON ONE FAIRY!!
?!
IT'S NOT ANGEL'S MERCY?!
I REMOVE TWO PARMALS, ZERIEL AND TETHYS, AND I SUMMON A FAIRY FROM THE GRAVEYARD!!

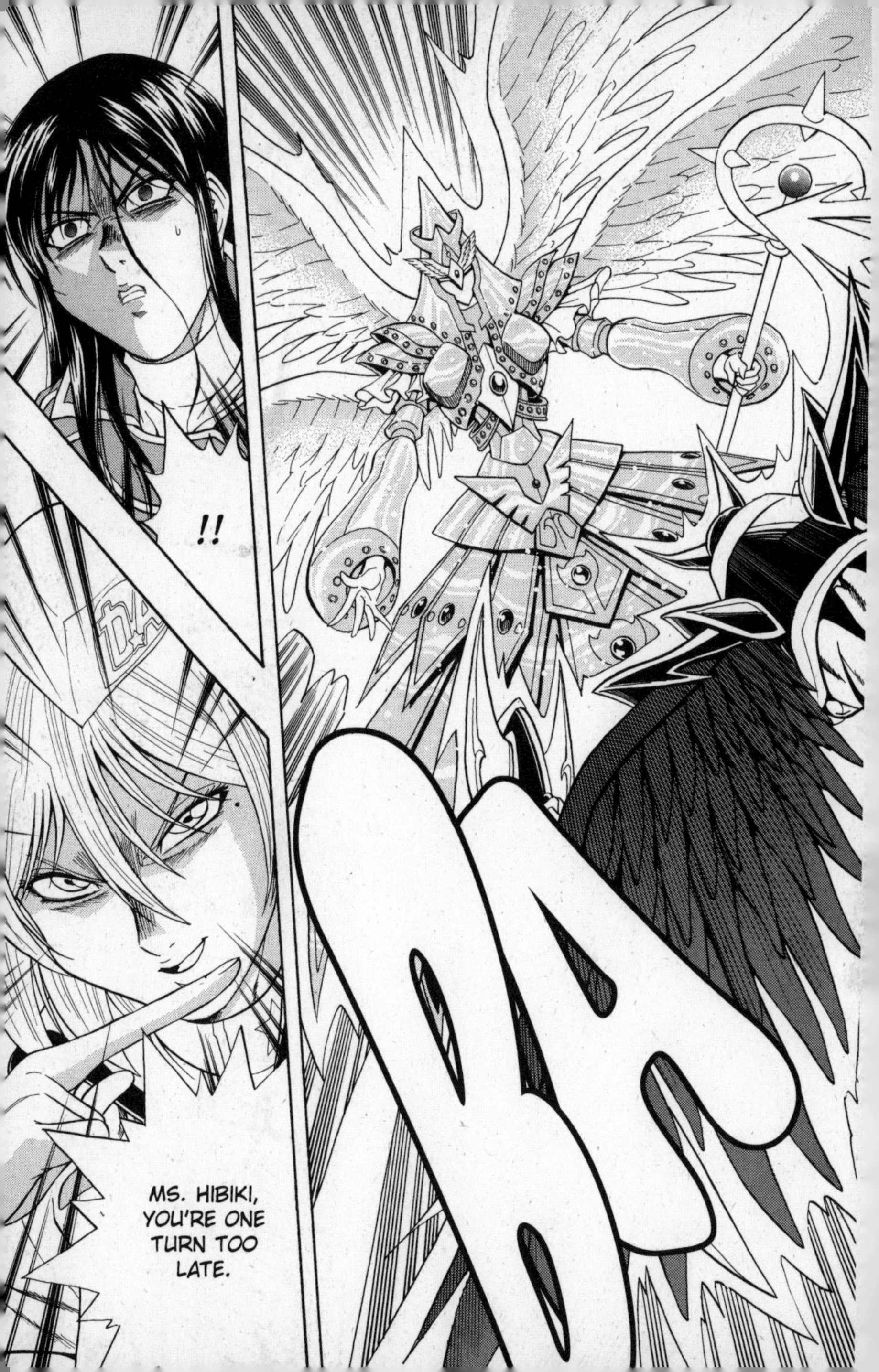
!!
MS. HIBIKI, YOU'RE ONE TURN TOO LATE.

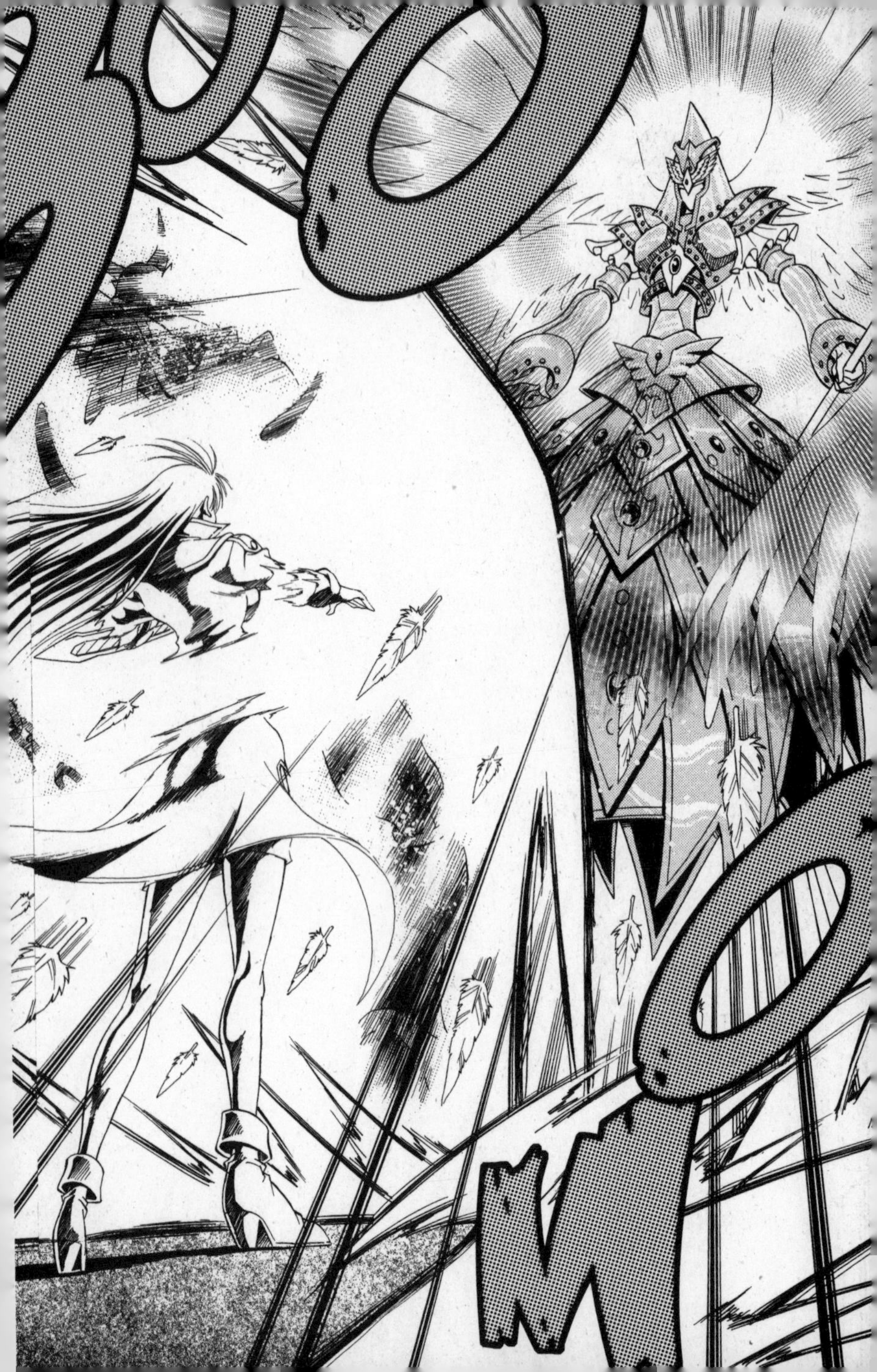

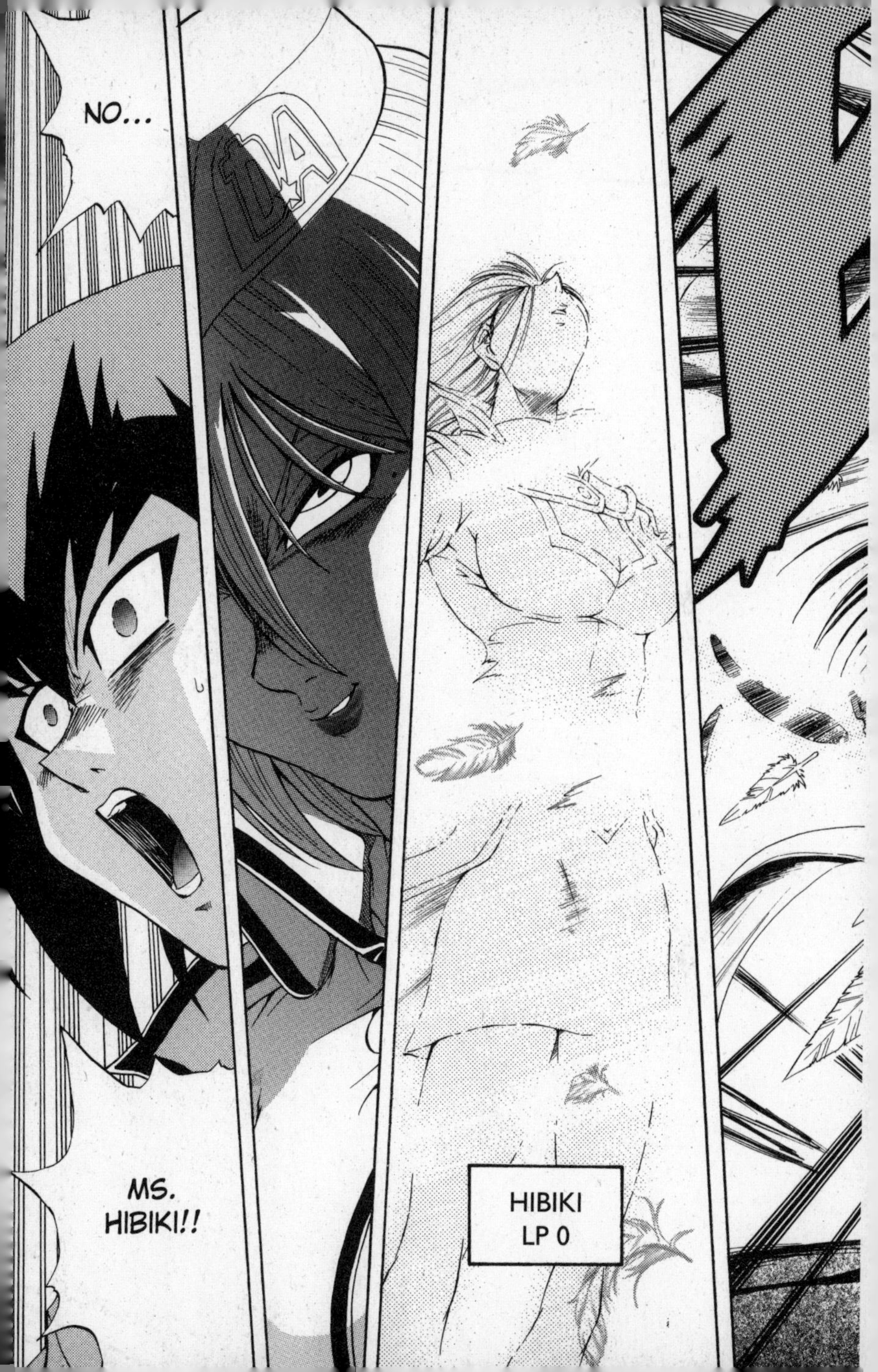
HIBIKI
LP 0
NO...
MS. HIBIKI!!

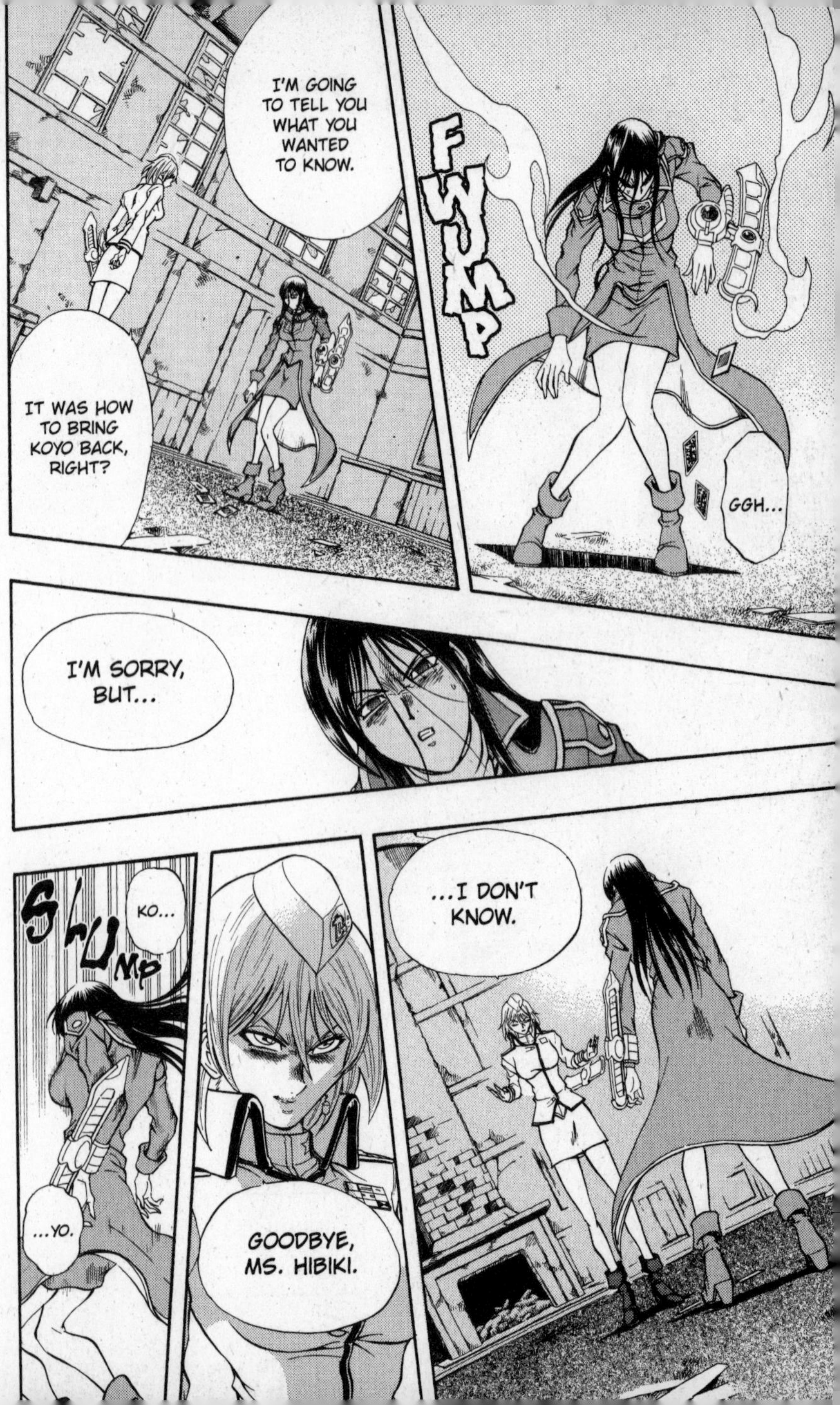
FWUMP
GGH...
I'M GOING TO TELL YOU WHAT YOU WANTED TO KNOW.
IT WAS HOW TO BRING KOYO BACK, RIGHT?
I'M SORRY, BUT...
...I DON'T KNOW.
GOODBYE, MS. HIBIKI.
KO...
SHUMP
...YO.

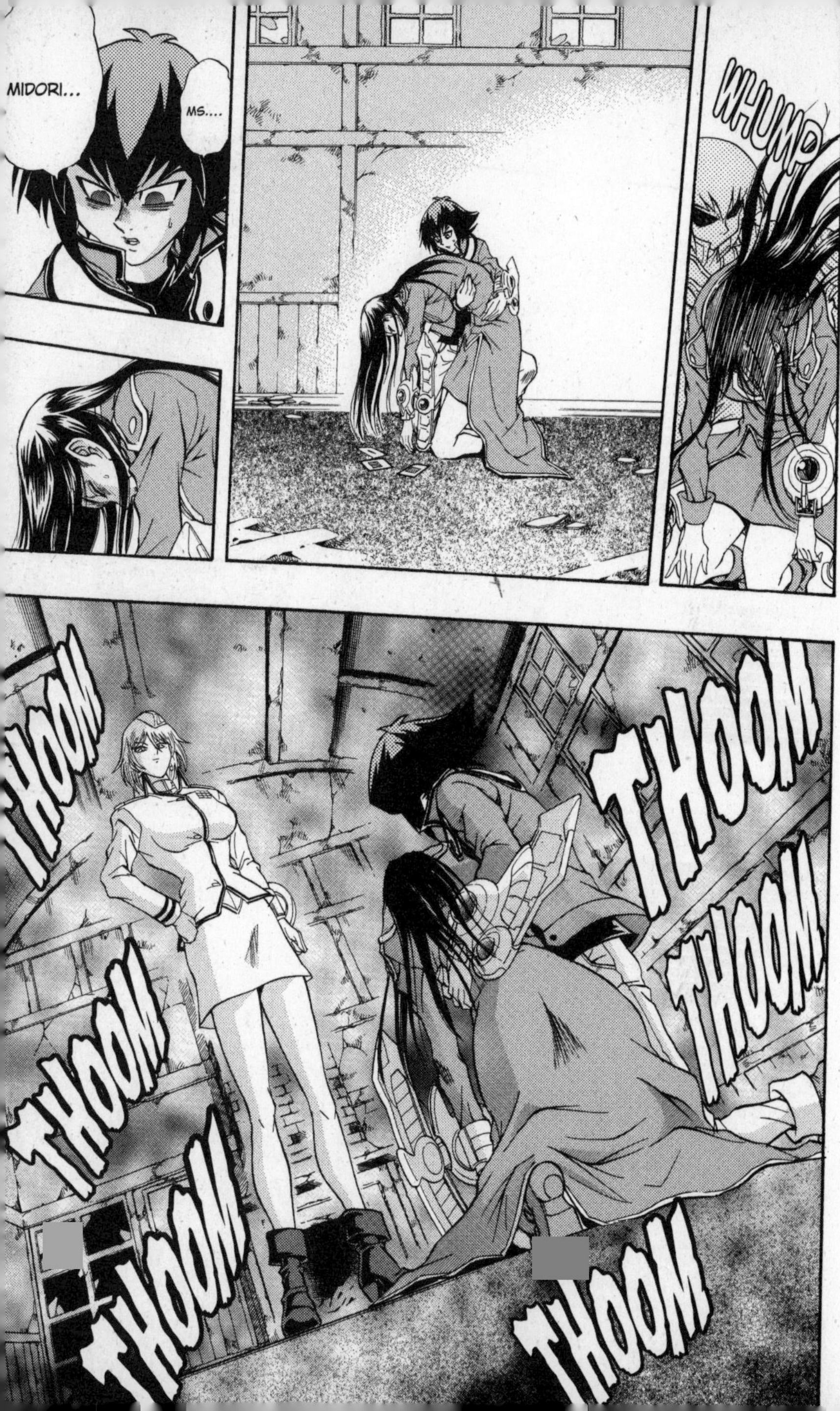
WHUMP
MS....
MIDORI...
THOOM
THOOM
THOOM
THOOM
THOOM
THOOM

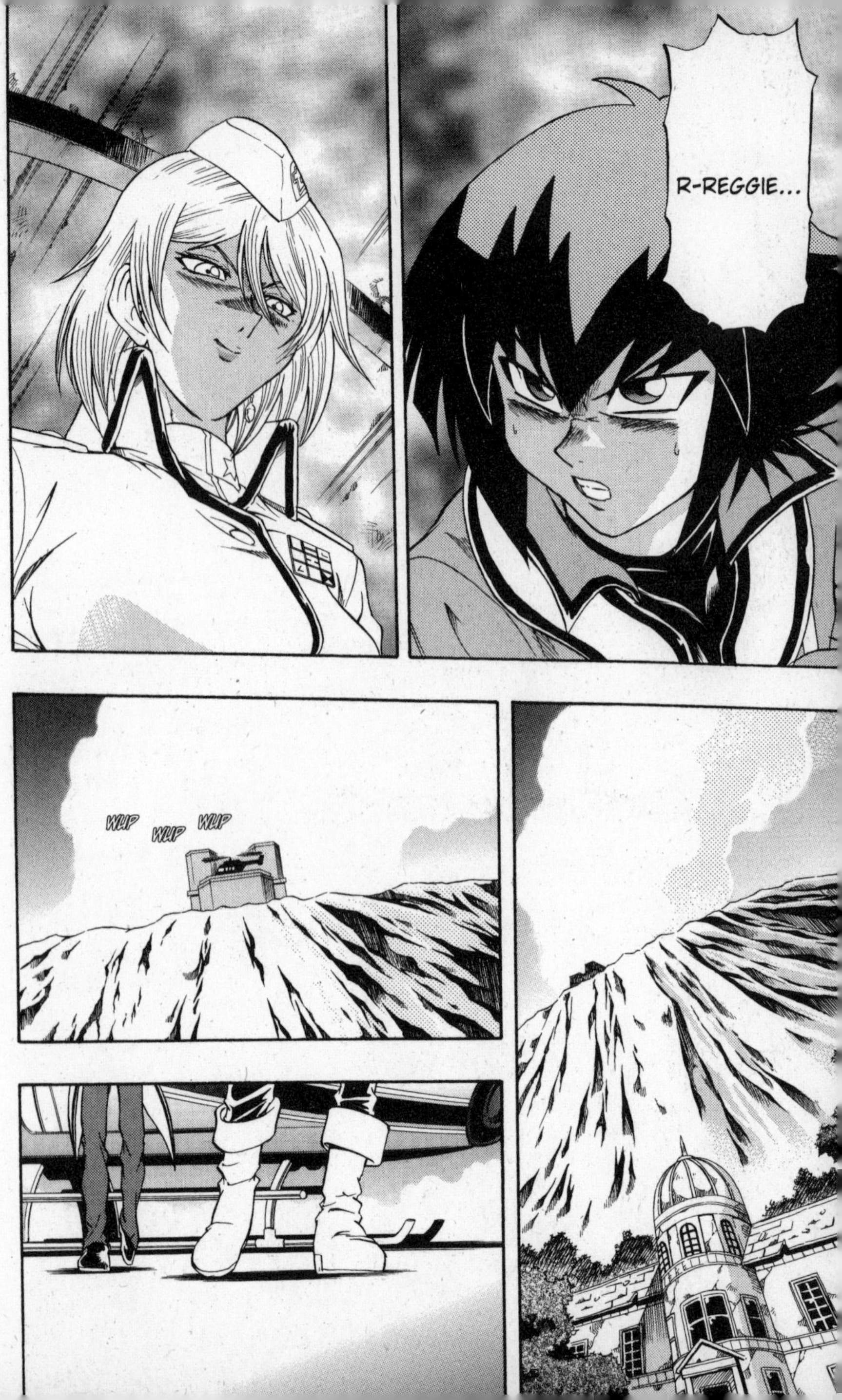
R-REGGIE...
WUP WUP WUP

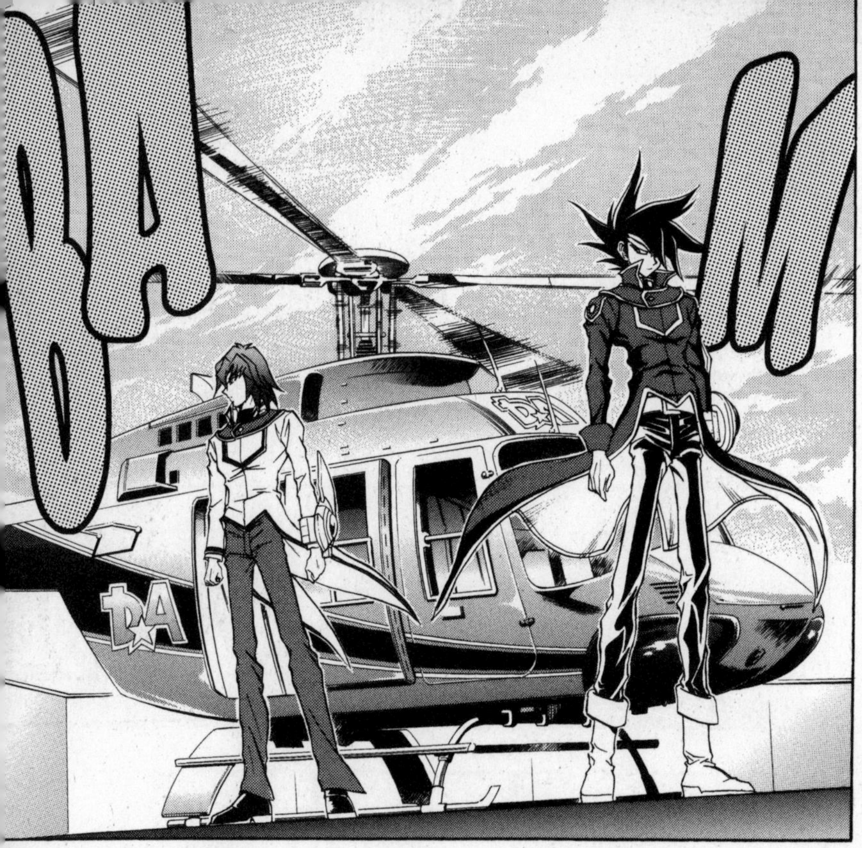
BAM

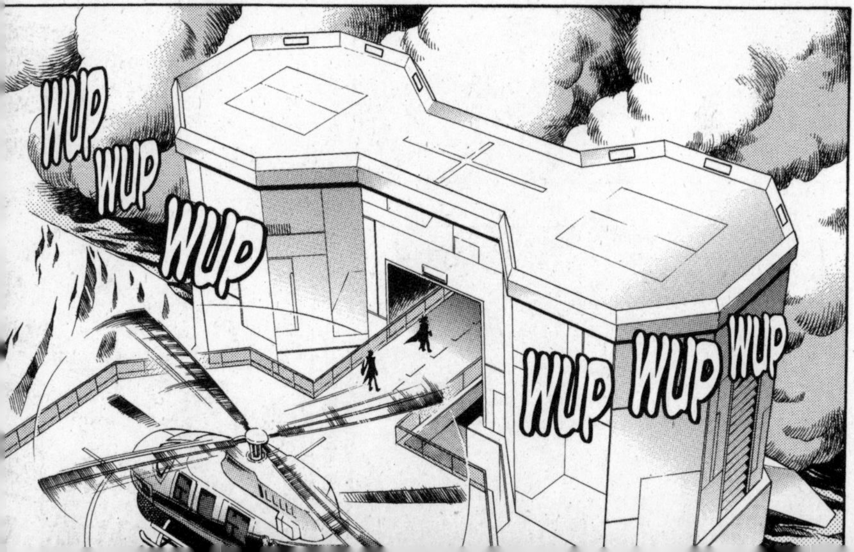
WUP WUP WUP
WUP WUP WUP

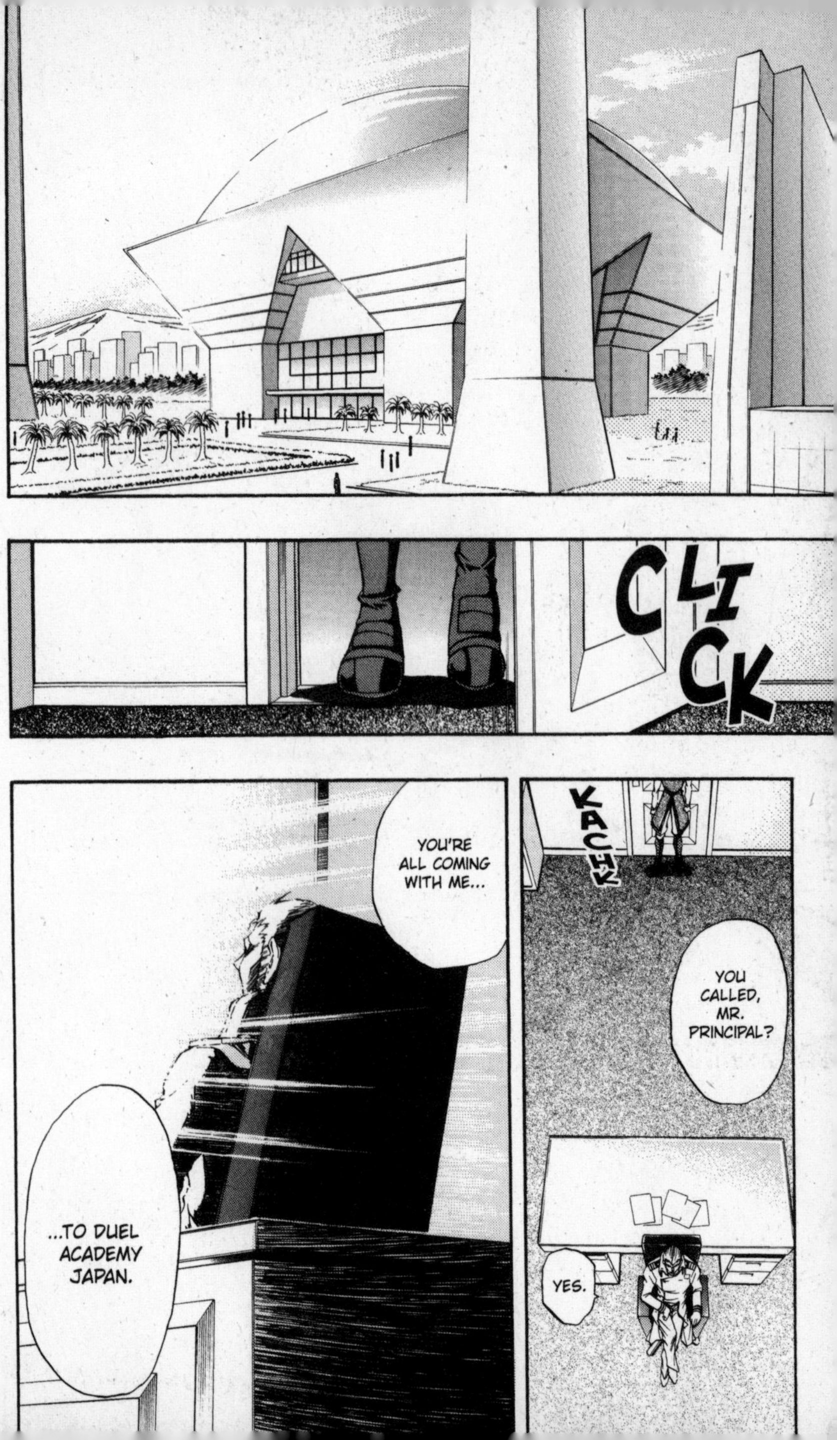
CLICK
KACHK
YOU CALLED, MR. PRINCIPAL?
YES.
YOU'RE ALL COMING WITH ME...
...TO DUEL ACADEMY JAPAN.

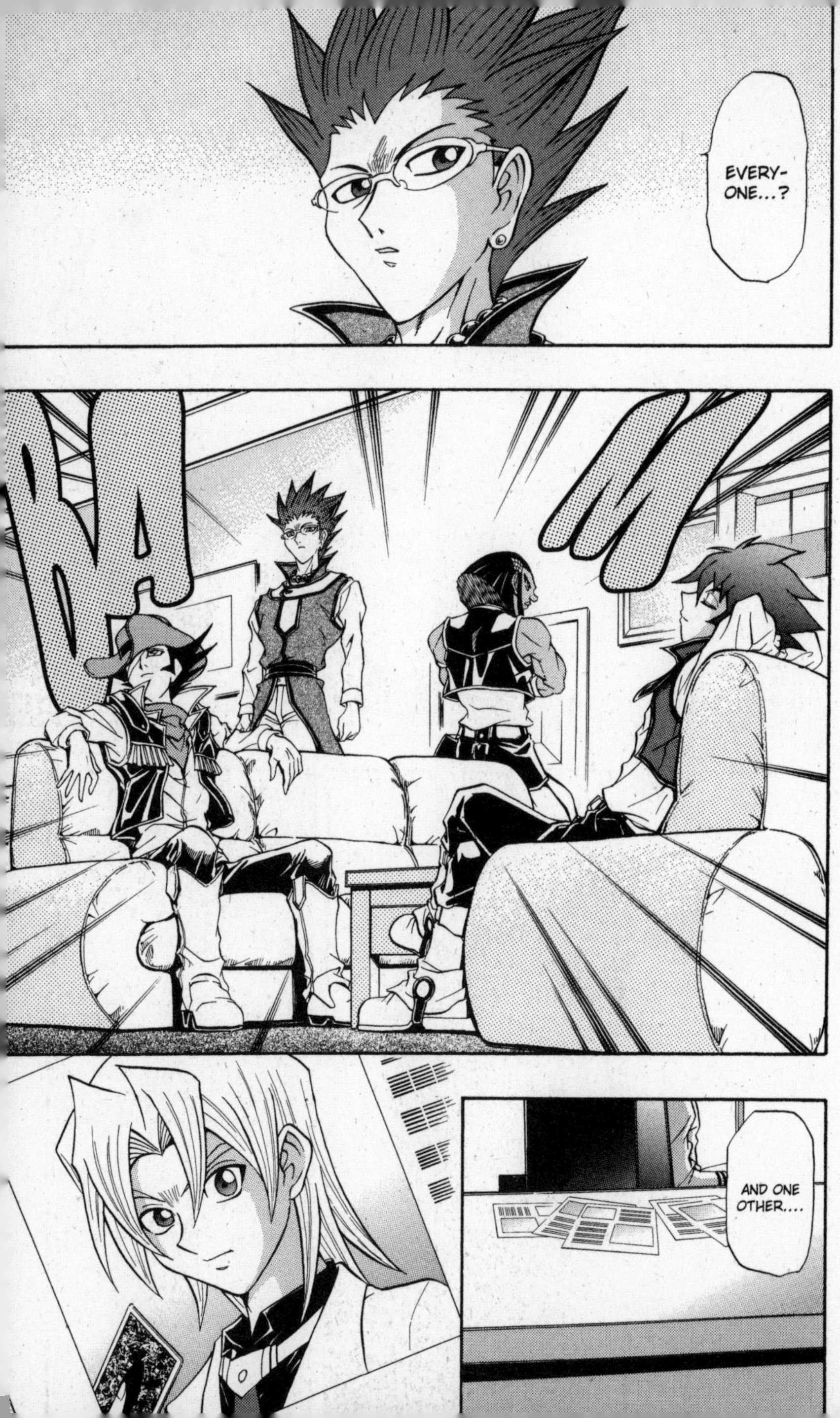
EVERY-
ONE...?
BAM
AND ONE
OTHER....

MOVING DAY

OCTOBER 2008
GOOD WORK TODAY, GUYS.
TODAY WAS OUR LAST DAY AT OUR OLD WORKPLACE, STUDIO DICE.
WE'D BEEN THERE SINCE AROUND THE END OF THE PEGASUS STORY ARC, SO...
...ABOUT TEN YEARS.
YU-GI-OH!, YU-GI-OH! R, YU-GI-OH! GX...
CLICK
LIONS
WE MADE THEM ALL IN THIS STUDIO.
THANKS FOR ALL YOUR HARD WORK, STUDIO.

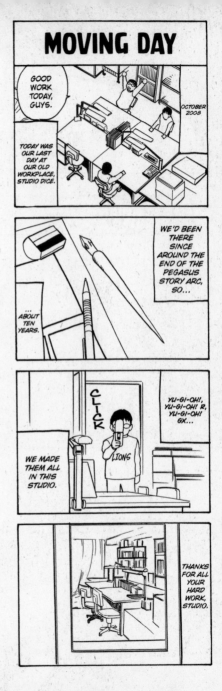

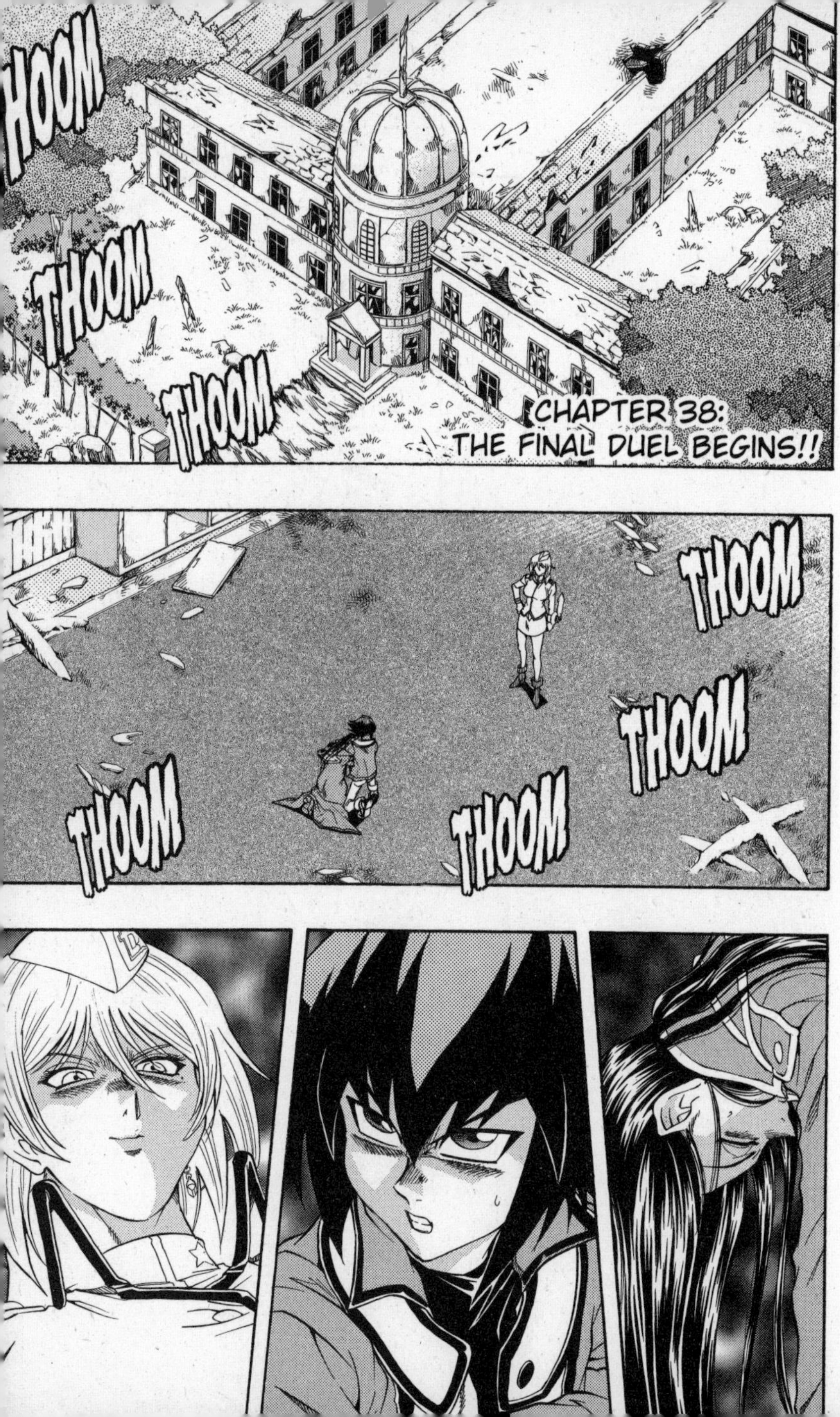
HOOM
THOOM
THOOM
CHAPTER 38:
THE FINAL DUEL BEGINS!!
THOOM
THOOM
THOOM
THOOM

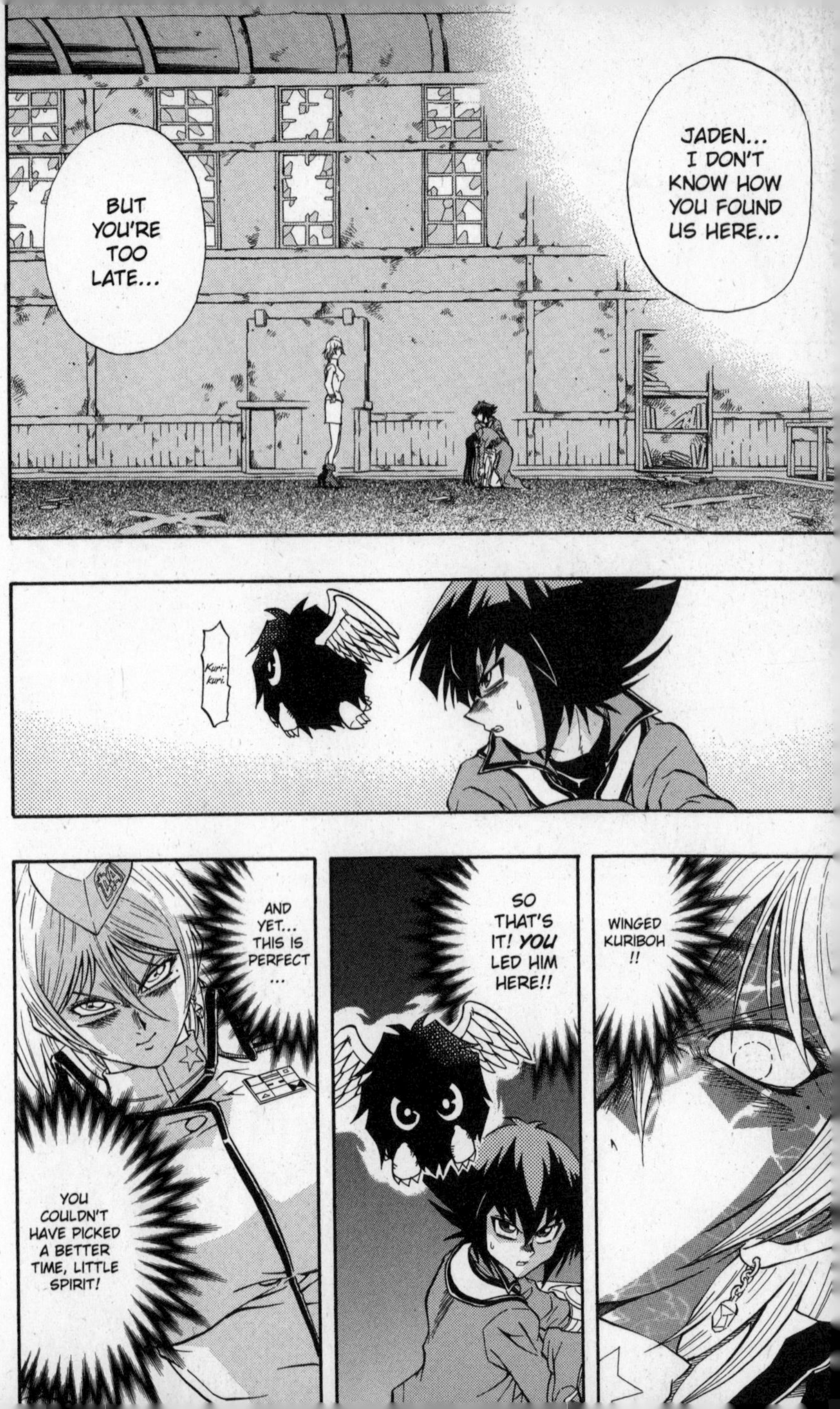
JADEN... I DON'T KNOW HOW YOU FOUND US HERE...
BUT YOU'RE TOO LATE...
Kuri-kuri.
WINGED KURIBOH !!
SO THAT'S IT! ***YOU*** LED HIM HERE!!
AND YET... THIS IS PERFECT ...
YOU COULDN'T HAVE PICKED A BETTER TIME, LITTLE SPIRIT!

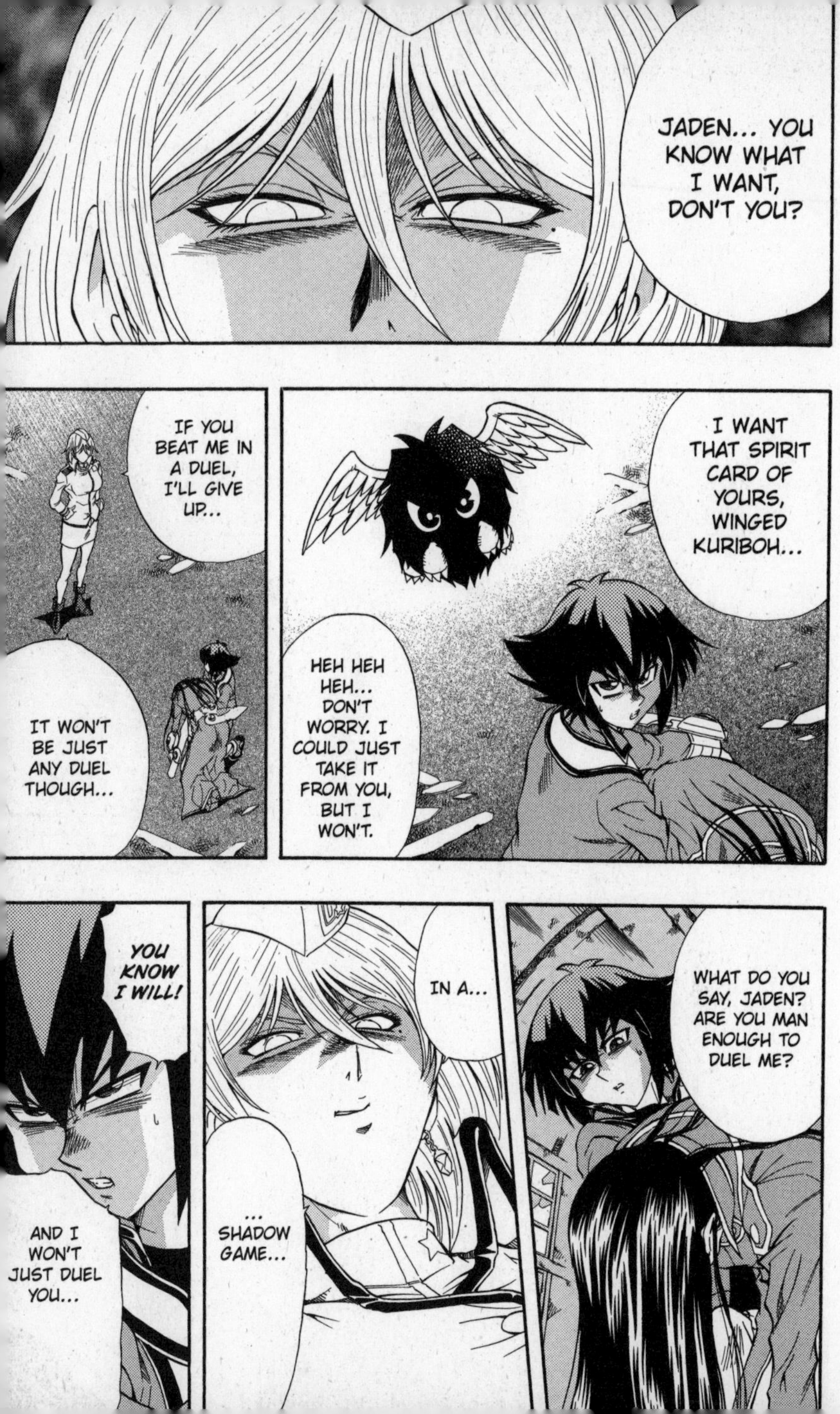
JADEN... YOU KNOW WHAT I WANT, DON'T YOU?
I WANT THAT SPIRIT CARD OF YOURS, WINGED KURIBOH...
HEH HEH HEH... DON'T WORRY. I COULD JUST TAKE IT FROM YOU, BUT I WON'T.
IF YOU BEAT ME IN A DUEL, I'LL GIVE UP...
IT WON'T BE JUST ANY DUEL THOUGH...
WHAT DO YOU SAY, JADEN? ARE YOU MAN ENOUGH TO DUEL ME?
IN A...
...SHADOW GAME...
YOU KNOW I WILL!
AND I WON'T JUST DUEL YOU...

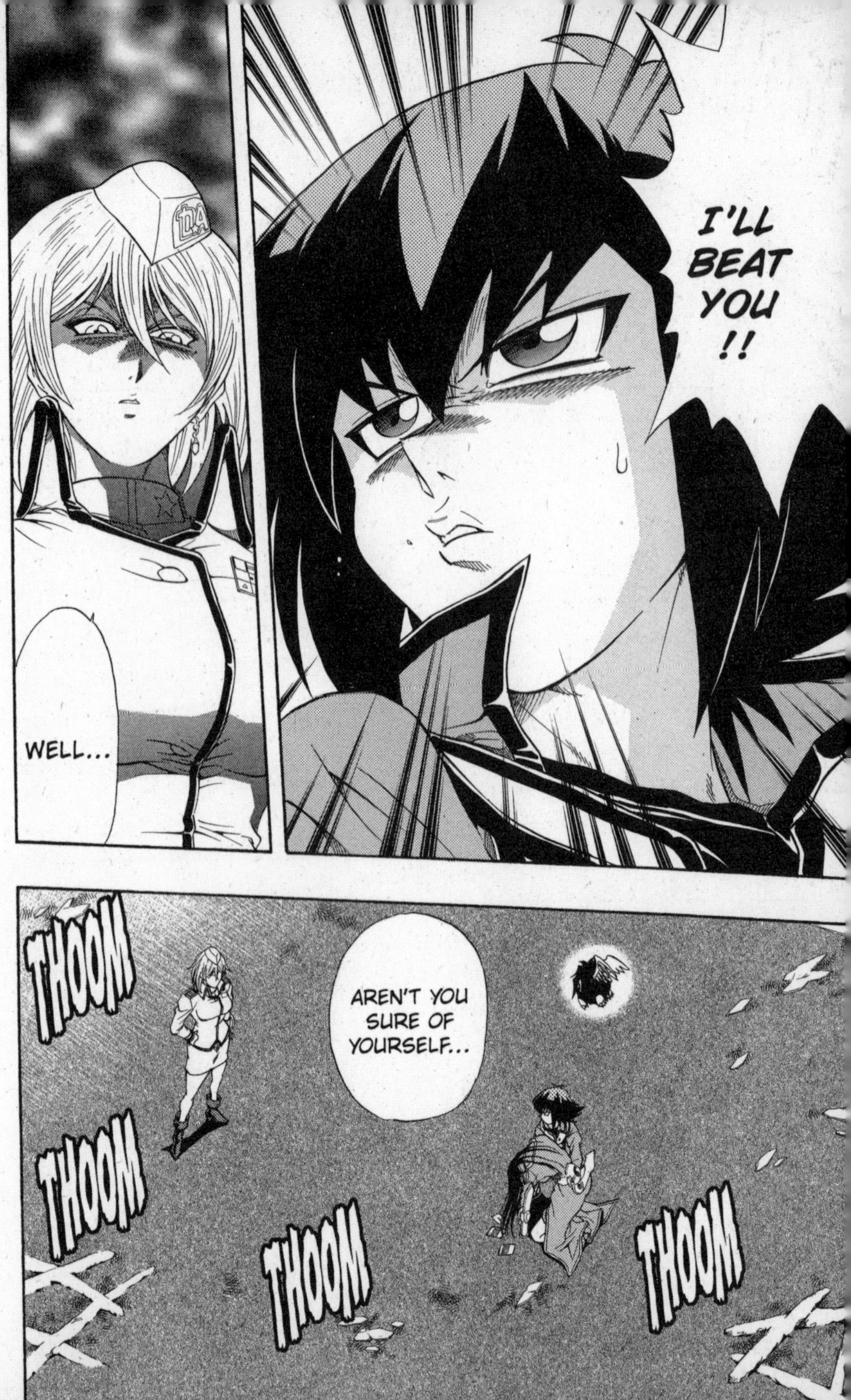
I'LL BEAT YOU !!
WELL...
AREN'T YOU SURE OF YOURSELF...
THOOM
THOOM
THOOM
THOOM

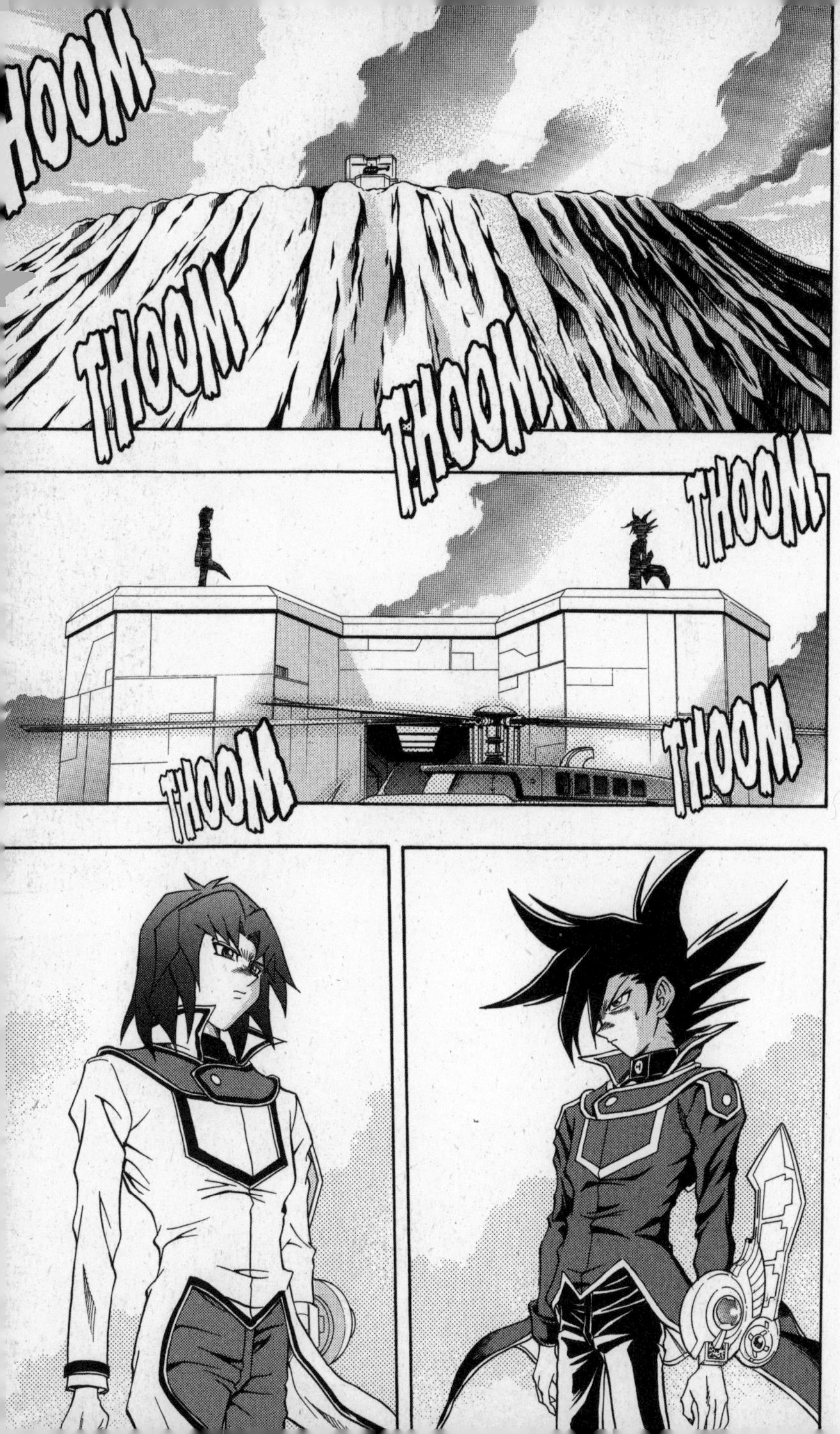
THOOM
THOOM
THOOM
THOOM
THOOM
THOOM
THOOM

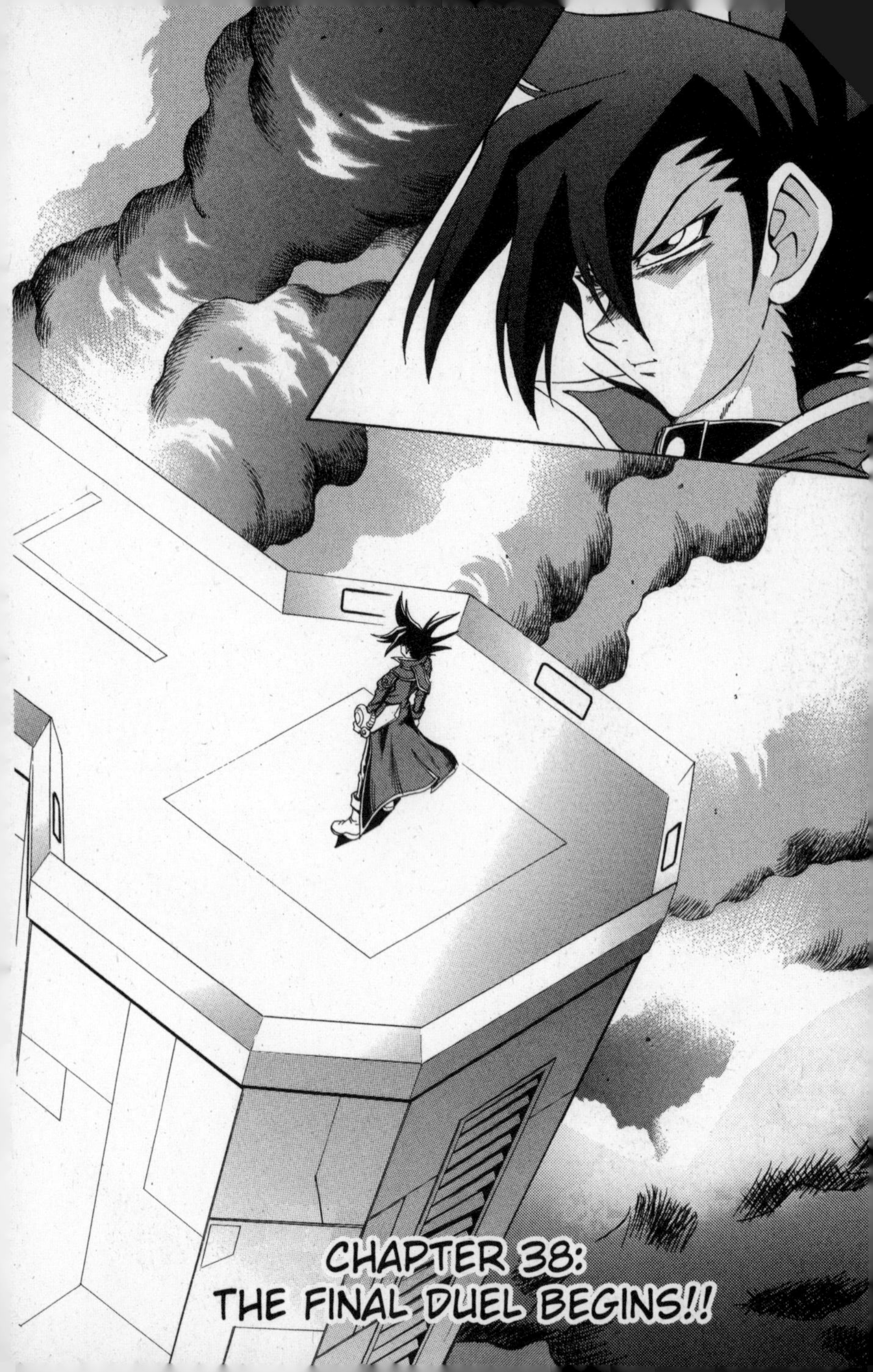
CHAPTER 38:
THE FINAL DUEL BEGINS!!

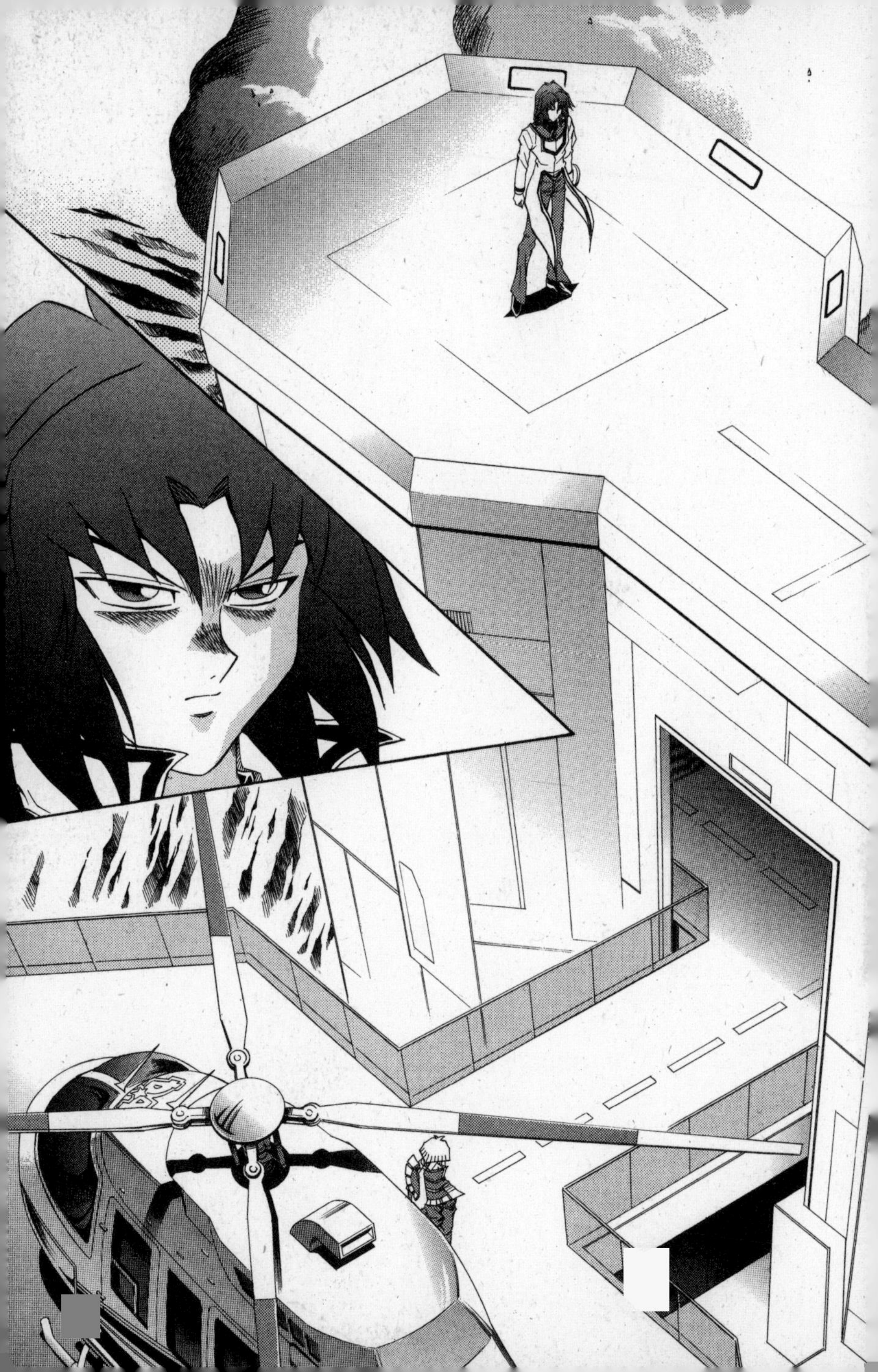

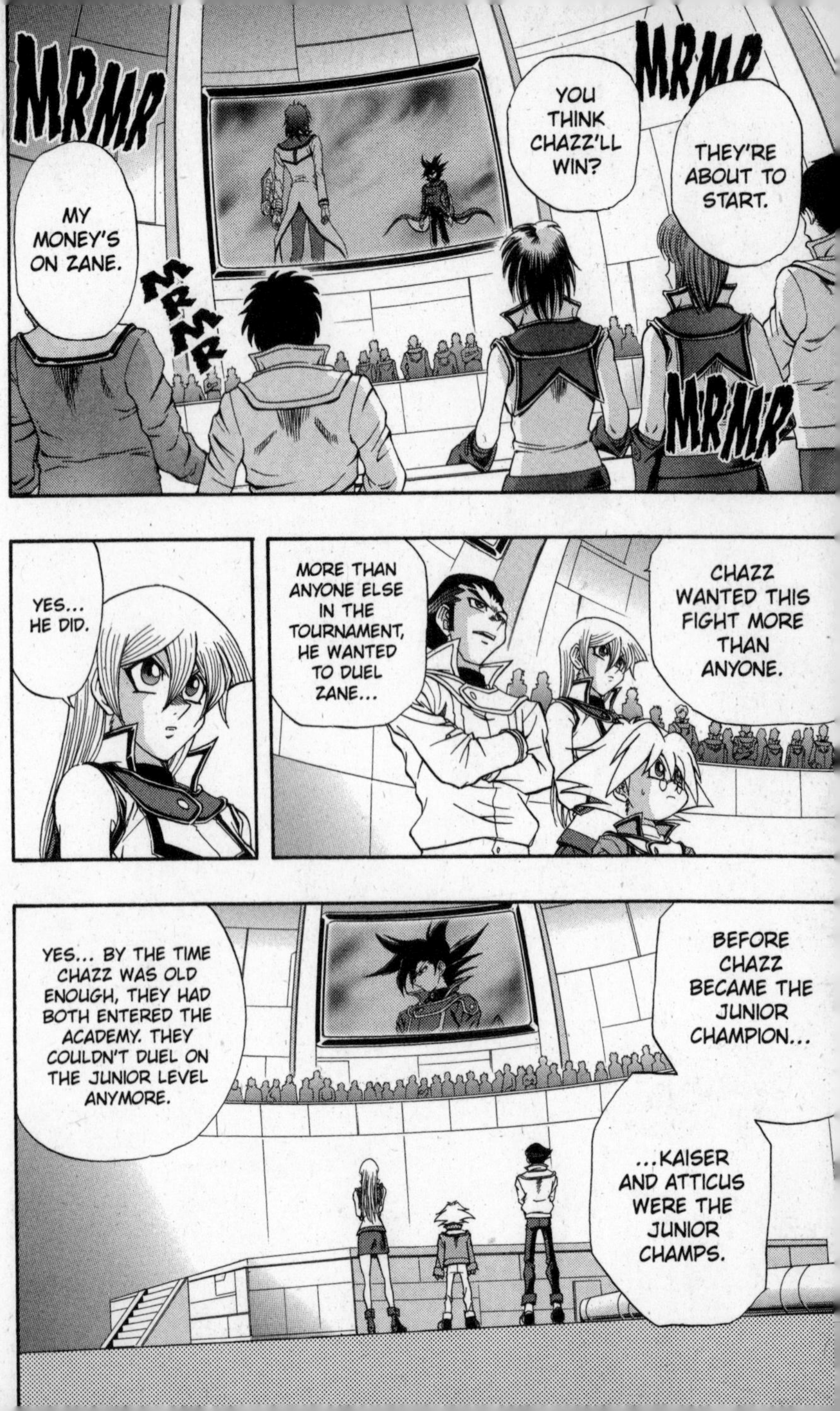
MRMR
THEY'RE ABOUT TO START.
YOU THINK CHAZZ'LL WIN?
MRMR
MY MONEY'S ON ZANE.
MRMR
MRMR
CHAZZ WANTED THIS FIGHT MORE THAN ANYONE.
MORE THAN ANYONE ELSE IN THE TOURNAMENT, HE WANTED TO DUEL ZANE...
YES... HE DID.
BEFORE CHAZZ BECAME THE JUNIOR CHAMPION...
...KAISER AND ATTICUS WERE THE JUNIOR CHAMPS.
YES... BY THE TIME CHAZZ WAS OLD ENOUGH, THEY HAD BOTH ENTERED THE ACADEMY. THEY COULDN'T DUEL ON THE JUNIOR LEVEL ANYMORE.

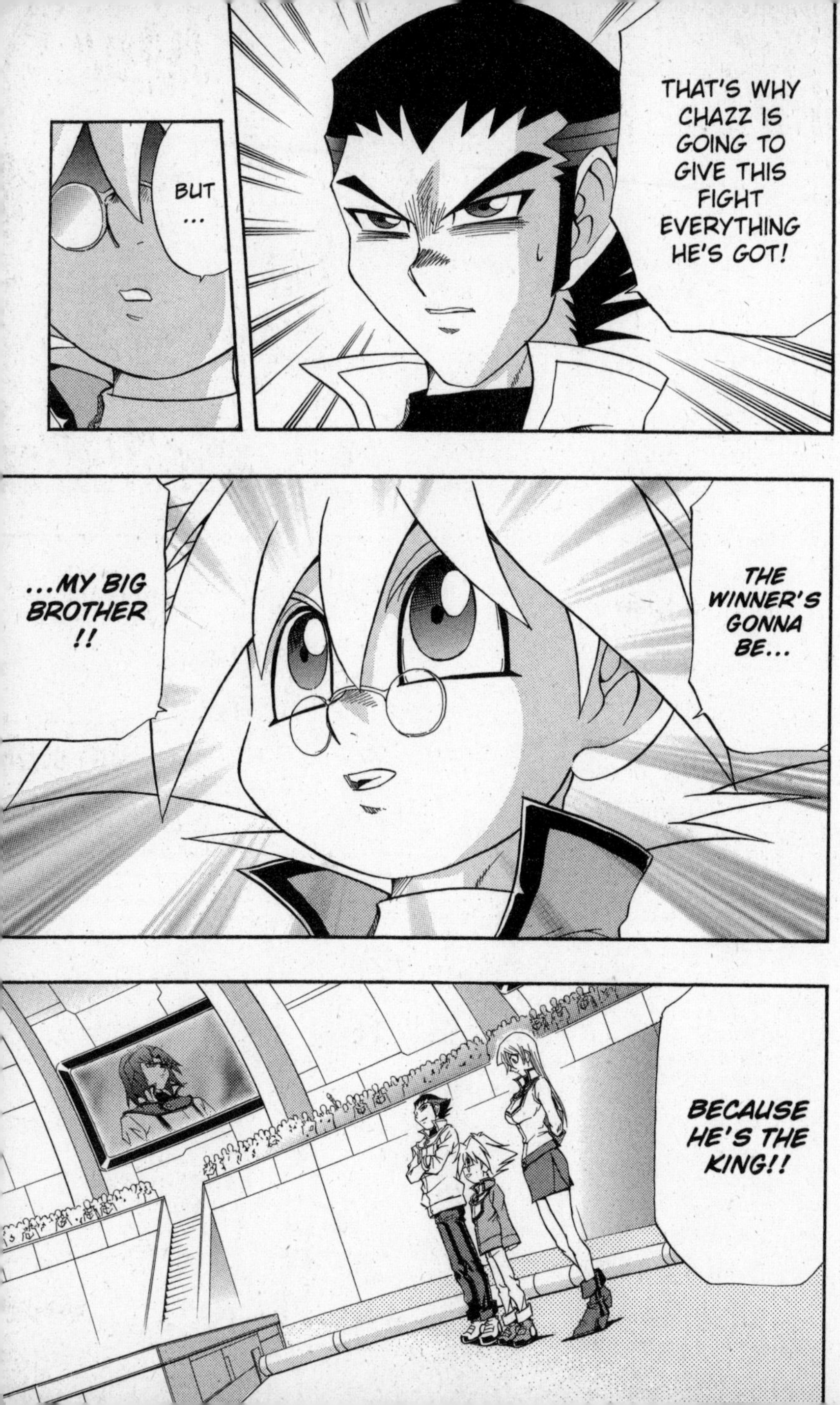
THAT'S WHY CHAZZ IS GOING TO GIVE THIS FIGHT EVERYTHING HE'S GOT!
BUT ...
THE WINNER'S GONNA BE...
...MY BIG BROTHER !!
BECAUSE HE'S THE KING!!

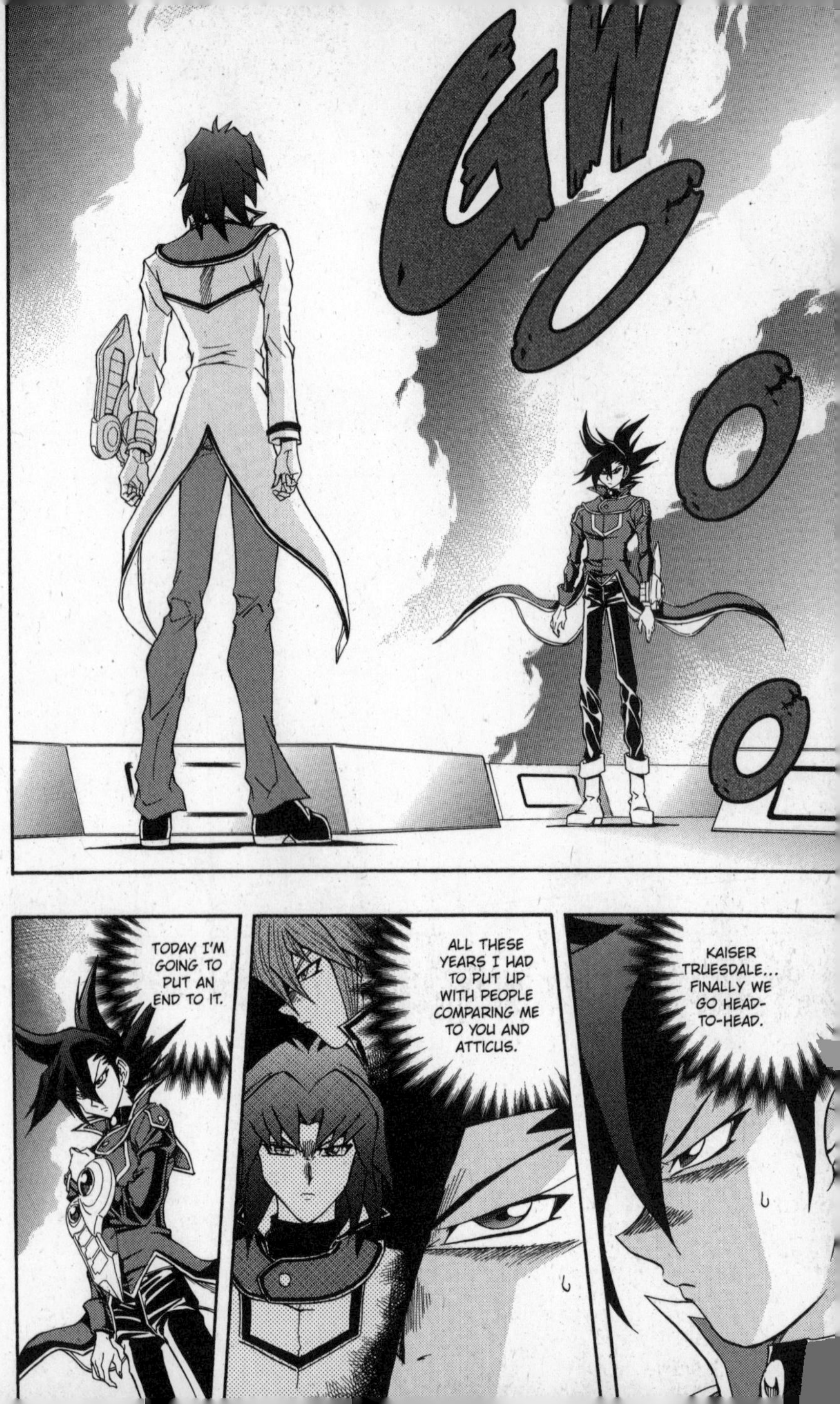
GWOOO
KAISER TRUESDALE... FINALLY WE GO HEAD-TO-HEAD.
ALL THESE YEARS I HAD TO PUT UP WITH PEOPLE COMPARING ME TO YOU AND ATTICUS.
TODAY I'M GOING TO PUT AN END TO IT.

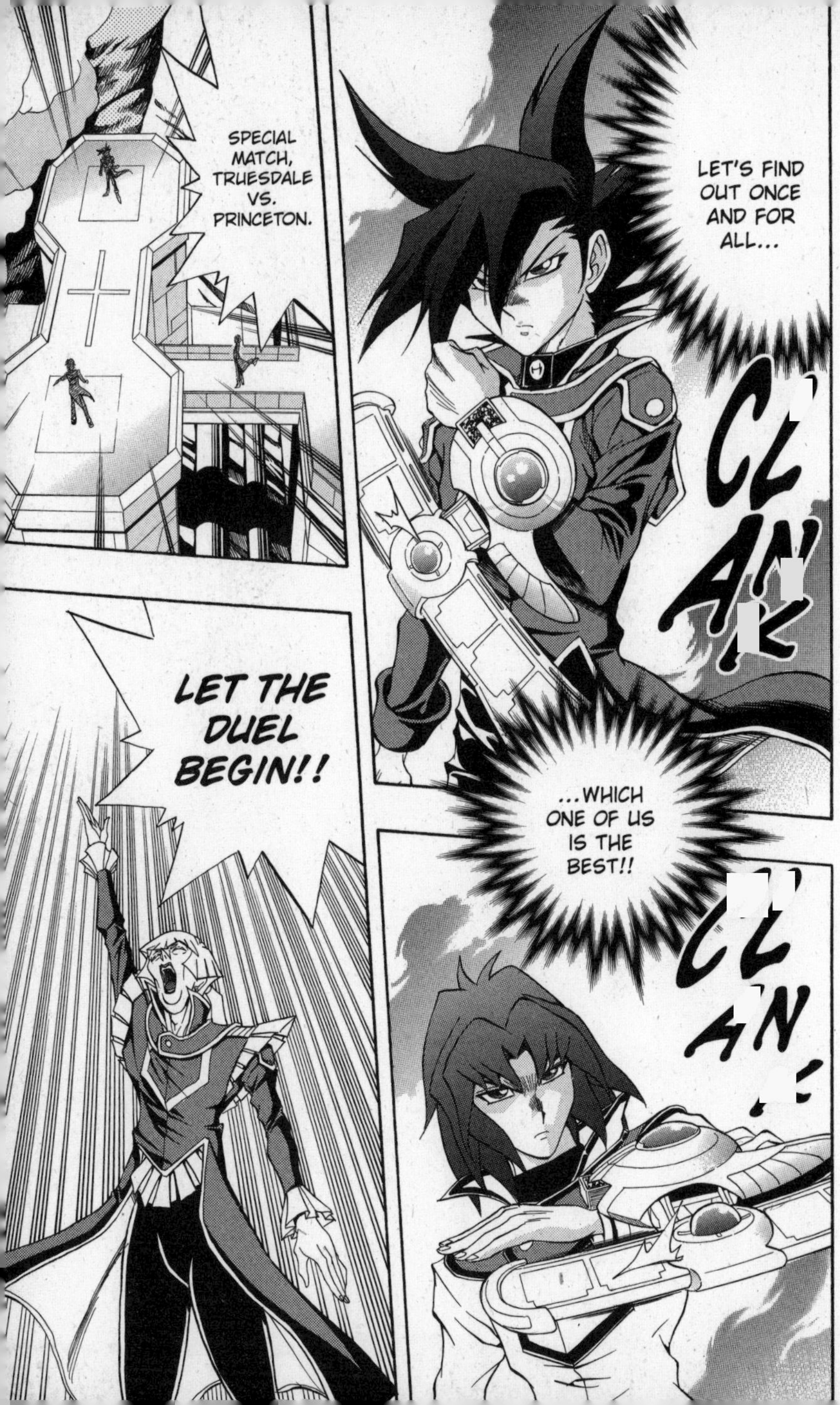
LET'S FIND OUT ONCE AND FOR ALL...
CLANK
SPECIAL MATCH, TRUESDALE VS. PRINCETON.
...WHICH ONE OF US IS THE BEST!!
LET THE DUEL BEGIN!!

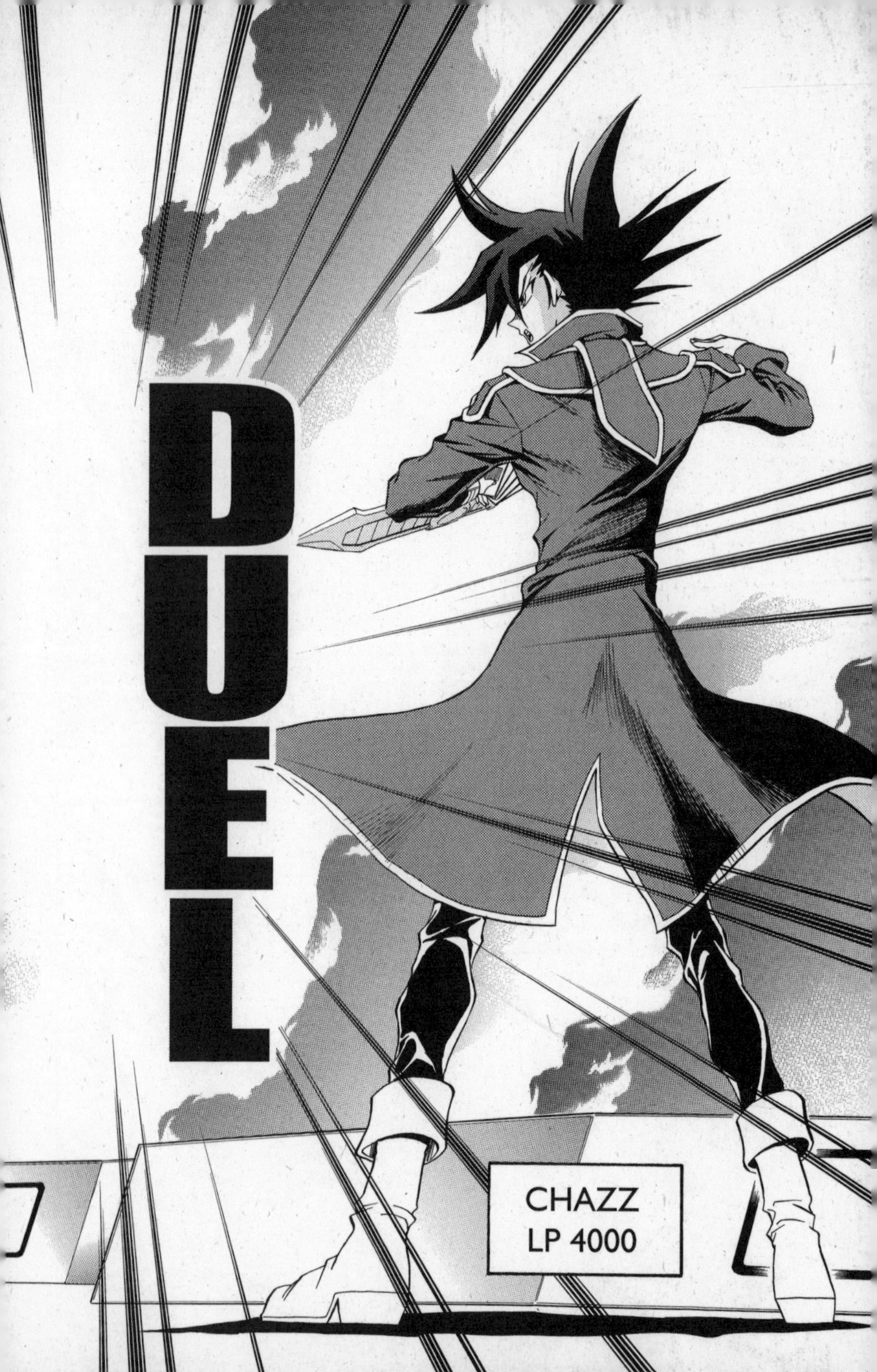
DUEL
CHAZZ
LP 4000

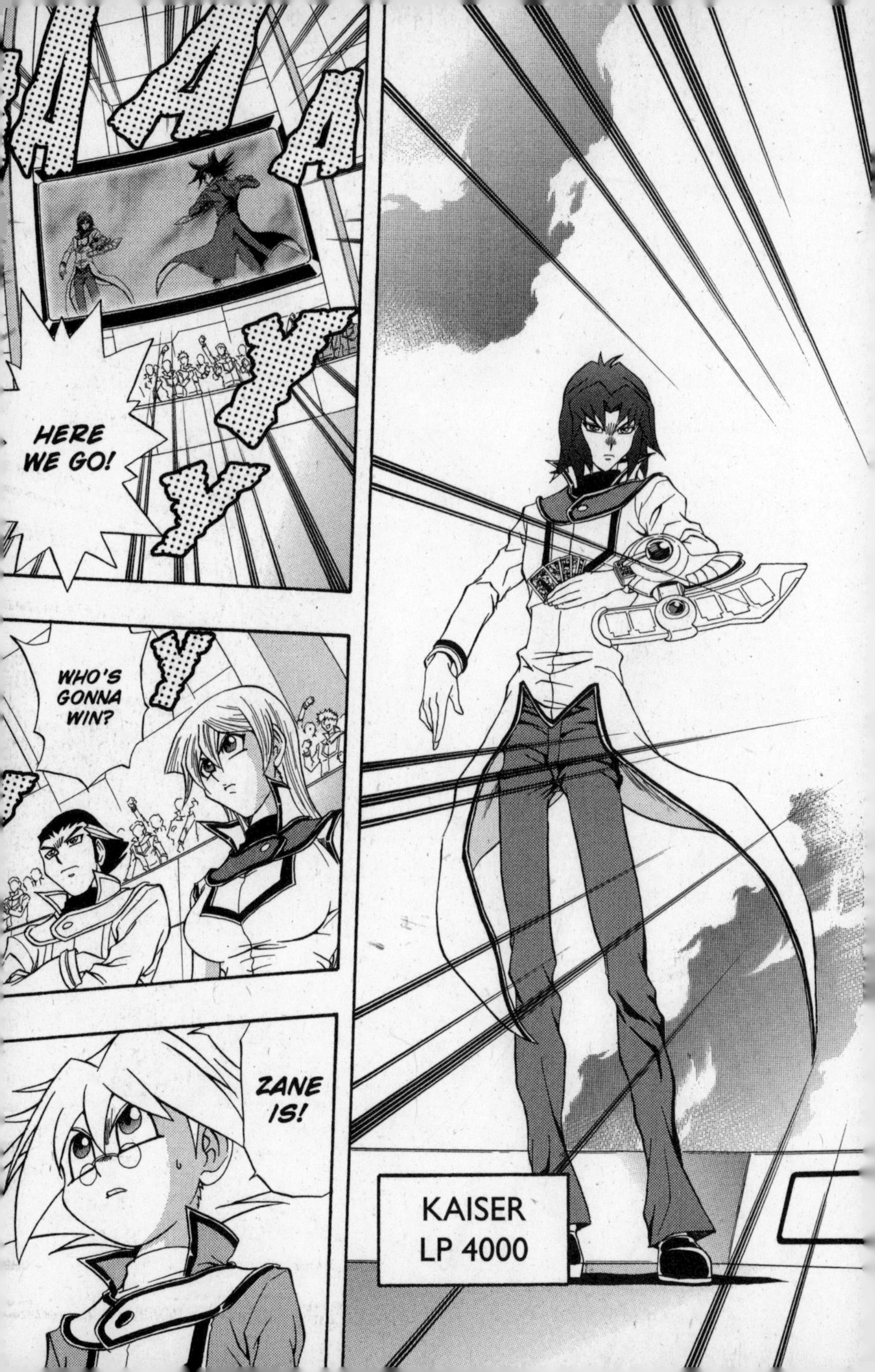
KAISER
LP 4000
HERE WE GO!
WHO'S GONNA WIN?
ZANE IS!

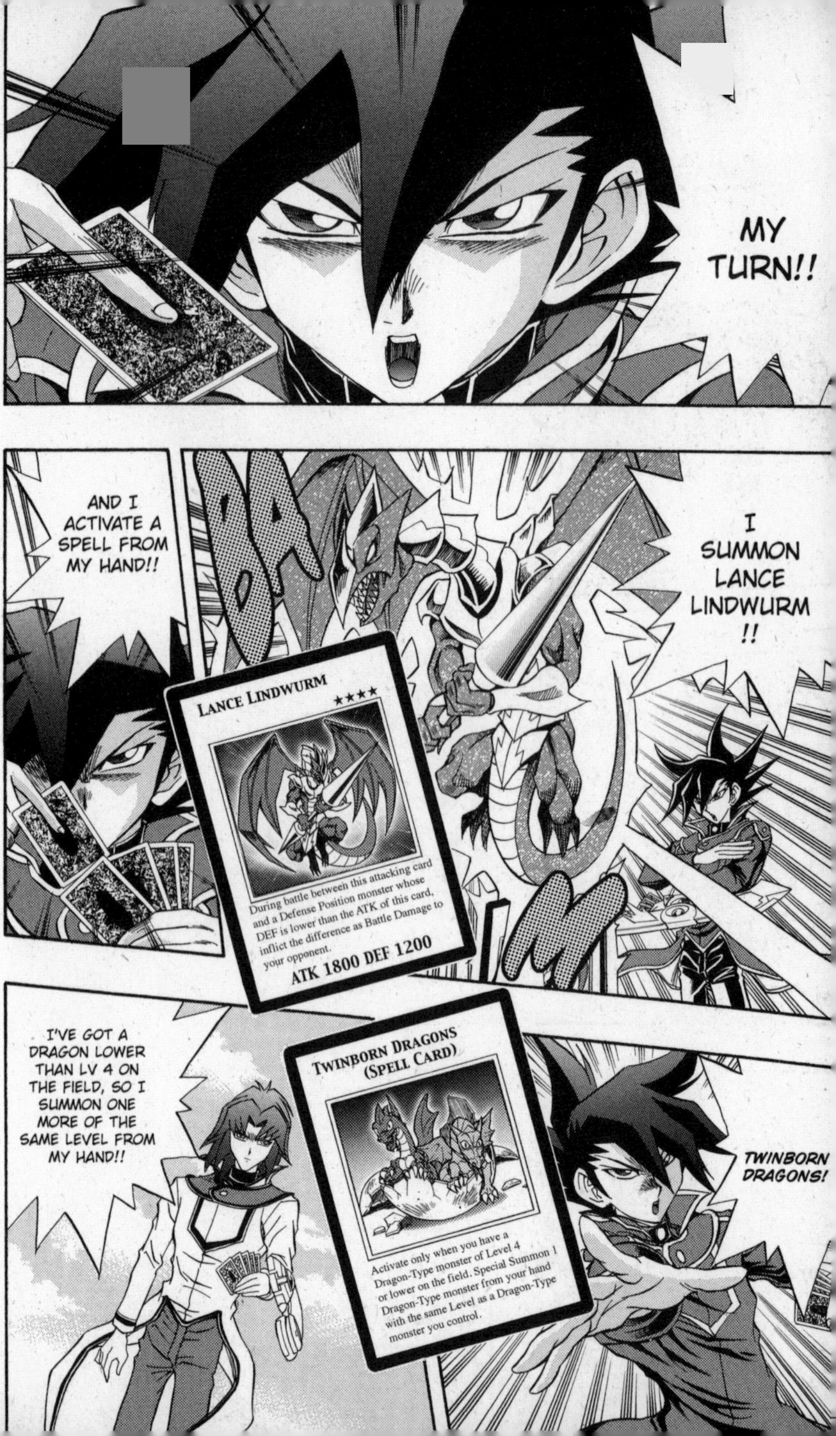
MY TURN!!
I SUMMON LANCE LINDWURM !!
LANCE LINDWURM ★★★★
During battle between this attacking card and a Defense Position monster whose DEF is lower than the ATK of this card, inflict the difference as Battle Damage to your opponent.
ATK 1800 DEF 1200
AND I ACTIVATE A SPELL FROM MY HAND!!
TWINBORN DRAGONS!
TWINBORN DRAGONS (SPELL CARD)
Activate only when you have a Dragon-Type monster of Level 4 or lower on the field. Special Summon 1 Dragon-Type monster from your hand with the same Level as a Dragon-Type monster you control.
I'VE GOT A DRAGON LOWER THAN LV 4 ON THE FIELD, SO I SUMMON ONE MORE OF THE SAME LEVEL FROM MY HAND!!

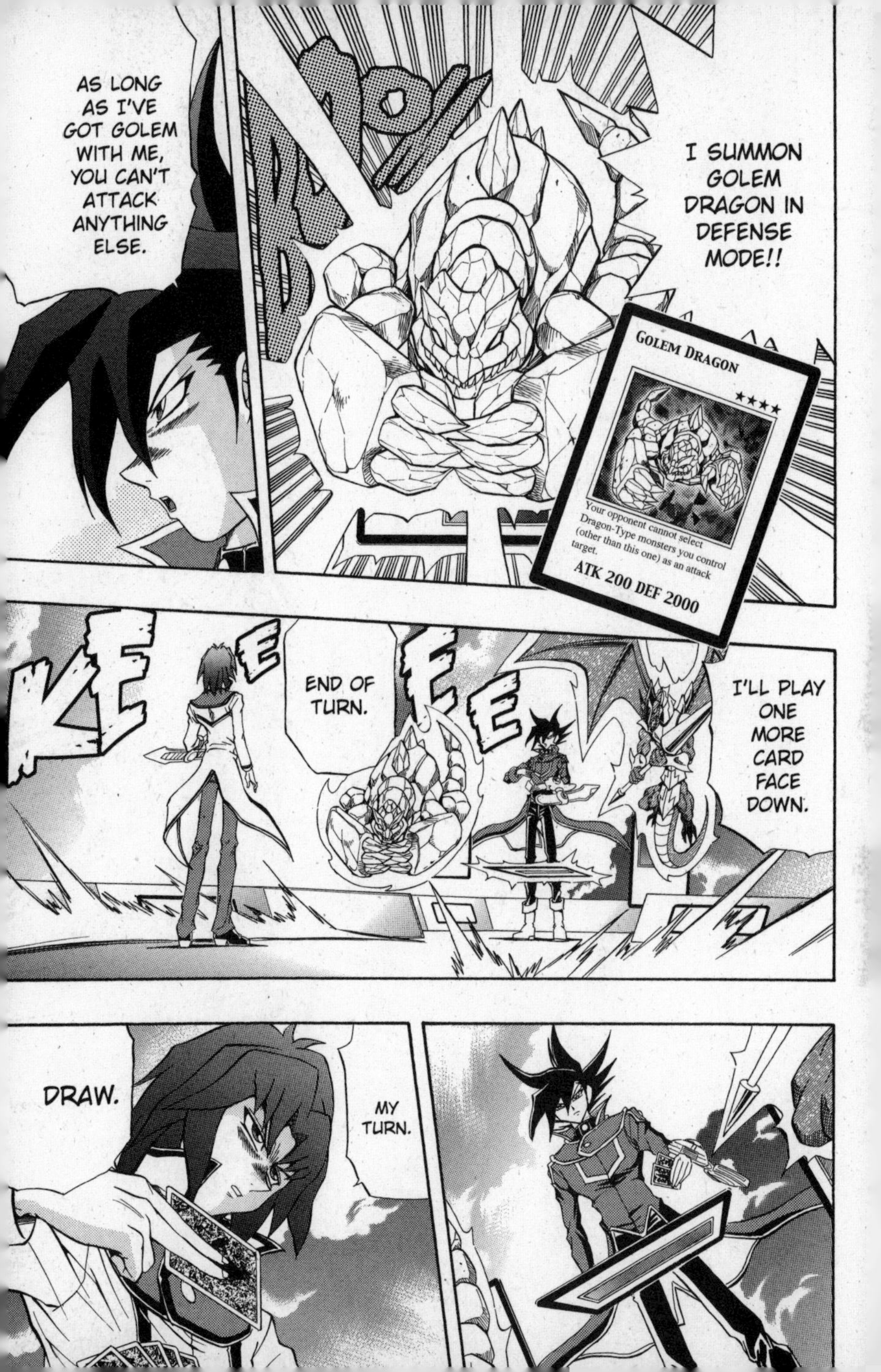
I SUMMON GOLEM DRAGON IN DEFENSE MODE!!
GOLEM DRAGON
Your opponent cannot select Dragon-Type monsters you control (other than this one) as an attack target.
ATK 200 DEF 2000
AS LONG AS I'VE GOT GOLEM WITH ME, YOU CAN'T ATTACK ANYTHING ELSE.
I'LL PLAY ONE MORE CARD FACE DOWN.
END OF TURN.
MY TURN.
DRAW.

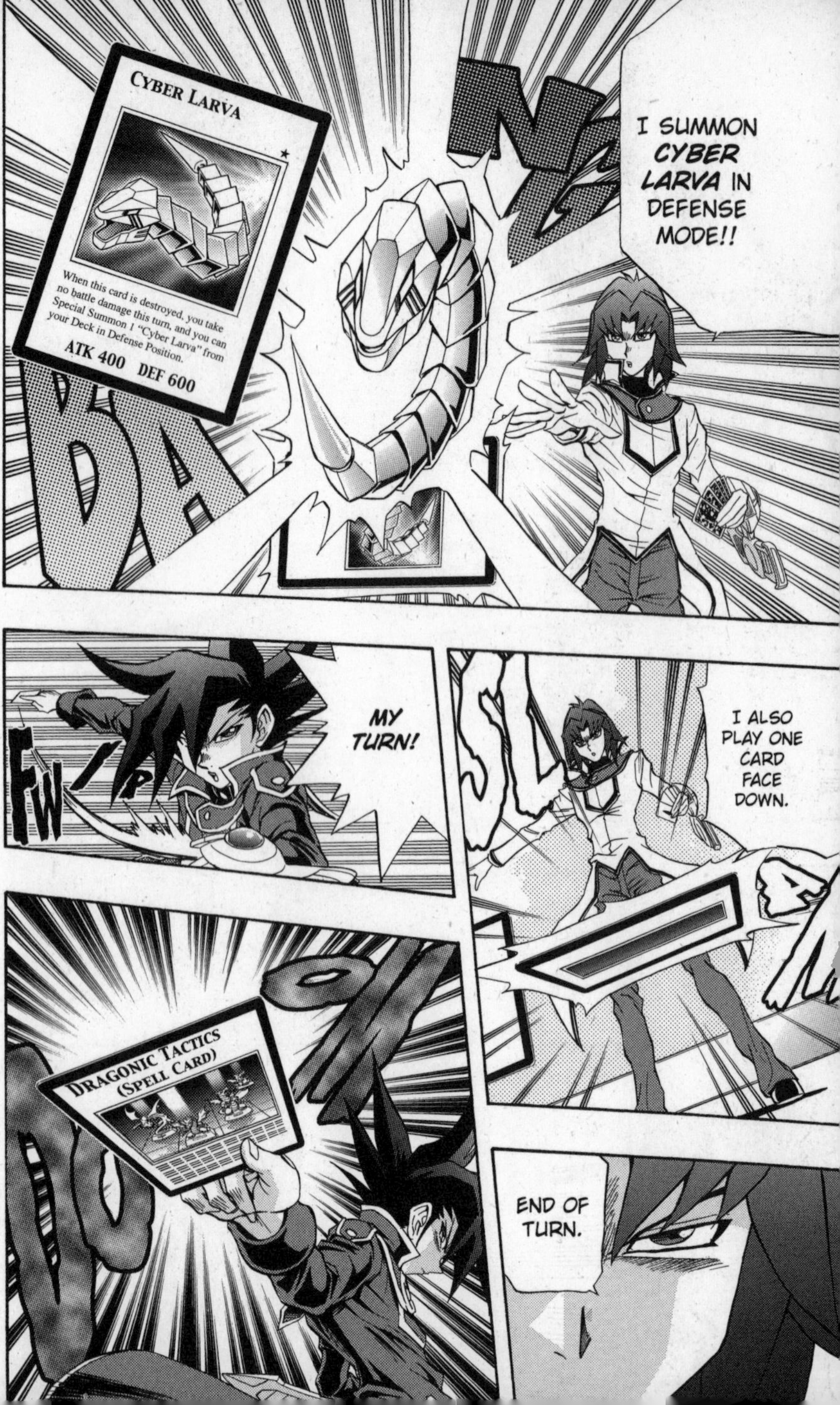
I SUMMON CYBER LARVA IN DEFENSE MODE!!
Cyber Larva
When this card is destroyed, you take no battle damage this turn, and you can Special Summon 1 "Cyber Larva" from your Deck in Defense Position.
ATK 400 DEF 600
I ALSO PLAY ONE CARD FACE DOWN.
END OF TURN.
MY TURN!
Dragonic Tactics (Spell Card)

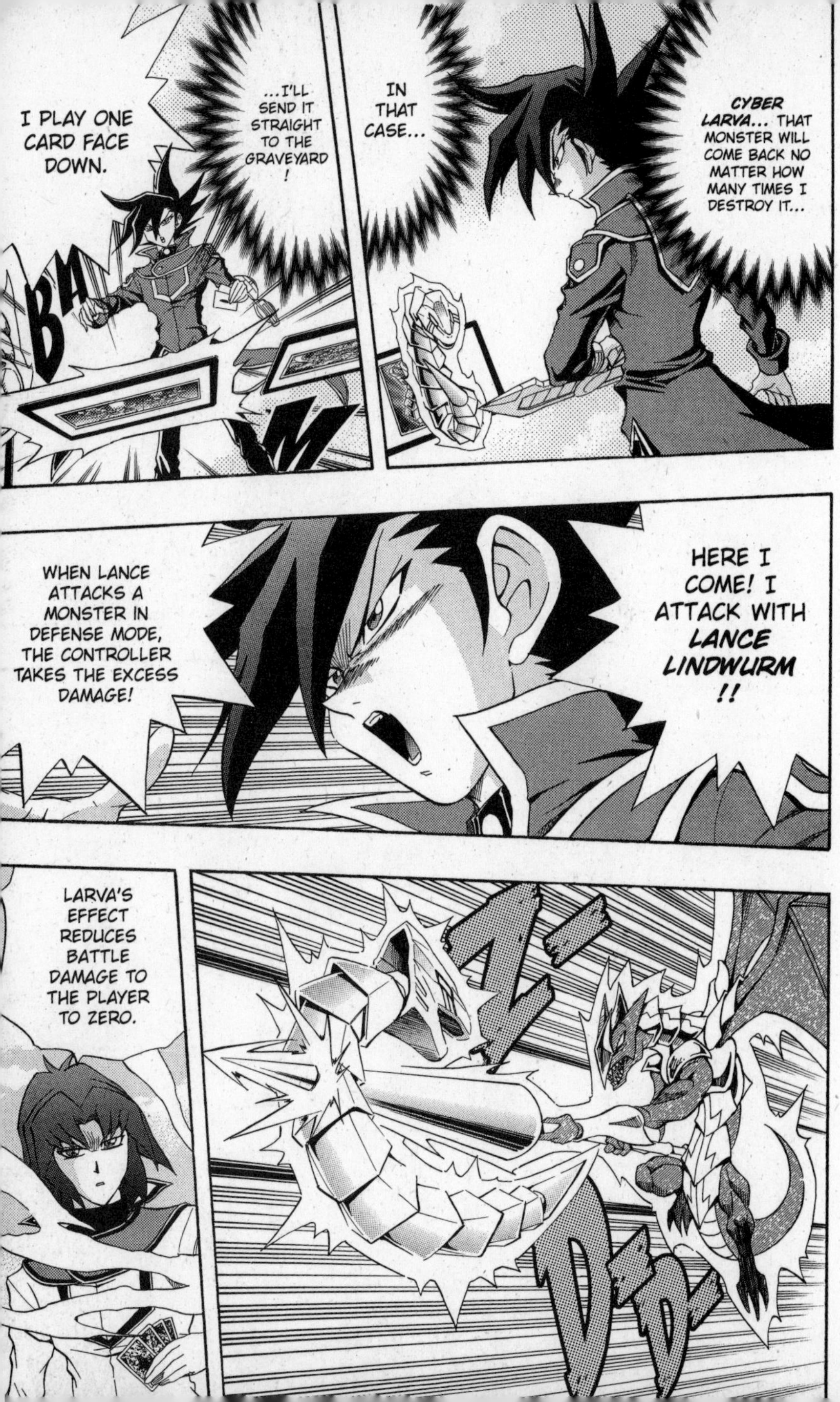
CYBER LARVA... THAT MONSTER WILL COME BACK NO MATTER HOW MANY TIMES I DESTROY IT...
IN THAT CASE...
...I'LL SEND IT STRAIGHT TO THE GRAVEYARD!
I PLAY ONE CARD FACE DOWN.
BA
HERE I COME! I ATTACK WITH LANCE LINDWURM!!
WHEN LANCE ATTACKS A MONSTER IN DEFENSE MODE, THE CONTROLLER TAKES THE EXCESS DAMAGE!
LARVA'S EFFECT REDUCES BATTLE DAMAGE TO THE PLAYER TO ZERO.

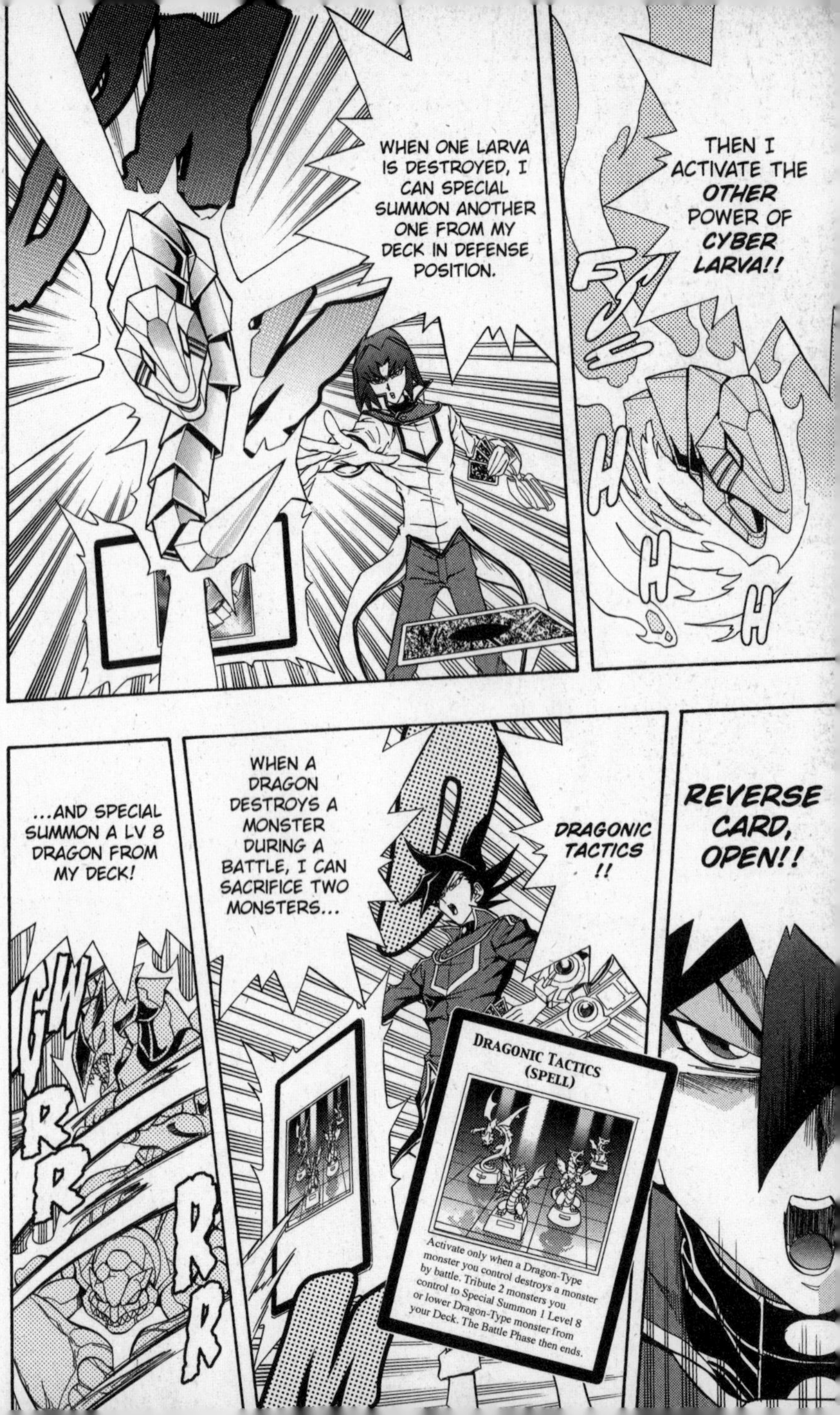
THEN I ACTIVATE THE OTHER POWER OF CYBER LARVA!!
WHEN ONE LARVA IS DESTROYED, I CAN SPECIAL SUMMON ANOTHER ONE FROM MY DECK IN DEFENSE POSITION.
REVERSE CARD, OPEN!!
DRAGONIC TACTICS !!
WHEN A DRAGON DESTROYS A MONSTER DURING A BATTLE, I CAN SACRIFICE TWO MONSTERS...
DRAGONIC TACTICS
(SPELL)
Activate only when a Dragon-Type monster you control destroys a monster by battle. Tribute 2 monsters you control to Special Summon 1 Level 8 or lower Dragon-Type monster from your Deck. The Battle Phase then ends.
...AND SPECIAL SUMMON A LV 8 DRAGON FROM MY DECK!

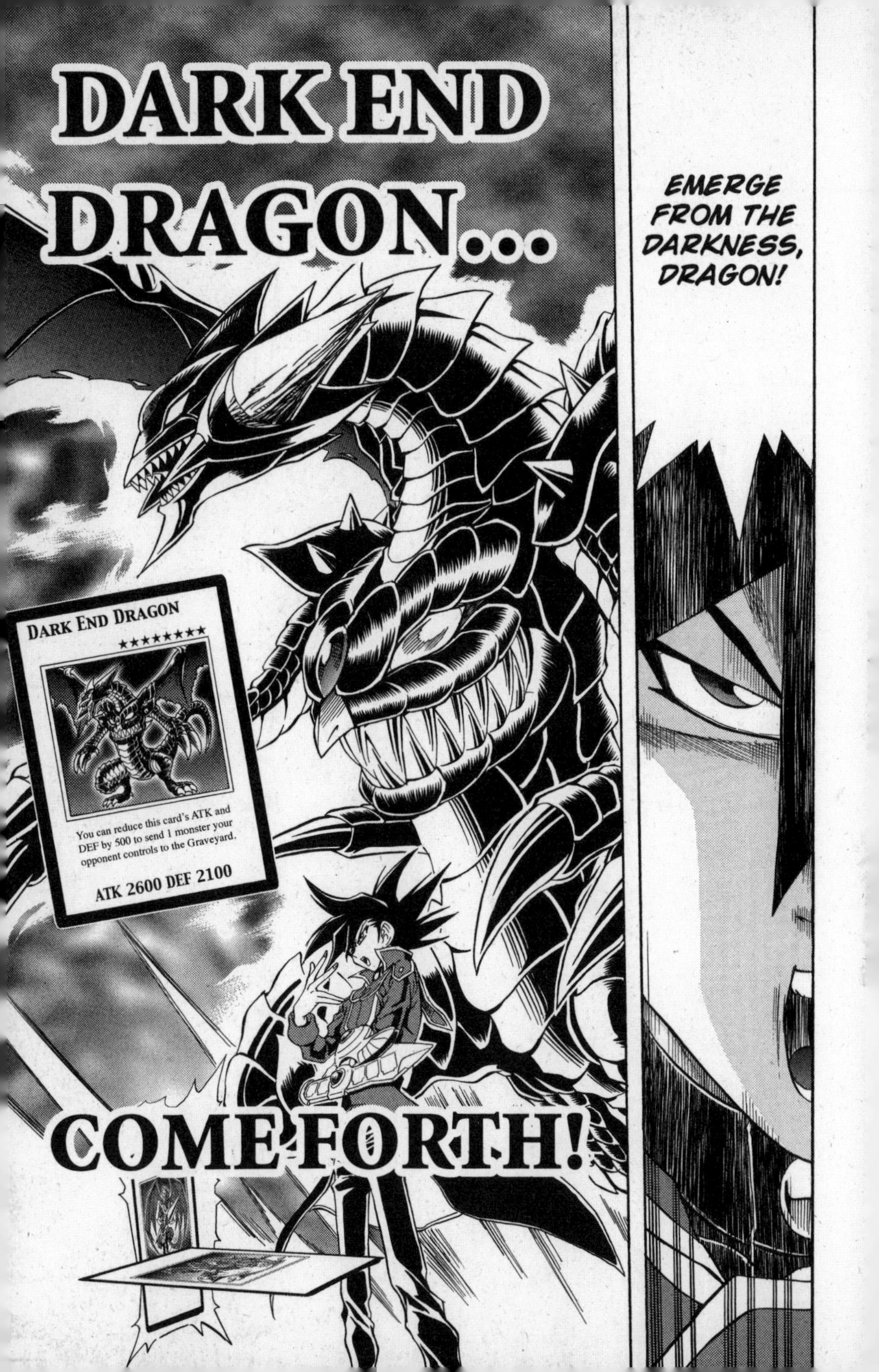
EMERGE FROM THE DARKNESS, DRAGON!
DARK END DRAGON...
DARK END DRAGON
You can reduce this card's ATK and DEF by 500 to send 1 monster your opponent controls to the Graveyard.
ATK 2600 DEF 2100
COME FORTH!

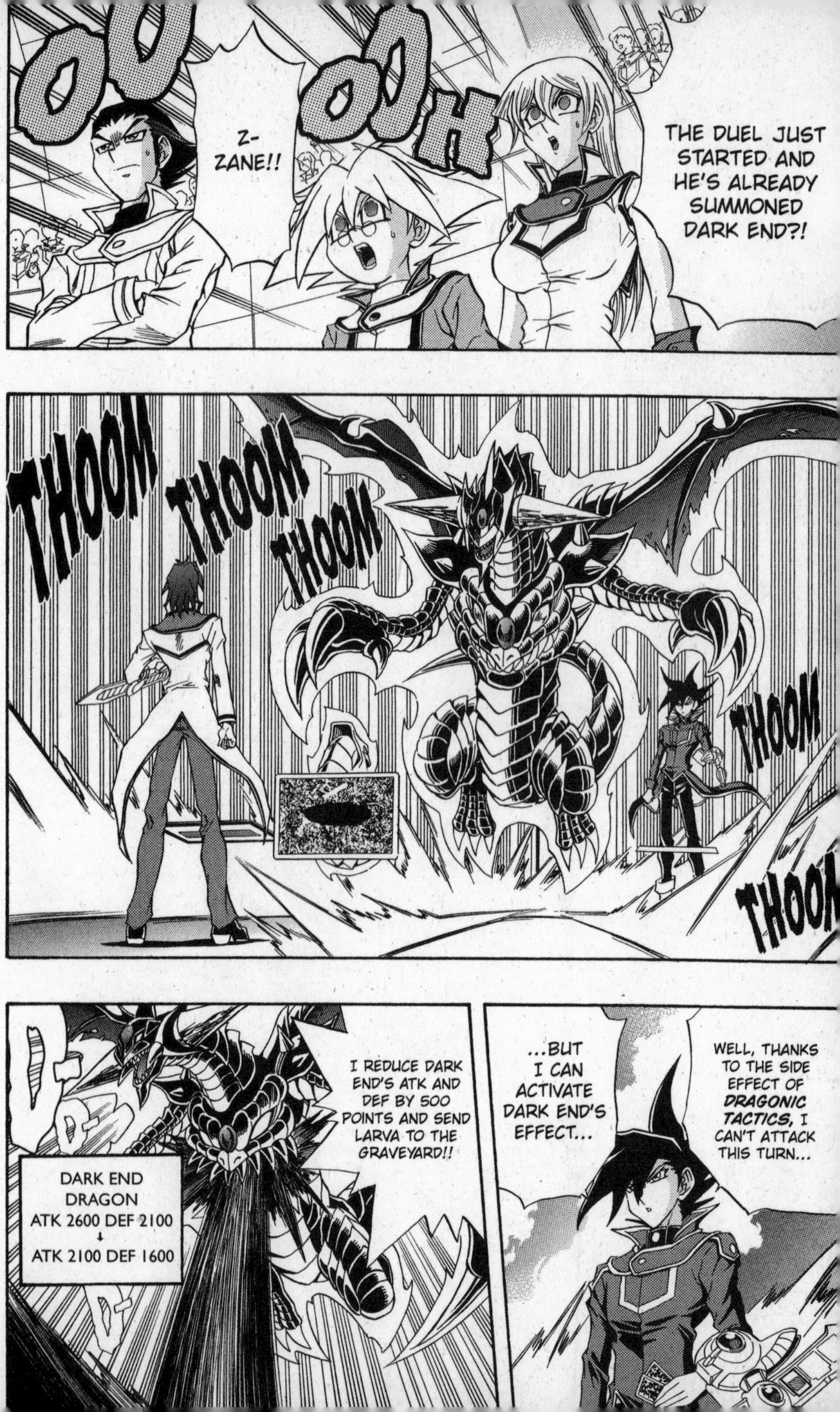
THE DUEL JUST STARTED AND HE'S ALREADY SUMMONED DARK END?!
OOOOH
Z-ZANE!!
THOOM
THOOM
THOOM
THOOM
THOOM
WELL, THANKS TO THE SIDE EFFECT OF *DRAGONIC TACTICS,* I CAN'T ATTACK THIS TURN...
...BUT I CAN ACTIVATE DARK END'S EFFECT...
I REDUCE DARK END'S ATK AND DEF BY 500 POINTS AND SEND LARVA TO THE GRAVEYARD!!
DARK END DRAGON ATK 2600 DEF 2100 ↓ ATK 2100 DEF 1600

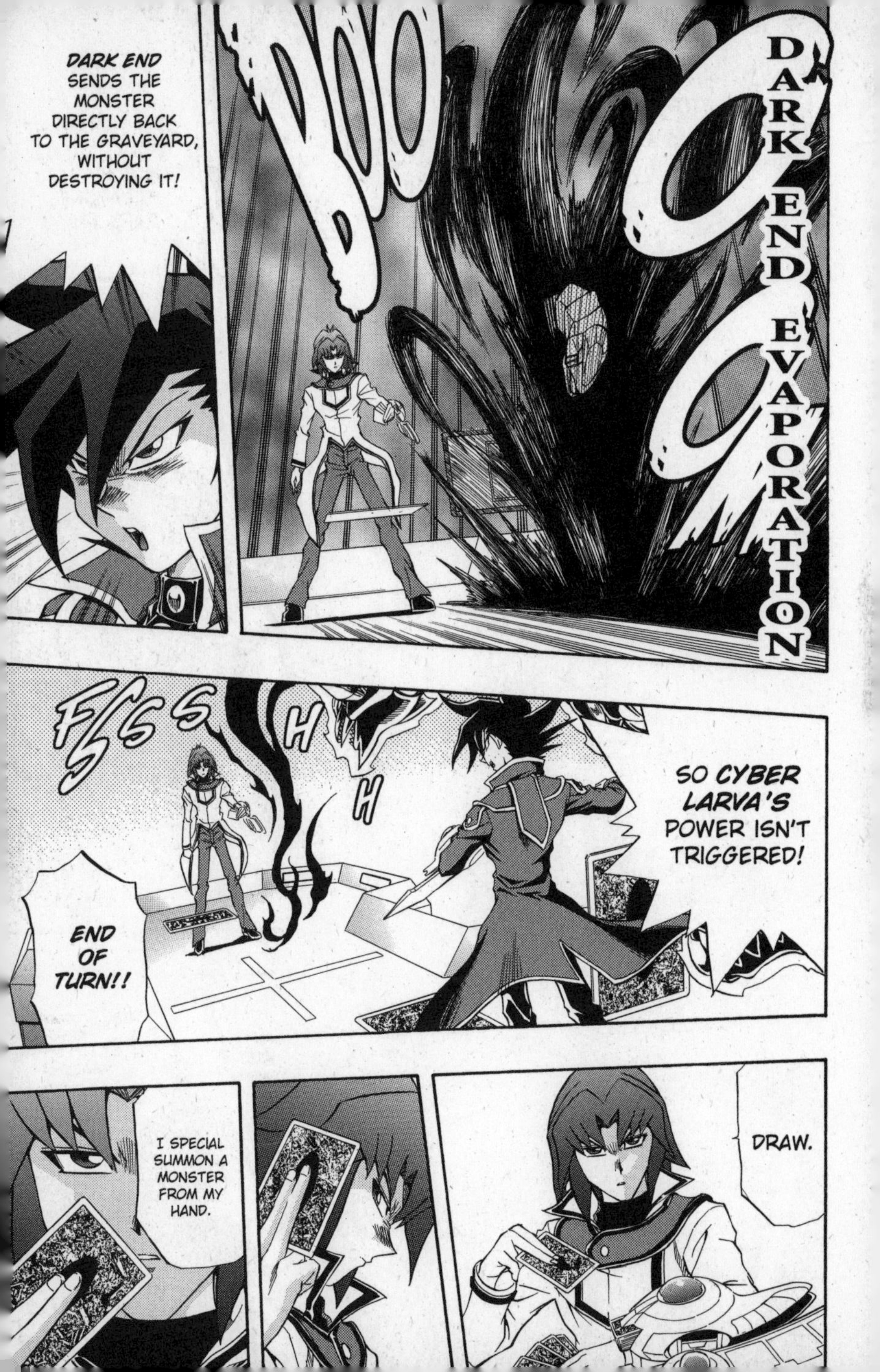
DARK END EVAPORATION
DARK END SENDS THE MONSTER DIRECTLY BACK TO THE GRAVEYARD, WITHOUT DESTROYING IT!
SO CYBER LARVA'S POWER ISN'T TRIGGERED!
FSSHH
END OF TURN!!
DRAW.
I SPECIAL SUMMON A MONSTER FROM MY HAND.

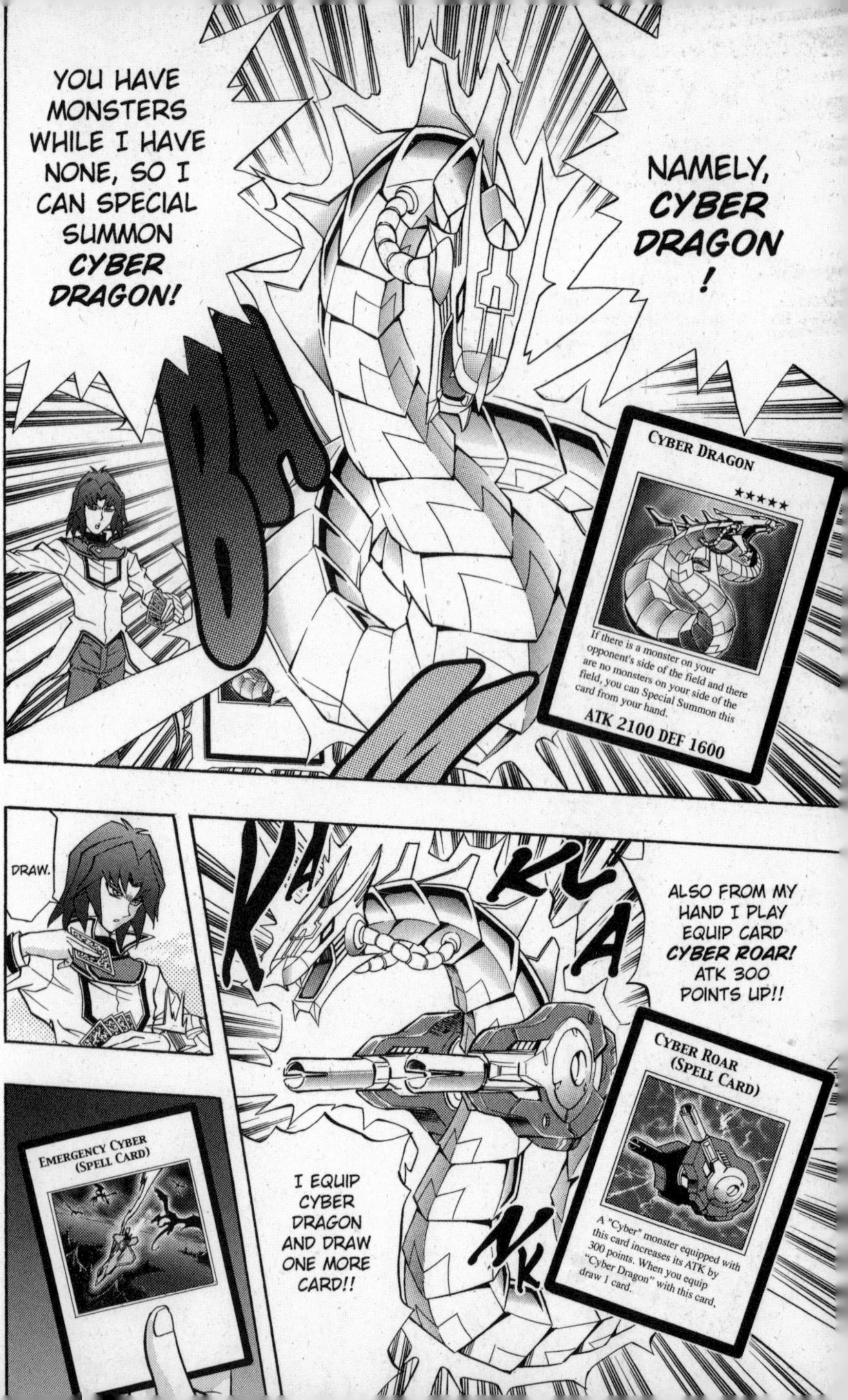
YOU HAVE MONSTERS WHILE I HAVE NONE, SO I CAN SPECIAL SUMMON CYBER DRAGON!
NAMELY, CYBER DRAGON!
CYBER DRAGON
★★★★★
If there is a monster on your opponent's side of the field and there are no monsters on your side of the field, you can Special Summon this card from your hand.
ATK 2100 DEF 1600
ALSO FROM MY HAND I PLAY EQUIP CARD CYBER ROAR! ATK 300 POINTS UP!!
CYBER ROAR (SPELL CARD)
A "Cyber" monster equipped with this card increases its ATK by 300 points. When you equip "Cyber Dragon" with this card, draw 1 card.
I EQUIP CYBER DRAGON AND DRAW ONE MORE CARD!!
DRAW.
EMERGENCY CYBER (SPELL CARD)

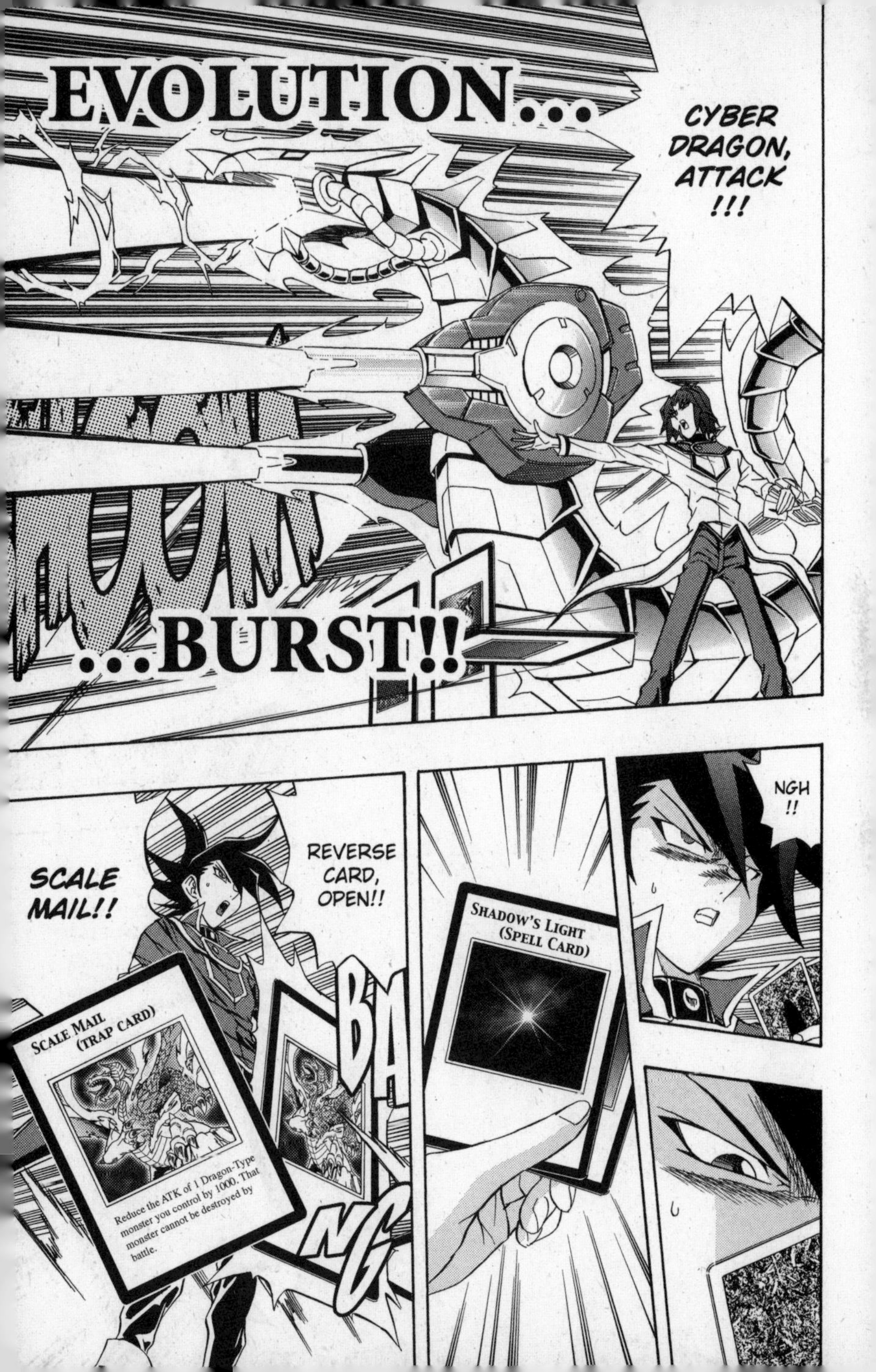
CYBER DRAGON, ATTACK!!!
EVOLUTION...
...BURST!!
NGH!!
SHADOW'S LIGHT (SPELL CARD)
REVERSE CARD, OPEN!!
SCALE MAIL!!
SCALE MAIL (TRAP CARD)
Reduce the ATK of 1 Dragon-Type monster you control by 1000. That monster cannot be destroyed by battle.

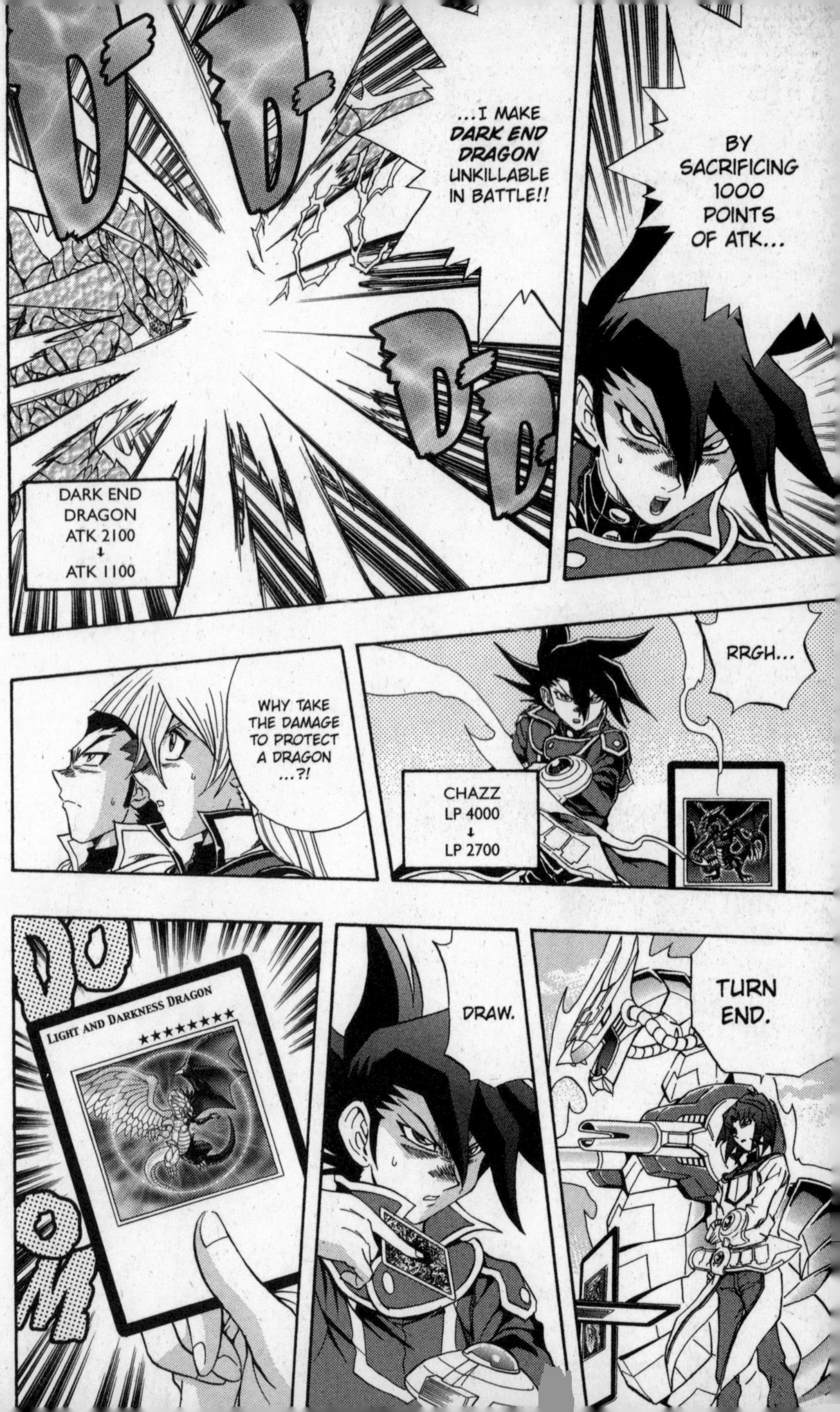

BY SACRIFICING 1000 POINTS OF ATK...
...I MAKE DARK END DRAGON UNKILLABLE IN BATTLE!!
DARK END DRAGON ATK 2100 ↓ ATK 1100
RRGH...
CHAZZ LP 4000 ↓ LP 2700
WHY TAKE THE DAMAGE TO PROTECT A DRAGON ...?!
TURN END.
DRAW.
LIGHT AND DARKNESS DRAGON

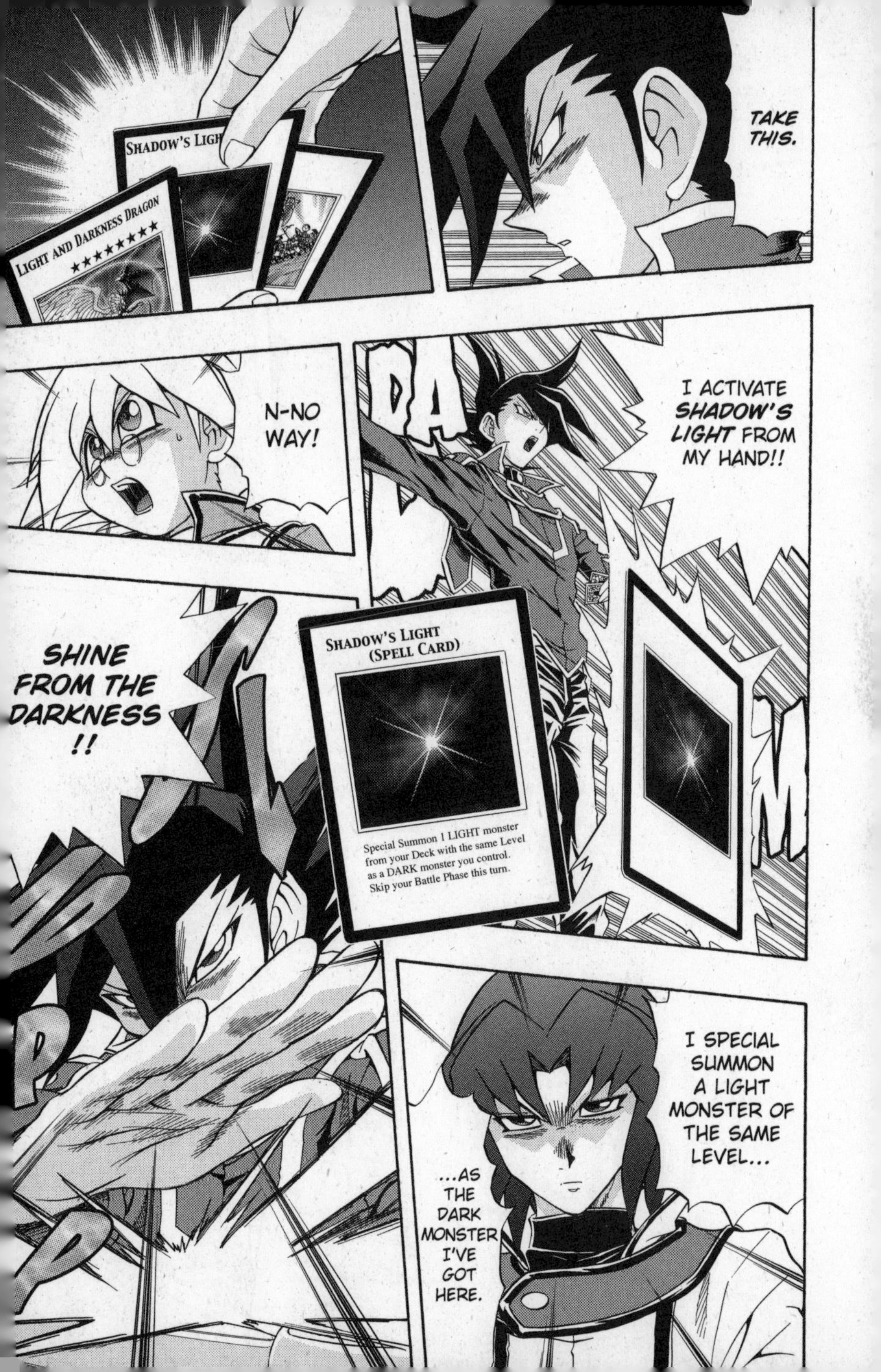
TAKE THIS.
SHADOW'S LIGH
LIGHT AND DARKNESS DRAGON
I ACTIVATE SHADOW'S LIGHT FROM MY HAND!!
N-NO WAY!
SHADOW'S LIGHT (SPELL CARD)
Special Summon 1 LIGHT monster from your Deck with the same Level as a DARK monster you control. Skip your Battle Phase this turn.
SHINE FROM THE DARKNESS !!
I SPECIAL SUMMON A LIGHT MONSTER OF THE SAME LEVEL...
...AS THE DARK MONSTER I'VE GOT HERE.

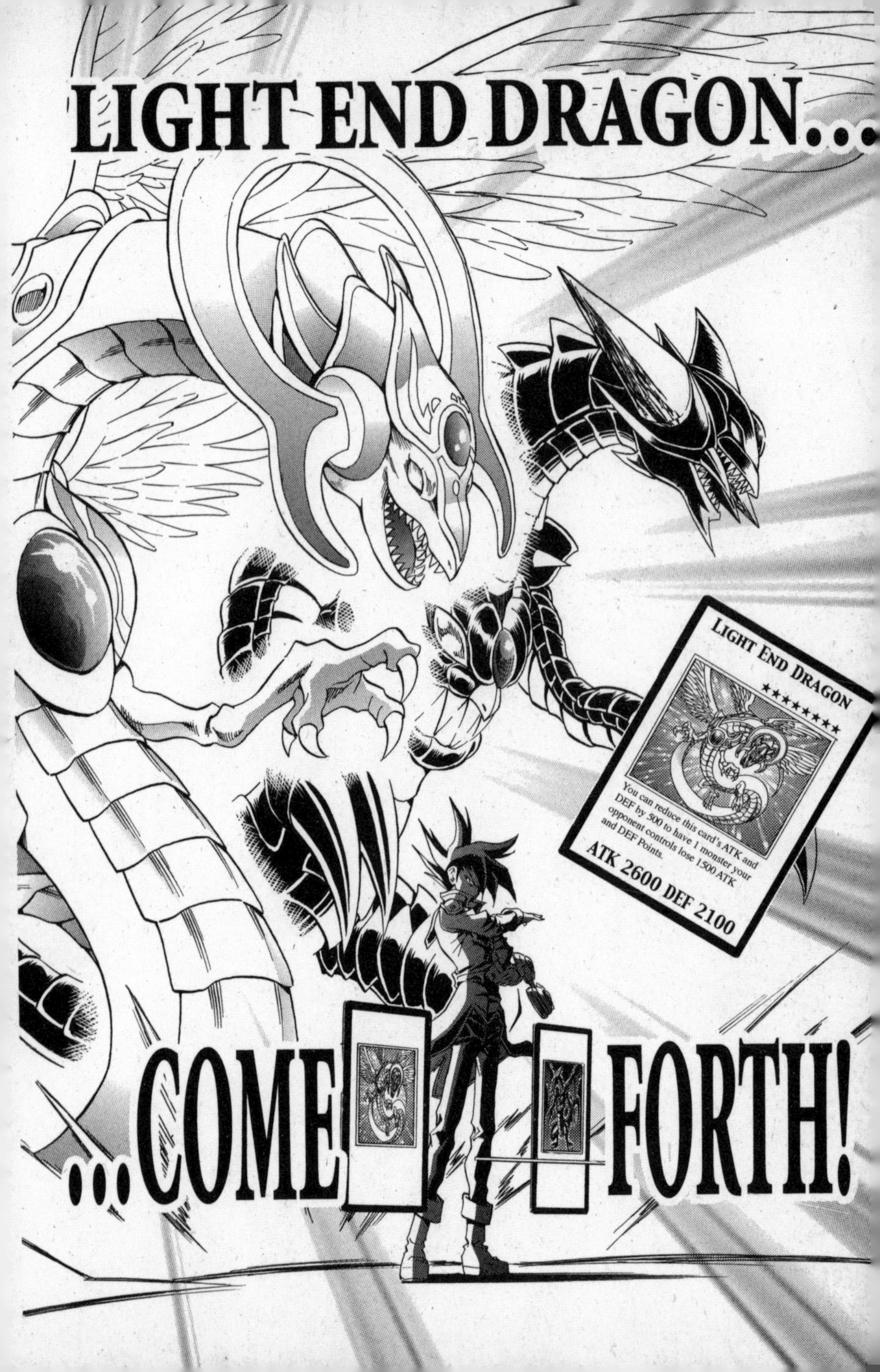
LIGHT END DRAGON...
LIGHT END DRAGON
★★★★★★★★
You can reduce this card's ATK and DEF by 500 to have 1 monster your opponent controls lose 1500 ATK and DEF Points.
ATK 2600 DEF 2100
...COME FORTH!

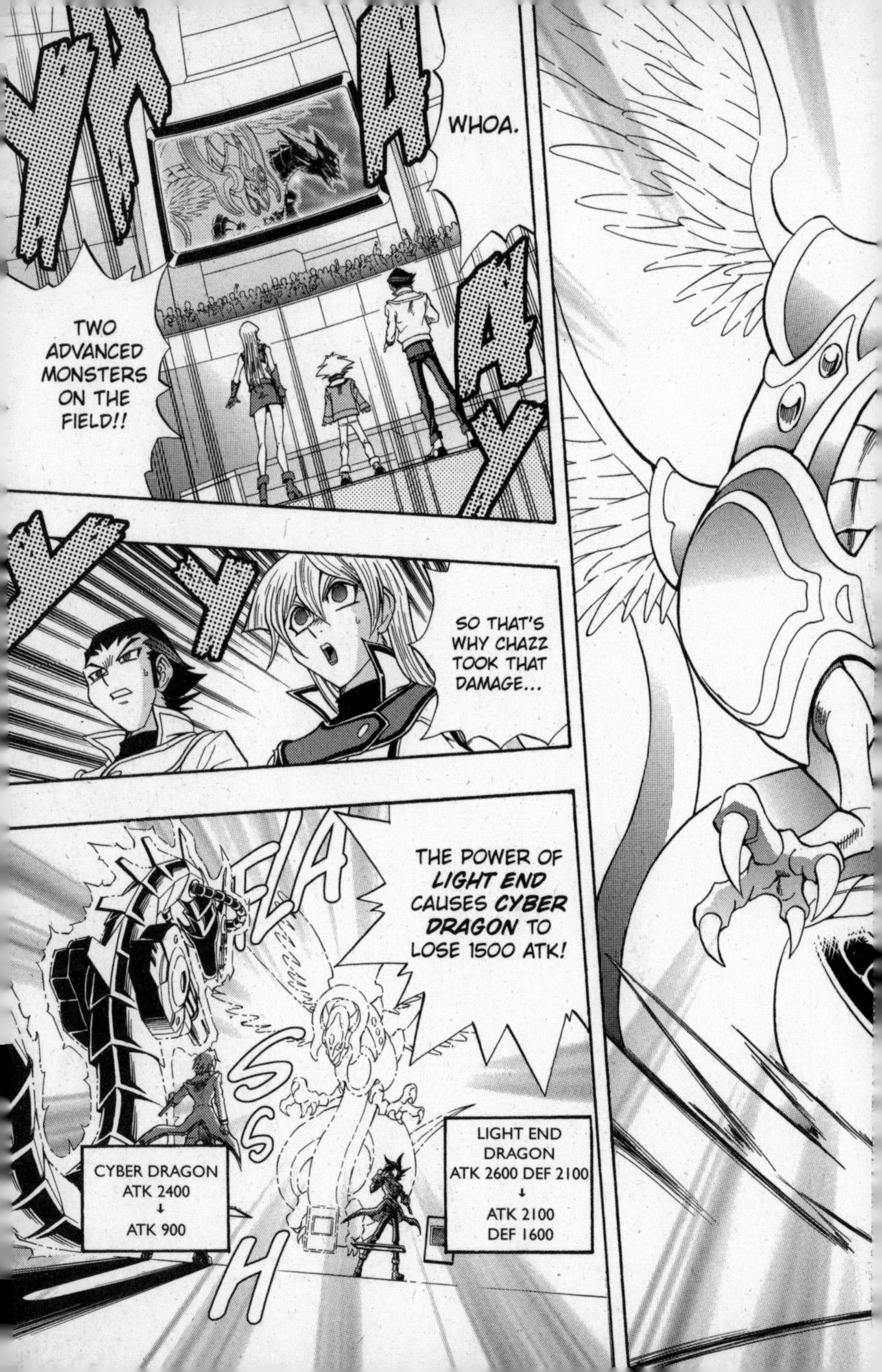
WHOA.
TWO ADVANCED MONSTERS ON THE FIELD!!
SO THAT'S WHY CHAZZ TOOK THAT DAMAGE...
THE POWER OF ***LIGHT END*** CAUSES ***CYBER DRAGON*** TO LOSE 1500 ATK!
LIGHT END DRAGON ATK 2600 DEF 2100 ↓ ATK 2100 DEF 1600
CYBER DRAGON ATK 2400 ↓ ATK 900

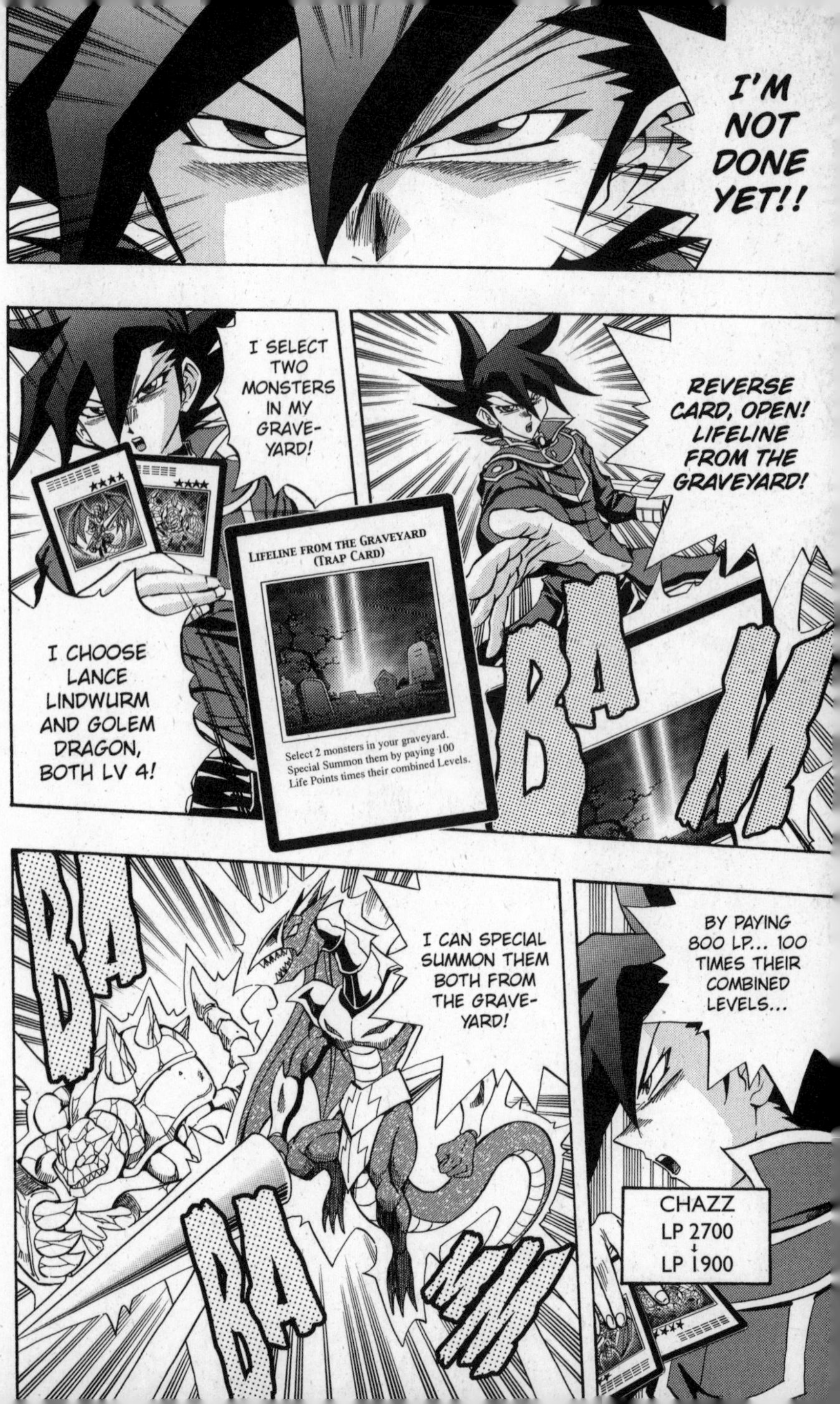
I'M NOT DONE YET!!
REVERSE CARD, OPEN! LIFELINE FROM THE GRAVEYARD!
BAM
I SELECT TWO MONSTERS IN MY GRAVE-YARD!
LIFELINE FROM THE GRAVEYARD (TRAP CARD)
Select 2 monsters in your graveyard. Special Summon them by paying 100 Life Points times their combined Levels.
I CHOOSE LANCE LINDWURM AND GOLEM DRAGON, BOTH LV 4!
BY PAYING 800 LP... 100 TIMES THEIR COMBINED LEVELS...
CHAZZ
LP 2700
↓
LP 1900
I CAN SPECIAL SUMMON THEM BOTH FROM THE GRAVE-YARD!
BA
BAMM

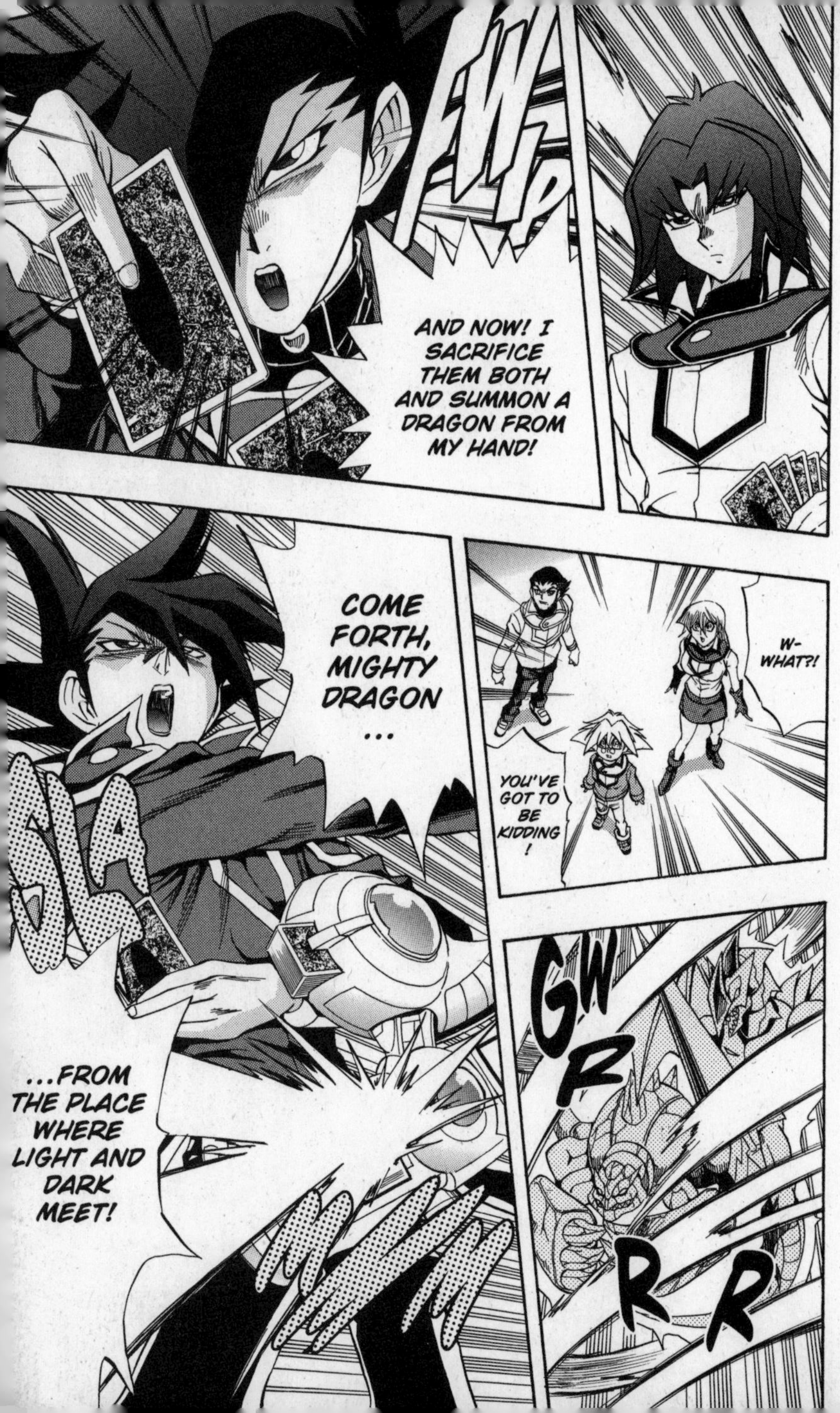
AND NOW! I SACRIFICE THEM BOTH AND SUMMON A DRAGON FROM MY HAND!
W-WHAT?!
YOU'VE GOT TO BE KIDDING!
GWRRR
COME FORTH, MIGHTY DRAGON ...
...FROM THE PLACE WHERE LIGHT AND DARK MEET!

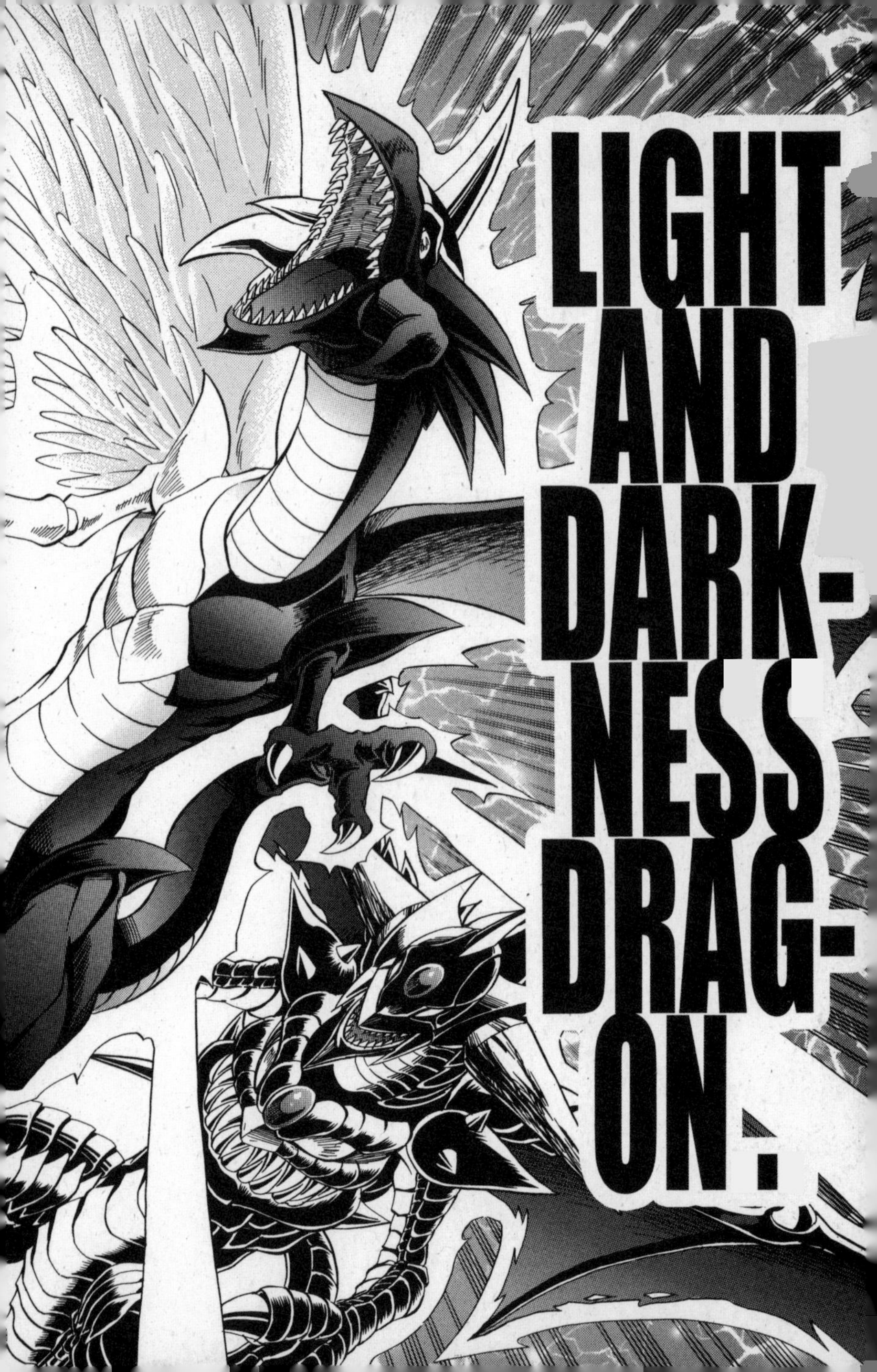
LIGHT AND DARK-NESS DRAG-ON.

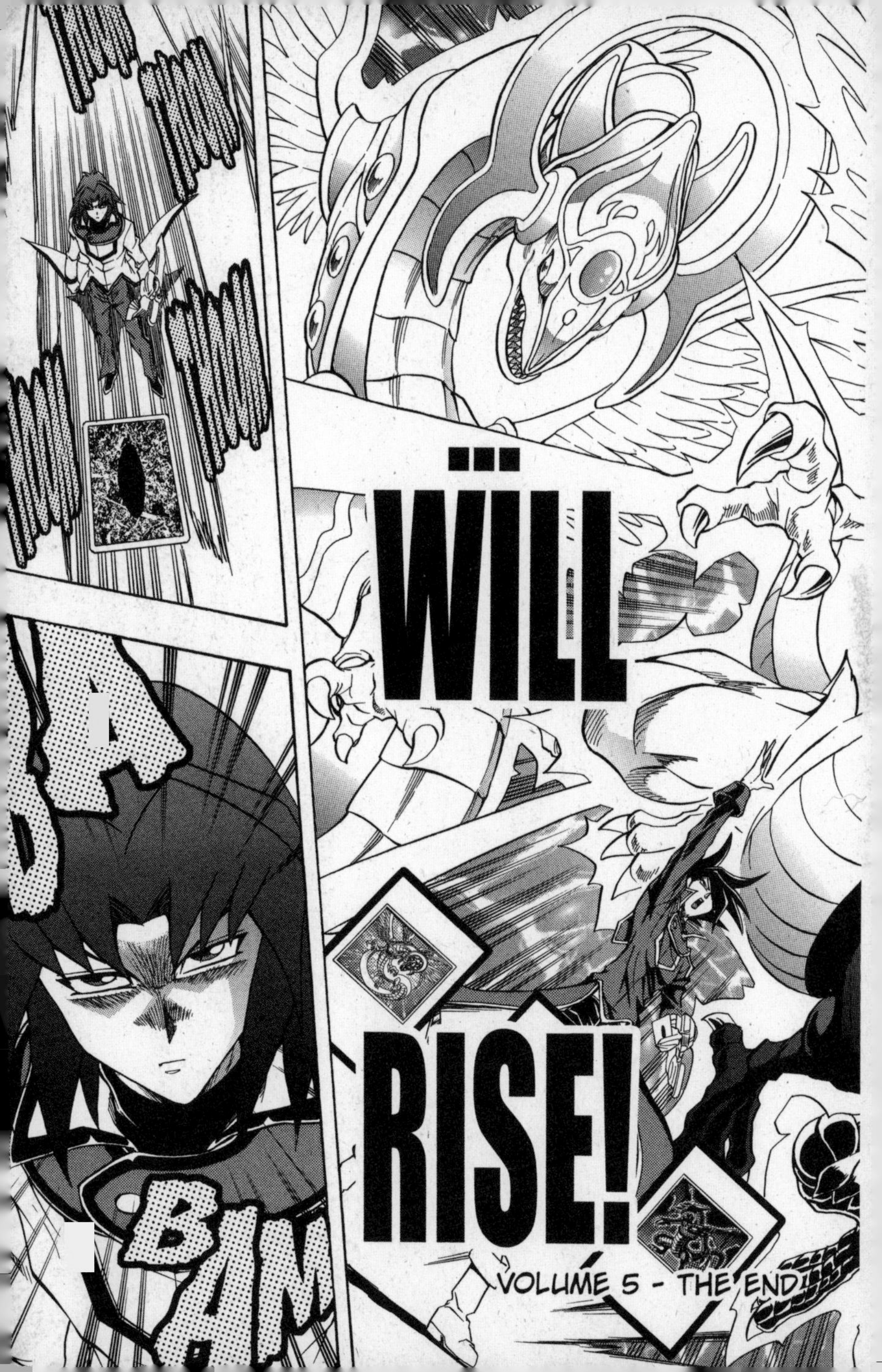
...WILL
RISE!
VOLUME 5 - THE END
THMM THMM THMM THMM
BAM

STAFF

MASAFUMI SATO
AKIHIRO TOMONAGA
AKIRA ITO

DUEL COMBINATION COOPERATION

MASAHIRO UCHIDA

COLORING

NABETARO

EDITOR

DAISUKE TERASHI

MASTER OF THE CARDS

Jaden Yuki and the rest of the next generation of Duelists have introduced their own cards into the *Yu-Gi-Oh!* TCG, which also make their first appearance here in the fifth volume of the *Yu-Gi-Oh! GX* manga! As with all original *Yu-Gi-Oh!* cards, names can differ slightly between the Japanese and English versions, so we're showing you both for reference. Plus, we show you the card even if the card itself doesn't show up in the manga but the monster or trap does! And some cards you may have already seen in the original *Yu-Gi-Oh!*, but we still note them the first time they appear in this volume anyway!

First Appearance in This Volume	Japanese Card Name	English Card Name <<!>> = Not yet available in the TCG.
p.7	*Dragonic Enrage* ドラゴニック・エンレイジ	Dragon's Wrath <<!>>
p.7	*Dark End Dragon* ダークエンド・ドラゴン	Dark End Dragon
p.7	*Elemental Hero Ice Edge* E・HERO アイス・エッジ	Elemental Hero Frost Blade <<!>>
p.15	*Bomb Dragon* ボム・ドラゴン	Dynamite Dragon <<!>>
p.15	*Elemental Hero Ocean* E・HERO オーシャン	Elemental Hero Ocean
p.16	*Spell Books in a Pot* 壺の中の魔術書	Spell Books from the Pot <<!>>
p.16	*Polymerization* 融合	Polymerization
p.17	*Light End Dragon* ライトエンド・ドラゴン	Light End Dragon
p.18	*Elemental Hero Absolute Zero* E・HERO アブソルートZero	Elemental Hero Absolute Zero
p.24	*Light and Darkness Dragon* 光と闇の竜	Light and Darkness Dragon
p.26	*Element Change* エレメント・チェンジ	Element Conversion <<!>>
p.30	*Dragon's Lair* 竜の巣窟	Dragon's Lair <<!>>

p.34	*Residual Reflection* 残留思念	Residual Reflection <<!>>
p.34	*Parallel World Fusion* 平行世界融合	Parallel World Fusion <<!>>
p.36	*Elemental Hero The Earth* ***E・HERO***ジ・アース	Elemental Hero Terra Firma
p.47	*Red Wyrm* レッド・ワイアーム	Red Wyrm <<!>>
p.48	*Earth Firma Gravity* アース・グラビティ	Terra Firma Gravity
p.51	*Dragon's Bond* 竜の絆	Dragon's Bond <<!>>
p.52	*Wish Dragon* ウィッシュ・ドラゴン	Wish Dragon <<!>>
p.53	*Hero's Legacy* *HERO*の遺産	Hero's Legacy <<!>>
p.54	*Dragon Cry* ドラゴン・クライ	Dragon's Roar <<!>>
p.54	*Another Fusion* アナザー・フュージョン	Alternate Fusion <<!>>
p.54	*Transcendent Wings* 進化する翼	Transcendent Wings
p.54	*Hero's Bond* *HERO'S*ボンド	Hero's Bond
p.56	*Ability Limitation* アビリティ・リミテイション	Power Shackle <<!>>
p.61	*Winged Kuriboh* ハネクリボー	Winged Kuriboh
p.66	*Dragon's Magic Eyes* 竜の魔眼	Dragon's Gaze <<!>>
p.94	*Court of Justice* コート・オブ・ジャスティス	Court of Justice <<!>>
p.95	*Divine Spirit Parmal* 聖神パーマル	Divine Spirit Parmal <<!>>

p.95	*Mighty Angel Virch* 力天使ヴァーチ	Mighty Angel Virch <<!>>
p.97	*Koushin Teteus* 光神テテュス	Tethys, Goddess of Light
p.97	*Dark Lightning* 電闇石火	Dark Lightning <<!>>
p.99	*Prison Flame* 獄炎	Prison Flame <<!>>
p.100	*Castle of the Gods, Valhalla* 神の居城-ヴァルハラ-	Valhalla, Hall of the Fallen
p.106	*Holy Sanctuary* ホーリー・サンクチュアリ	Divine Sanctuary <<!>>
p.107	*Light to the Temple* 神殿への光	Light to the Temple <<!>>
p.109	*Archangel Christia* 大天使クリスティア	Archlord Kristya
p.110	*Dark Mist* ダーク・ミスト	Dark Mist <<!>>
p.112	*Cyclone* サイクロン	Mystical Space Typhoon
p.114	*Fallen Angel Descends* 堕天使降臨	Darklord Descends <<!>>
p.115	*Fallen Angel Asmodeus* 堕天使アスモディウス	Darklord Asmodeus <<!>>
p.115	*Fallen Angel Superbia* 堕天使スペルビア	Darklord Superbia <<!>>
p.117	*Fallen Angel Ede Arai* 堕天使エデ・アーラエ	Darklord Ede Arai <<!>>
p.119	*Fallen Angel Bewitching* 堕天使の幻惑	Darklord Bewitching <<!>>
p.126	*Zeriel* ゼリエル	Zeriel <<!>>
p.133	*The Splendid VENUS* ザ　スプレンディッド　ヴィーナス	Splendid Venus

p.140	*Fallen Angel in Darkness* 闇に堕ちた天使	Fallen Angel in Darkness<<!>>
p.141	*Angel's Mercy* 天使の慈悲	Angel's Mercy <<!>>
p.142	*Angel Sing* エンジェエル・シング	Angelic Choir <<!>>
p.145	*Fallen Angel Yukoback* 堕天使ユコバック	Darklord Ukobach <<!>>
p.146	*Angel Bow* エンジェル・ボー	Angelic Bow <<!>>
p.152	*Fallen Angel Desire* 堕天使ディザイヤ	Darklord Desire <<!>>
p.156	*Angel Tear* エンジェル・ティア	Angel's Tear <<!>>
p.180	*Lance Lindwurm* ランス・リンドブルム	Lance Lindwurm <<!>>
p.180	*Twinborn Dragons* 双生の竜	Twinborn Dragons <<!>>
p.181	*Golem Dragon* ゴーレム・ドラゴン	Golem Dragon <<!>>
p.182	*Cyber Larva* サイバー・ラーバァ	Cyber Larva <<!>>
p.182	*Dragonic Tactics* ドラゴニック・タクティクス	Dragonic Tactics <<!>>
p.188	*Cyber Dragon* サイバー・ドラゴン	Cyber Dragon
p.188	*Cyber Roar* サイバー・ローアー	Cyber Roar <<!>>
p.188	*Emergency Cyber* エマージェンシー・サイバー	Emergency Cyber <<!>>
p.189	*Shadow's Light* 陰の光	Shadow's Light <<!>>
p.189	*Scale Mail* スケイル・メイル	Scale Mail <<!>>
p.194	*Lifeline from the Graveyard* 墓地からの命綱	Lifeline from the Graveyard <<!>>

IN THE NEXT VOLUME...

It's dragon breath vs. cyborg steel as the fiery duel between Chazz and Zane continues! Meanwhile, away from the spotlight and the roar of the crowd, Jaden gives his all in a desperate duel to save Miss Hibiki from Reggie's dark magic! Then four new faces arrive at Duel Academy, and one of them conceals a terrible secret...

COMING MARCH 2011!

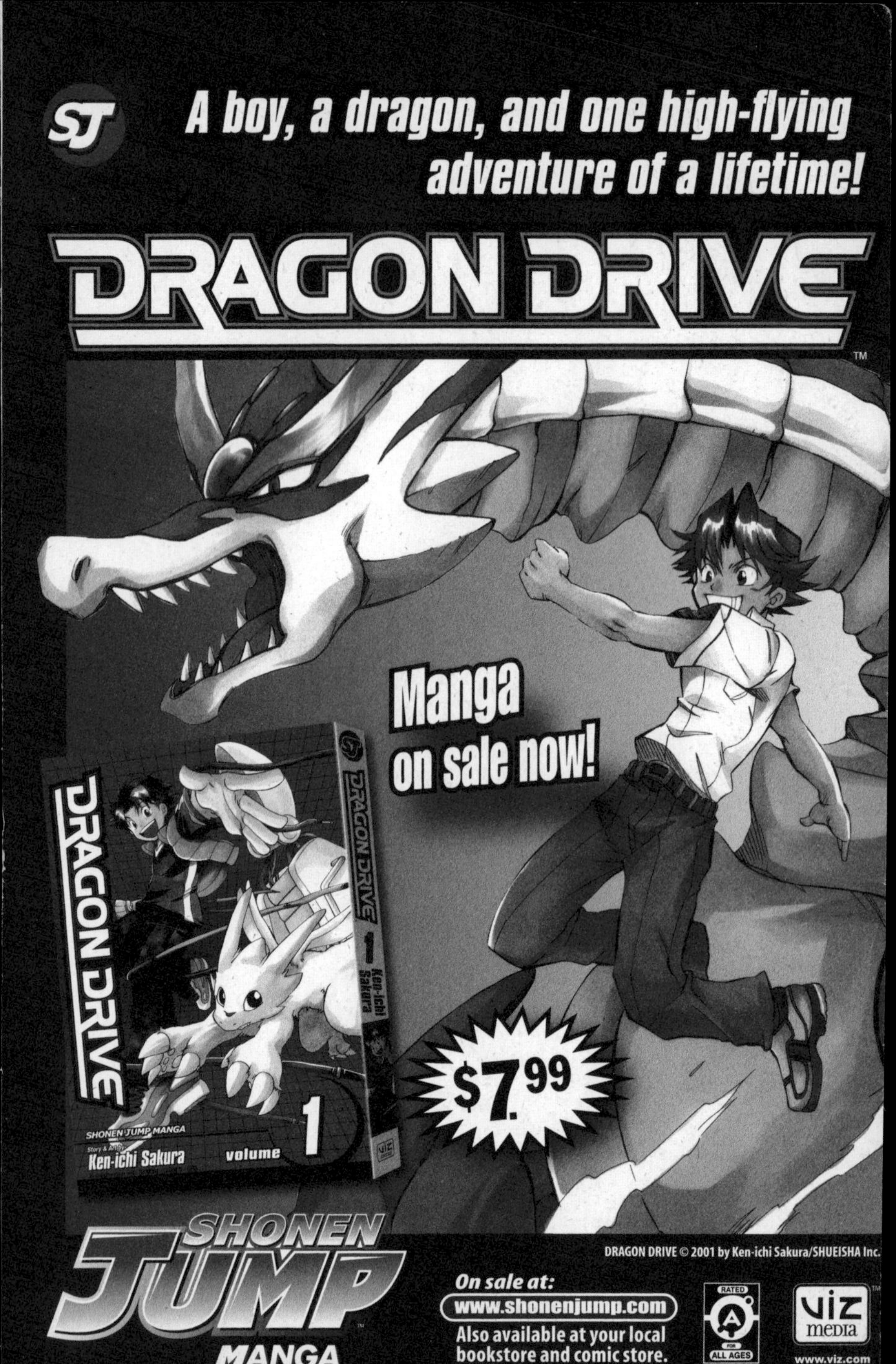

SJ
A boy, a dragon, and one high-flying adventure of a lifetime!
DRAGON DRIVE™
Manga on sale now!
$7.99
DRAGON DRIVE
SHONEN JUMP MANGA
Ken-ichi Sakura
volume 1
SHONEN JUMP MANGA
DRAGON DRIVE © 2001 by Ken-ichi Sakura/SHUEISHA Inc.
On sale at:
www.shonenjump.com
Also available at your local bookstore and comic store.
RATED A FOR ALL AGES
VIZ media
www.viz.com

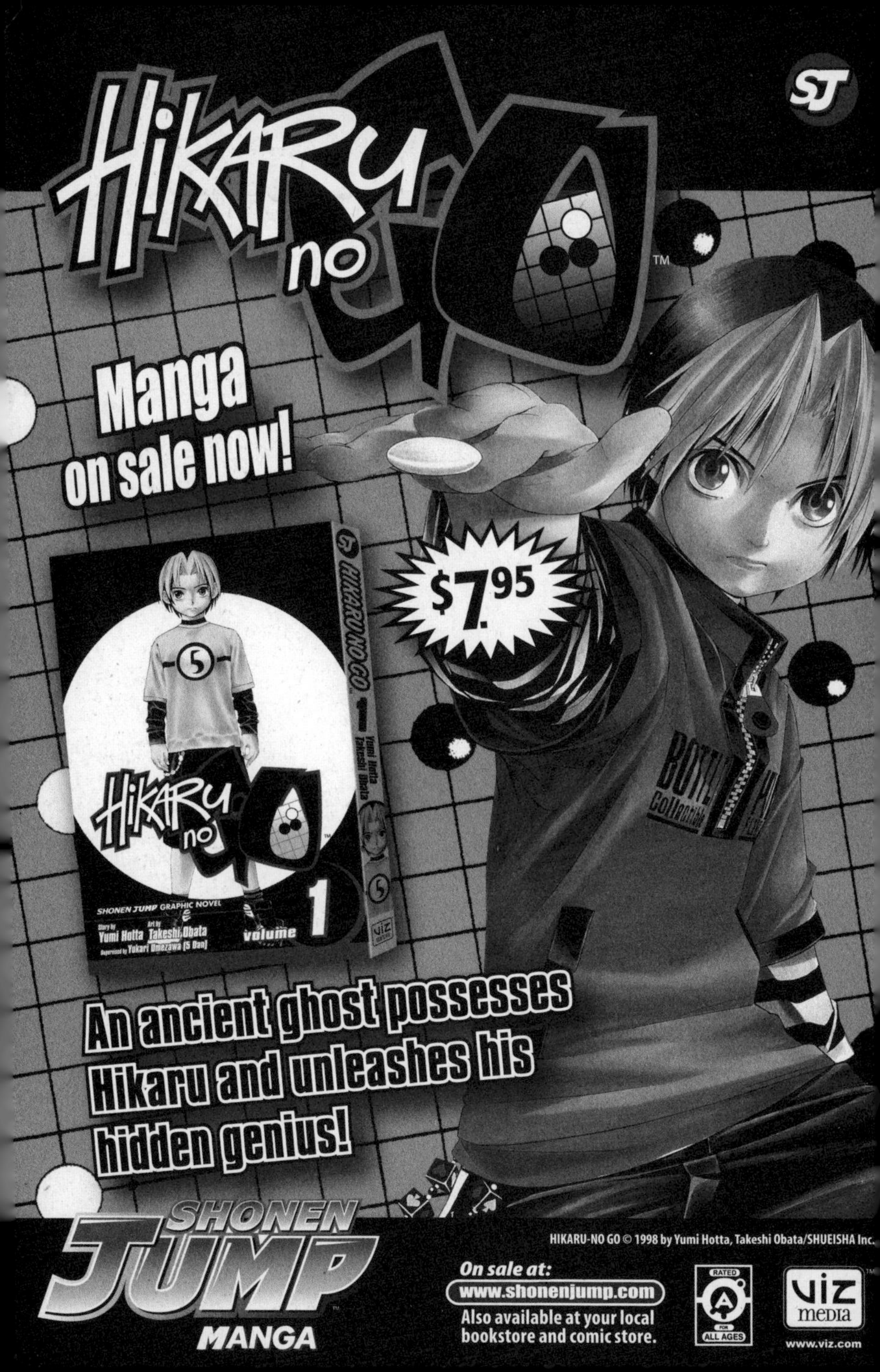

SJ
HIKARU no GO™
Manga on sale now!
$7.95
SJ HIKARU NO GO 1 Yumi Hotta Takeshi Obata
HIKARU no GO
SHONEN JUMP GRAPHIC NOVEL
Story by Yumi Hotta Art by Takeshi Obata
Supervised by Yukari Umezawa (5 Dan)
volume 1
An ancient ghost possesses Hikaru and unleashes his hidden genius!
SHONEN JUMP MANGA
HIKARU-NO GO © 1998 by Yumi Hotta, Takeshi Obata/SHUEISHA Inc.
On sale at:
www.shonenjump.com
Also available at your local bookstore and comic store.
RATED A FOR ALL AGES
VIZ media
www.viz.com

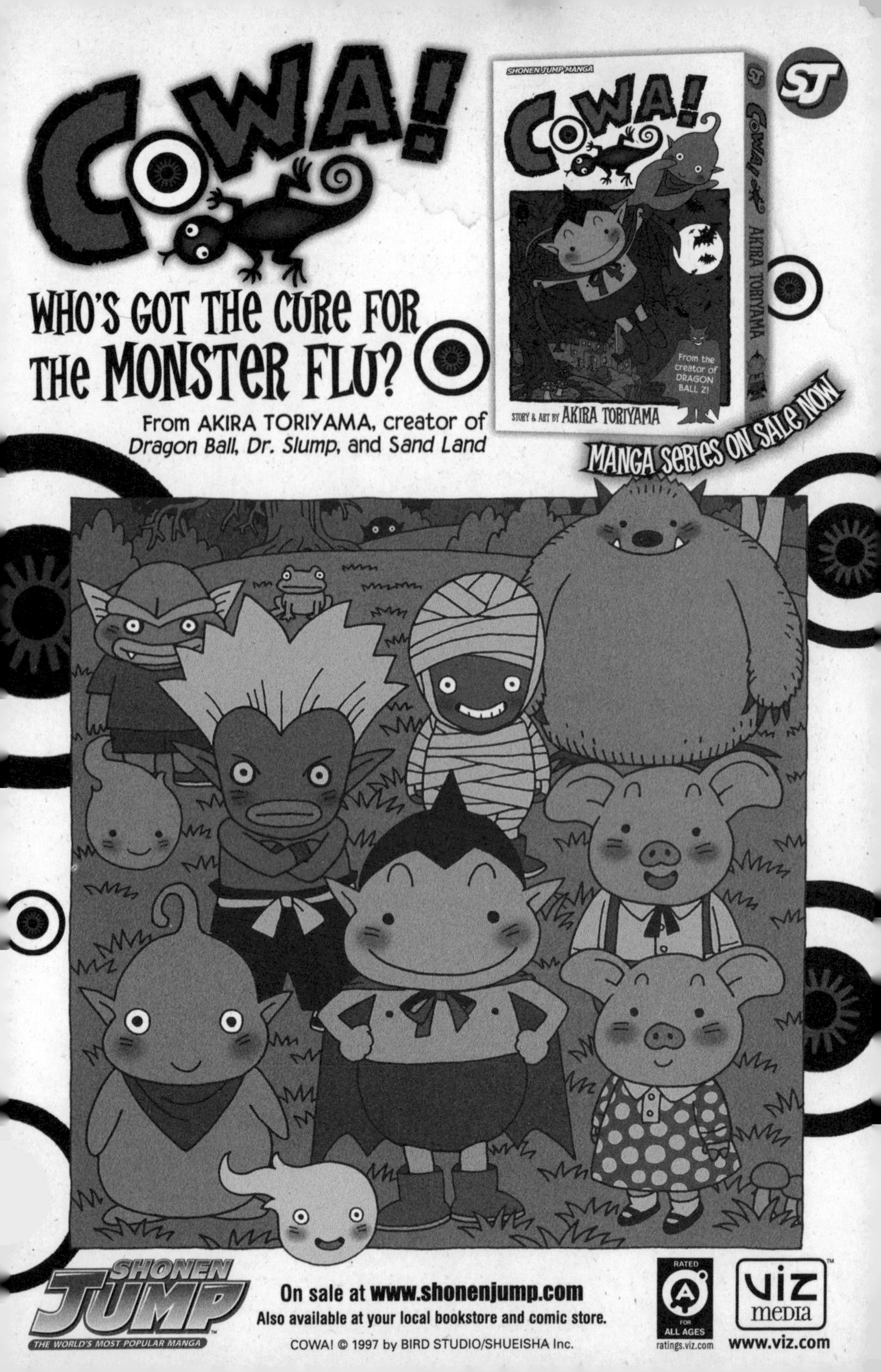
COWA!
WHO'S GOT THE CURE FOR THE MONSTER FLU?
From AKIRA TORIYAMA, creator of Dragon Ball, Dr. Slump, and Sand Land
SHONEN JUMP MANGA
SJ
COWA!
AKIRA TORIYAMA
From the creator of DRAGON BALL Z!
STORY & ART BY AKIRA TORIYAMA
MANGA SERIES ON SALE NOW
SHONEN JUMP
THE WORLD'S MOST POPULAR MANGA
On sale at www.shonenjump.com
Also available at your local bookstore and comic store.
COWA! © 1997 by BIRD STUDIO/SHUEISHA Inc.
RATED
A
FOR ALL AGES
ratings.viz.com
VIZ media
www.viz.com